CONTROLLING EATING DISORDERS WITH FACTS, ADVICE, AND RESOURCES

Raymond Lemberg, Ph.D.
Consulting Editor

ORYX PRESS
1992

The rare Arabian Oryx is believed to have inspired the myth of the unicorn. This desert antelope became virtually extinct in the early 1960s. At that time several groups of international conservationists arranged to have 9 animals sent to the Phoenix Zoo to be the nucleus of a captive breeding herd. Today the Oryx population is nearly 800, and over 400 have been returned to reserves in the Middle East.

Library of Congress Cataloging-in-Publication Data

Controlling eating disorders with facts, advice, and resources /
    Raymond Lemberg, consulting editor.
        p. cm.
    Includes bibliographical references and index.
    ISBN 0-89774-691-0 (pbk. : alk. paper)
    1. Eating disorders. 2. Eating disorders—Treatment. 3. Eating disorders—Treatment—United States—Directories. 4. Eating disorders—Bibliography. I. Lemberg, Raymond.
RC552.E18C66   1992
616.85′26–dc20   91-42850
                                                            CIP

Contents

▼
▼
▼
▼

Foreword
If You Have an Eating Disorder....

▼
▼
▼
▼   by Jean Bradley Rubel, Th.D.

So here you are. You've picked up the book. Now why should you read it?

Well, maybe someone has told you that you have an eating disorder. Maybe you've denied it, but underneath you're scared they might be right, or maybe you are a concerned loved one or a therapist.

In this book you'll learn the danger signs that point to an eating disorder. You'll also learn what to do to recover. Most important of all, you'll learn that you can recover.

An eating disorder can ruin your life and even kill you. Remember, though, that thousands of people have recovered. In the following pages you'll learn what you have to do to conquer your eating disorder. You'll find lots of hope, too.

Maybe you don't have an eating disorder, but someone you care about does. Maybe you're worried about a friend or someone in your family. Maybe you're feeling guilty because nothing you say or do helps. In fact, your best efforts have probably met with denial, hostility, withdrawal, or all three.

In this book you'll learn what you can, and can't, do to help. You'll learn that eating disorders are not just fads or pesky habits. You'll learn why the best resource for a person with an eating disorder is a team of physicians and psychotherapists. You'll also find reasons to give up your guilt. After all, you wouldn't expect to do surgery on a friend who had appendicitis, would you? Then don't expect to fix your friend's eating disorder. You can, however, learn how to support treatment and the hard work that recovery demands.

Maybe you're a schoolteacher, counselor or psychotherapist, youth worker, or someone who cares about young people and their problems. Read on to learn when you should be alarmed and what to do with your concern. Learn when to refer, where to refer, and how to find resources.

And finally, read this book if you want to be part of the solution instead of part of the problem. You've probably noticed that we live in a society that's preoccupied with physical appearance. Many people believe that success and self-confidence belong only to trim, muscled men and slim, fit women.

In this book you'll learn that social pressure to have a perfect body encourages a simplistic myth: "If I can control my body and make it fit the cultural ideal, I'll feel good about myself and find success and happiness."

You'll also learn that eating disorders are attempts to meet basic needs by people who find themselves overwhelmed by life's demands. People who feel lonely, anxious, bored, or trapped may eat for comfort, fun, and release. Others who feel inadequate may lose weight to feel special and important. Those who have survived devastating loss or abuse may binge or starve to

Jean Bradley Rubel, Th.D. is the president of Anorexia Nervosa and Related Disorders, Inc. (ANRED), and the editor of the organization's newsletter, *ANRED Alert*.

numb their depression and rage. Some try to release those feelings by vomiting, exercising, or using laxatives to induce diarrhea.

In all cases people are doing the best they can to take charge of their lives and feel better. In this book you'll see the futility of trying to do that through food or diets. You'll also see how much we need, both individually and as a society, healthy, effective ways to deal with the confusing and demanding times in which we live. With this information you can begin to take charge of your own life and in so doing become a healthy role model for those around you.

Foreword
Locating a Therapist or Treatment Program

▼
▼
▼
▼　　　　## by Vivian Meehan

Although there are many excellent therapists and treatment programs, the advice of the National Association of Anorexia Nervosa and Associated Disorders (ANAD) is buyer beware when a person with an eating disorder or his/her family starts to search for a therapist or treatment center. Eating disorders is a relatively new field, and there are currently no adequate guidelines or certification required in order for any therapist or institution to treat patients. You should learn as much as possible about therapists, treatment facilities, and costs before you embark upon treatment.

Since there are many philosophies concerning the treatment of eating disorders and many personality differences in both patients and therapists, ANAD strongly recommends that you select the therapist from a very personal standpoint to ensure finding the one who can work best with you or you and your family. The therapist's rapport with an individual (and family, if this applies), and confidence in the proposed treatment approach are important considerations.

ANAD believes that your best approach is to familiarize yourself, through reading, with all the phases of eating disorders and the treatment approaches and then select a therapist or treatment program that makes the most sense for your circumstances. This book is one good place to start.

FINDING A THERAPIST OR TREATMENT CENTER

To find a therapist or treatment center, first seek sources available to you. While ANAD does not endorse any therapy or therapist, it has compiled a list of over 2,000 individual therapists, hospitals, and clinics in the United States that treat eating disorders. This information is free and available to individuals and families. Part 4 of this book, "Facilities and Programs," lists some 200 treatment centers. Other resources may be available by calling psychiatrists, psychologists, social workers, or medical doctors listed in your phone book.

If insurance is a factor in treatment, be sure that the insurance carrier approves any treatment prior to the commencement of treatment. Insurance coverage is sometimes determined by how the illness is defined by the treating physician or therapist. You may need to fight for insurance coverage. If you do not have it, you must consider that the treatment for eating disorders requires a long-term commitment (usually one to two years). You may need to consider choosing a competent clinical specialist whose charges can be met over a period of time rather than engage someone with whom you may not financially be able to continue.

Vivian Meehan is president and founder of ANAD—National Association of Anorexia Nervosa and Associated Disorders.

QUESTIONS TO ASK

When talking with an employee of a treatment center or an individual therapist with a private practice, ask specifically about:

- Philosophy of treatment;
- Number of eating disorder patients treated;
- Average length of treatment;
- Costs;
- How long in business;
- Academic credentials and experience in the eating disorders field of *all* the professionals who will be treating the patient; and
- Success rate.

If you are an in-patient, ask for a description of treatment programs offered on a daily basis.

Hospital treatment programs may offer either in-patient or out-patient or both. Multidisciplinary treatment programs should include individual, group, and family therapy wherever possible. Regular medical monitoring should be included as a part of treatment for both out-patient hospital programs and individual psychotherapy. The internist or primary physician should understand eating disorders and be willing to give adequate time and attention to this population.

IF YOU HAVE PROBLEMS WITH THERAPY

If your symptoms appear to you to be indicators of anorexia nervosa or bulimia but the therapist suggests that no problem exists, or recommends that the problem can be handled by you without treatment, do not hesitate to ask for another opinion.

Any therapist who is willing to work with an eating disorder sufferer on the problems of low self-esteem, depression, anxiety, and guilt should produce some positive results, providing a good therapeutic relationship has been established. You should not, however, hesitate to seek another therapist if, after a reasonable time, no progress is evident. Before changing therapists, this concern should be discussed with the present therapist. Having considered the therapist's views one can make a more informed decision on changing or not changing therapists.

If fees for treatment are too high, check local (state) (county) mental health facilities or private welfare agencies that operate on a sliding scale.

CHOOSING WISELY

Choosing a treatment facility should be based on the factors outlined above and not on strong advertising or promotional materials, hard sale pitches, attempts at intimidation, special discount offers, or offers of free transportation to and from treatment centers.

Anyone seeking free information about eating disorders, educational programs, support groups, hotline support, or treatment center guidelines may write or call ANAD (National Association of Anorexia Nervosa and Associated Disorders), Box 7, Highland Park, IL 60035, (708) 831-3438. The oldest nonprofit organization of this kind in the United States, ANAD is an association of professional and lay people dedicated to alleviating the problems of eating disorders. Association programs are free and serve millions of people. See page 212 for more information about this organization.

How to Use this Book

▼
▼
▼
▼

Controlling Eating Disorders with Facts, Advice, and Resources provides the reader with authoritative articles on a variety of aspects relating to eating disorders, including:

- Full descriptions of anorexia nervosa, bulimia nervosa, and compulsive overeating.
- Health and psychological problems related to these disorders.
- Causes.
- Types of treatment.

In addition, this reference book lists 200 facilities that specialize in the treatment of eating disorders and over 400 resources, including articles, books, audiovisual materials, journals, indexes, and organizations.

THE ARTICLES IN THIS BOOK

The 26 articles written for this book are arranged in three sections. Part 1, "Causes, Symptoms, and Effects of Eating Disorders" includes nine articles that explain the main types of eating disorders, how they may start, and how they affect the body. Part 2, "Personal, Social, and Cultural Issues," features four articles that describe psychological stresses that contribute to eating disorders. They include family problems and emotional, physical, and sexual abuse as well as social and cultural pressures to be physically attractive. The 13 articles in Part 3, "Treatment of Eating Disorders," describe a variety of treatments available for eating disorders. They range from individual psychotherapy to medication treatment to group

therapy to nutritional counseling to art therapy to integrated or holistic therapies.

Each of the articles in *Controlling Eating Disorders with Facts, Advice, and Resources* is designed to stand alone so that the reader can pick up the book at any point and learn about a topic without needing to start at the beginning. Consequently the overlap and redundancy among some articles is unavoidable. And, some of the authors in this book offer differing viewpoints of this field. However, the astute reader has something to gain by noting the many commonalities among the authors, all of whom are experienced professionals.

The field of eating disorders is brand new, having emerged over the last 15 years or so. Yet this book reveals consistency in the basic clinical wisdom and knowledge among authors about eating disorders, including the cultural pressures that lead to dieting and may create medical and psychological problems; the difficulties of growing up and becoming one's own person; the role of family conflicts and personal trauma in symptom development; the stress of men's and, particularly, women's roles changing in our society; and how the eating disorder, once begun, seems to develop a life of its own in terms of the strength of the symptom and the tragic loss of self-esteem and hope of recovery to the sufferer.

Most authors highlight the complex interplay of biopsychosocial factors that contribute to eating disorders and that must be addressed in treatment. The team approach is emphasized, which involves using professionals from different disciplines and confronting the multitude of problems that go along with anorexia nervosa, bulimia nervosa, and compulsive overeating.

For the person with an eating disorder, and concerned loved ones, this book is a guide to help readers understand that overcoming an eating disorder is not based on "finding more willpower," but instead on recognizing the importance of emotional, interpersonal, and biological factors that produce shame, guilt, depression, and worsening of physical health. Many authors in this book, as working clinicians, have described what happens in treatment to promote an understanding of the recovery process.

For the clinician, this volume is a condensation of clinical wisdom and knowledge and as a result represents a review for some and also a good reference on specific, practical components of treatment. It is striking how clinicians and researchers contributing to this volume, from throughout the United States, have come to develop independently such similar views of the etiology and treatment of eating disorders.

THE FACILITIES LISTED IN THIS BOOK

The 200 listings in Part 4 of this book, "Facilities and Programs," are programs found in hospitals, universities, outpatient psychiatric and psychological services, and stand-alone facilities in the United States. Information was compiled from questionnaires mailed August through November 1991 and some telephone interviews. Each entry provides, at a minimum, name, address, telephone number, and type of eating disorder treated. Most entries give other information including contact person, hotline number, FAX number, date established, type of treatment, setting, program length, number of patients program can

treat, number of patients served last year, and type of follow-up evaluations available. The directory is arranged geographically by state and city, and an alphabetically arranged list of facility names follows.

Please note: The listings in Part 4 are by no means comprehensive, and readers should consult their physicians, local hospitals, medical schools, state medical and psychological associations, and the national eating disorder associations listed in Part 5 of this book for further suggestions. See two articles in this book, "Locating a Therapist or Treatment Program" (p. vii) and "How to Find Treatment for an Eating Disorder" (p. 83), for more information. Readers should also carefully check any eating disorder program before enrolling. Type of treatments available, staff, reputation of facility, price, and setting, should all be investigated. A listing in this book does not imply endorsement by The Oryx Press or any contributor to this book.

RESOURCES AND INDEX

Part 5 of *Controlling Eating Disorders with Facts, Advice, and Resources* offers a variety of information resources to help the reader find out more about eating disorders. There are 419 articles, books, and audiovisual materials listed. Popular, as well as some professional, titles are cited. Major eating disorder journals are identified, and indexes and subject searching methods are described. Six national and regional eating disorder organizations are listed. These organizations, which offer a wealth of helpful material, as well as offering support groups, referral lists, and professional training, research, and conferences, can be extremely useful to the person suffering from an eating disorder.

The book concludes with a comprehensive index.

Introduction: What You Should Know about Eating Disorders

▼
▼
▼
▼

by Raymond Lemberg, Ph.D.

Anorexia nervosa, bulimia nervosa, and compulsive overeating are eating disorders that usually require professional help. However, during one's lifetime an individual may experience some eating *problems* which do not necessarily require intervention. It is not coincidental that eating habits are tied to emotions. We know that depressed feelings, for example, often lead to overeating or the loss of appetite.

The hypothalamus, a small structure in the center of the brain, regulates such biological drives as thirst, hunger, and sex. The structure is part of a larger area in the brain called the limbic system, the "seat of emotions." Therefore, human emotions and biological drives are connected neurologically.

It has been reported that two-thirds of American adults binge eat at least twice a month; that is, eat not to satisfy hunger but to reduce stress and soothe the emotions.

DO DIETS LEAD TO EATING DISORDERS?

Dieting is one of the key forerunners for the development of eating disorders; particularly bulimia. With few exceptions, periods of *prolonged* dieting precede the development of binge-purge behavior.

A large number of Americans are dieters, with an estimated 30 billion dollars a year spent on dieting and weight loss products. Before age 13 in fact, 80 percent of girls report they already have dieted as compared with 10 percent of boys. Research has found that the teen years are particularly difficult for girls, who have severe pressures to control weight and appearance. By adolescence a large percentage of girls show a drop in self-esteem compared with adolescent boys.

Disordered eating does not always result in an eating disorder or require professional attention. There are "subclinical" eating disorders such as crash dieting or weekend binging which may be transient behaviors and which never become serious problems. The risk for progression to a serious eating disorder, however, is high.

WHEN TO GET HELP

The *severity* and *duration* of problematic eating behaviors are key indicators of whether an individual needs to seek help. Questions to ask about the severity of the eating problem include whether there has been a dramatic or rapid weight loss (greater than or equal to 15 percent of usual body weight or 10 pounds or more in a one-month period of time), or frequent binge behavior—two or more times a week—accompanied by out-of-control feelings, guilt, and the compulsion to "undo" the effects of overeating by vomiting, exercise, or other unhealthful dieting practices.

The degree of severity of an eating problem needs to be gauged by a person's psychological state and physical health risks. Serious depression, with loss of motivation, sleep disturbance, and suicidal thoughts, requires treatment. Dizziness, poor concentration, muscle spasms, and fatigue are all medical signs suggestive of the possibility of electrolyte imbalance and an increased risk for serious heart problems and even heart failure.

Even milder forms of any emotional problem require attention if the problem continues for a length of time. As a general "rule of thumb," if emotional problems continue three months or more, professional help should be considered.

There are other important considerations in recognizing whether an eating problem is of serious proportions. An individual with a true eating disorder becomes caught in a self-perpetuating vicious cycle in which attempts at trying to control eating through increased willpower result in increased guilt, overeat-

ing, obsession about weight loss, and, in bulimia or compulsive overeating, alternating cycles of starvation and out-of-control eating.

A final consideration in determining if an eating problem is serious is whether the eating behavior has become "bound up" in relationship issues, often involving the family system. There are few emotional problems or symptoms that occur in isolation. Often family conflict produces and promotes symptoms and/or symptoms become the focus for family concern ultimately resulting in power struggles and damage to interpersonal relationships. In these cases, outside professional intervention is usually indicated and can be very helpful.

Statistics about Eating Disorders

▼
▼
▼
▼

by Rosemary DePaolis Tso

Approximately eight million American teenagers and adults have some symptom of the life-threatening eating disorders anorexia nervosa and bulimia nervosa (Meehan, 1990). In *anorexia nervosa*, a person purposefully loses weight far beyond the normal range in order to become thin; in *bulimia nervosa*, a person excessively eats (binges) and then to prevent weight gain uses self-induced vomiting, laxatives or diuretics, and/or excessively exercises. Although considered relatively new diseases, dieting to feel in control of one's life is not new. There are much older references to observations of conditions similar to these modern-day eating disorders, according to Hilde Bruch, noted psychotherapist. One such observation was documented in 1689 by Richard Morton, who described an illness in which he referred to the patient as "a skeleton only clad with skin" (Bruch, 1978). It was about 100 years ago that this particular disease was given a name, anorexia nervosa, by British physician Sir William Gull (Bruch, 1978). However, in the last 20 years or so incidences of bulimia and anorexia have increased. A *New York Times* article cites a study that reported that three to five percent of women between puberty and the age of 30 are bulimic, and one percent are anorexic (Brody, 1990).

WHO SUFFERS FROM EATING DISORDERS

Who becomes bulimic or anorexic? Many studies have found similarities among those afflicted by these problems, most notably that more women are afflicted with these eating disorders than men. Historian Joan Brumberg, author of *Fasting Girls* (1989), projected that 90 to 95 percent of anorexics are women. One in 200 females between 12 and 18 years of age has had anorexia, according to an article in the *FDA Consumer* (Farley, 1986).

While anorexia used to be termed the disease of the affluent and appeared to be most common in white, upper-middle class teenage girls and young women, it is now clear that others, such as men and boys, older adults, blacks, other people of color, and the economically disadvantaged, are susceptible to eating disorders. According to an *FDA Consumer* article (Farley, 1986) five to 10 percent of bulimics and anorexics are men. The *New York Times* estimates that one in 10 people who seeks treatment at eating disorder clinics is male (Brody, 1990).

Why Do Some People Develop Eating Disorders?

Why are some people more susceptible than others? Some theories suggest that a combination of psychological, physiological, and cultural factors tend to have a major impact on people who are vulnerable. Those classified at high risk are individuals who place an emphasis on slimness, body image, or making a certain weight—for example, wrestlers, dancers, models, or long distance runners. Other people at risk are those, especially women, with socially demanding or powerful jobs. Eating-disordered people also tend to come from families who emphasize weight control or families with members who have eating disorders or who abuse alcohol or drugs. One study reports that one-half of people with eating disorders have been sexually abused as young children (Brody, 1990).

Society and the news media send out messages to young girls and women that slimness brings success and happiness. For example, the women in the Miss America Pageant have shown a seven percent decrease in weight over 15 years while the average American woman has had an increase of three to five percent, according to the *Campus Health Guide* (Otis & Goldingay, 1989). The *Guide* also found many studies have demonstrated that a woman's idea of her "ideal" weight is two to 15 percent less than her recommended weight. Although bulimics may be obese or very thin, they are usually within 15 pounds of their normal weight (Brody, 1990).

A study of schoolgirls in Michigan and Indiana shows that these psychological and cultural factors may play a large part in who becomes anorexic or bulimic (*Wall Street Journal*, 1986). The study found that 18 percent of underweight girls and 60 percent of average weight girls were dieting. In San Francisco another study of young women between nine and 18 years old found that more than one-half of all the girls were dieting (*Wall Street Journal*, 1986). The percentages were broken down by age groups: 50 percent of nine year olds, 80 percent of 10 to 11 year olds, and 90 percent of 17 year olds were dieting. Yet another survey of several private schools in Washington, DC, conducted by Dr. Sue Bailey, director of the Eating Disorders Clinic at the Washington (DC) Hospital Center, revealed that young girls showed a vulnerability to an eating disorder (Farley, 1986). Many of the girls surveyed responded that they had been dieting since age 13 and had been dissatisfied with their bodies since age 10. In one school, 28 percent of the eighth graders would consider vomiting to lose weight.

The first signs of anorexia often begin in girls between the ages of 13 to 17 (Jenish, 1989). Brumberg (1989) found that five to 10 percent of adolescent girls and young women are anorexic, and at some colleges that figure may rise as high as 20 percent.

Another study (Judith H. Swarth, Master Thesis, Department of School and Community Health, University of Oregon, 1984) concentrated on the attitudes of college-aged women on dieting. Eighty-two percent of the women wanted to lose weight, while as few as eight percent were actually overweight. To control their weight 13.5 percent vomited, 8.3 percent used laxatives, and 14.6 percent used diuretics. About 40 percent of those interviewed reported that their diets consisted of less than 800 calories—1200 calories per day is considered semi-starvation. Sixty-two percent of the women experienced uncontrollable desires to binge eat. The study also explored the women's attitudes toward food—29 percent believed most foods are fattening, and 55 percent often felt fat; over one-half (53 percent) preferred to avoid "starchy" foods.

With those attitudes about food it is not a surprise that 10 to 20 percent of women, and possibly more, who are not clinically diagnosed as having an eating disorder suffer from at least one symptom. The *Campus Health Guide* reports that researchers estimate one to 20 percent of college women have had fully developed symptoms of bulimia (Otis & Goldingay, 1989). A study by Kathleen Hart and Dr. Thomas Ollendick (1985) found about five percent of college women had bulimia. Some researchers, according to a *New York Times* article, estimate that one-half of all anorexics eventually become bulimic (Brody, 1990).

In the Hart and Ollendick study (1985) estimates of the bulimia syndrome dropped significantly as the researchers applied more diagnostic criteria. For example, estimates dropped from 41 percent to 27 percent for working women and from 69 percent to 54 percent for university women when they were asked if they had depressed and self-deprecating thoughts following binging. Prevalence estimates dropped again to 9 percent for working women and 17 percent for university women when the women were asked if binge eating was present in combination with self-deprecating thoughts and fears of not being able to stop eating voluntarily. When one last diagnostic criterion, the presence of self-induced vomiting on a weekly basis, was included with the three other criteria the rates were reduced further to one percent for working women and five percent for university women. Although the two samples experienced similar decreases, the working women showed lower frequencies of these behaviors than the university women.

The effects of bulimia and anorexia may have extreme consequences. Bulimia may last 10 to 20 years and cause throat and stomach problems among other afflictions. Both anorexia and bulimia can be life threatening: It has been estimated that six percent of people suffering from eating disorders die from these illnesses (Meehan, 1990).

RECOVERY FOR THOSE WITH EATING DISORDERS

For those who recognize their problem and seek help the recovery rate can be satisfactory, according to a study on long-term outcome of adolescent girls with anorexia nervosa by Richard E. Kriepe, M.D., Bruce H. Churchill, and Jaine Strauss, Ph.D. The average age of the subjects at follow-up was 22.7 years. Although 22 of 45 subjects acquired binge-eating patterns after hospitalization, 86 percent had a satisfactory outcome based on a developmentally oriented, multidisciplinary approach including inpatient and outpatient management in a pediatric service (Digest..., 1990).

Recovery is possible, but first victims must recognize and admit they have a problem. Studies on the number of bulimics and anorexics are not conclusive because the early stages of the eating disorders may go unrecognized for some time. It took Jane Fonda over 20 years to openly admit that she was bulimic (Janos, 1985). In the case of anorexia, victims may not be detected until they become extremely underweight. Although inconclusive, the studies do reveal an alarmingly high number of people afflicted with these life-threatening disorders and show that changes in attitudes about thinness and success are required.

REFERENCES

Brody, J.E. (1990). Personal health. Bulimia and anorexia, insidious eating disorders that are best treated when detected early. *The New York Times*, February 22, p. B9.

Bruch, H. (1978). *The golden cage: the enigma of anorexia nervosa*. Cambridge, MA: Harvard University Press.

Brumberg, J. (1989). *Fasting girls: the emergence of anorexia nervosa as a modern disease*. Cambridge, MA: Harvard University Press.

Digest—Long-term anorexia outcome (1990). *BASH Magazine, 9* (3), March, p. 86.

Farley, D. (1986). Eating disorders: when thinness becomes an obsession. *FDA Consumer*, May, 20-23.

Hart, K.J. and Ollendick, T.H. (1985) Prevalence of bulimia in working and university women. *American Journal of Psychiatry, 142*, 851-54.

Janos, L. (1985). Jane Fonda: finding her golden pond. *Cosmopolitan*, January, 168-71, 205.

Meehan, V. (1990). Testimony presented by Vivian Meehan, president of National Association of Anorexia Nervosa and Associated Disorders

(ANAD), at U.S. Congressional Hearing. September 24, 1990.

Rose, P. (1988). Hunger artists. *The Atlantic*, July, 82-85.

Swarth, J.H. (1984). *Relationship between food attitudes and dietary practices of college women.* Master Thesis. Department of School and Community Health, University of Oregon.

Wall Street Journal (1986). February 11, p. A1.

Contributors

▼
▼
▼
▼

▼ **Raymond Lemberg, Ph.D.,** consulting editor of *Controlling Eating Disorders with Facts, Advice, and Resources,* is a clinical psychologist maintaining a private practice in Scottsdale, Arizona. He is the executive vice-president of Willow Creek Hospital and Treatment Center in Scottsdale, a specialty hospital for the treatment of eating disorders. He has served as a consultant to various eating disorders programs, coauthored a children's book, and authored or co-authored numerous professional articles, including "Fat is Not a Feeling: Use of Reframing Techniques in the Treatment of Anorexia Nervosa and Bulimia"; "An Intensive Group Process-Retreat Model for Treatment of Bulimia"; "The Impact of Pregnancy on Eating Disorder Symptoms"; "Understanding Eating Disorders: A Guide for Family and Friends"; and "What Works in the Inpatient Treatment of Anorexia Nervosa and Bulimia: The Patient's Point of View."

▼ ▼ ▼

▼ **Sharon A. Alger, M.D.,** author of "The Obesities: Causes and Management," is an assistant professor of medicine at Albany Medical College in Albany, New York. Among her many articles on the subject of obesity are "Using Drugs to Manage Binge Eating among Obese and Normal Weight Patients," in *Opioids, Bulimia, Alcohol Abuse and Alcoholism* and "Nutrition and Gastroenterology: To Eat or Not to Eat" in *Current Gastroenterology, 1991.*

▼ **Arnold E. Andersen, M.D.** author of "Eating Disorders in Males: Critical Questions," is an internationally recognized expert in the study of anorexia and bulimia in males. Dr. Andersen is a professor of psychiatry at the University of Iowa, Iowa City, Iowa. Formerly an associate professor in the Department of Psychiatry at Johns Hopkins University, he is on the

editorial boards of the *International Journal of Eating Disorders* and *Eating Disorders Review.* He is a member of the National Advisory Council of the National Anorexia Aid Society and was the recipient of the Karen Carpenter Memorial Foundation Unrestricted Gift for Research. His many contributions to the medical literature concerning eating disorders include two books, *Practical Comprehensive Treatment of Anorexia Nervosa and Bulimia* and *Males with Eating Disorders.*

▼ **Carol Bloom, C.S.W.,** is coauthor of "The Truth about Dieting: A Feminist View." She is a member of the Women's Therapy Centre Institute in New York City, a training institute for the practice of feminist psychotherapy. With her coauthors, she is presently writing a book for practitioners on the feminist psychoanalytic aspects of eating problems, with an emphasis on compulsive overeating. Carol Bloom is also the author of "Bulimia: A Feminist Psychoanalytic Understanding" in *Fed Up and Hungry.*

▼ **Linda P. Bock, M.D.,** author of "The Hazards of Constant Undernutrition," "Secrets and Denial: The Costs of Not Getting Help," "Using Medications to Treat Anorexia Nervosa and Bulimia Nervosa," and "Using Individual Psychotherapy to Treat Anorexia Nervosa and Bulimia Nervosa," is the medical director of the Anorexia Bulimia Treatment and Education Center (ABtec) at St. John's Mercy Medical Center in St. Louis, Missouri, and is on the staff of DePaul Community Health Center. She also maintains a private practice. Dr. Bock has lectured widely to the lay and professional communities on the topics of anorexia nervosa and bulimia.

▼ **Irene Chatoor, M.D.,** author of "Child Development as It Relates to Anorexia Nervosa and Bulimia Nervosa," is the psychiatric director of the Eating Disorders Program and Infant Psychiatry Program at the Children's Hospital National Medical Center in Washington, D.C. She also serves as an associate professor of psychiatry and behavioral sciences and of child health and development at George Washington University School of Medicine and Health Sciences in Washington, D.C. She was recently granted the three-year Child and Adolescent Mental Health Academic Award by the National Institute of Mental Health, and has been widely published, specializing in infantile anorexia nervosa and eating disorders in early childhood.

▾ **Marjorie Crago, Ph.D.,** coauthor of "Eating Disorders among Athletes," is a research specialist in the Department of Family and Community Medicine at the University of Arizona College of Medicine in Tucson, Arizona. She is coeditor of *Psychotherapy Research: An International Review of Programmatic Studies* and coauthor of chapters on therapist variables in the *Handbook of Psychotherapy and Behavior Change* and the *Handbook of Social and Clinical Psychology*. She has also been the coauthor of a number of journal articles on eating disorders.

▾ **Alexandra O. Eliot, Ph.D., L.I.C.S.W., C.C.S.W.,** author of "More than Anorexia: An Example of an Integrated Treatment Approach for Adolescents," is an instructor in psychiatry at the Harvard Medical School and an adjunct assistant professor at the Simmons College School of Social Work, Boston, Massachusetts. She is codirector of the outpatient Eating Disorders Clinic at Boston Children's Hospital, where she is also chief social worker in the Division of Adolescent/Young Adult Medicine and a senior staff social worker in the Department of Psychiatry. Dr. Eliot also maintains a private practice and is vice-president and a board member of Anorexia Bulimia Care, Inc. in Lincoln Center, Massachusetts.

▾ **Nancy Ellis-Ordway, A.C.S.W.,** author of "Are You Really 'Too Fat? The Role of Culture and Weight Stereotypes," and "How to Find Treatment for an Eating Disorder," is the community coordinator for the Anorexia Bulimia Treatment and Education Center (ABtec) at St. John's Mercy Medical Center in St. Louis, Mis-

souri. She has also served as an instructor at the Washington University School of Medicine. Among her publications is "The Impact of Family Dynamics on Anorexia: A Transactional View of Treatment" in *The Addiction Process: Effective Social Work Approaches.*

▾ **Andrea Gitter, M.A., A.D.T.R.,** is coauthor of "The Truth about Dieting: A Feminist View." She is a member of the Women's Therapy Centre Institute in New York City, a training institute for the practice of feminist psychotherapy. With her co-authors, she is presently writing a book for practitioners on the feminist psychoanalytic aspects of eating problems, with an emphasis on compulsive overeating.

▾ **Susan Gutwill, M.S., C.S.W.,** is coauthor of "The Truth about Dieting: A Feminist View." A member of the Women's Therapy Centre Institute in New York City, a training institute for the practice of feminist psychotherapy, she is coauthoring a book on the feminist psychoanalytic aspects of eating problems, which will have an emphasis on compulsive overeating.

▾ **Adele M. Holman, D.S.W.,** is coauthor of "What Is Anorexia Nervosa? What Is Bulimia Nervosa?" Dr. Holman is the director of Clinical Projects at The Family Institute of Westchester in Mt. Vernon, New York and also maintains a family therapy practice in Teaneck, New Jersey. She is a vice president of the American Anorexia/Bulimia Association and is author of the book *Family Assessment: Tools for Understanding and Intervention.*

▾ **Annika Kahm, B.S.,** author of "Nutritional Counseling for Anorexic and Bulimic Patients," is the director of nutrition at the Wilkins Center for Eating Disorders in Greenwich, Connecticut. Ms. Kahm is also a board member of the American Anorexia/Bulimia Association, New York, New York, and maintains a private practice, treating patients with eating disorders, obesity, and pregnancy-related nutritional concerns.

▾ **Melanie Katzman, Ph.D.,** is coauthor of "Group Therapy for Bulimia Nervosa." Dr. Katzman is in private practice in New York and is also on the faculty at New

York Hospital—Cornell Medical Center. She serves as a board member of the American Anorexia/Bulimia Association. Dr. Katzman has done extensive research and therapy with bulimic women, addressing coping strategies, concurrent substance abuse, incest histories, and women's issues. Along with Dr. Lillie Weiss and Dr. Sharlene Wolchik, she has coauthored the books *Treating Bulimia: A Psychoeducational Approach,* and *You Can't Have Your Cake and Eat It Too: A Program for Controlling Bulimia.* She is currently writing a book on feminist approaches to the treatment of eating disorders.

▾ **Barbara P. Kinoy, Ph.D., C.S.W.,** is coauthor of "What Is Anorexia Nervosa? What Is Bulimia Nervosa?" Dr. Kinoy maintains a private practice in Brattleboro, Vermont in addition to her work as a senior consultant for the Wilkins Center for Eating Disorders in Greenwich, Connecticut. She has worked with the American Anorexia/Bulimia Association as both a board member and group leader and recently received an award for her contributions to this organization. Dr. Kinoy is author/editor of the book *When Will We Laugh Again—Living and Dealing with Anorexia Nervosa and Bulimia.*

▾ **Laura Kogel, A.C.S.W.,** is coauthor of "The Truth about Dieting: A Feminist View." She is a member of the Women's Therapy Centre Institute in New York City, a training institute for the practice of feminist psychotherapy. With coauthors, she is presently writing a book for practitioners on the feminist psychoanalytic aspects of eating problems, with an emphasis on compulsive overeating.

▾ **Cappi Lang, Ph.D.,** author of "Discovering, Re-Creating and Healing the Self through Art and Dreams: Help for Persons with Eating Disorders," is presently the director of Expressive Therapies at Willow Creek Treatment Center and Hospital in Scottsdale, Arizona. She is also in private practice. Her past experience includes positions in art and play therapy, and she has lectured widely on those topics. Dr. Lang is herself a professional artist.

▾ **John L. Levitt, Ph.D.,** author of "Assessment: Joining the Eating-Disordered Individual with the Right Professional," is

clinical director of the HELP Eating Disorders Program at HCA Woodlands Hospital, Hoffman Estates, Illinois. He is also program director and an associate at Partners in Psychiatry, Ltd., in Des Plaines, Illinois. He serves on the Chicago board of Anorexia Nervosa and Associated Disorders (ANAD) and among his many published articles are "Treating Adults with Eating Disorders by Using an Inpatient Approach" and "Eating Disorder Assessment Protocol." He has recently coauthored, with C. Stout and D. Rubens, the book *Handbook of Addictions.*

▾ **Margo Maine, Ph.D.,** author of "Eating Disorders and Behavior Change: How a Contract Can Help," is the program director of the Eating Disorders Service at Newington Children's Hospital in Connecticut, and also maintains a private practice. She writes a newsletter for professionals called *Eating Disorders in Focus* and is a member of the national board of Eating Disorders Awareness and Prevention, Inc. Dr. Maine founded and directs the Connecticut Eating Disorders College Task Force. She served as clinical consultant in development of the film *Wasting Away: Identifying Anorexia Nervosa and Bulimia,* and has written her first book, *Father Hunger: Fathers, Daughters, and Food.*

▾ **Bonnie Kathryn Marx, M.S.N.,** author of "Out of Balance, Out of Bounds: Obesity from Compulsive Eating," is a behavioral counselor and consultant for the Weight Management Program at the Institute of Medical Nutrition in Phoenix, Arizona. She also maintains a private practice in psychotherapy. Ms. Marx has done extensive work in designing treatment and training programs for the lay and professional communities regarding compulsive eating behaviors.

▾ **Diane W. Mickley, M.D., F.A.C.P.,** author of "Medical Dangers of Anorexia Nervosa and Bulimia Nervosa," is founder and director of the Wilkins Center for Eating Disorders in Greenwich, Connecticut. She also serves as president of the American Anorexia/Bulimia Association and is a member of the Connecticut State Task Force on Eating Disorders. She is a research associate in the Department of Psychiatry at the Yale University School of Medicine and has been a member of the faculty of the national meetings of the American College of Physicians. Among her publications are "Alprazolam in the Treatment of Bulimia".

▼ **James M. Parsons, M.D.** is coauthor of "Eating Disorders: A Holistic Approach to Treatment." He is former medical director of the New Life Center for the treatment of depression, anxiety, and eating disorders at Orlando General Hospital, a Division of Florida Hospital, Orlando, Florida. Currently, he is with Charter Hospital, Orlando South, Kissimmee, Florida. Dr. Parsons has written articles for professional journals and made presentations at medical colleges on the subject of pituitary/adrenal metaoblism and eating disorders.

▼ **Bonnie L. Pelch, A.C.S.W.,** author of "Eating-Disordered Families: Issues between the Generations," is a psychiatric social worker for the Anorexia Bulimia Treatment and Education Center (ABtec) at St. John's Mercy Medical Center in St. Louis, Missouri. She provides group and family therapy and trains medical professionals in family therapy for eating-disordered patients. She also maintains a part-time practice specializing in couple and family therapy.

▼ **Jeanne Phillips,** author of "Self-Help Groups in the Treatment of Eating Disorders," is the founder and director of SHED (Self-Help for Eating Disorders), which provides support for individuals who are either anorexic of bulimic. She also facilitates a family support group for significant others as well as an adolescent group therapy for teens with anorexia nervosa or bulimia. She is a frequent speaker to the lay and professional communities and has coauthored several articles on eating disorders.

▼ **Kenneth Rockwell, M.D.,** author of "Eating Disorder Treatment: The Importance of Research," directs the Anorexia Nervosa/Bulimia Treatment Program and is an assistant professor of psychiatry in the Department of Psychiatry at Duke University Medical Center, Durham, North Carolina. Among the many articles written by Dr. Rockwell are "Pharmacological Approaches to the Treatment of

Eating Disorders," in *Eating Disorders (New Directions for Mental Health Services)* and "The Electrocardiogram in Anorexia Nervosa."

▼ **Marie C. Shafe, Ed.D.,** coauthor of "Eating Disorders: A Holistic Approach to Treatment," is a clinical consultant to the eating disorders program at Charter Hospital—Orlando South. She was previously program director/clinical director, The New Life Center for Depression and Eating Disorders, Florida Hospital, Orlando, Florida. Additionally, she is a professor of graduate studies and counseling, Rollins College, Winter Park, FL. Dr. Shafe has conducted numerous workshops and presentations internationally and is currently working on a workbook for treatment professionals to use with groups on sexuality and relationships. She recently coauthored "Brain Chemistry in Eating Disorders."

▼ **Catherine M. Shisslak, Ph.D.,** coauthor of "Eating Disorders among Athletes," is an associate professor of Family and Community Medicine at the University of Arizona College of Medicine, Tucson, Arizona, and the director of the University of Arizona Health Sciences Center Eating Disorders Program. Her major clinical and research interests include anorexia nervosa and bulimia, family therapy, and sports psychology. She is a consultant on eating disorders to both local and national organizations, as well as being a consultant to the Stanford University School of Medicine Center for Disease Prevention and Health Promotion, where she was also a Visiting Scholar. She has been the recipient of several research grants and special awards and her continuing research in eating disorders and exercise has been published in *The New England Journal of Medicine* and several other books and journals.

▼ **Adrian H. Thurstin, Ph.D.,** author of "Symptoms of Eating Disorders: Behavioral, Physical, and Psychological," is an associate professor and director of training of the Psychology Training Consortium in the Department of Psychiatry at the University of Alabama School of Medicine at Birmingham. Among Dr. Thurstin's articles on the subject of eating disorders are "Issues in the Diagnosis and Treatment of

Anorexia Nervosa and Bulimia," and "In Pursuit of Thinness: Starving and Purging."

▾ **Rosemary DePaolis Tso,** author of "Statistics about Eating Disorders," is an editor and writer who lives in Flagstaff, Arizona. She has worked for the A.M. Best Co. in New Jersey, an insurance rating and publishing company.

▾ **Susan Wagner, Ph.D.,** author of "Eating Disorder Treatment Stories: Four Cases," maintains a private practice in White Plains, New York and is a voluntary faculty member of the Eating Disorders Unit of the Westchester Division of New York Hospital-Cornell Medical Center. Her published works include the article "The Sense of Personal Ineffectiveness in Patients with Eating Disorders: One Construct or Several?"

▾ **Lillie Weiss, Ph.D.,** is the coauthor of "Group Therapy for Bulimia Nervosa." Dr. Weiss is in private practice in Phoenix, Arizona and is an adjunct associate professor in the Department of Psychology at Arizona State University in Tempe. She has also served as interim director of the university's Clinical Psychology Center. Along with Dr. Melanie Katzman and Dr. Sharlene Wolchik, Dr. Weiss has done extensive research and therapy with bulimic women. They are coauthors of the books *Treating Bulimia: A Psychoeducational Approach,* and *You Can't Have Your Cake and Eat It Too: A Program for Controlling Bulimia.*

▾ **Sharlene Wolchik, Ph.D.,** is coauthor of "Group Therapy for Bulimia Nervosa." Dr. Wolchik is a professor in the Department of Psychology at Arizona State University. Along with Dr. Melanie Katzman and Dr. Lillie Weiss, Dr. Wolchik has done extensive research and therapy with bulimic women. They are coauthors of the books *Treating Bulimia: A Psychoeducational Approach,* and *You Can't Have Your Cake and Eat It Too: A Program for Controlling Bulimia.*

▾ **Lela Zaphiropoulos, A.C.S.W.,** is coauthor of "The Truth about Dieting: A Feminist View." She is a member of the Women's Therapy Centre Institute in New York City, a training institute for the practice of feminist psychotherapy. With coauthors, she is presently writing a book for practitioners on the feminist psychoanalytic aspects of eating problems, with an emphasis on compulsive overeating. She is also coauthor of *Solving Your Child's Eating Problems* (formerly published as *Are You Hungry?*).

PART 1
Causes, Symptoms, and Effects of Eating Disorders

What Is Anorexia Nervosa?
What Is Bulimia Nervosa?

▼
▼
▼
▼

by Barbara P. Kinoy, Ph.D. and Adele M. Holman, D.S.W.

Anorexia nervosa is an eating disorder characterized by a purposeful weight loss far beyond the normal range. Fear of being fat is almost always an overriding factor in this pursuit. A desire to perfect one's self, through one's body, and by extension in every other way, is also a strong characteristic and can supersede the reality of body structure and function (resulting in a distorted body image). This pursuit can also displace or change other requirements of living, such as family and social relationships.

A list follows of actual behavioral, physical, and emotional symptoms and changes that are a part of the picture of anorexia nervosa. Many of these symptoms and changes are discussed in other parts of this book. This list is meant to be a basic checklist, after which will be discussed some of the history and development of anorexia nervosa. Bulimia nervosa, or bulimia, will also be reviewed. Similar to anorexia nervosa, bulimia has often been linked with it, and an overlap will be found in the discussion of the two disorders. People do not always fit exactly into the categories of anorexia or bulimia, however, and thus the line between them may be fine or hardly distinguishable. In addition, anorexia and bulimia may coexist, or develop sequentially.

ANOREXIA NERVOSA

Symptoms of anorexia nervosa include the following.

A. Intense fear of becoming obese, which does not diminish as weight loss progresses.

B. Disturbance in body image; e.g., seeing one's self as fat even when bone thin or emaciated.

C. Weight loss of at least 15 percent of the expected body weight of a person, adjusted for height, body build, and age.

D. Refusal to maintain normal weight.

E. A cessation of the menstrual cycle, sometimes before an appreciable weight loss.

F. Hyperactivity; i.e., one is busy all the time, hardly ever coming to rest.

G. Fasting, vomiting, or laxative use, often following binging, but sometimes after ordinary intake of food.

H. Determined and/or repetitive rituals and thoughts called compulsive and obsessive behaviors; among them, a preoccupation with thoughts of food, weight, and exercise, to the extreme. Exercise goes far beyond the purpose of pleasure or fitness; it is used to "burn off" calories, to diminish whatever fat remains, and to affirm one's control over the nature of one's body.

I. Appearance of depression.

Proceeding from the above are these changes, which are more marked and severe:

- A disturbance in cognitive ability (thinking).

- Family and social relationships becoming absent or dysfunctional; or conversely, poor family relationships contributing to the onset of the weight loss.
- Social activity diminishing or or stopping entirely.
- An overt increase in depression. While this state is suggested by some to be a part of anorexia nervosa and/or even an underlying cause, the disorder itself often seems to act as a substitute for overt depression.
- The development of fine body hair (*lanugo*).
- Feeling cold (hypothermia).
- Lowered blood pressure.
- A slowed pulse rate.
- An imbalance in the body chemistry, called an electrolyte imbalance. For example, excessive purging or laxative use can reduce potassium content in the body to a dangerous degree. Medical attention is required to ascertain this information.
- Occurrence of dental problems, most often in those who vomit, because the acid content of the vomitus erodes tooth enamel.
- The possible occurrence of death if the process remains unabated. Suicide is not an uncommon consequence of the despair and depression connected with this condition.

History of the Knowledge of Anorexia Nervosa

In its restrictive and binging aspect, diet control has been around for a very long time. In early humans it was perhaps purposeful and adaptive in times of sparse food and in times of plenty. In the Middle Ages there was a religious connotation attached to starving one's self in the context of self-denial, sacrifice, and mortification of the flesh for holy and spiritual affirmation. By the late 1800s, however, anorexia nervosa was fairly well established as a medical condition with emotional factors. While Sir William Gull in England described

its physical attributes, it was Charles Lasegue in France, around the same time, who noted the marked emotional qualities accompanying the physical symptoms. He called it "anorexie hysterique," while Sir William called it "anorexia nervosa." Anorexia actually means loss of appetite, which is not accurate, as appetite is denied, at least initially. While hunger may be denied, the anorexic often feeds others and becomes obsessive about everything related to food. A present German term, "Pubertatsmagersucht," or "leanness passion of puberty" is perhaps concisely descriptive of a segment of the anorexic population.

Causes of Anorexia Nervosa

Anorexia nervosa mainly affects females, and usually in the adolescent years, although the overt onset may occur as early as 10 or 11 (and occasionally even earlier), and as late as the post-menopausal years. There is usually a trigger that marks the acute onset, such as the refusal or inability to stop dieting; a critical remark about weight or appearance from a significant person, relative, or peer; a sexual threat; or a trauma such as the loss of a parent or sibling, a divorce, or illness.

The trigger, however, is not necessarily the cause, but only the last straw. Causation is very complex and may not always be specifically known or identified. This is an area where mind and body are closely interrelated. Medical experts, as described in other parts of this book, look for and have found certain physiological clues. Psychological experts have added their findings. It is important to understand that no one thing causes anorexia nervosa. It is more likely that the exquisitely timed convergence of many external and internal forces promotes the anorexic process and allows it to predominate. Some of these key factors are seen to be the following.

Growing up is frightening for some girls when the body becomes round, curvy, and capable of sexual activity and reproduction. One strives to perfect oneself for the monumental task ahead that is adulthood. A tendency to "hold back" the passage of time is also noted in the anorexic's resistance to maturing, as if to ensure that the early constellation of parent and child need not change.

In addition, there are indications that anorexia is unknowingly fostered in very close parental/family relationships that do not encourage the development of one's own thoughts or opinions. In some instances certain issues are secret and simply not discussed.

Anorexic individuals may have grown up with an inordinate need to please others before themselves, or may never have been sure of their own perceptions in relation to their parents'. Described as extra sensitive, they often have been the caretakers of other needy family members or of the family's emotional balance.

Families in which there have been alcoholic or addictive problems appear to be more at risk for eating disorders. Often the anorexia nervosa of a child replicates some form of problem of impulse control or depression in a parent or previous generation. The significance of these findings is uncertain. At most, they suggest there may be a predisposition to eating disorders in certain families. Family expectations, or the perception of such hopes, may be instrumental in exerting pressure upon the anorexic-to-be.

Anorexia Nervosa as a Present-Day Disorder

Anorexia nervosa is now present in post-industrial countries where the presence of food is generally ensured. In these countries achievement and financial success are part of the cultural value system. In our own country there has been tremendous emphasis on slim female bodies and using them as sexual,

seductive charms to sell p   as provide a romantic al ness/happiness/success.   T ment of television, movie zines with these cultural   has reinforced an ideal that only a few can manage to achieve. Thus, the vulnerable find themselves striving for the perfection that is an impossible dream.

It is also thought that the status of females in our society has influence on the marked presence of anorexia nervosa. The new voices of assertion and independence that have been heard in the last decade or two are additional challenges to be absorbed into the emerging female character. Often, sexuality, motherhood, achievement, assertion, independence, dependence, appearance, and weight all get mixed up in one big confusing picture of "how to be." Anorexic thinking and behavior evolve as one way to retreat from this confusion, and one way of handling the accompanying depression.

Men and boys who suffer from anorexia nervosa are much fewer in number. They, too, have similar vulnerabilities in their histories and similar struggles in the present-day world. Masculine identity is undergoing changes, too, as women change. The old concept of the macho male is not always the ideal or the reality. As young boys struggle with their place in society, success, achievement, and maleness are often associated with fitness and slimness. Among athletes the necessary fitness may be carried to extremes when other factors come into play. It is suspected that more males suffer from anorexia nervosa than come to health professionals' attention. Those who do appear are deeply enmeshed in the destructive process of anorexia nervosa.

BULIMIA NERVOSA

Bulimia, or bulimia nervosa, as it is officially called in the standard diagnostic manual of the American Psychiatric Association (*DSM-III-R*), is an eating

...order that is closely linked to anorexia nervosa. The first reference to bulimic behavior was in early Roman times when binge eating and purging were described. In 1903, the French psychiatrist Pierre Janet wrote about a patient who binged and purged compulsively but never lost her appetite (Janet, 1903). An American authority on obesity, Dr. Albert Stunkard, was the first to identify bulimia in contemporary terms in 1959. The American Psychiatric Association characterized bulimia nervosa as a distinct disorder in 1980, describing the following characteristics:

A. Recurrent episodes of binge eating.
B. A feeling of lack of control over eating behavior during the eating binges.
C. The regular need to either self-induce vomiting, use laxatives or diuretics, diet severely or fast, or exercise vigorously in order to prevent weight gain.
D. A minimum average of two binge eating episodes a week for at least three months.
E. Persistent overconcern with body shape and weight.

Description of Bulimia Nervosa

Bulimia is an emotionally based disorder in which food is used as a means of satisfying inner needs. In contrast to anorexics who restrict food as a means of gaining control over problems in their lives, bulimics react to distress by eating unusually large amounts of food—binging—and then purging. The word bulimia derives from the Greek, meaning "insatiable appetite." The troubled person feels a powerful urge to eat and is driven by the belief that only by giving in to a craving for food that is much more intense than normal feelings of hunger can satisfaction be achieved.

Binging usually involves the rapid consumption of high-calorie foods that are often sweet and of a texture that is easily swallowed. Binges may last several minutes or several hours and may be planned or unplanned. If the urge to eat is felt suddenly, any available food may be gobbled down quickly. At other times, binges are planned, and the person decides in advance to do it at a specific time and place. For many people with this problem, an uncontrollable pattern of binging develops into a daily routine; as this becomes a habit, the body loses its ability to signal satisfaction and consequently eating is no longer in response to physiological hunger.

Rapid consumption of large amounts of food brings on considerable physical discomfort. There is abdominal discomfort and a bloated feeling. Relief can be brought about by purging, that is, ridding the body of the food and fluids. Most often, this is accomplished by vomiting. Ordinarily it is planned and self-induced, but for some people who have purged this way over a long period of time, just thinking about it brings on vomiting. Some bulimics purge by using laxatives or diuretics or a combination of means. Often tolerance to laxatives builds, leading to the use of extraordinarily large quantities, such as over 100 doses a day. Usually purging reduces the physical discomfort and assures the binger that since the food has been eliminated there is less to fear in gaining weight. What the binger does not know is that many calories are absorbed, even with purging, leading to confusion about why weight is usually maintained. What was begun as an "ideal" way to eat and lose weight frequently becomes the basis for a very persistent and disturbing self-reinforcing pattern of behavior.

Many bulimics engage in daily strenuous exercise routines, as anorexics do, as another means of controlling weight gain. The strong drive to exercise often contributes to a self-punishing regime. When half an hour is seen as good, an hour is seen as better, and more than that is better yet.

All of these behaviors are accurately felt by the bulimic person to be bizarre and unnatural. Therefore, there is usually an element of secrecy involved in carrying them out. Considerable effort is spent in obtaining food, consuming it, getting rid of it, and excessively exercising. Bulimics often go to great lengths to conceal these activities from others to avoid shame and guilt, although these feelings become internalized anyway.

There is a form or stage of bulimia that combines restrictive aspects of anorexia with those of bulimia and has sometimes been referred to as "bulimarexia." This is characterized by periods of starving in order to lose weight, alternated with periods of binging and purging. Typically, restricting food begins the process, and then either under pressure to give it up from within or from an outside source, the person shifts to binging and purging. This is sometimes interspersed with periods of normal eating but then the pattern of fasting or binging begins again. As a result, there are often marked weight fluctuations.

There are a number of physiological effects of this self-inflicted behavior, some of which are very serious and irreversible and potentially fatal. These will be discussed in greater detail later in this book, but should be mentioned here as well. These problems include menstrual cessation and irregularities; digestive disturbances; dehydration of the hair, nails, and skin; dizziness; electrolyte imbalance; muscle cramps; fatigue; enlargement of the parotid (salivary) gland; dental problems, especially permanent erosion of the enamel; poor circulation; heart irregularities; and heart failure. When proper nutrition is restored, many of these problems are reversible; however, permanent damage may be done. Therefore, early detection and treatment are extremely important.

Who Is Likely to Become Bulimic?

Bulimia can be better understood by knowing who is likely to engage in this behavior and the underlying dynamic reasons that encourage people to develop these symptoms. Research has shown that persons with bulimia will probably be female, although a small percentage are male. Unlike the anorexic, the bulimic's appearance is not ordinarily an indicator of the problem. Usually, bulimics are within a normal weight range, although some weigh 10 or 15 pounds within normal.

Although bulimia and anorexia nervosa are closely linked, there are significant differences shown in each disorder. The bulimic person is likely to have a more accurate perception of body image than the anorexic person and is more likely to acknowledge abnormal eating patterns. Bulimics also tend to be more impulsive; however, they are more apt to refer themselves for treatment. Bulimics are more likely to be in a relationship, or to be married, than persons suffering from anorexia nervosa.

The families of bulimics are drawn from various class and ethnic groups. Often there is a history of physical or sexual abuse in these families and a higher than usual incidence of substance abuse. There is very likely to be depression in one or both parents and an association between depression in a parent and in a bulimic offspring. Some research suggests that there is a greater predisposition to bulimia in families where depression is present than where it is absent. However, it should be noted that a small percentage of families seem to be without dysfunction.

Generally the problem develops in the late adolescent or early adult years, but there is evidence that some people develop it later in life. Surveys have shown that between 10 to 30 percent of college students admit to some bulimic thoughts or actions (Halmi, Falk, & Schwartz, 1981; Pyle, Mitchell, & Eckert, et. al., 1983; Evo Shoshana, 1985). Early history of bulimic individuals shows that they have been deeply concerned with weight and appearance. They have reacted to values expressed in movies, in magazines, on television, and by their friends and families. Bulimics are frequently people who have been overweight previously or who have family members who have been overweight. Thus, weight and appearance become a focus for their disappointments and frustrations.

The bulimic person usually has feelings of low self-worth and dissatisfaction with various aspects of life. Typically, there is loneliness, fear, and lack of emotional fulfillment. Interest in sexual activity is often minimal. Significant depression, over a period of time, is sometimes so severe that suicide attempts are made.

Characteristically bulimics are dependent and compliant people who are especially concerned with acceptance and approval. They may adopt a confident and independent manner in order to mask their deep feelings of inadequacy. Also, they show an eagerness to win approval by striving for perfection in the activities that they undertake. Failure to achieve their goals creates disappointment and anxiety and often results in taking irresponsible and unreasonable actions. Escape is sought through the substitute satisfactions of eating large quantities of food. Binging, and then purging, become the means of making the bulimic's world feel more in control by providing temporary comfort and security. Bulimics struggle with the need to control, and, at the same time, feel out of control.

The pattern of seeking comfort and escape in binge eating can be compared to seeking relief from anxiety through the use of alcohol or drugs. Consequently, bulimics are considered by some to be "food addicts." Indeed, their uncontrollable need to binge and purge is clearly characteristic of the addicted person.

Psychologically, the gorging of food is understood as having a numbing effect on anger and anxiety. At the same time, the guilt that accompanies the eating and the self-disgust that accompanies the purging contribute to further distress. However, the physical and emotional relief from purging may be so great that it provides an emotional "high" and may become a desired end in itself. This, then, promotes a repetitive cycle of a self-perpetuating habit whereby the bulimic cannot stop thinking about binging and purging and feels compelled to act on these thoughts. This is seen as obsessive-compulsive behavior.

SUMMARY

Experience has shown that both bulimia and anorexia nervosa are very complex disorders with physical and emotional complications. It is essential for them to be taken very seriously. One or more forms of treatment are required to recover. The various forms of treatment are medical, nutritional, and psychological. Psychological treatment may be individual, group, or family therapy or a combination of therapies. In addition to therapy, participation in a self-help group for people with eating disorders can be very beneficial. These modes of treatment and their application are discussed in Part 3 of this book.

REFERENCES

American Psychiatric Association. (1980). *Diagnostic and Statistical Manual of Mental Disorders* (3rd ed.). Washington, DC: American Psychiatric Association Press.

Evo Shoshana, N.E. (1985). Bulimic symptoms: Prevalance and ethnic differences among college women. *International Journal of Eating Disorders, 4,* 151-168.

Halmi, K.A., Falk, J.R., & Schwartz, E. (1981). Binge eating and vomiting: a survey of a college population. *Psychological Medicine 11*, 697-706.

Janet, P. Les obsessions et la psychasthénie (1903). Paris: Felix Alcan.

Pyle, R.L., Mitchell, J.E., Eckert, E.D., et al., (1983). The incidence of bulimia in freshman college students. *International Journal of Eating Disorders 2*, 75-85.

Stunkard, A. (1959). Eating patterns and obesity. *Psychiatric Quarterly, 33*, 284-295.

Child Development as It Relates to Anorexia Nervosa and Bulimia Nervosa

▼
▼
▼
▼ by Irene Chatoor, M.D.

There is growing evidence in the western part of the world that the prevalence of eating disorders among young girls is on the rise. To understand why this should be happening in our culture requires answering another question: Why are increasing numbers of young girls susceptible to an eating disorder while others who diet are able to undertake the developmental tasks of adolescence?

People who have anorexia nervosa and bulimia nervosa have these characteristics in common: gross disturbances in eating behavior, intense fear of obesity and disturbance of body image, and a feeling of being "fat," even when slim or emaciated. However, these two disorders differ in the eating pattern displayed. Whereas anorexics restrict their food intake by counting calories and forcing themselves into eating less and less, bulimics tend to alternate between dieting, fasting, and binge eating. They display a roller coaster type of eating pattern with great variations in the timing and amount of food eaten. The hallmark of bulimia is recurrent episodes of binge eating characterized by the rapid consumption of a large amount of usually high-calorie, easily ingested food, such as ice cream, cookies, cakes, breads, or any food available at the time. The binge episode is usually ended by abdominal pain, sleep, or social interruption. Whereas the binge eating appears to serve as a distraction and to provide comfort and pleasure, at the end of the episode the individual usually experiences physical and emotional distress and severe guilt and panic over the amount of food eaten. This panic frequently leads to *purging* in the form of vomiting, taking laxatives or diuretics, or it may lead to a new cycle of starvation followed by another binge episode. Both eating disorders can cause disturbances in hormonal regulation. Anorexia nervosa, as it progresses toward malnutrition, leads to amenorrhea—the absence or suppression of menstruation. The menstrual pattern in bulimia nervosa tends to be irregular and fluctuates in a manner similar to weight.

CAUSES AND ORIGINS OF ANOREXIA AND BULIMIA

Both eating disorders begin most commonly during adolescence, a time when a young person needs to meet major developmental tasks and master the developmental issues of separation and becoming an individual. A young girl needs to adapt to puberty when her body proportions change from those of a child to those of a young woman. She needs to make the transition between loosening the ties with her parents and increasing her dependency on her peers. In order to find her place in her peer group she needs to deal with personal and cultural values regarding body image, sexuality, and achievement—key areas where young girls with eating disorders appear to struggle.

While the exact etiology, or causes, and mechanisms of anorexia nervosa and bulimia nervosa are not known, most experts will agree with Garfinkel and Garner (1982) that these eating disorders are the product of the interplay of a number of forces. There appear to be *predisposing factors* that combine with *precipitating events* in the individual's life that may lead to the expression of an eating disorder. One way to understand the developmental crisis of adolescence as it shows up in these eating disorders is to look at the individual, family, and cultural factors that enhance or interfere with the preparation of the child for the developmental tasks of adolescence.

Signals in Infancy

Hilde Bruch, a pioneer in the field of eating disorders, hypothesized that anorexia nervosa and juvenile onset of obesity are related to a disturbed awareness of inner processes among these individuals. They do not recognize when they are hungry or satiated, nor do they differentiate the need for food from other uncomfortable sensations and feelings (Bruch, 1973). These individuals need signals from outside of them—external—to know when and how much to eat because their own inner awareness has not been programmed correctly. Reconstructing the developmental histories of her patients, Bruch concluded that there was a lack of appropriate and confirming responses by the parents to the child's signals which reflected his or her needs and other forms of self-expression. Bruch hypothesized that appropriate responses to cues from the infant, whether biological, intellectual, social, or emotional, are necessary for the child to organize the significant building blocks for the development of self-awareness and self-effectiveness. If a parent's reaction is frequently inappropriate, be it neglectful, overly solicitous, inhibiting, or indiscriminately permissive, the child will experience perplexing confusion (Bruch, 1973).

In my work with infants and toddlers with eating disorders and failure to thrive I found evidence confirming Bruch's hypothesis. James Egan and I

have observed an eating disorder in infants and toddlers that closely resembles the anorexia nervosa of the adolescent; we call it infantile anorexia nervosa (1988, 1989). Onset is usually between six months and three years, with a peak onset around nine months of age. The disorder occurs with the infant's thrust for autonomy during the first period of separation and individuation. As the infant develops motor skills, parent (usually the mother) and infant need to negotiate who is going to put the spoon in the infant's mouth. The parent's appropriate responses to the infant's signals of hunger and fullness versus the infant's cues for autonomy and self-control in the feeding situation create an essential interplay in negotiating this period of transition to self-feeding successfully. The parent needs to determine whether the infant wants to nurse because of hunger or for comfort and whether he or she refuses to open the mouth because of anger, desire for attention, or satiety. If the mother, because of her own anxiety or her conflicts over issues of control, is unable to interpret the infant's cues correctly, and if she overrides his or her signals by trying to coax, cajole, or force the infant into eating her way, the infant will confuse internal signals of hunger and satiety with intense emotions aroused by the interactions with the mother. As a result, meals become a battleground between parent and child, where the infant's food intake is controlled by emotions instead of physiological sensations of hunger and fullness. The infant does not develop *somatopsychological differentiation*, which in this case is the ability to differentiate between feelings, such as anger, frustration, love, and affection on one hand, and sensations of the body, such as hunger and fullness, on the other.

Differentiating between Mind and Body Signals

Difficulty with somatopsychological differentiation appears to be a primary basis of all eating disorders. In the eating-disordered individual, eating is controlled by emotions and external cues instead of internal physiological signals. Interestingly, preliminary data from our ongoing research reveal a striking tendency of anorexic, restricting individuals to be unable to eat when they experience negative emotions, such as anger, frustration, or anxiety, whereas bulimic individuals report that they seek food and eat in response to the same feelings.

Temperament of Children Who Become Anorexic

The question remains as to what went wrong in the development of mind-body differentiation in individuals with eating disorders. My hypothesis is that, among individuals with anorexia nervosa, temperament is a decisive factor. I observed a striking difference in temperament between the infantile and the adolescent anorexics. Whereas the infants tend to be strong-willed, persistent, and demanding in the expression of their wants (which leads to conflicts in the early phase of separation and individuation), adolescent anorexic girls are usually described to have been easygoing, adaptive, and obedient infants and children. The parents usually do not remember any oppositional behaviors or temper tantrums during the early phase of separation and individuation. This difference in temperament appears to determine infantile versus adolescent onset of anorexia nervosa.

Parents' reports about the anorexics' infancy and childhood indicate that these children have not challenged their parents by expressing their own wishes and wants in opposition to the parents' demands. They have usually eaten what was put on their plates, just as they have performed in school what was expected from them. As they have failed to strongly express their feelings and wants, they have failed to receive distinct confirmation or rejection of what they wanted or did not want. They have

remained unaware of their inner feelings and strivings and consequently have failed to develop a sense of self.

In my work with adolescent anorexic girls I have been impressed by their simultaneous sensitivity to verbal and nonverbal cues of others and their unawareness of their own feelings. It appears that these youngsters have perfected the art of focusing on others and reading their cues while remaining unaware of their own needs and emotions. Their temperamental characteristics, perceptiveness, passivity, and adaptability, have allowed them to grow up as extensions of their mothers and to fulfill their parents' wishes and expectations without developing senses of self. (There has been some recent confirmation for this hypothesis regarding temperament as a risk factor for anorexia nervosa by Casper [1990], who reported that recovered anorexic women showed a temperamental disposition toward greater restraint in emotional expression and initiative and rated higher on risk avoidance when compared with their sisters and a control group.)

The Role of Depression and Anxiety

Another factor that can contribute to the disturbance in mind-body differentiation and lead to confusing the feelings of anger, sadness, loneliness, and fear of rejection with hunger and satiety is the experience of an anxiety or depressive disorder. Several studies have reported on the presence of mood disturbances among patients with anorexia nervosa or bulimia nervosa. Herzog's (1984) research has revealed that 55 percent of the anorexic patients and 23 percent of the bulimic patients met criteria for major depressive disorders. Piran, et al. (1985) have reported on the high incidence of panic disorder in patients with bulimia nervosa. Many studies have reviewed the frequency of psychiatric illness among relatives of patients with anorexia nervosa or with bulimia nervosa.

Whether depression or the eating disorder comes first, however, can vary from patient to patient. There is evidence that malnutrition leads to mood disturbances and that binge eating is frequently followed by intense negative emotion; on the other hand, depressive and anxious moods affect the awareness of hunger and fullness and can interfere with eating. Whatever comes first, the eating or the mood disorder, one affects the other with a compounding effect.

Family Influence on Eating Disorders

If temperament and mood disorders are considered risk factors for these eating disorders, certain family and cultural factors have been implied as well. Parents of children with any type of psychiatric disorder frequently feel responsible for or guilty about the child's problems. However, family studies of patients with anorexia nervosa indicate that some of these families reveal no specific psychopathology and demonstrate no more interactional problems than other families with healthy adolescents. Family distress may be an effect of the adolescent's eating disorder rather than its cause. However, there seem to be certain family characteristics that join with cultural factors to contribute to the adolescent's conflicts. Families in which there is rigid adherence to rules and conservative values, avoidance of open conflict, and lack of conflict resolution seem to produce more patients with anorexia nervosa (Minuchin, Rosman, & Baker, 1975). On the other hand, families with severe parental conflict and inconsistency of rules and values also threaten the adolescent process of identity formation (Kog & Vandereycken, 1989). Interestingly, many families of eating-disordered patients appear preoccupied with food and gourmet cooking, weight and dieting, thus drawing attention to food as representing more than nutrition.

Cultural Changes and Eating Disorders

Finally, the cultural changes over the last 20 years, the sexual revolution, the entrance of women into the work force, the emphasis on thinness as the ideal for a woman's beauty, and the general indulgence in food, have led to a potpourri of values and ideals with which any young person would have difficulty. Young girls confront food at home, at parties, at the movies, wherever they go. At the same time, they are expected to embody the ideal of thinness modeled in the fashion magazines. They have been brought up to believe in religious and interpersonal values that often clash with a world of violence, fast food, and fast sex. Many have grown up in a home where mother fulfilled everybody's needs while foregoing her own ambitions. As adolescents they confront choices of careers as professionals or as housewives, the conservative roles their own mothers may have filled. They tend to think that in order to be perfect, they should master both roles at the same time.

One can see how adolescents with temperamental vulnerabilities or tendencies for depressive and anxiety disorders, when exposed to conflicting family and cultural values, become frightened of growing up. When subjected to what might seem a minor trauma, such as the loss of a best friend, a change of school, or rejection by a peer group, they often find control of their eating and weight a welcome escape and turn it into their solution to the overwhelming task of growing up and finding their place in a world that appears so frightening. Their eating and their body size is something they strive to control when the rest of their life seems so much out of control.

REFERENCES

Bruch, H. (1973). *Eating disorders: Obesity, anorexia nervosa, and the person within.* New York: Basic Books, Inc., pp. 66-86.

Casper, R.G. (1990). Personality features of women with good outcome from restricting anorexia nervosa. *Psychosomatic Medicine, 52,* 156-170.

Chatoor, I., Egan, J., Getson, P., Menvielle, E., & O'Donnell, R. (1988). Mother-infant interactions in infantile anorexia nervosa. *Journal of the American Academy of Child and Adolescent Psychiatry, 27,* 535-540.

Garfinkel, P.E., & Garner, D.M. (1982). *Anorexia nervosa: a multidimensional perspective.* New York: Brunner/Mazel.

Herzog, D. (1984) Are anorexic and bulimic patients depressed? *American Journal of Psychiatry, 141,* 1594-1596.

Kog, E., & Vandereycken, W. (1989). Family interaction in eating disorder patients and normal controls. *International Journal of Eating Disorders, 8,* 11-23.

Minuchin, S., Rosman, B., & Baker, L. (1978). *Psychosomatic families: anorexia nervosa in context.* Cambridge, MA: Harvard University Press.

Piran, N., Kennedy, S., Garfinkel, P.E., & Owens, M. (1985). Affective disturbance in eating disorders. *Journal of Nervous and Mental Disorders, 173,* 395-400.

Symptoms of Eating Disorders: Behavioral, Physical, and Psychological

▼
▼
▼
▼

by Adrian H. Thurstin, Ph.D.

While the emaciation that accompanies anorexia nervosa is easily observed by family and friends, many behavioral, physical, and psychological signs and symptoms of the disorder go unnoticed. The same can be said of bulimia nervosa and compulsive overeating, because only the most obvious signs such as severe obesity or major weight changes are recognized. As each disorder shares some common symptoms and signs, the discussion that follows will necessarily seem repetitious. To provide a complete picture of the individual disorders, however, the behavioral, physical, and psychological aspects of each disorder must be examined separately; a general description would not be appropriate.

ANOREXIA NERVOSA

Behavioral Features

During the initial stages of anorexia nervosa, the individual's behavior may be difficult to distinguish from that of a normal dieter. There are some simple reasons for this: People attempting to lose weight avoid certain foods (for example, fats, sweets, and breads), and normal dieters reduce portions of other food groups. Unlike normal dieters, however, the young person (usually a woman) with anorexia nervosa will continue such food restrictions after others have resumed more flexible eating patterns after having achieved a "normal" body weight. In addition to the continued re-striction of intake, the anorexic individual will display eating behaviors that are not characteristic of healthy dieters. Most people who are dieting enjoy meals and eat what they are permitted (and sometimes more!), but careful observation of the anorexic reveals that she or he typically eats less than what is on the plate and may not eat more than a few bites. Frequently, anorexics will appear to be eating when, in fact, they are spending most of their time simply moving food around on the plate. Alternatively, they will cut food into tiny servings or take small bites while chewing slowly and drinking noncaloric, non-nutritive liquids. If confronted with the lack of nutritional intake, they often claim to have eaten earlier and to feel full.

Not only do anorexics exhibit atypical eating behaviors as described above but they also display unusual responses to eating or to eating situations. Instead of looking forward to being with others at meals, they will find excuses for eating alone. At first, they may isolate themselves only at mealtimes, but later they begin to withdraw from social contact more completely. Another behavior that may be seen is an exaggerated interest in recipes and cooking for others. Some individuals go to great trouble to prepare gourmet meals that are served to others but not to themselves. Finally, after eating even a small meal, anorexics may become very anxious and complain of feeling "stuffed."

In addition to the behaviors associated with eating, many anorexics over-exercise. As with some eating behaviors, exercise patterns may seem appropriate initially, but, over time, the amount of exercise may increase to clearly excessive levels. In some cases, three to four hours a day is not uncommon. Typically, an anorexic girl will involve herself in an aerobics class, spend an hour walking/running alone, and/or complete a series of calisthenics. The level of activity is frequently related to what the individual has eaten that day. If she or he has eaten very little and nothing "fattening," an hour of aerobics may be enough. On the other hand, if she or he believes to have overeaten, the anorexic is prone to increase substantially the exercise time in order "to make up for the extra calories." Occasionally, anorexics exercise in more subtle ways such as walking stairs frequently, running in place while watching television, or by stretching.

In general, individuals with anorexia nervosa act in ways that minimize caloric consumption and maximize energy output. Thus, in this context, the food "taboos," increased exercise levels, and unusual eating behaviors are easily understood. Because the body has a tendency to preserve itself, which often provokes even more severe caloric restriction and exercise activity, behaviors that may emerge in anorexics over an extended period are binge eating and possibly purging. Also, laxative and/or diuretic abuse can occur as the anorexic seeks alternative ways to lose weight.

Physical Features

The physiological changes associated with anorexia nervosa are very similar to the alterations of physical functioning that follow a prolonged period of malnutrition and starvation. Some of the effects of nutritional restriction are observed fairly early in the course of the illness, while others are not seen until an extended time has elapsed. The most readily recognized change is the very rapid weight loss that

often occurs. It is not unusual to see a young anorexic lose 20 pounds in a month and as much as 20 to 25 percent of total body weight over several months. With the very serious decline in body weight and nutritional status, menstrual changes in women quickly emerge; a woman with relatively regular cycles will soon cease having a menstrual cycle at all.

Given the emphasis that individuals with eating disorders place upon physical appearance, it is ironic that many of the results of anorexia tend to diminish physical attractiveness. With a protein deficiency as a consequence of caloric restriction, the anorexic will experience a decrease in the quality of hair, skin, and nails. Both hair and nails will become brittle, leading to much breakage. The hair also will begin to thin as new hair is not grown to replace the lost hair. Skin changes are similar, as dry, scaly skin develops from the lack of nourishment. Another problem is the declining condition of teeth and gums. Cavities and gum disease frequently occur secondary to the lack of calcium and nutrients as well as a consequence of vomiting in some individuals.

In addition, anorexia nervosa contributes to problems associated with fluid depletion as well as temperature regulation. For anorexics who abuse laxatives and/or diuretics, significant dehydration and potassium loss is quite frequent. The immediate outcome of such behavior is typically muscle cramping, fatigue, and low blood pressure on standing. The problems listed are not just found in laxative/diuretic users but are magnified by substance abuse. Finally, the body is not able to warm itself without fuel or needed layers of body fat, and anorexics will be overly sensitive to cool environmental conditions. In fact, an anorexic may need a sweater to be comfortable when others are in shorts and t-shirts. As the condition progresses, some people grow fine, soft hair over much of the body, presumably the body's response to the need to maintain warmth.

Most of the physical features so far described above are not life-threatening but they still constitute serious health problems. There are, however, long-term consequences of anorexia nervosa that do have an impact on the quality and quantity of life. With prolonged starvation, nearly all major bodily functions are impaired, including the heart, the liver, kidneys, stomach and bowels, muscles and bones, reproductive system, and the brain. Each of the organs is affected by anorexia because the body doesn't just burn fat to make up for needed calories, it also burns muscle and other tissue. Heart problems may develop as a result of using heart muscle for fuel and are compounded by dehydration and potassium loss. The anorexic may have a fatal heart attack, although this is rare. Other long-term health problems include kidney failure, osteoporosis (loss of bone density), infertility, and intellectual decline. Laxative abuse may also result in chronic bowel impairment.

Psychological Characteristics

The psychological characteristics associated with anorexia nervosa can be divided into those traits that are outcomes of the illness and those that are related to its development. Although not the cause of anorexia nervosa, high achievement orientation seems to be a common finding in young women with anorexia. The desire to be "the best" at whatever they are doing and to do things perfectly appears to contribute to the disorder. The perfectionism displayed in school and recreational activities is applied to personal appearance. The extreme demands for the ideal body lead to preoccupation with even the most minor "flaws." The distorted body image that anorexics have is a logical result of their focus upon the smallest amount of body fat.

Anorexics exhibit denial of their disorder as well as negative feelings. They are often described by parents as "model" children willing to do what is asked and never complaining. Anorexics attempt to please others in any way possible to avoid conflict and will deny feeling angry or frustrated, afraid that others will not like them if they are not everything they are expected to be. Inside, the anorexic may feel unloved, unaccepted, and deficient. Depressed mood and negative self-esteem are often seen once the disorder progresses beyond the initial stages. Lastly, the individual who was an "A" student begins having trouble completing assignments because of preoccupation with food and concentration and memory loss secondary to his or her malnutrition.

BULIMIA NERVOSA

Behavioral Features

Like anorexics, the eating behaviors of people with bulimia differ from those of normal people and not just as they relate to binge episodes. Friends and relatives will rarely observe the binge-eating episodes that are the hallmark of the disorder. On the contrary, what is usually seen is a very restrained, controlled caloric intake when in public. In fact, the restraint displayed by bulimic young women (most bulimics are young women) is so extreme that others may wonder how they can keep from losing weight. During "public" meals they will studiously avoid fats, sweets, and "fattening" foods, while limiting themselves to low-calorie vegetables, fruits, and small amounts of lean meat. Their exhibition of self-control is a mask that conceals the chaotic eating patterns engaged in when alone as well as the fear they experience about food. Once away from scrutiny, the bulimic individual may consume huge quantities of the very foods so carefully avoided earlier. The loss of control during a binge stands in stark contrast to her public restraint and is the source of much of her negative self-image.

As the disorder progresses, a bulimic woman becomes increasingly socially isolated as binge eating and purging consumes ever more of her time and energy. An outgoing, sociable woman will begin turning down invitations to parties, dinners, or other activities involving food. If they live with other people, bulimics will isolate themselves by withdrawing to their rooms rather than watching television, playing games, or conversing. Frequent excuses include needing to study, feeling tired, or having work to do. Typically, it is during such isolation that a binge may occur. A parent, sibling, or friend may later discover empty food containers hidden under a bed, stuffed in a closet, or in a trash can. In addition, following meals, bulimics often immediately excuse themselves to the bathroom. Because of their fear of gaining weight and of binge eating later, they feel compelled to vomit even modest amounts of food. If prevented from purging, bulimics will grow increasingly anxious as time passes; situations in which vomiting is not possible can be especially anxiety-provoking and may result in panic.

Physical Features

The physiological problems associated with bulimia nervosa are numerous and related in large part to the severity of the disorder and to the methods of purging used by the individual. Because the vast majority of bulimic women are at normal or slightly above normal weight, menstrual irregularities will be observed initially, with amenorrhea, loss of menstrual periods, developing as time passes and the woman's nutritional status deteriorates. Rapid changes in weight will also be observed as a function of alternating periods of fasting and binge eating. Large weight fluctuations may occur because of laxative and/or diuretic abuse, which affects the individual's fluid balance. Other frequent complaints involve sore throats, mouth and gum ulcers, dry and cracked lips, and tooth decay. Bulimics may also experience constipation, fatigue, weakness, generalized swelling and salivary gland irritation. Although none is life-threatening, these conditions are signs that more serious damage may be occurring. For example, a chronic sore throat with occasional blood in vomit may be a sign that the esophagus is tearing or ulcers are developing, which can be quite serious.

The constipation can be either a short-term outcome of the disorder or may signify more chronic effects of the illness. With frequent vomiting and laxative usage, the bulimic runs the risk of "paralyzing" the digestive tract. Because the muscles involved in digesting and eliminating food are bypassed or hyperstimulated by vomiting and laxative use, respectively, the young person with bulimia may lose the ability to move food through the body efficiently. Thus, she or he will experience "feeling full" for longer than most people and may have bloating without the relief of a bowel movement. Additionally, chronic laxative abuse may result in colitis, an inflammation of the colon. The most serious consequence of binge eating is stomach rupture which, although it rarely occurs, usually leads to death.

The digestive tract is not the only system subject to harm by bulimia. With prolonged diuretic abuse in order to increase urination, kidney functioning can be impaired, muscle cramping can occur, and heart rhythms may be disrupted. These problems are primarily related to potassium depletion, which allows for the proper functioning of muscle tissue. Many people get muscle cramps during strenuous exercise, which go away with rest and fluid replacement; however, for laxative- and diuretic-abusing bulimics, the body stores of potassium can become dangerously low and result in irregular heart beats. Replacing potassium is essential to correct imbalances and to restore regular heart functioning, but such replacement can be hazardous if not monitored by a physician. Too much or too little may lead to a heart attack.

Psychological Characteristics

Predominant among the psychological characteristics of many bulimics is an impaired sense of self-worth and self-confidence. They tend to see themselves as less attractive, less capable, and less interesting than others. Associated with low self-esteem are strong achievement motivation and perfectionism. Because they believe that they are not as competent as others, bulimics attempt to compensate by doing things perfectly, because by being perfect, they believe they can escape any possible criticism. Unfortunately, bulimics are neither able to recognize their own successes nor to accept the recognition of their successes by others. For bulimics, the security of knowing they have done well lasts only until the next task is undertaken or the next request is made. Although coworkers will describe them as compulsive, demanding, and rigid, bulimics also have trouble setting limits on what is asked of them. They are terribly afraid that they will disappoint someone, and, subsequently, be disliked.

Not surprisingly, bulimics often suffer from anxiety and depression. Because they are so concerned about performance and people's acceptance of them, bulimics appear to be tense, highstrung, and worried. They are particularly sensitive to any indications that someone is dissatisfied, because they assume that it is their responsibility to make sure everybody is happy. Consequently, the bulimic individual is continuously vigilant for sources of potential conflict or frustration to others. She or he fears anger and its expression. If others are angry or upset, the bulimic frequently accepts the "blame" and tries to correct the problem. Since it is impossible to anticipate all

needs, bulimics will encounter constant frustration in their efforts to control the environment, and both guilt and depression are the direct result of this personal "failure." Specific frustrations leading to guilt and depression are failure to control their weight, stop binge eating, maintain healthy relationships, and "do a good job" (by their own standards).

As was noted, anger is an emotion that frightens a bulimic individual and is rarely expressed. However, as the disorder develops and becomes more intense, she or he becomes increasingly hostile and irritable toward others. The once compliant, passive, and accommodating young person may become aggressive and hostile. The emergence of resentment and anger represents only the tip of the iceberg of the rage harbored within, resulting from feeling unloved, unappreciated, and abused by others.

COMPULSIVE OVEREATING

Behavioral Features

Compulsive overeaters share several characteristics with bulimics. Like bulimics, compulsive overeaters experience loss of control over food, frequently resulting in binge eating episodes. However, there is a significant difference between bulimics and compulsive overeaters in the nature of such binges. For the bulimic, a binge generally consists of food that is of limited nutritional value such as sweets or "junk food"; for compulsive overeaters, binge eating may involve foods that are otherwise healthy as well as sweets and junk food. The compulsive overeater may sit with others and consume an appropriate amount during a meal but may lose control later while clearing the table of leftovers. He or she may eat what other people leave on their plates, finish what remains in serving dishes, or continue to eat while putting food away. Another pattern of the compulsive overeater involves continuous snacking, especially during evening hours, when food takes on the role of a "soothing companion."

People with compulsive overeating habits often have trouble saying no to the requests of others, often forgetting their own plans to try to respond to other people's needs. Rarely will compulsive overeaters ever suggest that something would be inconvenient or an imposition. At work, they will assume extra responsibility and are always ready to be of assistance no matter how heavy the load. The simplest description of the compulsive overeater's attitude is "people pleasing." If it makes someone else happy, she or he will take care of whatever is needed.

Physical Features

As a direct result of compulsive overeating, individuals with the disorder have weight problems involving inability to maintain a stable weight or become severely to morbidly obese. Teenagers and younger adults who are just developing the problem may not have reached the stage of serious obesity but will be significantly overweight. Because they are not engaging in purging behaviors, compulsive overeaters do not have the sore throats, cracked lips, or dry skin of bulimics. The effects of compulsive overeating are not generally observable until a number of years have passed, and the individual develops problems associated with obesity. Long-term consequences involve development of diabetes, high blood pressure, heart disease, stroke, and cancer. In addition, arthritis may be exacerbated by the stress of carrying excess weight.

Psychological Characteristics

The psychological traits of compulsive overeaters are very similar to those of both anorexics and bulimics. Those with the disorder tend to experience anxiety, *dysphoria* (feeling unwell or unhappy), perfectionism, and low self-esteem. To those around them, they may appear happy and content; however, when alone, compulsive overeaters describe themselves as sad, lonely, and frustrated. They lack the security of knowing that others love and accept them. Compulsive overeaters attempt to ensure acceptance by doing for other people, being "people pleasers," or by completing tasks perfectly. They are chronically tense as they are afraid that something they have done will not be satisfactory. Finally, they are neither able to set limits on the demands placed upon them by others, nor can they express anger or frustration. The compulsive overeater is simply afraid that the expression of negative emotions will result in rejection.

Eating Disorders in Males: Critical Questions

▼
▼
▼
▼

by Arnold E. Andersen, M.D.

INTRODUCTION

Eating disorder in males makes up a fascinating, sometimes neglected area of clinical and research interest, of greater importance in the current day when pressures on males to change in weight and shape are increasing.

Anorexia nervosa was first described in 1694 by Dr. Richard Morton. At the historical moment of publication of these first two cases of anorexia nervosa in English, half of the cases were male, and the outcome of treatment in the male was satisfactory. These two points remain important to any discussion of the subject of eating disorders in males today.

Sir William Gull, in his detailed study on anorexia nervosa in the mid-19th century, also includes mention of males suffering from this disorder. Why has there been so little mention made of them in the century after Gull? First, some psychodynamically based theories of anorexia nervosa required the presence of a "fear of oral impregnation" which would, therefore, exclude males. Other criteria required the presence of amenorrhea (abnormal absence of menstruation), thereby also restating a gender bias in diagnosis.

On a less theoretical level, males with eating disorders may have sought professional help so infrequently in the past that sometimes the fact that they could develop anorexia nervosa was lost sight of because of their statistical rarity. Finally, there are socioculturally determined stereotypes on the part of both patients and clinicians that males do not develop eating disorders, which results in this diagnosis simply being overlooked, whereas similar symptoms in a female would prompt a correct identification.

Beginning in the 1960s, Crisp and others noted the occurrence of anorexia nervosa in male subjects, and interest has been increasing since. Bulimia nervosa was only defined as a clinical syndrome in the late 1970s. Study of bulimia in males is still in its early stages.

CRITICAL QUESTIONS

The following are some provocative questions and tentative answers, based on currently available information.

1. Do Males Develop Eating Disorders?

The answer is a definite "yes." The three essential requirements for the diagnosis of anorexia nervosa pertain equally well to males and females: (1) self-induced weight loss of a substantial degree; (2) the presence of a morbid fear of becoming fat; and (3) an abnormality of reproductive hormone functioning.

The diagnosis of bulimia nervosa likewise can be equally applied to males and females. The essential diagnostic features are compulsive binge eating, followed by remorse and/or physical distress, a fear of fatness, and a variety of compensating efforts to avoid weight gain.

2. How Many Males Suffer from an Eating Disorder?

We have reported that almost exactly 10 percent of cases presenting to Johns Hopkins Hospital Eating and Weight Disorders Clinic were males. A recent community-based study from Sweden found an almost identical incidence of ten females to one male having an eating disorder. The number of individuals with an eating disorder in the 75,000,000 young people aged five to 25 in the U.S. ranges from two to five percent, depending on the criteria used, with one-tenth of these being male.

3. Why Do So Few Males Develop Eating Disorders?

The following four factors have been suggested as reasons why males are less likely to develop eating disorders.

First, some recent studies have suggested that males may respond differently to intravenous doses of L-tryptophan, an amino acid precursor to the neurotransmitter serotonin, when compared with females. Second, the male hypothalamus from early in fetal life produces a steady-state rather than a cyclical, "pulsed" pattern of sex hormones. Third, the presence of a high testosterone to estrogen ratio in the developing male appears to contribute to the increased ratio of lean muscle mass to body fat. Fourth, in this area of biological differences, men have a substantially lower percentage of body fat than women.

Having recognized these four well-documented biological differences between males and females, which probably are not significant in regard to development of eating disorders, it can still be stated that current evidence weighs heavily in favor of psychological and social reasons, rather than biological, causing the differential rate of eating disorders in males and females. Hsu (1989) has examined the "gender gap" in eating disorders and concludes that "eating disorders are more prevalent in the female because more of them are dieting to lose or control weight." Other support in this direction comes from studies by DiDomenico and Andersen (1990). When the 10 popular magazines most frequently read by men were compared with the 10 most often read by women, they found a ratio of 10.5 to 1 in women's vs. men's magazines for articles and advertisements concerning weight loss. This ratio duplicates almost exactly the ratio of eating-disordered women to men. Men, however, are disportionately influenced toward changing body shape, especially to achieve a hyper-masculine, inverted-V upper body appearance.

The hypothesis that females are encouraged more than males by society and culture to lose weight is well supported. Every significant difference in gender-related frequency of behaviors related to body weight or shape change can be correlated with existing sociocultural values. Where a sociocultural norm is equally distributed between the sexes, the behavioral response is roughly equal in both sexes. These behavioral disorders, it appears, are primarily triggered by our society and culture, not caused by neurological problems, although there may possibly be important secondary biological contributions to perpetuation of illness.

4. Why Do Certain Males Develop an Eating Disorder?

The major risk factors that have been associated in general with the development of an eating disorder are:

a. Living in an industrialized country where there is a sociocultural norm for the attainment of slimness and the avoidance of fatness.
b. An increased incidence of affective (emotional) disorders in the family of patients.
c. The presence of a vulnerable personality, either from Cluster B of

from Cluster B of the *Diagnostic and Statistical Manual* (*DSM-III-R*) of the American Psychiatric Association (narcissistic-histrionic-borderline) or Cluster C (sensitive-avoidant-obsessional).

d. Dieting behavior, especially during the critical adolescent and early adult years.

e. Dysfunctional family patterns in which eating disorder produces a stabilizing effect.

f. Membership in a vulnerable subgroup where weight loss is required.

g. A history of sexual abuse, the emergence of "sex disgust" during adolescence, or the presence of other issues in sexuality which are made more tolerable by patterns of weight loss and strict self denial.

In addition, there are three major dieting factors in which males are overrepresented compared with females:

First, in contrast to women who, in general, *felt* fat before they dieted, males who went on to develop eating disorders *were*, generally, medically obese at some time, usually in the mild to moderate range, especially if the eating disorder included any bulimic features.

Second, men more often than women dieted either to attain certain goals in sports or to avoid the possible weight-gaining effects of a sports-related injury that caused them to decrease their physical activity for awhile.

Third, more men than women have in our experience dieted in order to avoid potential medical complications, especially ones they have seen develop in their parents and have heard their parents warned about. No young women in our series dieted to avoid future medical illness, and only one older woman in her 40s did so.

5. Are There Differences in the Natural History of Males and Females in the Development of Eating Disorders?

Tables 1 and 2 suggest a series of stages through which anorexia nervosa and bulimia nervosa appear to progress in both males and females. The process of development from relatively normal behavior to a clinically recognizable eating disorder appears to progress in a regular step-wise fashion, but the mechanisms to explain this transition are not well understood.

TABLE 1
Stages of Development of Anorexia Nervosa

Stage 1: A NORMAL BEHAVIOR.
Normal, voluntary dieting behavior.

Stage 2: A DIAGNOSABLE DISORDER.
Dieting not under personal control and/or dieting has serious medical, social, psychological consequences. Characterized by morbid fear of fatness. DSM-III-R criteria met.

Stage 3A: AUTONOMOUS BEHAVIOR.
The disorder does not resolve even if conditions stimulating its origin have resolved. Behavior not susceptible to any degree of personal control. Secondary mechanisms frequently present.

Stage 3B: ILLNESS BECOMES AN IDENTITY.
The patient identifies with being the illness, not only having the illness (I *am* anorexic). Prospect of loss of illness leads to existential fears of nothingness.

TABLE 2
Stages of Development of Bulimia Nervosa

Stage 1A: NORMAL DIETING BEHAVIOR.
Similar to anorexia nervosa, Stage 1.

Stage 1B: INVOLUNTARY BINGE BEHAVIOR.
Dieting behavior and weight loss lead to this, based on response to hunger.

Stage 2: A DIAGNOSABLE DISORDER.
The trigger for binge behavior generalizes from hunger to a variety of painful mood states. Marked fear of fatness is present. Meets DSM-III-R criteria. May have serious medical, social, psychological consequences.

Stage 3A: AUTONOMOUS BEHAVIOR.
Binges autonomous, frequent, large. Secondary mechanisms often present.

Stage 3B: ILLNESS BECOMES AN IDENTITY.
The thought of living without bulimic behavior provokes great fear, leading to an existential lack of identity and fear of inability to cope.

6. What Is the Nature of Sexuality in Males with Eating Disorders?

There appear to be, in our experience, more issues in sexual identity associated with teenage onset in males while later life issues, such as marital and work-related conflicts, may dominate the picture in those of older onset men. Herzog, Bradburn, and Newman (1990) have noted that, "anorexic males display a considerable degree of anxiety with regard to sexual activities and relationships." Low levels of sexual activity have been noted among anorexic males before and during the onset by Fichter and Daser (1987).

Bulimic males, as with bulimic females, are generally more sexually active both before the onset of bulimia and at the time of their illness. Burns and Crisp (1990) have associated the outcome of anorexia nervosa in males with the frequency of pre-eating disorder sexual activity. The worst outcome occurred in those with the least pre-eating disorder sexual activity. While some studies suggest there is an increase in gender identity conflict and sexual orientation in males with eating disorders, there is lack of agreement about the degree to which these findings are present.

Several studies have documented that anorexia nervosa in males is associated with a decrease in plasma testosterone. In contrast to the "on-off" phenomenon of amenorrhea in females, the decreased testosterone in males is more linearly proportional to the decrease in the male's weight.

7. What Are the Psychological Characteristics of Males with Eating Disorders?

Both males and females with eating disorders appear more likely to have other major psychiatric disorders as well as personality disorders. The most common diagnoses are mood disorders, drug and alcohol abuse, and anxiety syndromes.

What is the reason for the increased incidence of eating disorders and mood disorders in the same individuals and in the same families? It can be argued (Andersen, 1990) that there has been an increased incidence of mood disorders in these individuals and families with eating disorders because the behaviors of the eating disorders stablize and temporarily improve abnormal mood states that occur for a variety of reasons.

Numerous studies have shown an increase in the frequency of personality disorders with eating disorders. There is also some differential frequency of the type of personality disorders with sub-type of eating disorder. Piran, et al. (1988) have documented with careful studies an association that many clinicians have noted anecdotally, namely that bulimic patients, compared with anorexic patients, have a higher probability of having abnormal personality features from Cluster B, the narcissistic-histrionic-borderline category. In contrast, food-restricting anorexics have a higher probability of deriving their personality disorder, when present, from Cluster A, with the characteristic obsessional, sensitive, perfectionistic, and obsessive-compulsive features.

In our experience, males share with females many similar features in regard to the central dynamic aspects of their illness but also have some important separate issues reflecting male vulnerabilities and social pressures in our society. First, the experience of males with actual obesity, rather than feared obesity, especially in males with sensitive features of personality during critical phases of development, means that they are more apt to have psychodynamic vulnerability.

Second, low self-esteem, whether from personality vulnerabilities or from crucial family interactions, can lead males to attempt to attain through dieting a stereotypical, inverted-triangle shape, which they fantasize will make them feel more masculine, in greater control of themselves, and more commanding of respect from those around them.

TABLE 3
Stages in Treatment of Eating Disorders

---

1. Decision regarding in-patient vs. out-patient treatment.
2. Accurate diagnosis and exclusion of differential diagnoses (e.g., swallowing disorders, primary medical illness, primary mood disorder).
3. Medical evaluation and stabilization.
4. Diagnosis of Axis I and Axis II co-morbidities and comprehensive treatment plan.
5. Nutritional rehabilitation to restore healthy body weight, including weight reduction if needed.
6. Interruption of binge-purge behavior and identification of "triggers."
7. Psychological testing.
8. Appropriate psychopharmacology.
9. Sequence of psychotherapy according to patient needs.
10. Identification and treatment plan for unique male issues.
11. Behavioral practice re: choosing meals, purchasing clothing, planning everyday activities, etc.
12. Extended follow-up.

8. Treatment of Males with Eating Disorders: How Are They Similar, How Are They Different?

Table 3 summarizes the essential steps of treatment of males with eating disorders. Treatment involves working with a series of interactive methods and multiple focuses, appreciating both the shared and the unique features of males and females; the biological, psychological, and sociocultural contributions to illness; and the need for individual, group, and family methods.

Most males with bulimia nervosa can be treated out of hospital, with numerous exceptions, while most patients meeting criteria for anorexia nervosa need to be treated in the hospital, again, there being exceptions. Medical assessment should be followed by prompt medical stabilization. The most pressing initial issues are usually treatment of severe starvation, with its associated medical dangers, and treatment of the systemic effects of hypokalemia (too little potassium in the blood) and other metabolic disorders that are secondary to vomiting and/or purging behavior.

A variety of approaches to nutritional rehabilitation have been tried without definitive studies to confirm that one particular method is clearly superior. In general, we favor the approach of "normal food eaten normally." A weight restoration of two and one-half to three and one-half pounds a week can usually be safely accomplished.

A program of close supervision of patients during the vulnerable phase after admission to in-patient care will promptly interrupt binging and purging behavior. The next and considerably more difficult goal is to translate this externally imposed restraint into the patient's own will so that stopping binging and purging behavior becomes a self-, rather than other-governed, practice. For many patients, this transition requires identifying clearly the triggers for binge behavior and learning to choose alternative or incompatible behaviors. All-or-none reasoning tends to lead patients to think that any relapse, or an occasional binge, is a sign of failure and, therefore, dissuades them from persevering. We encourage the approach of simply "shaping" binge-related behaviors toward decreased frequency, recognizing that progress often occurs in a "sawtooth" manner, rather than by the less achievable "gone for good" belief that leads to demoralization if relapse occurs.

Patients with personality disorders generally benefit from an approach that helps them increase their strengths and decrease their weaknesses. Identifying and working with those aspects of personality that are functioning effectively in order to deal with those features that are problematic and vulnerable remain the essence of treatment of a personality disorder.

A reasonable argument can be made that the fundamental center of treatment of eating disorders is psychotherapeutic work—persuading people to understand the origin and course of their eating disorder; the purpose it serves; how to "trade in and trade up"; how to act sanely in a weight- and shape-preoccupied culture of narcissism and densely packed calories; how to deal in a healthy way with their own life development issues, and relationships; and how to decrease their overvalued ideas and misbeliefs. In order to arrive at the point of beginning effective psychotherapeutic work, however, many hurdles need to be overcome. First of all, starvation needs to be treated so that thinking can be freed from the nonspecific apathy and food-focused attention caused by starvation. Metabolic abnormalities need to be corrected. Comorbidities that interfere with psychotherapy, such as a mood disorder, anxiety states, and alcohol and drug abuse, need to be effectively treated. Table 4 suggests a four-stage approach to psychological treatment.

TABLE 4
Sequence of Psychotherapy Methods for Most Eating-Disordered Males

---

Method	*Comment*
1. Supportive and Psychoeducational Work	For restoration of morale, re-integration of existing defenses, and education concerning nature of illness. (First two weeks)
2. Cognitive-Behavioral Methods	For identification and replacement of abnormal beliefs and thoughts leading to painful mood states and self-defeating or dysfunctional behaviors. (Several weeks to months.)
3. Psychodynamic Psychotherapy	To make "connections" and bring resolution of central dynamic conflicts. (Several months to one to two years.)
4. Existential Psychotherapy	To explore issues in meaning, values, and suffering. To develop purpose and spiritual dimensions. (Several months to one year.)

CONCLUSION

More questions than answers exist regarding males with eating disorders. In the meantime, adequate information is now available to allow clinicians to diagnose accurately eating disorders in males and to organize comprehensive treatment, appreciating the multidimensional aspect of these illnesses. A practical approach to males with eating disorders will appreciate those aspects of illness that are shared with women as well as features of illness unique to males. There is no evidence currently that males with eating disorders have a worse prognosis or outcome than females. Virtually every aspect of these illnesses is treatable to some degree. A stance of optimism tempered with realism will guide current practice until well-designed research inquiries into causes, mechanism, and treatment lead to more fundamental understanding in the future.

REFERENCES

Andersen, A.E. (1990). A proposed mechanism underlying eating disorders and other disorders of motivated behavior. In A.E. Andersen (Ed.), *Males with Eating Disorders*, pp. 221-254. New York: Brunner/Mazel.

Burns, T., & Crisp, A.H. (1990). Outcome of anorexia nervosa in males. In A.E. Andersen (Ed.), *Males with Eating Disorders*, pp. 163-186. New York: Brunner/Mazel.

DiDomenico, L., & Andersen, A.E. (1990). Why so few males with eating disorders: a comparison of men's and women's magazines. Abstract presented at the Fourth International Conference on Eating Disorders, New York, NY, April 1990.

Fichter, M.M., & Daser, C.C. (1987). Symptomatology, psychosexual development, and gender identity in 42 anorexic males. *Psychol Med 17*, 409-418.

Herzog, D.B., Bradburn, I.S., & Newman, K. (1990). Sexuality in males with eating disorders. In A.E. Andersen (Ed.), *Males with Eating Disorders*, pp. 40-53. New York: Brunner/Mazel.

Hsu, L.K.G. (1989). The gender gap in eating disorders: why are the eating disorders more common among women? *Clinical Psychology Review* 9, 393-407.

Piran, N., Lerner, P., Garfinkel, P.E., et al. (1988). Personality disorders in anorexic patients. *International Journal of Eating Disorders* 7, 589-599.

Eating Disorders among Athletes

▼
▼
▼
▼

by Catherine M. Shisslak, Ph.D. and
Marjorie Crago, Ph.D.

INTRODUCTION

The advantages of exercise are well known and include such benefits as reductions in blood pressure and cholesterol levels and increase in cardiac output. Beneficial psychological effects of exercise such as reductions in depression and anxiety and increases in feelings of well being and self-fulfillment are also well documented. However, in recent years, some negative consequences of exercise have become more evident. For example, a number of researchers have found that exercise can become an addiction or compulsion having harmful effects on the individual (DeCoverley Veale, 1987, Sacks & Sachs, 1981). Reinforcing the notion that exercise may become an addiction is the fact that many individuals experience withdrawal symptoms when prevented from exercising because of illness or injury (Robbins & Joseph, 1985, Little, 1969). Another negative effect of exercise brought to light recently is that excessive exercise may lead to an eating disorder in certain individuals.

PREVALENCE OF EATING DISORDERS AMONG ATHLETES

A dramatic increase in eating disorders over the last two decades has led to a number of studies aimed at determining how much these disorders affect various segments of the population. One group that appears to be more at risk is athletes. Research on this topic is based on individual case studies of athletes who have developed eating disorders, group comparisons of athletes and eating disorder patients, and laboratory studies of the relationship between exercise and eating disturbances in animals.

Preoccupation with Weight

One of the ways many athletes resemble eating disorder patients is in their extreme preoccupation with body weight. Since many sports such as gymnastics or distance running require a lean body build for optimal performance, it is not surprising that athletes who participate in these sports show extreme concern about gaining weight. But does this concern sometimes go beyond a desire to maximize performance in one's sport? Some studies suggest that it may. Dummer & associates (1987), for example, surveyed 487 female competitive swimmers and found that the reason given by 81 percent of the swimmers for wanting to lose weight was to look better.

Unhealthy Weight Control Methods

Unhealthy weight control methods used by people with eating disorders, such as restrictive dieting, self-induced vomiting, laxatives, diuretics, and diet pills, are also used by many athletes. Rosen & associates (1986) surveyed 182 female collegiate athletes participating in a variety of sports and found that 32 percent of the athletes reported using at least one of these weight control methods on a regular basis. In addition, 70 percent of the athletes using these methods believed them to be harmless. There are indications that the percentage of athletes using these weight loss methods may be even higher in certain sports such as gymnastics. Of 42 female gymnasts, 62 percent reported regularly using at least one unhealthy weight loss method, usually self-induced vomiting, diet pills, or fasting (Rosen & Hough, 1988). The percentage of male athletes losing weight this way is considerably less than female athletes, usually ranging from 10 to 20 percent (Black and Burckes-Miller, 1988).

Unhealthy weight loss methods are used more frequently by athletes participating in sports requiring leanness. However, many athletes in sports not requiring extreme thinness such as field hockey, softball, volleyball, and tennis have also reported using these methods (Rosen, McKeag, Hough & Curley, 1986). Using one or more of these ways to lose weight over a period of time can lead to negative health consequences such as severe dehydration with accompanying electrolyte disturbances, kidney damage, cardiac arrhythmias, and loss of endurance (Garner & Rosen, in press). These adverse consequences eventually impair athletic performance, increase the risk of injury, and, in some cases, can lead to death (Rosen & Hough, 1988).

Finding Eating Disorders among Athletes

Screening Tests. A number of athletes have obtained scores that indicate significant eating abnormalities when they were administered screening tests for eating disorders. In a group of 112 female dance students, 31 (28 percent) obtained scores on the Eating Attitudes Test (EAT) as high as those of anorexia nervosa patients (Garner & Garfinkel, 1978). In another study, 20 percent of female gymnasts and 17 per-

cent of female athletes in a variety of sports scored in the anorexia nervosa range on the EAT, in contrast to 12 percent of the female nonathlete control group who scored in this range (Warren, Stanton, & Blessing, 1990). In a group of 26 male wrestlers, 4 (6.5 percent) had scores on the EAT that were indicative of a possible eating disorder, but none of the control group of 21 male swimmers and skiers had scores in this range (Enns, Drewnowski, & Grinker, 1987).

Self-Reports by Athletes. Other studies of the prevalence of eating disorders among athletes are based on reports by the athletes themselves. In a group of 55 female dancers, one-third of the dancers reported having had either anorexia nervosa or bulimia nervosa at some time in their lives (Brooks-Gunn, Warren, & Hamilton, 1987). Among elite women runners, 13 percent reported a history of anorexia nervosa, and 34 percent reported atypical eating patterns (Clark, Nelson, & Evans, 1988).

Several well-known athletes have described their struggles with eating disorders. Cathy Rigby, the Olympic gymnast, became obsessed with losing weight while training for the Olympics. She learned to control her weight by vomiting after eating and usually vomited about six times a day. However, after retiring from gymnastics her bulimic behavior did not stop but became worse until the majority of her day was spent eating junk food and throwing up. Bulimia has also been a problem for Tiffany Cohen, an Olympic swimmer. She was recently hospitalized for nine weeks in order to be treated for her bulimic disorder (Thornton, 1990).

Diagnoses of True Eating Disorders by Clinicians. Although a number of athletes resemble eating disorder patients in such ways as preoccupation with body weight, use of unhealthy weight loss methods, and high scores on screening tests for eating disorders, only a portion of these athletes *actually* fulfill the criteria for an eating disorder when interviewed by an eating disorder specialist. For example, of 112 female dance students, six (five percent) were diagnosed as anorexic when interviewed by a clinician, although 31 (28 percent) had obtained high scores on a screening test for eating disorders (Garner & Garfinkel, 1978). In another study involving 183 female dance students, 69 (37.7 percent) had high scores on a screening test for eating disorders, but only 12 (6.5 percent) of the students were diagnosed as anorexic during a clinical interview (Garner & Garfinkel, 1980). These differences may suggest that while a significant number of athletes are at risk a lesser group have actually developed a true eating disorder. The at-risk individuals are viewed as a "subclinical" group and may be subject to the development of the full eating disorder syndrome at a later time.

Why the Numbers Vary. Estimates of how widespread eating disorders are among athletes vary from less than 1 percent to as high as 25 percent (Thornton, 1990). There are several reasons for such vast differences in estimates. One of the most important factors is the type of information on which the estimate is based. Estimates will vary greatly depending on whether they are based on scores from eating disorder screening tests, self-reports by athletes, or diagnosis by an eating disorder specialist. Another factor is that eating disorders are often successfully hidden from family, friends, and teammates, which makes it difficult to estimate the actual prevalence of these disorders. Also, some sports seem to have a higher incidence of eating disorders than others so estimates will vary depending on which sport is the focus of study.

HOW ATHLETES DEVELOP EATING DISORDERS

Does Exercise Cause Eating Disorders?

One of the questions that researchers are attempting to answer is whether strenuous exercise in itself causes eating disorders or whether individuals who are prone to eating disorders gravitate toward sports that require a low body weight. Evidence for exercise-induced eating disorders is found in individual case studies, comparisons of athletes and eating disorder patients, and laboratory studies of animals. Two cases of male long-distance runners who developed anorexia nervosa after they became serious runners are described by Katz (1986). Both men later became depressed and bulimic when they were forced to curtail their running because of injury. Smith (1980) described a case of a male rower who became anorexic after engaging in restrictive dieting in order to qualify for a light-weight rowing competition.

Types of Sports Where Eating Disorders Are Often Found

Athletes participating in sports that emphasize leanness such as gymnastics, wrestling, diving, figure skating, distance running, and ballet appear to be at greater risk for the development of eating disorders than athletes participating in nonleanness sports (Garner & Rosen, in press; Yates, 1991; Yates, Shisslak, Crago, & Allender, 1991). In addition to an emphasis on leanness, other characteristics of a sport that may contribute to the development of an eating disorder are its competitiveness, its emphasis on form and appearance, the amount of stress placed on the body, and an emphasis on individual effort rather than team performance (Yates, 1991, p. 69, Hamilton, Brooks-Gunn, &

Warren, 1985). Sports such as dance, gymnastics, and figure skating which emphasize not only ultraleanness but appearance as well may have a larger percentage of athletes with eating disorders (Brooks-Gunn, Burrow, & Warren, 1988; Yates, 1991).

Personality Traits Combined with Certain Sports May Lead to Eating Disorders

The characteristics of a sport such as an emphasis on leanness or individual competition may interact with the personality traits of the athlete to start and perpetuate an eating disorder. Some of the personality traits exhibited by athletes are similar to the traits manifested by many eating disorder patients. For example, both groups tend to be characterized by high self-expectations, perfectionism, persistence, and independence (Yates, 1991, p. 110). It may be that these very qualities, which enable these individuals to succeed at athletics, also put them at greater than average risk for the development of an eating disorder (Yates et al., 1991).

Follow-up studies of anorexia nervosa in dance students provide further evidence that strenuous exercise may bring about eating disorders in vulnerable individuals. In 12 cases of anorexia nervosa in female ballet dancers, all but one case developed the disorder while studying dance (Garner & Garfinkel, 1980). In a follow-up study of 35 female ballet students who were interviewed between two and four years after initial assessment, nearly 40 percent met the criteria for an eating disorder or a partial eating disorder syndrome at follow-up (Garner, Garfinkel, Rockert & Olmsted, 1987). Thus, these disorders were not merely benign or temporary adaptations to the ballet subculture but continued over a several-year time period. Further follow-up studies are needed to determine the progression of these disorders over longer periods of time.

Anorexia and Exercise

Other evidence for the association of strenuous exercise and eating disorders comes from studies of anorexic patients. In several studies it was found that more than half of the anorexic patients had begun exercising excessively prior to the onset of the anorexic disorder (Kron, Katz, Gorzynsky, & Weiner, 1978; Touyz, Beumont, & Hook, 1987). These anorexic patients had progressed from normal exercising to compulsive overexercising which they were no longer able to control.

Epling & Pierce (1988) have also proposed that a significant number of cases of anorexia nervosa may be activity induced. In extensive laboratory studies of animals, Epling and Pierce found that rats who were put on a restrictive diet spent increasing amounts of time running on an activity wheel. As their running increased more and more, the animals ate less and less. Consequently, they lost a great deal of body weight. This process, if allowed to continue, eventually led to the animal's death from self-starvation. Control animals who were put on the same restrictive diet, but not allowed to run, survived. These results suggest that excessive exercise and food restriction can become a deadly combination, as evidenced by the fact that mortality rates among anorexics are higher than among any other psychiatric group (Herzog, Keller, & Lavori, 1988).

PREVENTION AND TREATMENT OF EATING DISORDERS AMONG ATHLETES

Since there is a subgroup of athletes who have eating disorders or who are engaging in behaviors that could lead to an eating disorder, such as restrictive dieting or the use of other unhealthy weight loss methods, it is important for coaches, trainers, teammates, teachers and others associated with athletes to be aware of certain behaviors which may signal an eating disorder. Some of these indicators of a possible eating disorder are listed below. Since eating disorders are more difficult to treat the longer they progress, early intervention is important. Most important of all, however, is the prevention of circumstances or factors which could *lead* to an eating disorder (Shisslak, Crago, Neal, & Swain, 1987).

Warning Signs of a Possible Eating Disorder

1. Stealing or hoarding of food
2. Consuming large amounts of food without gaining weight
3. Avoidance of eating in public
4. Frequent trips to the bathroom (especially immediately after eating)
5. Excessive weight loss
6. Preoccupation with food, weight, and appearance
7. Frequent weighing
8. Repeated periods of restrictive dieting or fasting
9. Extreme weight fluctuations over short time periods
10. Excessive physical activity
11. Minor theft of food, money or equipment
12. Social withdrawal
13. Loss or thinning of hair
14. Tendency toward stress fractures or shin splints
15. Swollen salivary glands
16. Loss of menstrual periods in females
17. Claiming to feel fat even when normal weight or underweight
18. Denial of hunger
19. Use of drugs to control weight (laxatives, diet pills, diuretics, emetics)
20. Refusal to maintain even a minimal normal weight
21. Complaints of bloating or water retention
22. Depressed mood following eating
23. Preoccupation with the eating behavior of other people
24. Evidence of self-induced vomiting
25. Numerous physical complaints such as headaches, weakness, dizziness, muscle cramps, or gastrointestinal problems

If an Athlete Shows Warning Signs

If an athlete shows several of the eating disorder warning signs listed above, the coach or trainer should meet with the athlete privately and express his/her concerns about the athlete's eating behavior. It is important that the athlete be reassured that the admission of an eating problem will not result in him or her being dropped from the team or being prevented from further competition, unless the athlete's health has been seriously compromised.

If an Athlete Admits to an Eating Disorder

If the athlete admits to having an eating problem or admits to the misuse of certain unhealthy weight loss techniques it is important for the coach to educate him or her about the negative effects which an eating disorder can have on athletic performance. Some of the physical and psychological complications of an eating disorder which will eventually impaire athletic performance are dizziness, muscle weakness, lack of endurance, depression, inability to concentrate, and possible loss of bone density. It may be necessary for the coach to meet with the athlete periodically to check on the athlete's progress in improving eating behavior.

If an Athlete Denies There Is a Problem

If the athlete refuses to admit to having an eating problem in spite of evidence to the contrary or if the problem behavior continues in spite of the coaches' efforts to persuade the individual to modify the behavior, it may be necessary for the coach to refer the athlete to a clinician who specializes in treating eating disorders. Early intervention is extremely important since an eating disorder becomes more difficult to treat once it has become firmly established. While the athlete is in treatment the coach should continue to stay in contact with the athlete and be as supportive as possible. During the recovery process, which can be stormy and disruptive, the athlete will need to be reassured that she/he is still an important member of the team.

Education Is the Key to Prevention

Based on what is known about the development of eating disorders in athletes, various recommendations can be made for the prevention of these disorders. Perhaps most important is the *education* of athletes, trainers and coaches about the principles of proper nutrition for optimal athletic performance. Ideally, a dietitian or nutritionist should be included on the training staff to help the athlete design a weight loss program that is effective in reducing body fat while not adversely affecting strength or endurance.

Athletes, coaches, and trainers should be educated about the warning signs of an eating disorder as well as its medical complications and the long-term risks associated with these disorders. The early detection and treatment of mild disturbances in eating behavior could prevent the development of a full-blown eating disorder later on. Eating disorders which have gone on for a period of time often require more extensive treatment such as hospitalization and drug therapy as well as psychotherapy.

Why Coaches and Trainers Are Important

Coaches and trainers can play an important role in the prevention of eating disorders since athletes tend to trust them and rely on their advice. Because coaches and trainers often tell athletes how much to weigh, they are in a good position to tell athletes who have lost too much weight that they have to gain a certain number of pounds. When the coach has to tell an athlete to lose weight, it would be helpful if a dietitian or nutritionist were available to assist the athlete in designing an effective but healthy weight loss program. Many athletes have reported that they began excessively restrictive diets or the use of other unhealthy weight loss techniques after being told by a coach or trainer that they had to lose a certain amount of weight (Zucker et al., 1985).

Since the success of a coach is dependent upon the athlete's performance, some coaches may be reluctant to refer an athlete with an eating disorder to a specialist for treatment because of fear that treatment will take away not only the eating disorder but the athlete's drive to compete as well. Although this has indeed happened with some athletes (Zucker et al., 1985), in general, the overall good health of an athlete will ensure better athletic performance in the long run than the use of quick and unhealthy weight loss methods. Since depression and suicide attempts are common among eating-disordered individuals it is best not to ignore the warning signs of a possible eating disorder in an athlete. In this, as in other areas, the health of the athlete should be the highest priority.

REFERENCES

Black, D.R., & Burckes-Miller, M.E. (1988). Male and female college athletes: Use of anorexia nervosa and bulimia nervosa weight loss methods. *Research Quarterly for Exercise and Sport, 59,* 252-256.

Brooks-Gunn, J., Burrow, C., & Warren, M.P. (1988). Attitudes toward eating and body weight in different groups of female adolescent athletes. *International Journal of Eating Disorders, 7,* 749-757.

Brooks-Gunn, J., Warren, M.P., & Hamilton, L.H. (1987). The relation of eating problems and amenorrhea in ballet dancers. *Medicine and Science in Sports and Exercise, 19,* 41-44.

Clark, N., Nelson, M., & Evans, W. (1988). Nutrition education for elite female runners. *Physician and Sports Medicine, 16,* 124-136.

DeCoverley Veale, D.M.W. (1987). Exercise dependence. *British Journal of Addiction, 82,* 735-740.

Dummer, G.M., Rosen, L.W., Heusner, W.W., Roberts, P.J., & Counsilman, J.E. (1987). Pathogenic weight control behavior of young, competitive swimmers. *Physician and Sports Medicine, 15,* 75-86.

Enns, M.P., Drewnowski, A., & Grinker, J.A. (1987). Body composition, body size estimation and attitudes towards eating in male college athletes. *Psychosomatic Medicine, 49,* 56-64.

Epling, W.F., & Pierce, W.D. (1988). Activity-based anorexia: a biobehavioral perspective. *International Journal of Eating Disorders, 7,* 475-485.

Garner, D.M., & Garfinkel, P.E. (1978). Sociocultural factors in anorexia nervosa. *Lancet* (Sept.), 674.

Garner, D.M., & Garfinkel, P.E. (1980). Sociocultural factors in the development of anorexia nervosa. *Psychological Medicine, 10,* 647-656.

Garner, D.M., Garfinkel, P.E., Rockert, W., & Olmsted, M.P. (1987). A prospective study of eating disturbances in the ballet. *Psychotherapy and Psychosomatics, 48,* 170-175.

Garner, D.M., & Rosen, L.W. (in press). Eating disorders among athletes: research and recommendations. *Journal of Applied Sport Science Research.*

Hamilton, L.H., Brooks-Gunn, J., & Warren, M.P. (1985). Sociocultural influences on eating disorders in professional female ballet dancers. *International Journal of Eating Disorders, 4,* 465-477.

Herzog, D., Keller, M., & Lavori, P. (1988). Outcome in anorexia nervosa and bulimia: a review of the literature. *Journal of Nervous and Mental Disease, 176,* 131-143.

Katz, J.L. (1986). Long-distance running, anorexia nervosa, and bulimia: a report of two cases. *Comprehensive Psychiatry, 27,* 74-78.

Kron, L., Katz, J.L., Gorzynski, G., & Weiner, H. (1978). Hyperactivity in anorexia nervosa: a fundamental clinical feature. *Comprehensive Psychiatry, 19,* 433-440.

Little, J. (1969). The athlete's neurosis: A deprivation crisis. *Acta Psychiatrica Scandinavica, 45,* 187-191.

Robbins, J.M., & Joseph, P. (1985). Experiencing exercise withdrawal: possible consequences of therapeutic and mastery running. *Journal of Sport Psychology, 7,* 23-39.

Rosen, L.W., & Hough, D.O. (1988). Pathogenic weight-control behaviors of female college gymnasts. *Physician and Sport Medicine, 16,* 140-146.

Rosen, L.W., McKeag, D.B., Hough, D.O., & Curley, V. (1986). Pathogenic weight-control behavior in female athletes. *Physician and Sports Medicine, 14,* 79-86.

Sacks, M.H., & Sachs, M.L. (1981). *Psychology of Running.* Champaign, IL: Human Kinetics Publishers, Inc.

Shisslak, C.M., Crago, M., Neal, M.E., & Swain, B. (1987). Primary prevention of eating disorders. *Journal of Consulting and Clinical Psychology, 55,* 660-667.

Smith, N.J. (1980). Excessive weight loss and food aversion in athletes simulating anorexia nervosa. *Pediatrics, 66*, 139-142.

Thornton, J.S. (1990). Feast or famine: eating disorders in athletes. *Physician and Sports Medicine, 18*, 116-122.

Touyz, S.W., Beumont, P.J.V., & Hook, S. (1987). Exercise anorexia: a new dimension in anorexia nervosa? In P.J.V. Beumont, G.D. Burrows, and R.C. Casper (Eds.), *Handbook of eating disorders, Part I* (pp. 143-157). New York: Elsevier Science Publishers.

Warren, B.J., Stanton, A.L., & Blessing, D.L. (1990). Disordered eating patterns in competitive female athletes. *International Journal of Eating Disorders, 9*, 565-569.

Yates, A. (1991). *Compulsive exercise and the eating disorders.* New York: Brunner/Mazel.

Yates, A., Shisslak, C., Crago, M., & Allender, J. (1991). *Compulsive athleticism and the eating disorders: is there a relationship?* Manuscript submitted for publication.

Zucker, P., Avener, J., Bayder, S., Brotman, A., Moore, K., & Zimmerman, J. (1985). Eating disorders in young athletes. *Physician and Sports Medicine, 13*, 89-106.

Medical Dangers of Anorexia Nervosa and Bulimia Nervosa

▼
▼
▼
▼ by Diane W. Mickley, M.D.

Eating disorders involve a complex interplay of physical and emotional factors. The medical complications of anorexia and bulimia can be life-threatening but may give no outward warning symptoms. Attention to health realities must accompany (or even precede) therapy to provide the time and safety for recovery.

ANOREXIA NERVOSA: UNDERSTANDING THE EFFECTS OF STARVATION

Most patients with anorexia nervosa do not see themselves as starved because they do eat, often very healthy foods such as salads. But just as a car with the best tires and oil can't run without gas, so no amount of "healthy" foods can make up for inadequate calories. Without enough calories, the body slows its metabolism, compromises vital functions such as circulation, and uses up its muscle to provide the fuel that isn't coming from food.

A well-known study done by the U.S. military simulated prisoner-of-war camps by subjecting healthy men to starvation. This study, Ancel Keyes's "Minnesota Experiment," is described in *The Biology of Human Starvation* (Minneapolis: MN: University of Minnesota Press, 1950). The men's behavior soon showed many "anorexic" features: They obsessed about food constantly, ate their meals slowly and with strange rituals, felt depressed and tired, and once allowed to resume normal eating binged for months afterwards. Some anorexic symptoms we can understand as

a biologic defense against starvation. Thus, preoccupation with food, fatigue, and sometimes depression can be tolls of malnutrition which improve with weight gain.

Patients with anorexia often find that constant thinking about food and weight becomes plaguing. They may experience depression, fatigue, and sleep difficulty as well as feel cold, bloated, or constipated, or they may grow fine hair on the body (called *lanugo*). Many anorexics, however, insist that they feel fine, or minimize their discomforts and continue to work hard, get good grades at school, perform athletically, or exercise compulsively. This makes it hard for patients, family, and friends—and sometimes even doctors—to realize the danger of their situation.

Not only do anorexic patients perform in a vigorous fashion, which may hide the severity of their illness, but the price of starvation may not show on simple exam; the electrocardiogram may not show the kind of heart weakening that occurs; and blood tests often are normal or only seem mildly amiss. Because of this, anorexics often insist that they are healthy or are mistaken to be healthy when they are not.

When Is Low Weight Unhealthy?

Being underweight takes a major toll on the body. But what is underweight? Anorexics often feel that other women or models prove that very low weights are acceptable. To estimate *ideal weight*, a young woman of average bone size should weigh 100 pounds plus approximately four pounds for every inch over five feet in height (108 pounds for 5'2", 116 pounds for 5'4", 124 pounds for 5'6", and so on). For a very slight bone size, this is adjusted down to add three pounds for every inch (106 pounds for 5'2", 112 pounds for 5'4", etc.). For a very solid frame size, adjust up to five pounds for every inch over five feet (110 pounds for 5'2", 120 pounds for 5'4," etc.).

The term *critical weight* is used to define a minimum amount that the body needs to function healthily. Critical weight is about 90 percent of ideal weight. An average sized, 5'5" female would have an ideal weight of 120 pounds and a critical weight which is 10 percent less (so 120 pounds minus 12 pounds), or 108 pounds. Critical weight may not be enough for a person to have menstrual periods or do competitive sports, but it gives us a rough guideline. Certainly, below critical weight we know that major physical compromises are occurring regardless of how well a person feels.

Two other factors are important in evaluating weight. First, youngsters not finished with puberty may not lose weight; they may just get taller without gaining the weight they need to go along with it. These preteens will fail to gain weight and ultimately stop growing, but they may not actually lose weight. Second, individuals who are overweight to begin with may lose dangerous amounts of weight and show some of the physical damages of anorexia but not seem as dramatically underweight because of the extra pounds with which they began.

Physical Tolls of Anorexia

One of the most obvious consequences of anorexia for women is the loss of menstrual periods. For up to a third of anorexics, periods stop *before* weight loss begins. We used to consider the absence of periods a harmless reminder that an anorexic had work to do

to recover. Now, however, we know that the absence of estrogen that it reflects causes bone thinning after as little as six months time. This may lead to osteoporosis and a lifelong risk of fractures. For this reason, hormone replacement is now considered an important part of medical treatment for anorexics with prolonged absence of periods.

Anorexia's effects on the heart are especially worrisome. Heart muscle is reduced with malnutrition, just as arm and leg muscles are. The heart is smaller and weaker. Blood pressure falls, and the heart cuts back on circulation to the periphery to protect vital central organs. This is seen in the bluish-purplish appearance (called *acrocyanosis*) of the toes and then the fingers (especially in cold weather) of anorexic patients. Another serious consequence of cardiac impairment is the inability of the heart to increase oxygen delivery to the tissues in response to exercise. Because of this, continued exercise in underweight patients is especially dangerous.

The metabolism slows progressively as weight is lost. Feeling cold, tired, constipated, and depressed are complaints heard from patients with underactive thyroids, and anorexic patients often have low values on screening tests of thyroid functions. In fact, however, low thyroid function is just a compensation for starvation, slowing the body to conserve energy. This improves without treatment once caloric intake is better.

The stomach is also affected by anorexia. Many patients feel full easily or bloated, and indeed there is delayed stomach emptying so that food stays in the stomach many hours beyond normal. Liquids are better digested than solids, and frequent small portions are more comfortable than large meals. This too corrects with better nutrition, but medication (usually metoclopromide) is sometimes useful temporarily if symptoms are severe.

All sorts of other abnormalities can occur in anorexia. CT scans show that there is often loss of brain mass at very low weights. Cholesterol may be increased, liver tests may be amiss, and blood counts may be low (both for red cells and white cells). Nerve palsies can occur, causing "foot drops."

The important things to remember are not the specifics. The simple fact is that being underweight is physically dangerous, often in ways that are not apparent. Most of these physical problems resolve completely with recovery. But regaining weight is critical for both safety and recovery. It may be possible for anorexics to gain weight by working with a physician and a dietitian on an out-patient basis, but sometimes hospitalization is necessary. Exercise should usually be stopped temporarily. Medication can sometimes be useful. Going to therapy to understand the causes of weight loss is of great importance. But restoration of weight cannot be put off in the meantime—it is the cornerstone of recovery.

UNDERSTANDING BULIMIA NERVOSA

Anorexia nervosa and bulimia nervosa sometimes overlap. About half of patients with anorexia develop bulimic symptoms during their illness, but the great majority of patients with bulimia are of normal weight; in fact, some have had difficulty being overweight. Bulimics binge—sometimes on large volumes of food, but sometimes just a normal meal or a forbidden kind of food is experienced as a binge. Fearing weight gain, bulimics then purge, sometimes through strict fasting or excessive exercise, but most often by vomiting. Laxatives, diet pills, or water pills may also be used in futile efforts to lose weight.

Though some patients with bulimia feel well, many do not. Most patients also feel uncomfortable emotionally: ashamed, secretive, isolated, depressed, out of control. Like anorexics, most bulimics are preoccupied with food and weight in a constant, bothersome way that soon intrudes on other spheres of

their lives. Patients with bulimia may also experience a wide range of physical symptoms, including weight swings, insomnia, weakness, abnormal menstrual periods, heartburn, bloating, swollen cheeks, dental decay, and so on.

Physical Tolls of Bulimia

Bulimia can have pervasive physical consequences. Patients who fast between binges slow their metabolisms and set up a cycle in which their undereating drives the body to binge again. Thus, treatment often involves learning to regularize eating and, temporarily, to avoid excess dieting.

Bulimia may cause women to have irregular or no menstrual periods. However, this usually does *not* impair fertility. Because of the myth that birth control pills may cause weight gain, many patients with eating disorders avoid them, often resulting in unwanted pregnancies. In fact, the very low doses of hormones in most modern oral contraceptives can be taken without fear of weight gain. Some studies show worrisome consequences of eating disorders during pregnancy, and patients with such disorders clearly require special care.

Most bulimic patients purge by vomiting, which causes many physical dangers. The teeth develop cavities and the lingual surfaces erode. The loss of electrolytes during vomiting may cause low potassium, which may cause muscle weakness or, without symptoms, lead to fatal cardiac arrhythmias or respiratory paralysis. Detection requires periodic blood tests to monitor the need for potassium replacement. The likelihood of low potassium is compounded by low weight or abuse of diuretics or laxatives.

Patients with bulimia often experience swelling of the parotid glands, producing a "chipmunk cheek" appearance. The submandibular glands under the chin may enlarge as well. This often affects both sides, is painless, and usually resolves once patients stop vomiting.

The esophagus often becomes inflamed from being bathed in stomach acid during vomiting. This can cause heartburn, which may be helped by medication. Tears or even rupture of the esophagus, which causes vomiting of blood, as well as pain, are other feared complications. The stomach tends to empty poorly in bulimics, causing a feeling of bloating after eating.

Most patients who abuse laxatives choose those with phenolphthalein, a drug which tends to work for the bowel, causing it to be unable to function on its own after a while. The very high doses used by some patients can even cause pancreatitis or encephalitis in rare cases. Ironically, though laxatives are believed to reduce weight, studies show that *laxatives do not remove calories*. They only cause water loss, as calories are already digested by the time food gets to the part of the colon affected by laxatives. Both laxatives and diuretics do cause loss of potassium. In addition, the dehydration they produce causes rebound fluid retention each time they are stopped. This leads to uncomfortable weight swings in many bulimic patients.

Most deadly among the forms of purging is the abuse of Ipecac, a syrup used to treat poison victims. Many patients who try it once find it so unpleasant they avoid further use. However, the emetine in this medicine accumulates in the body, so repeated use, even on a two- or three-times-a-week basis, can cause high levels in the body. This can produce a myopathy with arm and leg weakness, or affect the heart and cause sudden death.

Up to 20 percent of patients with bulimia may have problems with alcohol or drug abuse, which may already have been dealt with by the time these patients come for eating disorder treatment. Obviously, however, patients who have active alcohol intake have a whole additional set of medical risks, especially to their livers and blood counts. In-hospital treatment can be especially useful in this setting.

SUMMARY

Both anorexia and bulimia have specific physical dangers, and both require careful medical monitoring. Some patients will feel quite ill, others deceptively well. All should have a physical examination, including blood tests and an electrocardiogram. Other special studies are sometimes useful as well. Although these exam results may appear to be normal, we know that this in no way shows the patient to be free of danger. Medical treatment is geared to averting these risks, lessening symptoms, and promoting recovery.

The Hazards of Constant Undernutrition

▼
▼
▼
▼

by Linda P. Bock, M.D.

The extreme forms of restrained eating in anorexia nervosa and bulimia nervosa usually begin with simple dieting. Dieting, or caloric restriction, very quickly can lead to nutritional deprivation, often with serious and significant problems. Obviously, not all dieting results in eating disorders. The fine line between common social behavior (95 percent of Americans have dieted at some time in their life) and illness is marked by the autonomous nature seen in the illness. When the dieter "loses control" and the dieting has "a life of its own," this behavior is seen as abnormal, or pathologic.

Along the way to full-blown anorexia nervosa and bulimia nervosa, there is a spectrum of signs and symptoms—some of which are physical and others of which are psychological. The interplay between psyche (mind) and soma (body) is interesting to observe.

The classic scientific observation of human starvation in 1944 by Ancel Keyes illustrates the interplay of body and mind during starvation and differentiates findings involving malnutrition in "normal" people from the findings seen in individuals with the severe psychiatric illnesses of anorexia nervosa and bulimia nervosa. In this "Minnesota Experiment" by Keyes, 32 normal men volunteered to lose 25 percent of their body weight. In the weight loss phase of the experiment, there were both psychological responses and physical responses to starvation.

PSYCHOLOGICAL RESPONSES TO STARVATION

While the men in the "Minnesota Experiment" were content with their bodies and not longing to become thin, they chose to participate in this study to help prepare to rescue starving Europe as World War II was ending. Even though they weren't "dieting," the men became preoccupied with food. All their free thoughts revolved around food. They could continue to perform well at intelligence tests and academic tasks, but their simple activities would be interfered with by intrusive and interrupting obsessions about food. They lost interest in usual activities and even became dishonest about food. They collected recipes, talked about food, and even dreamed about food. They used so much coffee, tea, and gum that these substances had to be limited by the researchers conducting the study. This group of volunteers from the Quaker religion, usually a friendly and social group, became quarrelsome and irritable isolationists. They did not sleep well. They had no energy at some times, and at other times they were agitated, pacing, and anxious. They had mood swings, at times nearly euphoric, but eventually depressed. Interest in sex decreased. They ate with odd habits, cutting and arranging their food in patterns on their plates; practiced rituals of chewing; and excessively salted and seasoned their food.

The 32 Quaker men had been selected from 1,000 volunteers and each had tested as "normal." In spite of their normality, starvation made these men behave like very emotionally disturbed individuals. To summarize, the psychological symptoms of starvation seen in the 1944 study included:

- Preoccupation with food (recipes, coupon collecting).
- Odd food handling behaviors and rituals.
- Anhedonia (inability to be happy).
- Poor judgment, dishonesties.
- Excessive use of nonfood satisfiers (gum, coffee, etc.).
- Moodiness (irritability, euphoria, depression).
- Difficulty sleeping.
- Disturbed energy (agitated or apathetic).
- Decreased interest in sex.

PHYSICAL RESPONSES TO STARVATION

The physical changes among the men in the study were also interesting. They all had gastrointestinal problems—bloating, belching, and constipation. Although all the men had high-protein starvation meals, they all lost muscle mass. One highly visible area of muscle wasting was the temporal area just above the cheekbones. Heart muscle was not spared, and heart size also decreased. The heart rate slowed and the blood pressure decreased. The men had muscle weakness and cramps. There were also signs of dehydration. The scalp hair thinned and fine, downy hair, called *lanugo*, covered the body. Body temperature decreased, and the men felt cold all the time. The most prominent effect was the decrease in basal metabolic rate by 40 percent. Before focusing on this slowing in metabolism, here is a summary of the physical sequelae, or aftereffects, of starvation:

- Gastrointestinal symptoms—bloating, constipation.
- Muscle mass loss.

- Temporal muscle wasting.
- Muscle weakness and cramps.
- Decreased heart size.
- Slowed heart rate, decreased blood pressure.
- Dehydration.
- Hair loss.
- Lanugo.
- Decreased metabolic rate, coldness.

Basal metabolic rate refers to the rate at which energy is used to run the body at its "base" or resting state. This means the energy to keep the body warm, the energy to run cellular chemical systems, and the energy to do all the involuntary work of the body. In times of inadequate food, drought, famine, or during diets, the metabolic rate falls. All systems go on a work slowdown. This has been called hibernation metabolism.

HIBERNATION METABOLISM

When caloric intake for humans falls below 25 kcal (or calories) per day the body shifts to conserve energy. The best example of this hibernation metabolism is in animals that sleep all or part of the winter. Bears, squirrels, and chipmunks eat very little in the cold winter months, and they sleep a lot. Many body functions shut down. Hair does not grow well. The heart beats slowly. The bowels become inactive. The body temperature falls. Very commonly, the overall body weight does not go down because the body does less work to "get by" on less fuel, fewer calories.

The more a person diets, the more the body shifts to get by metabolically and weight is maintained. The body fights weight loss. Not only is excessive dieting futile, the dieting-nondieting cycle is very dangerous. After a diet ends and metabolic rate is low, regaining of the lost weight is very easy and occurs quickly. Further, with each subsequent substantial diet, weight will be lost more slowly and regained even more readily than with early diets.

SUMMARY

Restrained eating, chronic undernutrition, and extreme dieting for weight loss do not work. The dangers, physically and psychologically, are many. The fertile soil of starvation during dieting may spawn the very serious illnesses of anorexia nervosa and bulimia nervosa.

REFERENCE

Keyes, A., Brozek, J., Henschel, A., Mickelsen, O., & Taylor, H.L. (1950). *The biology of human starvation.* Minneapolis, MN: University of Minnesota Press.

Out of Balance, Out of Bounds: Obesity from Compulsive Eating

▼
▼
▼
▼

by Bonnie Kathryn Marx

There are times when all of us overeat and gain some extra weight. There are times when we all wish we were thinner, shorter, taller, huskier, more shapely, less shapely, whatever. Experiences like these are pretty normal and usually come and go without much ado. Experiences like these need not signal danger and vary greatly from the experiences of compulsive eaters, as will be seen.

Six women meet to form a self-help group. They are concerned about their overweight condition and their constant inability to manage dieting. They have several things in common. They all describe themselves as compulsive eaters. They all dislike their bodies and disassociate from their bodies in some way. They feel off balance, buffeted about between a compulsion to eat and a command to diet. They feel anxious and out of control around food. They all confess to some form of overeating followed by feelings of shame, guilt, and self-hate. They have all dieted and lost weight many times only to regain it. They all engage in secret eating.

As the women work together it is apparent that they are eager to find out "why" and "from where" their problems arise. They look at family and social attitudes, messages, and patterns that may have contributed to their uneasiness about their bodies, their weight, and the significance of food in their lives. These excursions into the past lend a new meaning and understanding to the present problem. However, after a number of weeks of self-study, a disturb-

ing new question arises: "What now?" Their expanded awareness has not altered the fact that they still feel hopeless and powerless to control their behaviors around food.

The experiences of these women are not unique. Countless people in our society, women and men, engage in this struggle with the intake of food in order to perfect their bodies by eating less and becoming thin. In their attempts to do so, they have tried the latest diets, frequented the nation's weight loss and/or exercise centers, talked with physicians and therapists, read every book on the subject, and joined Overeater's Anonymous or other support groups such as the one described earlier. By these routes, some have succeeded in breaking the cycle of events associated with compulsive eating. There are many others, however, who have tried it all, not succeeded, and like the women in the story, are asking, "What now?"

What a hard question! What makes change so difficult for these people is the complexity of a disorder that is too often dismissed simply as a "weight problem" or "medical condition" and treated as such. To do so diminishes the painful experiences of every person who struggles with this disorder. If not a weight problem, then what is obesity from compulsive eating?

A DEFINITION OF COMPULSIVE EATING

As an entity distinct from anorexia nervosa and bulimia, compulsive eating has never been strictly defined, though it does contain some features of both (Arenson, 1984; Orbach, 1978; Reiser, 1985; Wardle and Beinart, 1981). Like the other eating disorders, it can be characterized very simply as gross disturbances in eating behaviors. More precisely, it is a complex phenomenon descriptive of a set of beliefs, feelings, and behaviors associated with body image, self-image, and the consumption of food. Compulsive eaters are often not even fully aware of many of these beliefs, feelings, and behaviors. What they are acutely aware of, however, and what they present when they come into treatment, is a history that includes some, or all, of the following:

1. Being chronically overweight with a long history of dieting behaviors.
2. Body image disturbances (hating their bodies, ignoring or otherwise disassociating from their bodies, distorting size and/or shape of their bodies).
3. A self-image based on body weight.
4. An inability to diet and lose weight (or maintain a goal weight after dieting and losing weight).
5. A strong desire to eat unrelated to any sense of physical hunger.
6. An inability to sense physical hunger.
7. Being aware of "feeling fat for as long as I can remember," even when in a healthy weight range.
8. Feeling empty and using food to fill the void.
9. Feeling addicted to food and helpless to change.
10. Being obsessed with food, weight, and dieting, yet feeling compelled to eat.
11. Feeling driven into the above activities as if from forces outside of themselves.
12. Being erratic, inattentive, thoughtless, or impulsive about feeding themselves.
13. Eventually feeling ashamed and guilty about eating *anything*.

14. Overeating after periods of restricting intake (i.e., after trying "to be good and diet").
15. Feeling big, out of place, left out, unable to fit in.
16. Engaging in overeating (or what is perceived as overeating), which is unwanted, unacceptable, and followed by shame, guilt, depression, self-condemnation, and self-hatred.
17. Engaging in secret eating.
18. Using rigid, perfectionistic structures in attempt to control the obsessive-compulsive energy.

(Arenson, 1984; Marx, 1985; Marx, 1989: Bruch, 1973; Rau and Green, 1975; Orbach, 1978; Wardle and Beinart, 1981).

From this list of beliefs, feelings, and behaviors it is obvious that obesity from compulsive eating is a serious and debilitating problem. The problem is made worse by the health risks associated with obesity: diabetes mellitus, hypertension, gallbladder disease, *hypercholesterolemia* (excessive cholesterol in the blood), arthritis and gout, certain cancers, and longevity (Kohl, 1991).

WHAT CAUSES COMPULSIVE EATING?

Because it is not defined or studied as a distinct entity in most of the literature (Arenson, 1984 and Orbach, 1978, excepted), the causes remain speculative. Via its association with the major eating disorders, components of compulsive eating have been theoretically linked with obsessive-compulsive disorders (Bychowski, as cited by Orbach, 1978; Mount, et al, 1991); addictive disorders (Milkman and Sunderwirth, 1983; Scott and Baroffio, 1986); fear of thinness (Orbach, 1978); neurologic dysfunction (Rau and Green, 1975); and hypothalamic dysfunction (Lundberg and Wolinder, 1967; Templar, 1971).

That obesity from compulsive eating does exist as more than a medical problem and as a condition separate from the major eating disorders may be debated. However, its reality is probably best reflected in Bruch's (1973) description of "thin fat people," and more recently in the work of Arenson (1984), Orbach (1978), and all the clinicians who have described the thousands of people they see who are searching for release from this battle with themselves about food. These thousands have been distinguished from the population of compulsive eaters who are not obese and from the population of obese who are not compulsive eaters.

Knowing that it exists and speculating about the causes does not tell much about obesity from compulsive eating. To fully explore the nature of this disorder demands a different question: What is it about?

The experiences of people who eat compulsively give clues as to the nature of compulsive eating and to issues central to its development. Sequences in these experiences may highlight and reflect stages in that development. It makes sense, then, to look first to the earliest remembered experience reported by compulsive eaters, e.g., dissatisfaction with their bodies and the body image (body image disturbances).

Most compulsive eaters have distorted views of themselves in relationship to their bodies. Because they hate their bodies and see them as fat and ugly, they disassociate themselves from their bodies in some way. Some live in their bodies from the neck up, disowning themselves from the neck down (Orbach, 1978). Others feel that they do not "have" a body, but that they "are" their bodies, perpetuating the idea that they will be acceptable only when their bodies are acceptable in size and shape (Arenson, 1984). Still others believe that their "true" selves are hidden beneath layers of fat to be revealed to them only when the fat is eliminated (Orbach, 1978). Since they do not belong with or take ownership of or feel responsibly connected with their bodies, it is no wonder that compulsive eaters feel no sense of control over them.

Boundary and Control Issues

Splitting of the body from the self and subsequent boundary and control problems make up the core issues confronting compulsive eaters. The critical issue, of course, is one of control. Compulsive eaters feel powerless and out of control about food, their bodies, themselves, and their potential to change. Such a disturbance of body image then interferes with the development of the self-concept and the capacity to accept oneself as a whole, integrated person in charge of self and environment (Hardy 1982). Without the body there are no physical boundaries and without physical boundaries there is no place to live and "be" in the world, no place to experience themselves as separate from others, no place to "feel" in, and consequently, no sense of control over what happens to them. What has happened to create this disruption?

In nearly every case what has happened is that compulsive eaters came to believe that their bodies and their experiences were somehow not their own, that they belonged to someone else or were too insignificant to attend to. The belief (most often unconscious) developed over time after receipt of many "messages," spoken and unspoken, to support it. Some received these messages when their bodies were used and abused for incest or other forms of sexual trauma. Some received the messages through beatings and/or other kinds of physical abuse and neglect. Some received messages in subtler, more insidious ways so "natural" to the context of their lives that they went unnoticed. What became noticeable though, were the effects of these messages: never feeling good enough, smart enough, responsible enough, perfect enough; feeling pressure to take on roles and responsibilities in the family that the adults in the system failed to perform; feeling responsible for everything and everybody; feeling discounted, unworthy, ashamed, alone, unlovable, abandoned. Simply, never feeling safe and sound in the world.

It is impossible for anyone to feel safe and competent when the foundation of their early experiences in the world has been built with harshness or confusion. When people have not been well taken care of, a question about self-worth (and in some cases even their right to exist) develops. It is very difficult for these people to learn how to take good care of themselves and their needs, to learn to make choices for their own well-being. In their attempts to take care of themselves they often develop systems that seem to help them feel safe and in control at the time but which fail to provide safekeeping in the long run. Obesity from compulsive eating is one such self-care system. For these compulsive overeaters, focusing on weight and food and constantly looking for the perfect diet is an attempt to treat what ails them. Their treatment focus, however, is way off the mark when the whole picture of their problems comes into view.

TREATMENT OF COMPULSIVE EATING

What comprises adequate treatment for obesity from compulsive eating? Traditionally, treatment approaches for obesity and overeating as "medical conditions" were all that were available to compulsive eaters. These approaches focused on the presenting problem, overweight, and were based on self-control and stimulus control (Stuart and Davis, 1972; Mount, 1987; Wardle and Beinart, 1981). In some cases, attempts were made to treat the underlying causes of distress that produced the overweight and compulsive eating through some form of psychotherapy (Bruch, 1973; Stunkard, 1959). Other treatment interventions, alone or in combination, such as exercise programs, hypnosis, cognitive-behavioral management, and even drastic surgical procedures were also employed to help compulsive eaters lose undesired weight and gain control over eating patterns.

At best, these interventions have provided relief from the cycle of events and issues associated with compulsive eating. However, relapses are frequent, particularly when treatment focuses on weight reduction and self-control alone. That approach deals with only the tip of the iceberg and does little to promote long-lasting results. Treatment must eventually address the major psychological issues and support development of a healthier system of self-care. Inherent in any treatment must be the idea of ownership, of reclaiming and reparenting the body, and reacquainting with it as part of the self. The recovery process requires it.

Compulsive eaters, often seekers of the "quick fix," must accept that *recovery is a process*. It is not a quicky diet plan guaranteed to take off 50 pounds in two weeks! It is not a magic pill to swallow that will forever halt the need to eat. For compulsive eaters it is a movement out of fear, helplessness, and victimization supported by a willingness to learn how to "reparent" themselves, to learn to take good care of their physical, emotional, and mental needs. The treatment of choice for recovery may vary but the treatment path must always lead compulsive eaters to develop healthy responses to question such as:

- Who am I?
- What are my *own* thoughts, ideas, values, feelings?
- What are my *own* wants and needs?
- What scares me, angers me, pleases me, saddens me?
- What can I do when I feel fear, anger, joy, or sorrow besides eat?
- How can I stop obsessive thoughts and compulsions to eat?
- What stresses me and makes me tense?
- What can I do when I feel tense and stressed besides eat?
- How can I ask for what I need and want?

- How can I learn to accept that I have a right to ask for what I need and want?
- How can I learn not to abandon myself all the time for the sake of others?
- How can I learn to accept myself and be patient and harmless with myself while I heal?
- How can I learn to forgive myself?

Good treatment by professionals provides the safety, instruction, guidance, and atmosphere necessary to do this kind of work. The compulsive eaters in turn must provide the will and the courage to persevere. It is hard work, but it is freeing and fulfilling. It is like coming home.

REFERENCES

Arenson, G. (1984). *Binge eating* (1st ed). New York: Rawson Associates.

Bruch, H. (1973). *Eating disorders* (1st ed). New York: Basic Books, Inc.

Hardy, G.E. (1982). Body image disturbances in dysmorphophobia. *British Journal of Psychiatry, 141* 181-185.

Kohl, Debra MS, RD, CNSD. (1991). Consulting Nutritionist, Institute of Medical Nutrition, Phoenix, Arizona, 1991.

Lundberg, O., & Wolinder, J. (1967). Anorexia nervosa and signs of brain damage. *International Journal of Neuro-Neuropsychiatry, 3,* 165-173.

Marx, B.K. (1985). The evolution of a holistic treatment program for people who are compulsive eaters. University of Wisconsin, Madison.

Marx, B.K. (1989). Obese patient population analysis for N.I.M.H. survey. St. Luke's Medical Center, Phoenix, Arizona.

Milkman, H., & Sunderwirth, S. (1983). The chemistry of craving. *Psychology Today*, October, 36-44.

Mount, D.R., Neziroglu, F., & Taylor, C.J. (1991). An obsessive-compulsive view of obesity and its treatment. *Journal of Clinical Psychology, 46*(1).

Mount, D.R. (1987). A comparison of stimulus control and exposure with responsive prevention for control of obesity in clients with obsessive-compulsive eating tendencies. *Dissertation Abstracts International, 47*(11).

Orbach, S. (1978). *Fat is a feminist issue* (1st ed). New York: Paddington Press Ltd.

Rau, J.H., & Green, R.S. (1975). Compulsive eating: a neuro-psychologic approach to certain eating disorders. *Comprehensive Psychiatry, 16*(3) 223-231.

Reiser, L.S. (1985). Compulsive eating: obesity and related phenomena. Fall meeting, American Psychoanalytic Association, New York, December 21, 1985.

Scott, R.L., & Baroffio, J.R. (1986). An MMPI analysis of similarities and differences in three classifications of eating disorders: anorexia nervosa, bulimia, and morbid obesity. *Journal of Clinical Psychology, 42*(5).

Stuart, R.B., & Davis, B. (1972). *Slim chance in a fat world* (1st ed.). Champaign, IL: Research Press.

Stunkard, A.J. (1959). Eating patterns and obesity. *Psychiatric Quarterly, 33,* 284-292.

Templar, D. (1971). Anorexic humans and rats. *American Psychology, 26,* 935.

Wardle, J., & Beinart, H. (1981). Binge eating: a theoretical review. *British Journal of Clinical Psychology, 20* 97-109.

The "Obesities": Causes and Management

▼
▼
▼
▼

by Sharon A. Alger, M.D.

The prevalence of obesity has increased dramatically in western societies over the past 50 years. In the United States, obesity affects approximately 34 million adults and is a risk factor for the development of other health problems such as diabetes, hypertension, heart disease, and stroke. Genetic, psychological, emotional, and environmental factors are all believed to play a role in the etiology, or causes, of obesity, and attempts at a long-term treatment or prevention have met with limited success.

This chapter will focus on defining the factors associated with the development of obesity: the various types of "obesities," their causes, and strategies for long-term management of this disorder.

WHAT IS OBESITY?

Obesity exists when adipose (fat) tissue makes up a greater than normal percentage of total body weight. This has been defined as a body fat content greater than 30 percent for women, and greater than 25 percent for men. However, accurate methods to measure body fat such as underwater weighing or impedance, a technique using electric current to determine body composition, are not readily available in many health care centers. Therefore, obesity is often measured by means of the body mass index (BMI), which assesses body weight in relation to height. According to this index, values of BMI between 20-25 represent acceptable weight, 25-30 mild obesity, 30-40 moderate obesity, and over 40 severe obesity. The risk of dis-

ease and death from obesity-related health problems is significantly increased in individuals with a BMI greater than 30 (Gray, 1989).

The *distribution* of body fat is genetically determined and is also a very important factor in establishing health risks. Central obesity, in which a large proportion of excess fat is stored in the abdominal area, occurs more commonly in males and is associated with the development of hypertension, diabetes, and heart disease. Peripheral obesity, in which excess body fat is stored in the hip and thigh area, is more common among females and less likely to lead to the development of serious health problems. Central obesity is defined as a waist-to-hip ratio greater than 0.9.

WHAT CAUSES OBESITY?

Obesity represents a positive energy balance in which excess nutrients (from food) are stored as body fat. It requires an intake of calories in excess of energy expenditure. However, the balance between energy intake and expenditure is widely variable among individuals and is influenced by a variety of genetic, environmental, and psychological factors.

Energy Intake

There is no good evidence to suggest that overweight people consistently eat more or eat faster than lean individuals. Studies on taste preference suggest that the obese may prefer foods with a higher fat content than normal weight people (Drewnowski, Brunzell, Sande, et al., 1985). Some of this difference in taste, however, may relate to the diet status of the individual rather than to body weight, because restrictive dieting is known to increase the preference for highly palatable "forbidden foods" (Rodin, Moskowitz, & Bray, 1976). These high-fat foods pose a greater risk for weight gain than calories from carbohydrate or protein sources because dietary fat is readily converted to stored body fat.

Diet-induced cravings for high-calorie foods may also contribute to the development of binge eating in a subset of the obese population. Between 25-46 percent of overweight individuals have been reported to engage in binge eating at least twice weekly (Marcus & Wing, 1987). In one study, 97 percent of those who indicated serious problems with binge eating met the *DSM-III-R* (*Diagnostic and Statistical Manual*, 3rd edition, revised, of the American Psychiatric Association) criteria for bulimia. These obese bingers had food attitudes, personality traits, and depressive symptoms very similar to normal weight bulimics and quite different from non-binging obese individuals (Marcus & Wing, 1987).

Frequency of meals and snacks also seems to influence body weight in a certain way. Many obese individuals limit their food intake to one meal a day in an effort to restrict calories. The meal is often in the evening, after the activities of the day are completed. This pattern of eating may actually hinder the weight loss effort because the amount of energy burned off by the body as heat is reduced, and therefore, the body becomes more efficient at storing energy as fat.

Energy Expenditure

The second half of the energy balance equation involves the way the body uses food. The basal metabolic rate accounts for the majority of daily energy expenditure (60-70 percent in a sedentary individual). The basal metabolic rate represents the energy burned by the body under resting conditions and in a fasted state; it is the "idling" speed of the body. The thermic (or heat) effect of food accounts for an additional 10-15 percent of daily energy expenditure, which is energy used by the body for the metabolic processing of ingested nutrients (food). The thermic effect of food is increased with a high carbohydrate intake and with increased meal frequency. The energy used by voluntary physical exercise is the most variable and adjustable component of daily energy expenditure and is dependent upon the intensity and duration of the exercise as well as on the individual's body weight. Exercise can account for between 15 and 30 percent of the body's energy expenditure.

Basal metabolic rate varies greatly and is largely determined by the fat-free mass, fat mass, age, and sex of the individual (Ravussin, Zurlo, Ferraro, & Bogardus, 1991). However, recent evidence suggests that basal metabolic rate is also related to family membership and is therefore at least partially genetically determined (Bogardus, Lillioja, Ravussin, et. al., 1986). Individuals with a low basal metabolic rate are at increased risk for weight gain. Genetic factors, therefore, partially determine the rate at which food is burned as energy or stored as body fat. Metabolic rates may be related to differences in sympathetic nervous system activity (Peterson, Rothschild, Weinberg, et al, 1988) or possibly to genetically determined differences in muscle fiber types (Wade, Marbut, & Round, 1990).

In summary, differences in daily food intake patterns and energy expenditure result in wide variations in the energy balance equation between individuals. For example, a 20-year-old male, at a height of 5'10" with no family history of obesity, may consume 3000 kcal/day (calories per day) to maintain his usual body weight of 160 pounds. In contrast, his next-door neighbor, a

45-year-old woman of the same height but with a strong family history of obesity, has maintained her weight of 210 pounds with a dietary intake of only 1500 kcal/day!

These two individuals have maintained their weight at markedly different levels of energy intake. Several possible explanations for this are:

1. They ate different kinds of food. (High-fat foodstuffs may increase the risk of weight gain.)
2. They had different eating patterns. (One meal a day vs. multiple meals throughout the day.)
3. They had different rates at which ingested nutrients, food, are burned as fuel. (Their basal metabolic rate and thermogenesis were dissimilar.)
4. They had different levels of voluntary physical activity.

MANAGEMENT STRATEGIES FOR WEIGHT LOSS

In planning an appropriate weight loss program, it is important to assess the severity of obesity and the potential for development of obesity-related health problems. The risk of hypertension, cardiovascular disease, and diabetes is much greater in individuals at a BMI greater than 30 and with a central distribution of body fat. Individuals in this category may significantly reduce their risk of long-term health problems through weight reduction. Individuals with a peripheral distribution of body fat or a BMI of less than 30 may benefit from instruction in healthful eating and exercise patterns but should be discouraged from *severely* restrictive weight loss regimens. The health risks with this degree of obesity are less significant and greater emphasis should be placed on helping the individual accept his or her body shape.

A history of binge eating, multiple fad diets, or abuse of diet pills or laxatives is a warning signal for the development of a serious eating disorder. Severely restrictive diet plans should be discouraged in these individuals. Careful screening by a multidisciplinary team before beginning a weight loss program will aid in determing the combination of nutritional, psychological, and behavioral interventions appropriate for each individual.

Dietary Modifications

Nutrient intake should include a high-carbohydrate, low-fat regimen (a ratio of 55:25:20, carbohydrate, fat, and protein respectively). Carbohydrate is less calorically dense than fat (4 kcal/gm for carbohydrate vs. 9 kcal/gm for fat), and therefore allows more food to be eaten for an equal number of daily calories. A high-carbohydrate diet will also lead to more calories being burned as heat (increased "dietary-induced thermogenesis") than a high-fat diet and is less likely to result in storage of nutrients as body fat. Meals should be eaten at regular intervals throughout the day, and periods of fasting should be avoided. Fasting may result in a reduction in metabolic rate, with fewer calories burned off as heat. Eating more meals a day increases dietary-induced thermogenesis. The level of caloric restriction recommended is variable, depending on an individual's body weight, activity level, and pattern of food intake.

Exercise

Exercise should be strongly encouraged (after medical approval, if indicated). Regular exercise enhances weight loss and increases the capacity of the muscle to use fat as a fuel, hence decreasing the likelihood of fat accumulation. Physical exercise, because it increases energy expenditure, helps to offset any decline in energy expenditure that may occur from a weight-reducing diet.

Behavioral/Psychological Treatment

Obesity is a complex disorder with multiple factors contributing to weight gain. In some individuals, environmental and psychological factors and attitudes about food and eating patterns may be the primary factors associated with weight gain, whereas, in others, genetic backgrounds and a decreased level of energy expenditure may be the primary cause or etiologic factor.

The psychologist, as part of the multidisciplinary treatment team, can be very helpful in determining the psychological factors involved in the development or maintenance of obesity. Binge eaters, for example, are at increased risk for depression, food phobias, and anxiety disorders. Binge-eating behavior may be associated with a family history of alcohol abuse, drug abuse, or sexual and/or physical abuse. Early detection and initiation of psychological counseling in these individuals is critical to long-term recovery and weight control.

Cognitive-behavioral techniques, which attempt to modify psychological and environmental factors associated with obesity, have shown positive results in achieving short-term weight loss. Individuals involved in a behavioral group program may benefit from the supportive nature of the group and the increased sense of control over their lives (Rodin, Schank, & Striegel-Moore, 1989). Behavioral interventions, such as eating in only one place, learning to control the rate of eating, avoiding "buffet-style" meals, etc., are also effective in controlling the enhanced response to food cues noted in some individuals. Binge eaters may respond well in behavioral programs but tend to regain weight more rapidly than non-bingers once the treatment is completed (Marcus & Wing, 1987). This may reflect a return to the old habits of dietary restriction, followed by binge eating.

Obese individuals have recently been treated with antidepressant medications such as desipramine and fluoxetine. These medications have proved useful in the control of binge eating among normal-weight bulimics and may also be helpful in normalizing eating behavior in the obese population. Further research is needed to appropriately match the needs of the individual with the wide variety of treatment approaches currently available.

REFERENCES

Bogardus, C., Lillioja, S., Ravussin, E., et al. (1986). Familial dependence of the resting metabolic rate. *New England Journal of Medicine, 315,* 96-100.

Drewnowski, A., Brunzell, J.D., Sande, K., et al. (1985). Sweet tooth reconsidered: taste responsiveness in human obesity. *Physiological Behavior, 35,* 617-622.

Gray, D.S. (1989). Diagnosis and prevalence of obesity. *Medical Clinics of North America, 73* (1), 1-13.

Marcus, M.D., & Wing, R.R. (1987). Binge eating among the obese. *Annals of Behavioral Medicine, 9*(4), 23-27.

Peterson, H.R., Rothschild, M., Weinberg, C.R., et al. (1988). Body fat and the activity of the autonomic nervous system. *New England Journal of Medicine, 318* (17), 1077-1083.

Ravussin, E., Zurlo, F., Ferraro, R., & Bogardus, C. (1991). Energy expenditure in man: determinants and risk factors for body weight gain. In: *Recent Advances in Obesity Research: Proceedings of the 6th International Congress on Obesity.* London: J. Libbey, Publishers.

Rodin, J., Moskowitz, H.P., & Bray, G.A. (1976). Relationship between obesity, weight loss and taste responsiveness. *Physiological Behavior, 17,* 591-597.

Rodin, J., Schank, D., & Striegel-Moore, R. (1989). Psychological features of obesity. *Medical Clinics of North America, 73*(1), 47-66.

Wade, A.J., Marbut, M.M., & Round, J.M. (1990). Muscle fibre type and aetiology of obesity. *Lancet, 335,* 805-808.

PART 2
Personal, Social, and Cultural Issues

Eating Disorder Treatment Stories: Four Cases

▼
▼
▼
▼

by Susan Wagner, Ph.D.

The following case descriptions are taken from out-patient psychotherapy. Some of the details have been altered to protect the identities of the patients.

BULIMIA NERVOSA

Maria began therapy with me at age 24. She had several failed attempts at psychotherapy but felt she was not ready to work on her problems. She had bulimia nervosa, with an eight-year history of binging and vomiting as often as three times a day. She had never gone longer than two weeks without doing this. Her physical exam and laboratory studies were normal, but she admitted to having lost some of her hair over the past year.

Maria was extremely attractive, intelligent, and witty, with a good figure on the slim side of normal. She was also moody, sensitive, and prone to temper tantrums. She had attended an Ivy League college, where she managed only moderately good grades. Her pattern of skipping classes and staying up all night in order to binge and vomit clearly interfered with her academic and social life. She had friends, but she never told them about her problem. Even her boyfriend, with whom she was "unofficially" living, had no idea she was in trouble.

When Maria was 16, she had felt deeply insecure. She was 10 or 15 pounds overweight. Boys were not interested in her, and her only friends were other "brainy" girls who were not socially successful. Her family life was stormy: Her sensitive, intelligent, irritable parents were often critical of Maria,

her friends, each other, and anyone else who entered their lives. Her older sister coped with the parents by quietly withdrawing into her studies. Maria's response was the opposite: relentless arguments, screaming matches, and chronic frustration. Yet, she wanted her parent's approval very badly.

As part of a self-improvement campaign, Maria began to diet. She did well at first. Then she began to eliminate too many foods, which caused her to have intense food cravings. In this way, the binge/purge cycle began: The cravings led to binges; the binges led to a fear of becoming fat, which led to making herself vomit after a binge. Maria also found that immersing herself in food and then throwing it up gave her a calm, serene sort of feeling. As her illness progressed Maria was binging and purging not only because her dieting was far too restrictive, but because she could soothe herself this way when life (her parents, school, boys) upset her. Although she knew in some way that the binging and purging was "wrong," it remained her secret way of "getting by."

When Maria entered therapy with me, she was tired, ashamed, and sick of being sick. She was willing to risk gaining a few pounds for the sake of getting well. To get her parents to pay for previous treatments, Maria had told them about her problem but had made it seem much milder than it really was. This time, she allowed me to tell them the details. At first, her parents became angry and very critical of Maria (and of me). As time passed, however, they settled down and were supportive of Maria's efforts to get well.

Maria and I met once a week. We worked out a program of slow but steady elimination of binge/purge behavior. The decision about how much to cut back on binging and purging from week to week was always hers. She made an effort to eat three reasonable meals every day, and she sometimes kept a food diary, which she would share with me. She also went for brief nutritional counseling with a nutritionist who had years of experience counseling bulimics. Within a few months her binging and purging had stopped. She had gained five to 10 pounds, which bothered her; but she accepted this weight gain as a fair price for regaining her health. The remainder of the year's therapy sessions were spent on developing new ways of dealing with stress, which meant that Maria had to learn how to recognize what was bothering her. She had never had to do that, since her answer to every kind of discomfort had been the same: binge and vomit. Now Maria began to develop a healthy respect for some basic realities: her own needs and wishes, the needs of others, the limits of her ability to influence others, and the limits of others' abilities to respond to her needs. Maria learned to identify her needs and to think about ways of taking care of them. She also learned to evaluate whether particular people in her life were likely to help her meet those needs, or if they instead might interfere with her efforts to take care of herself. She learned that she did not have to sacrifice her preferences and beliefs to get approval.

Maria terminated psychotherapy with me after one year. She wanted to go back to school for an advanced degree, and she felt ready to apply what she had learned in treatment. We both assumed that she would return to therapy at some future point.

ANOREXIA NERVOSA

Tracy came to therapy at the age of 19, in her sophomore year of college, where she was getting good grades. She had a boyfriend from high school but had made few friends at college. Tracy stood 5'6" tall and weighed about 98 pounds. She had started losing weight deliberately about two years earlier, although she had been thin even then, weighing about 120. She just started eating less and less; losing weight became the most important thing in her life, although she couldn't explain why. When she came to me Tracy was frankly unhappy about the prospect of gaining weight, but she was also frightened by feelings of fatigue, the loss of her period for over six months, and her difficulty in being able to concentrate on school work.

As the younger sister of an unpredictable, rebellious, angry girl, Tracy felt obligated to be a "problem-free" child for her parents. She had witnessed countless fights between her parents and sister and listened endlessly to her parents complaining about her sister. Tracy was praised by her parents for being a good student, responsible, and considerate. Tracy had become entirely oriented toward pleasing others. She learned to hide her negative feelings, conceal different opinions, and become exceptionally intuitive about other people's wishes and needs.

Whenever possible, Tracy kept her problems to herself. She carried her silence even to the point of telling no one when she was attacked and raped on the way home from school when she was 14.

As high school graduation grew closer, Tracy began to restrict her food intake. She counted calories constantly, began to eliminate whole food groups from her diet, and spent hours inspecting her body for fat. She knew that she was afraid to go away to college. She feared that her mother would become depressed without her. She felt guilty about starting a life of her own and confused about what her parents really wanted her to do about going to college. Tracy did not realize that her overwhelming terror of making a mistake played a major part in her anorexia nervosa.

Family and friends expressed concern about Tracy's weight loss, but she held them off with excuses and with promises to gain. She decided on her own to pursue psychotherapy because of worries about her physical health. After Tracy and I discussed her diagnosis of anorexia nervosa, we agreed to the following treatment plan: a complete medical evaluation by a physician familiar with eating disorders; weight gain at the rate of one to two pounds a week; a target weight of 122; weekly "weigh-ins" at the doctor's office (in a hospital gown, after voiding, and supervised by the doctor or nurse); and psychotherapy once or twice weekly, depending on her progress.

Tracy took over one-and-a-half years to reach her target weight. She would gain and lose. For a long time, she described her food intake as "huge," when in fact she was eating under 2,000 calories per day (on which she could not gain). Her fatigue and poor concentration, which she correctly understood as the effects of malnutrition, helped motivate her to stop restricting her food.

Psychotherapy centered on three broad topics: her "addiction" to food restriction and how to recover from it, her feelings about her family and about herself as a part of her family, and her body image problems.

Tracy was able to grasp the concept of "addiction to restriction" very easily. She also saw that she would have to learn new coping skills in place of her "addiction." She remained, however, very guarded on the topic of her family. She was able to express some resentment toward her sister, but she just couldn't acknowledge any negative feelings toward her parents. Her body image problems had a lot to do with the rape at age 14. Tracy did come to feel and express her reactions to that trauma, her self-blame, her shame, and last of all, her anger.

Tracy achieved her goal weight and maintained it for over six months before ending her psychotherapy. She would return to anorexic ways of thinking when pressured or stressed, but she could resist the temptation to restrict her food. She had also expanded her social network at school, was able to participate in "fun things," share intimate stories with friends, and be silly when she felt like it.

ANOREXIA, BULIMIA, AND DRUG ABUSE

When I first met Allie she was 22, and her eating disorder had put her in the hospital four times: three for medical emergencies and once, for an entire year, for psychiatric treatment. Her problems with food had begun at about age 12. Allie had also abused cocaine for over two years. Although she drank alcohol infrequently, when she did, she drank to get drunk.

Over the years, Allie had seen a number of qualified out-patient therapists, only to become frustrated with them and drop out of treatment. She had, however, been trying to stick it out with her most recent therapist, who had then moved to another state. She told me that she had benefited a lot from her year in the hospital and that she was serious about getting well. Her perseverance with her previous therapist seemed to be a positive sign against a not very hopeful picture.

At 5'7" tall, Allie's weight had ranged from 87 to 128 pounds. She would make herself vomit after eating almost anything: an apple was as good an excuse as a huge binge on cake, ice cream, and candy. At times she used laxatives (up to 20 times the recommended dose), medicines to bring on vomiting, and appetite suppressants (over-the-counter or street drugs). She had often vomited blood and had blood in her stool. On occasion, Allie had intentionally cut or burned herself and once had made a suicide attempt.

Allie's background was brutally traumatic. Her parents separated when she was six, after years of vicious fighting. Her older brother was often left in charge, and he regularly beat her. During and after their separation, the parents made Allie and her brother deliver messages from one parent to the other. Sometimes those messages included threats or insults that provoked a rageful response from the recipient. The parental combat continued unabated throughout the time that Allie came to see me; it seemed to heat up whenever they could get the children or their friends to watch.

When Allie was eight, two older neighborhood boys picked on her for what became years of sexual abuse. At first, they approached her nicely, which she found flattering and confusing. As they attempted to coax her into sexual acts, she became more reluctant and afraid. Their tactics changed from gentleness to force and threats of more force. They warned her never to "tell" or they would hurt her mother. She was raped, sodomized, made to perform fellatio, called names and forced to call herself names, such as "slut" and "pig." Allie was pretty sure the abuse began to taper off during her 10th year, and she recalled no further abuse after the age of 11.

Allie was a good student in grammar school and well-liked because of her intelligence, wit, and beauty. By junior high school she was skipping classes, cutting school altogether, and sampling many drugs. She also began to binge, to induce vomiting, and to lose weight. It was at this point that school authorities insisted that her parents take her for psychiatric treatment.

Allie was helped very little by outpatient therapy, in-patient hospital treatment, medication therapy, or me. She and I worked together intensively (two to three sessions per week). She attended eating disorders group once a week. However, her symptoms lessened only temporarily. After nearly a year, she had yet another medical crisis (dehydration, with an electrolyte imbalance), and I referred her for another in-patient eating disorders treatment.

Further information about her progress is not available.

People like Allie sometimes die of their illnesses, but some do get better. Many factors contribute to their ability to recover. Parents who continue to abuse the patient or blame the patient are hard to fight. Friends who support recovery can help a lot; sticking with friends who abuse food or drugs can undermine treatment. People give up addictions when they "hit bottom"; this point seems to be harder to reach for those who have been the most severely abused.

LONG-TERM TREATMENT OF BULIMIA NERVOSA

This case represents a successful treatment. It took three-and-a-half years, half of which the patient spent in twice-weekly therapy, and a year during which the patient was also treated with antidepressant medication for her binge urges.

Jamie was 23 when she came to me for psychotherapy. She had a five-year history of binging and inducing vomiting while maintaining a normal weight. She was a graduate student, continuing a college romance which was now "long distance," had a number of good friends, and a dog she adored. When Jamie started therapy she was binging and purging about four times per week. She felt "fat" all of the time and devalued her looks overall. Her only previous treatment occurred at age 15 when she saw a psychiatrist three times after she had made a suicide attempt.

An only child, Jamie believed that family was especially important to her. She was close to her mother and stepfather (her parents divorced when she was seven), father, and maternal grandmother. Her friends and boyfriend saw her with her parents frequently and thought they were all "great."

It was not surprising to find that Jamie was better at recalling events in her history that made her happy rather than those that hurt her. She was accepted at a special grammar school for gifted children and enjoyed herself there very much. After her parents split up she saw her father most weekends and had a wonderful time with him. Although her mother would occasionally make insulting remarks about her father, neither her mother nor father was especially indiscreet in this area.

Jamie was popular throughout her schooling and was always free to invite other children to her home. When her mother remarried and moved, Jamie made friends easily and adjusted to the new school well.

In spite of her high intelligence, Jamie had practically no insight into her illness. She thought she had an eating disorder because she "liked to eat too much." As therapy progressed she reported that her mother frequently criticized her appearance, always begging Jamie to lose weight and be beautiful like her. (Her mother was quite beautiful and probably also had an eating disorder.) Jamie wanted to retract any bad reports she gave me about her mother and blamed herself for being so "one-sided" and felt guilty about being so "unappreciative" of all that her mother had done for her. Although she was much more comfortable poking fun at her father for being a rigid, compulsive person, she was unable to give examples of him rejecting or mistreating her.

The first six months of treatment helped Jamie reduce her binging and vomiting to once a week or every other week. We worked on regulating her eating habits, identifying signals that she was getting "bingey," and establishing alternative stress release behaviors. As we also worked on identifying "triggers" of binge urges, we found multiple examples that pointed to contact with her mother as a primary trigger. This made it easier for Jamie to give an honest account of her life with her mother.

Jamie had very few memories prior to her parents' divorce. Once her parents separated she remembered very well that

her mother would scream at her for no apparent reason, cry uncontrollably, and tell Jamie that she was a bad girl and a bad daughter. Sometimes her grandmother was there and intervened on Jamie's behalf. Most of the time her grandmother would explain that Jamie had to understand that her mother was going through a hard time. When Jamie was nine her mother remarried and became somewhat calmer. Even so, Jamie recalled that her mother would initiate fights with Jamie, Jamie would eventually become hysterical, and her stepfather would come home to a scene in which Jamie was out of control and her mother was cool, calm, and feigning ignorance about Jamie's upset. The other source of tremendous frustration came from her mother's teasing of her in front of a friend, persisting until Jamie would burst into tears. Both of these patterns were continuing in Jamie's adult life.

During the next six to 12 months, Jamie and I tried to develop strategies for Jamie to protect herself from such hurts by her mother. She tried very hard but never seemed to successfully preserve her self-respect in these encounters. The aftereffects of her contacts with her mother were still usually eating-disordered behavior. We agreed to have Jamie evaluated for treatment with medication for her binge urges. She began to take antidepressants, and within a month, all binging and purging had stopped. However, she found she could not handle her visits with her mother without feeling a loss of self-esteem and self-respect. At this point Jamie decided to cut off all contact with her mother, explaining to her that she needed time to get well and sort out her problems.

Into the third year of Jamie's treatment, she received a number of angry communications from her stepfather and grandmother berating her for her "cruel" treatment of her mother. She was able to tell them that she intended no harm to her mother but needed time for herself. They did not understand.

Now free of the continued pressure to be a "good daughter," Jamie worked hard on coming to terms with her past and present relationship with her mother. Feelings of hatred, fear, and hurt surfaced with intensity. In the final phases of our work together Jamie came to grips with the fact that her mother was emotionally impaired, which was probably caused by or worsened by her abuse of alcohol. She realized that the "closeness" she had felt with her mother was actually based on a one-sided relationship, and that her yearning to have a truly "motherly" mother would not be fulfilled.

Jamie was free of bulimic behavior, her body image was good, and she was maintaining her progress without medication. She stayed in touch with me for several years to tell me of her marriage and the birth of her first child. She had chosen to include her mother in these events but did not find herself reacting to her in the old ways.

Secrets and Denial: The Costs of Not Getting Help

▼
▼
▼
▼

by Linda P. Bock, M.D.

Chris was becoming thinner, and she avoided going out with her friends, especially if the event involved food. At school, Jane worried about Chris's not eating lunch. Jane confronted Chris: "You're just not eating." Chris replied calmly, "I'm fine. There's nothing wrong."

Jennifer always seemed to eat a lot. One day she ate a Big Mac, large fries, a shake, and a large Coke, then she and her friends went to the dairy where she had banana splits. Later at home she ate a whole bag of cookies. She went to the bathroom. Jennifer's friend Carol said, "Why do you go to the bathroom every time we eat?" Jennifer was scared but confessed, "I throw up." She told her story and ended by saying, "You're my friend and I trust you—don't tell anyone, it's a secret."

THE COSTS OF SECRETS AND DENIAL

The secrets of bulimia and the denial of anorexia have many forms, but both secrets and denial defend the sufferer from the truth that he or she is ill.

Giving up the denial or trusting the secret to open view makes the person feel vulnerable and anxious. If recovery is to be possible, secrecy and denial must stop.

A true friend or a loving sister, mother, father, or brother will confront their sick beloved: "I'm sorry, Chris, you are not fine. You are alone all the time, you never have fun, and you seem so tense and worried."

Or: "No, Jennifer, I can't keep this a secret. Throwing up your food is dangerous. Can I go with you to talk to your parents or do you want me to tell them myself?"

WHAT LOVED ONES CAN DO

Communicating with someone who has either anorexia nervosa or bulimia nervosa and who is in denial is not easy. Jerry Kreisman, M.D., who wrote a book entitled *I Hate You, Don't Leave Me* (1989) describes a technique of communication that is very applicable for people who by their illness say, "I'm hungry; don't feed me." In this technique, you, the concerned loved one, have three tasks—show support and concern, express empathy or understanding, and tell a truth.

Dr. Kreisman believes you must complete all three tasks, because if you omit the support statement, you seem uncaring. If the empathic statement is left out, the usual response will be, "you don't understand." If you don't tell your truth statement, the denial will persist.

To someone whose anorexia has made her dull, tired, and weak, a complete communication may be, "Susan, you seem so tired and exhausted, and you know I care about you deeply. I know you must be afraid to realize it and I am a little afraid too, but I need to insist that you are not well. You must get some help. We can work together on finding some help."

In this paragraph there is a statement of love and support. "I care about you." There are several statements that recognize the anorexic's point of view: "You are...tired...afraid." The truth is saved for the last and calls for action.

While very ill people with anorexia nervosa may refuse the truth or rage and bluster, you have said your truth in the most acceptable way. The positive effect may come later. Wait. Pray, if you choose to. Be ready to act when the moment of weakness in denial comes.

For someone who suffers with bulimia nervosa, the difficulty with eating and purging is readily felt as abnormal. The secrecy is the way bulimics defend themselves.

"Sharon, you know that I love you and I can't be a detective or policeman about your eating. My mother's heart tells me that these ways of yours—all the food, all the trips to the bathroom, your swollen red eyes—you can't feel safe or normal. I'm certain you could feel very afraid and embarrassed perhaps, but my love will never be embarrassed by you. The truth is all this is dangerous. Please get help now."

Such a speech could fall upon a ready heart and then the journey to recovery can begin. Remember that the illness did not begin overnight, and that recovery will take time. Be prepared with the names and phone numbers of resources. Be ready to rearrange your schedule to keep someone company at the first appointment. Have a plan of how to face the financial doubts. Pray. And as soon as you can, act.

To some, anorexia nervosa and bulimia nervosa can seem to be devastating failures in living. The only failure in these illnesses is to *not* learn from them.

Henry Ford said, "Failure is simply an opportunity to be again more intelligently." Those who face their illness and learn how to defeat it are in fact stronger than those who have never had challenge in their life. These illnesses are present because some things need to be changed. Maintaining denial and secrecy makes change impossible.

The secrets and denial must be set aside so that reality can be clearly visible. Only with such clarity of vision can real recovery begin.

REFERENCE

Kreisman, J. J., & Straus, H. (1989). *I hate you, don't leave me: understanding the borderline personality.* Los Angeles, CA: Price Stern Sloan, Inc.

OTHER USEFUL SOURCES

Bennett, W., & Gurin, J. (1982). *The dieter's dilemma: eating less and weighing more.* New York: Basic Books.

Garner, D.M., Rocket, W., Olmsted, M.P., Johnson, C.L., & Coscina, D.V. (1985). Psychoeducational principles in the treatment of bulimia and anorexia nervosa. In Garner and Garfinkel (eds.), *Handbook of Psychotherapy for Anorexia Nervosa and Bulimia*, pp. 513–572, New York: Guilford Press.

The Truth about Dieting: A Feminist View

▼
▼
▼
▼

by Carol Bloom, Andrea Gitter, Susan Gutwill, Laura Kogel, and Lela Zaphiropoulos

DIETING AS A SOLUTION

You have a test, you're nervous. Do you find yourself thinking about food, your body, or dieting?

You had a fight with your mother/ father/boyfriend/girlfriend. Do you find yourself thinking of dieting or of eating the whole chocolate cake?

You're shopping for clothes. You don't look like the models or the skinniest girl in the class. Do you start to think about dieting?

A magazine article promises you can lose five pounds in seven days. Do you feel tempted to try and think, "maybe this will work"?

You're nervous about putting on a bathing suit...about a blind date.... Is dieting a solution?

Your girlfriend asks you to go on a diet with her. Can you let her down?

Your parents promise you a new wardrobe if you lose 20 pounds. Don't you start thinking of dieting?

You wake up feeling lousy, begin your morning-mirror routine, worrying about what you ate last night or yesterday. Does dieting come to mind?

You feel depressed. It must be because you're too heavy, so you plan to diet.

DIETING AS A PROBLEM

Dieting may seem like a solution to all these moments—moments of tension, conflict, confusion, and unhappiness, but does it work? What does dieting really do for you?

Let's look at how diets work in society at large. Sixty-five million people and 85 percent of women in America are dieting at any given moment (Orbach, 1986, Brumberg, 1989, Schwartz, 1986). Ninety-five percent of all people who lose weight on a diet gain back more than they lost in every single case (Orbach, 1978, Goode, 1990, Miller, 1989). Hundreds of thousands of young women and increasing numbers of men are suffering from anorexia and bulimia (Brumberg, 1989). Dieting often leads to binging, which leads to a plan to diet again, a real yo-yo syndrome (Goode, 1988, Hirschmann and Munter, 1988, Bennett and Gurin, 1982, Polivy and Herman, 1983). In spite of how much dieting fails people, it channels $35 billion a year to an industry that very successfully sells the same thing to the same people over and over again (Schwartz, 1986, Miller, 1989). Unfortunately, the profits of this diet industry are made from people's insecure and uncomfortable feelings about themselves, their lack of self-confidence, and their lack of self-respect.

It is therefore no surprise that most girls and women (and even some boys and men) in our society feel something is very wrong with their bodies (Jacoby, 1990; Brumberg, 1989). We wonder if we can ever be shapely, thin, pretty enough? We wonder if we can ever relax and rest, or be comfortable in our own skins. Much of the reason we feel this way is because advertising seduces and frightens women; it thrives off women's senses of inadequacy. Throughout history women's bodies have been viewed as the property of others, as decoration for men, and as ways to attract men. Today, however, it seems we feel the perfect body is not just for men, for we have taken the culture so deeply into ourselves that it has become our own standard as well. We believe that we have to be thin to feel good. Over the last few decades, the standard women are supposed to attain continues to emphasize thinness. Today, TV, magazines, and all the news media have the ability to bombard us constantly with their images of beauty—the sleek, lean look that can never be thin enough, rich enough, toned enough.

The multibillion-dollar advertising industry uses women's bodies to sell its products: lipsticks, cars, clothes, computers, cigarettes, and liquor. These sales pitches are intentionally directed at women to sell us this year's image of how we are supposed to look and feel. In the face of this avalanche, women feel their uniqueness, their individuality, not to be their gift, but to be their failing in the ways they don't conform to the advertised image.

Unfortunately we get negative messages from our families as well, which can undermine our body images and our ability to feed ourselves. How we were seen and how we were cared for as small, vulnerable, dependent, and impressionable beings shapes our sense of self and how we care for ourselves. Parents, affected by their own parents as well as by social prejudices, visit their anxieties on their children. This is particularly true for mothers in relation to their daughters. As women in this world, mothers are made to feel insecure about their own senses of self, body, and of eating issues. Some mothers and fathers are overly wrapped up with their daughters, particularly over their appearance. Others are emotionally absent. In neither case does a daughter feel supported,

valued, or seen as an individual in her own right. Often these difficulties are expressed through food: Food is inappropriately used by parent or child to assert power, to show love, to gain control, to reward, and to punish.

Women's response to all of this pressure—from society and from their families—is often to diet in order to feel better. The business of becoming a woman in our world is a complicated, bumpy road to navigate. And diets seem like a way to get control over this difficult process.

But, what happens when you chronically diet and think about diets? As soon as you go on a diet you find yourself wanting to binge. Have you ever noticed that when someone tells you not to have a certain food, that's the food you really want? It seems special; you can't stop thinking about it, and it practically calls to you. Dieting makes you worried, scared, anxious, and fearful of temptation. Over time, you stop listening to your body's hunger signals and you start fearing them instead. You stop feeling you have any power to know your own hunger and satiation. Although at the beginning of a diet you may feel excited, hopeful, and high, you end up feeling defeated, inadequate, and out of control. You just don't trust yourself anymore. You buy magazines with diet articles, make pacts with girlfriends, and pay the many diet clubs, all the while feeling weaker and weaker in your own abilities. Eventually, not only do you feel like a "failed" dieter, but you feel like a "bad" person, out of control and "messed up."

Your body has become so much your focus that every insecure feeling—envy, fear, hate, every conflict with a friend, every difficulty in school and at home, every confusing relationship—all of these get translated into insecurity about your body and a fear of food and eating.

This is not your fault!

THE NATURAL SOLUTION: WHAT YOU CAN DO

We believe there is a way you can both eat food and enjoy and maintain a body size that is comfortable for you. How? First and foremost, find, discover, listen to, and respect your physical hunger. This is your body's gift to you about when to feed yourself. Just as people are learning about the need to respect and care for our natural environment, your hunger is a major part of your natural inner environment. You must not violate it or you begin a process of bodily misattunement and, eventually, harm.

Next, offer yourself all foods. No foods must be considered off limits. Any food that is denied becomes magical, too special, and triggers the next binge. You must be thinking we are crazy! No dieting, and you can eat sweets, pizza, etc! But, no, we are very, very serious. Over time, as you allow yourself off-limit foods, they will lose their magical powers and take their place as a food you enjoy without seducing or tempting you.

Finally, there is a way to know when your body has had enough. It is the feeling of satiation. If you eat when you are hungry, you will know when you have had enough. Satiation is another aspect of your body's environment that you can learn to trust. But it is essential that you not yell at yourself when you can't follow each step of this process. The yelling only makes you feel worse, and it is these "bad" feelings that can make you reach for food when you're not physically hungry.

Learning to eat when you're hungry and to stop when you're satisfied will be new experiences which, like using untapped muscles, need to be exercised to be developed. In other words, you may not be able to do this easily at first. But, if you keep practicing you will know just what to eat and when to stop. Slowly, you will be in tune with your personal environment. You will feel better, in control, and more self-reliant and secure about food, eating, and body image. This, then, may generalize into other aspects of how you feel about and treat yourself.

WHAT ABOUT MY SIZE?

A body that eats in tune with hunger and satiation will eventually come to its natural weight. This may not be what the magazines say you should be but, rather, what your body naturally is meant to be. If you are overweight, eating with hunger means you will slowly lose weight. If you have been starving yourself and are very skinny, as you gain a few pounds you will feel healthier and more confident.

IS THIS A HARD PROJECT?

Yes! But, many positive outcomes will accompany your effort! You can make your body a natural environment where food is what it's supposed to be—food, and not confuse it with feelings. Until now, food and feelings have been very entangled. You've eaten and dieted because you felt depressed, anxious, ugly, guilty, shameful, and envious. Now, you can learn not to eat in response to your feelings and, instead, to tolerate and even respect them despite how intense, complicated, or uncomfortable they often can be. You don't have to do this alone. You can share this idea with friends, speak to a professional who understands this philosophy, or form a self-help group.

It is a courageous act to give up the false and destructive idea that being thin and viewing food as an enemy will solve life's problems as well as make you a more desirable female. To stand apart from the cultural madness is to challenge it while affirming your own unique value.

REFERENCES

Bennett, W., & Gurin, J. (1982). *The dieter's dilemma.* New York: Basic Books.

Brumberg, J.J. (1989) *Fasting girls: the history of anorexia nervosa.* New York: New American Library.

Goode, E. (1988). When dieting is all that counts. *U.S. News and World Report*, May 9, p. 74.

Goode, E. (1990). Getting slim. *U.S. News and World Report*, May 14, p. 64.

Hirschmann, J., & Munter, C. (1988). *Overcoming overeating.* Reading, MA: Addison-Wesley.

Jacoby, S. (1990). The body image blues. *Family Circle*, February 1.

Miller, A. (1989). Diets incorporated. *Newsweek*, Sept. 11, pp. 56-60+.

Orbach, S. (1978). *Fat is a feminist issue.* New York: Paddington Press.

Orbach, S. (1986). *Hunger strike.* New York: W.W. Norton.

Polivy, J., & Herman, C.P. (1983). *Breaking the diet habit.* New York: Basic Books.

Schwartz, H. (1986). *Never satisfied.* New York: Free Press.

Seligman, J. (1990). The losing formula. *Newsweek*, April 30, pp. 52-61.

Are You Really "Too Fat"? The Role of Culture and Weight Stereotypes

▼
▼
▼
▼

by Nancy Ellis-Ordway

ATTRACTIVENESS MEANS THINNESS

Since the beginning of time, human beings have used food to serve many functions besides just providing nutrition. Food is used to celebrate special occasions, comfort in times of grief, provide a way to share within a common community, express love and affection, identify ethnic traditions, and express artistic creativity. Human beings are programmed from birth to enjoy food, especially sweet, salty, or rich foods. Our culture today continues to interact with food in all these ways. What is unique to our culture is that, for the first time in history, attractiveness is equated with thinness rather than plumpness.

"Compulsive overeating" is widely identified in our culture as an eating disorder. While there are some similarities in behavior, anorexia nervosa and bulimia nervosa are distinct illnesses that are very different from "compulsive overeating." However, it is impossible to understand any of these illnesses without also understanding something about society's attitudes toward obesity.

WEIGHT SETPOINTS

Within each individual there is a "setpoint," a genetically programmed desirable weight. If a person eats when hungry and stops when full, having access to a variety of foods, then that individual's weight will stay within a small range. The setpoint itself may change slightly with variables such as illness, age, or depression, but it is determined genetically. With few exceptions, if a person's parents are fat, then the individual will be fat. If the parents are thin, then the person will be thin. There is very little that can be done to change this. Whether a person overeats or undereats, the body compensates by changing the metabolism as well as the amount of hunger experienced to try to keep the body the same weight. (Bennett & Gurin, 1982).

Research studies have shown for years that fat people, on the average, do not eat more than thin people; that adopted children of thin biological parents who are placed with fat adoptive parents grow up to be thin and vice versa; and that people who engage in restrictive eating (commonly known as "dieting") regain the weight they lose. Studies that attempt to overfeed genetically thin people to make them fat have shown that it cannot be done. (Ciliska, 1990).

SOCIETY AND WEIGHT CONTROL

Yet our society persists in believing that weight can be controlled and therefore should be controlled. This belief is nurtured by a multibillion-dollar-a-year business that sells us products and services promising to make us thinner. As the fashionable ideal for attractiveness gets thinner and thinner, more and more people are vulnerable to the claims of advertisers that thinness is within the grasp of anyone who can find and afford the right product or program. When the person fails to lose weight, or regains the lost weight, he or she is criticized for "not having enough willpower."

In fact, the body reacts to a diet the same way our cave dweller ancestors reacted to famine. The metabolism becomes more efficient in order to conserve fuel, or calories. As the body learns to get by with less food, the dieter hits the proverbial "plateau." Eating becomes more restrictive and the dieter feels more deprived. When in the presence of food (and the food can be present simply in a magazine or television ad), the body reacts with increased hunger to try to ensure its own survival. Sooner or later the dieter, battling with the implacable capabilities of his or her own body, gives in and eats. The body continues to be ravenously hungry until the original, or setpoint, weight is reachieved. However, now the body is afraid of another famine, so it stores up a little extra, just in case. And the metabolism has learned to be more efficient so that the body can actually weigh more on less food. Dieters, beset with feelings of failure and worthlessness, set out on other diets, hoping that this time they have found the magic solution. The cycle begins again.

Reasons for Overeating

Everyone occasionally eats for emotional reasons. Thin people are not criticized for it. Everyone occasionally overeats. Thin people are not criticized for this either. Only when a person is genetically programmed to be heavier than the currently fashionable style do eating patterns come under scrutiny. "Compulsive overeating" is almost always a response to chronic dieting. This is not to underestimate the anguish felt by people who are involved in this kind of behavior. "Compulsive overeating" can feel very out of control and overwhelming, and the constant sense of

failure and shame is demoralizing and eroding to self-esteem. Yet treatment that focuses on food control and weight loss just reinforces the cycle. According to Ellyn Satter, it's like giving a person with a hand-washing compulsion a basin and a towel and saying, "Here, if you just get your hands clean enough, the problem will go away." Treatment that focuses on renormalizing eating and renormalizing weight is becoming more available all the time. The shift in attitude from focusing on dieting and controlling intake to responding to hunger can be difficult but successful in the long run. People who get this kind of treatment may never be thin, but they can be thinner, eat more, and feel relaxed and good about themselves.

Eighty to 90 percent of people on diets are women, in spite of research that shows most women have many fewer health risks associated with being heavy than men do. In fact, many women engaged in dieting behavior are actually within or below "ideal body weight range," as it is defined by statistics compiled by life insurance companies. Yet studies show that dieting behaviors can be observed in as many as half of fifth-grade girls, and that children in early elementary grades perceive being fat as worse than being disabled.

SOCIETY'S CRITICISM OF OVERWEIGHT PEOPLE

It is no longer acceptable in our society to discriminate against people for reasons of color, gender, religion, or ethnic background. Fat people are the only subgroup left to safely criticize. And they participate in their own persecution, believing that their failure to be thin is due to some flaw within themselves, some lack of willpower. Genetically thin people then feel smug about their own superior willpower.

This attitude has an insidious effect on everyone, including people who do not have a "weight problem." Individuals who are at their setpoints and are content with their weight nevertheless feel compelled to "watch" their weight. Normal-weight people especially feel guilty when eating and feel they have to forego or justify especially desirable foods. Historically, eating has been a source of great pleasure. Currently, it is increasingly a source of guilt. Advertisers recognize and capitalize on this with commercials promoting "guilt-free" foods.

It is not surprising, given the widespread societal disgust with people who are overweight, that some individuals choose to be anorexic or bulimic to avoid that fate. Recovery is much more difficult when the person is surrounded by the cultural attitude that weight gain is shameful and weak. Understanding the role of the news, entertainment, and advertising media is helpful, but the family members, friends, co-workers, and schoolmates of the recovering person are all still subjected to the same cultural message. After a long struggle in in-patient or intensive out-patient treatment, a girl may return to a family with several members on diets, boyfriends who make cruel comments about overweight peers, and uninformed friends who make comments on what great willpower she has when she does not eat.

Family members of people with eating disorders often confront them loaded with information about all the physical risks and side effects, expecting them to change. The reason that "scare tactics" do not work when trying to convince individuals to change their behavior is that often no threats of death, illness, or permanent physical impairment can be as terrifying as the thought of being fat.

The current preoccupation with weight loss now seems to be influenced by an emphasis on fitness rather than on thinness. Unfortunately, for people who are vulnerable to eating disorders this seems to translate into a dangerous exercise compulsion that can be just as disruptive as bulimia. Some social scientists predict that we have seen the extreme in the pursuit of thinness and that the pendulum will now swing back to more realistic standards. Only time will tell.

REFERENCES

Bennett, W., & Gurin, J. (1982). *The dieter's dilemma.* New York: Basic Books.

Ciliska, D. (1990). *Beyond dieting: psychoeducational interventions for chronically obese women: a non-dieting approach.* New York: Brunner/Mazel.

Satter, E. (1986). *Child of mine: feeding with love and good sense.* Menlo Park, CA: Bull Publishing.

Satter, E. (1987). *How to get your kid to eat... but not too much.* Menlo Park, CA: Bull Publishing.

PART 3
Treatment of Eating Disorders

Eating Disorder Treatment: The Importance of Research

▼
▼
▼
▼

by Kenneth Rockwell, M.D.

WHICH KINDS OF TREATMENT ARE BEST?

Many people in today's health field believe that the treatment of eating disorders is among the least satisfactory in medicine. A large group of people agrees with them—those with anorexia or bulimia nervosa who have tried a variety of treatments and their families and friends. A healthy response to the frustration felt all around has been the actions of hundreds of investigators, whose ultimate goals are to prevent eating disorders entirely or at least provide much more rapid and effective treatment, and sufferers, who are willing to participate in a series of research procedures from which they know they may not personally benefit in any way. As it has turned out, however, in the great majority of treatment studies whose conclusions form the basis for this chapter, the results have been positive: Most eating-disordered people have been helped at least some. But that isn't good enough. So, the same basic question still confronts researchers, caregivers, and patients: What specific treatment(s) will be most effective in the least amount of time and with the least pain and expense for an individual with an eating disorder?

There are two major classes of treatments that have been tried in eating disorders: medications and talk therapies. The former have included investigations using most classes of drugs that influence psychological conditions or appetite. In the latter are included "traditional psychotherapies," the newer cognitive and behavioral techniques, family therapy, and support groups. Talk therapies have been applied on an individual and group basis, both in some investigations.

Finally, it should be noted that anorexia nervosa has a long history of treatment research, while bulimia nervosa has a short one. Although the illnesses often co-exist or succeed one another, it is convenient to separate them for this review, which will include studies of (1) medication treatment of anorexia nervosa, (2) medication treatment of bulimia nervosa, (3) psychotherapy treatment, (4) a study comparing medication and psychotherapy treatments, and (5) family therapy.

MEDICATION TREATMENT FOR ANOREXIA NERVOSA

By way of background, it is interesting that at the time anorexia nervosa was named over 100 years ago it was thought by many to be a "nervous condition," whatever that phrase was taken to mean then. This view prevailed for more than 30 years, at which point it was discovered that failure of the pituitary gland, the most influential of the body's hormone producers, caused some symptoms that resembled anorexia nervosa; thereafter, the illness was thought to result from pituitary disease. It was about another 30 years until the trend

The work for this article was supported in part by the Tom and Sarah Kern Anorexia Nervosa Fund.

in thinking turned once again toward a psychological basis for anorexia nervosa, the view that prevails today. But separation of mind and body is not so neat, at least when it comes to treatment, and frequently "physical" treatments, which now usually mean medication, continued to be explored. In the not-so-distant past electroconvulsive therapy (ECT), implantation of calf's pituitary into the abdomen, and even brain surgery were tried. Such treatments may now seem unnecessary and extreme, but there was a theory behind doing each one, and those who proposed them and carried them out were serious in their attempts to help people in the desperate circumstance of facing death by starvation.

Types of Drugs Tried in Anorexia Nervosa Treatment

Imagine the excitement that must have prevailed in the mid-1950s, when the effects of a new drug, chlorpromazine, became known. Three reasons for trying this medication suggested themselves immediately: It might help persons with anorexia nervosa see themselves (or feel themselves to be) as others saw them—emaciated—rather than unattractively plump in certain places; it might enable persons to eat without their former fear; and, its use was beginning to be associated with weight gain, for uncertain reasons. Some initial successes with weight promotion were reported, but to the disappointment of all, the new drug did not help alter the basic attitudes toward food, weight, and shape, nor did it enable patients simply to eat fearlessly. Trials with other drugs of this class, neuroleptics (antipsychotics), have achieved basically similar results.

Numerous medications of different classes or with effects suggesting a potential for helping to reduce the symptoms of anorexia nervosa have been tried. Tricyclic antidepressants, so called for their three-ringed chemical structure,

were among the first. Like neuroleptics these medications were associated with weight promotion. In addition, many people with anorexia were also depressed, and in some of these people their depression lessened after treatment with these drugs. Again there were reports of some successes, but not in a great number of patients. One of the tricyclics, clomipramine, has anti-obsessive-compulsive, as well as antidepressant, actions, and it was thought that this drug might help reduce some of the disabling preoccupations and behaviors associated with anorexia nervosa. In one study, patients given a small dose of clomipramine during the time weight increase was being helped by an in-hospital behavioral program tended to maintain their weights better after discharge than those who had been on a placebo, but the reason for this was unclear. Yet, in another in-hospital study, only one of 10 patients on larger doses of clomipramine gained a substantial amount of weight, strongly suggesting that the medication by itself would not be a major factor in changing attitudes toward eating in the underweight anorexic patient. Some weight-restored patients feel and function better while on this medication but at present there is no systematic way of determining in advance who these individuals might be.

Another medication tried in treating eating disorders is lithium carbonate, a "salt" which is a mood regulator most often associated with the treatment of bipolar affective disorder ("manic-depressive" illness). Compared with placebo during an in-hospital study, lithium was actually associated more with favorable attitudinal and symptomatic changes than with weight increase, but the risks of complicating blood electrolyte problems in patients with eating disorders have dimmed interest in its use.

Drugs such as "minor tranquilizers" (diazepam, for example) and sleeping pills have been used often enough in general clinical practice without making any change in the basic processes of anorexia (or bulimia) so that they have not been reported in formal research trials.

Cyproheptadine, a drug marketed in Europe for years for weight restoration for a variety of medical conditions, has been studied in a relatively large number of patients. With respect to weight gain, results have tended to favor the drug over a placebo, most notably in a subgroup of patients that might represent the more severely ill. A major advantage of this medication is that very few side effects have been reported.

Finally, a brief trial, in-hospital, was given to delta-9-tetrahydrocannabinol (THC), the major psychoactive component of marijuana, because of its reported properties of appetite stimulation ("the munchies") and promotion of weight gain. Since the patients on THC felt worse in a variety of ways, the study was not extended beyond two weeks.

While some of the medication studies cited above were taking place, numerous hospital management trials were demonstrating that weight gain could be achieved without medication as rapidly as was physiologically and psychologically appropriate. Medications can be useful therefore to help reduce feelings of severe depression or anxiety, but in only a small minority of individuals do they seem to add something to the treatment of malnutrition as such. An important question is what beneficial effects drugs might have on feelings, attitudes, and behaviors in order for weight to be maintained *after* it is restored and the person to function to his or her own satisfaction. The response is that we are still in a trial-and-error period in which broad generalizations cannot be made. Thus, certain individuals may find a specific medication useful during a particular time. The same can be said of various psychotherapeutic approaches to the treatment of anorexia nervosa. Arriving at a correct judgment in this matter requires cooperation between patient and therapist and often takes a considerable amount of time.

MEDICATION TREATMENT FOR BULIMIA NERVOSA

During the past 11 years attention has turned to the study of the treatment of bulimia nervosa. Although the illness had been known prior to 1980, the American Psychiatric Association's characterization of it in that year as a distinct disorder certainly contributed to professional interest. Other contributing factors have been the greater numbers of bulimic patients coming for treatment (more people with the symptoms, plus, especially, more willingness to be treated) and greater responsiveness to treatment (more positive change[s] per unit of time). Medication therapy is one of the two major lines of treatment that has been investigated, psychotherapy being the other. Quite different types of drugs have been tried in the treatment of bulimia nervosa, each type tested because at the time there seemed to be a reason why it might work. Research scientists are accustomed to experiments that don't work or to early "successes" that later fizzle out. In trying to solve tough problems the question at first is "What can be learned from failure or only partial success?"

Even before the term bulimia nervosa became an official diagnosis with its own set of criteria, the condition was known, and some doctors thought that in at least some of the patients who were describing their symptoms, there were characteristics similar to the symptoms of epilepsy. This led to the use of phenytoin, a frequently prescribed anticonvulsant medication, in a number of patients. Although it was more effective than placebo in diminishing binging and vomiting behaviors in one study, the use of this medication has not been pursued. The connection between bulimia and epilepsy was not very great to begin with and also no relationship to the effectiveness of the medication was shown between those patients who had an abnormal EEG (brain wave test, often abnormal in epilepsy) and those who did not.

In assessing the effectiveness of a medication, the standard procedure is the double-blind, placebo-controlled trial in which neither therapist nor patient is told whether administered pills have the medication in them. Other aspects of the pill-taking trial are then presumably the same for the medication and placebo takers, and additional "active (treatment) ingredients" are eliminated as much as possible. There are, nevertheless, a number of so-called "nonspecific" elements of treatment involved, such as coming to a clinic, undergoing evaluation, filling out forms over the course of the study, and meeting with an interested professional person regularly, which may be beneficial to the patient. If so, the benefits may influence results. Thus, even placebo-controlled studies do not yield results in which drug effect is clearly isolated without the need for further scrutiny and interpretation.

Antidepressants and Bulimia

The finding that patients with bulimia nervosa are so often substantially depressed has led to study of the relationship between bulimia nervosa and depressive disorders—with inconclusive results so far about cause and effect. Nevertheless, this has led to the use of antidepressant medication. Placebo-controlled trials have now been made, or are underway, with all chemical classes of antidepressants. Among antidepressants tried have been "tricyclics" (imipramine, desipramine, amitriptyline), "monoamine oxidase inhibitors" (MAOIs) such as phenylzine and isocarboxazid, and others of different chemical make-up, including mianserin, trazodone, and bupropion. Fluoxetine is undergoing controlled trials with encouraging early results but clinical experience suggests it is not a panacea.

Treatment with antidepressants has resulted in reductions in binge eating from roughly two-thirds to 90 percent. On average, however, only around 30 percent of patients have been binge-free by the end of treatment. These results are close enough to results of psychotherapy studies that one cannot claim an advantage for medication treatment over psychotherapy in preventing binging behavior. If it were a matter of just handing out pills, then, medication treatment would appear to be quicker and cheaper and therefore "better" from a practical standpoint. But there are problems with this theory. For one, none of the drug treatment studies was done by the method of just handing out pills—more time and attention was spent with patients than that, as should be. Also, in the drug trials there was a much higher "dropout" rate of two kinds. First, it appears that more patients who contacted the drug treatment study teams failed to get beyond the contact and evaluation phase and into the drug-taking phase of treatment. The reasons for this are unclear but represent a difference of some sort between the characteristics of those who consider drug treatment and those who follow through on it. Second, far more people could not or would not tolerate some of the side effects of medication and stopped taking it. Although there are very few studies with follow-up beyond six months, what evidence there is suggests that failure to stick with medication continues to be a problem as time goes on: Side effects may begin weeks or months after medication is started; side effects which were tolerable over the short run become less tolerable, even when they are unchanged, as time goes on; people may become discouraged that only a limited effect has been obtained and discontinue medication (or any other treatment, for that matter) altogether; and there is the suspicion, not yet proven, that the beneficial medication effect may wear off in some individuals after a time. Finally, some people have tried a variety of medications and could not tolerate the side effects of any of them. Because of the foregoing reasons for those patients who did not benefit from medication, and for other patients who refuse to take medication in the first place, other modes of treatment are necessary if these patients are to be treated at all.

Opioid Antagonist Medications

Certain features of the behaviors and feelings exhibited in bulimic patients have led to trials of a type of medication entirely different from antidepressants. Many patients seem to become locked into a cycle of binging and vomiting from which they appear powerless to escape in the same way that alcohol and drug addicts do. It also has been known for some time that the brain manufactures its own narcotic-like substances called *endogenous opioids*. These substances are known to influence eating behaviors, with higher levels generally being associated with more food intake. The way endogenous opioids behave in patients with bulimia has been examined in a number of individuals but the results have been controversial so far. Nevertheless, there have now been several medication trials using naltrexone, a long-acting narcotic antagonist, to see if it would help reduce binging behavior. The results of these trials have likewise been controversial. This may be due at least in part to the way in which naltrexone acts on brain chemistry. In a dose that would be sufficient to block the effect of a narcotic given to a person, naltrexone may have little or no effect on bulimic symptoms. At doses two or three times as high, however, there has been substantial reduction of binge eating in a number of patients. This difference might be accounted for on the basis that at higher doses the action of naltrexone on the brain might be different from its action as an antagonist to endogenous opioids ("narcot-

ics"), yet effective in reducing bulimic symptoms. Another explanation might be that within the brain there are different types of molecules on nerve cells, called receptors, which interact with incoming substances in such a way as to affect the cells' activity. There are several different receptor types that interact with opioids, but one of the receptor types that appears to be more involved with the effect of opioids on eating behavior is less interactive with naltrexone, and hence, a higher dose of the medication may be necessary for effect.

A practical problem in using this medication, however, is that as dosage goes up so does the likelihood of a toxic effect on the liver, a very bad side effect. Nevertheless, some patients do not respond to any of the antidepressants, and naltrexone may prove to be an alternative treatment for this group. Defining the characteristics of such a group, called a "subgroup," would be particularly important, if it could be done before antidepressant treatment were even attempted. So far, no such subgroups of patients with bulimia nervosa have been identified—those who respond especially well to a particular form of treatment.

The Addiction Theory and Bulimia

Even a theory can have an unfortunate side effect, and the "addiction theory" for "the cause" of bulimia nervosa seems to have one. Many patients with bulimia nervosa have been told or have read that they have an addiction (to food) and will never be cured of it, that they will always be "addicts." This distorts the original definition of addiction beyond recognition—it was never intended to include dependence on and craving for substances essential to life, such as air, food, and water—and worse still, it fuels feelings of hopelessness and powerlessness, often at the worst possible time, and fuels them with an untruth. People with eating disorders do become cured, the majority of them so far as we know, completely and forever.

PSYCHOTHERAPY TREATMENT

More than 30 studies on psychotherapy for patients with bulimia nervosa have been reported and include approximately 500 patients. In all studies there was a positive result on at least one outcome measure. Outcome measures have typically included changes in eating behaviors such as number of binge and/or vomiting episodes per week and number of days per week abstinent, mood scales, and various attitude scales, including those toward eating and one's body and toward other aspects of one's self and outlook. Reduction in abnormal eating practices has been the major outcome variable under study, with change in depression scores second in interest. On average, 35 to less than 50 percent of treated patients were free of binging and vomiting at the end of the treatment period, with perhaps one-half of the rest experiencing a 50 to 75 percent reduction in binge-vomiting frequency. In follow-up reports less than one-half of patients were still free of binging and vomiting, and many of these people had had further treatment. Moreover, follow-up, if done, has most often been for six months or less, with only a few studies having a follow-up for up to two years. Increased feelings of being in control over the eating process have tended to accompany improvement in behaviors, but preoccupation with nutritional practice (content of diet and when, where, and how consumed), body weight and shape, and fear of fatness have tended to recede slowly and erratically. Depression scale scores have usually, but not always, declined along with the reduction in bulimic symptoms. Many other measures of changes in a variety of symptoms and attitudes have been taken. The results are too many and too inconsistent to be summarized here.

Problems with Comparing Types of Psychotherapy

Types of treatment have included behavioral, cognitive-behavioral, psychoeducational, insight-oriented (psychodynamic), and experiential. There are about an equal number of studies using one or more treatment forms, and some studies compare results of different treatments. However, among psychotherapists, treatment modalities are not pure, and features of one may be found in the others so that distinctions among treatments are often blurred. Another problem in assessing effects of psychotherapy is that of the "control group." How this treatment compares with no treatment at all is a basic question in establishing treatment effectiveness. Since there is no way of observing someone's change over time without establishing some sort of contact, a "waiting list" control is a method that is often used in treatment studies, but it has been used in a minority of bulimia nervosa studies. In these waiting list control studies treatment has proved to be superior to control.

Other problems in assessing and comparing the results of psychotherapy outcome studies include differences in the duration (length in time) and intensity (number of sessions per unit of time) of treatments, individual compared with group treatment, comparability of the patients who were treated, and comparability of therapists. In a substantial majority of the studies the number of treatment sessions was 20 sessions or less and lasted less than six months, which by most definitions qualifies these treatments as "brief," but even so, the variation in duration and intensity among studies is sufficient to complicate further the comparison of treatment methods. The number of patients ("sample size") included in most of the individual treatment outcome studies is so small, for example, that these could be considered "pilot" studies only, that is, pointing the way toward a treatment approach that might be tried with a larger number of patients with general or specific applicability of the method to be determined by these larger studies. Not all patients diagnosed as having bulimia nervosa were diagnosed in just the same way and even if they had been, not all patients with the same diagnosis respond uniformly to the same treatment. Other personal characteristics are influential. Least considered of all in these reports have been therapist characteristics, which although presumably very important, are an understudied aspect of psychotherapy research in general.

Designing and executing treatment studies is very difficult, so the foregoing comments are not meant as criticisms of the hard-working people who have done them and who are only too aware of their limitations. These and other limitations are what make it difficult at this time to determine which treatment method or methods have an advantage, even for some, if not all, patients. Some practitioners of cognitive-behavioral and behavioral therapy have claimed an advantage for this form of treatment over others, and these claims may be substantiated in whole or in part with further work, although it is still too early to tell. Certainly from the standpoint of current therapy cognitive-behavioral and behavioral treatments have been the most studied psychotherapies and, given that they have produced some positive results, this has been good for patient care.

PSYCHOTHERAPY COMPARED WITH MEDICATION

One study has compared group psychotherapy with antidepressant drug treatment directly plus examined the results of combining the two treatments. This study found group psychotherapy (combining cognitive, behavioral, and nutritional counseling techniques) superior to medication in reducing problem

eating behaviors and in improving some attitudes relevant to bulimia. Both treatments were superior to placebo with respect to reducing disordered eating behaviors and in decreasing symptoms of depression and anxiety; the two treatments being equally effective in reducing these latter two symptoms. The addition of medication to group treatment did not improve outcome on measures of eating behaviors but did reduce depression and anxiety more so than either treatment alone.

Since several different formats of psychotherapy and a variety of medications have been found to be effective, at least partially if not totally, with a majority of patients treated, studies directly comparing the effectiveness of different treatments are important. The design and execution of such studies is quite complicated and time consuming, however, and they require a large number of patients, so they are likely to accumulate slowly. Moreover, the number of possible comparisons is already quite large, since several different medications and several different psychotherapies have been found to be effective. It is therefore unlikely that each one will ever be compared with all the others. An additional complication in trying to compare one psychotherapy with another is the difficulty in finding, on the same team of investigators, two different kinds of therapists with relatively equal skill and experience in the type of treatment they do and in sufficient numbers to conduct the two treatments. Nevertheless, studies comparing treatments will be useful, as many as can be done.

FAMILY THERAPY

Family therapy has played a part in the treatment of patients with anorexia nervosa much more often than those with bulimia nervosa, presumably due to the greater availability for treatment of families of the former. This is probably because more anorexic patients have an earlier onset than bulimic patients, and anorexia often precedes bulimia. Adolescent anorexics are often forced into treatment because of the medical dangers, while bulimic adolescents hide their symptoms, usually until the late teen or early adult years. From a research standpoint, the question is not whether families should be included in the treatment of patients with eating disorders, since family involvement of some sort is usually a clinical fact of life, but rather how to involve the family in a way most beneficial to the patient. Then the questions become: "Is family treatment effective?" and "How does family treatment compare with other treatments?"

It appears that for nutritional rehabilitation of severely malnourished patients with anorexia nervosa, family therapists, like therapists employing other treatments, have considered in-hospital programs the treatment of choice. Effectiveness of family treatment in comparison with other treatment types is measured by weight maintenance and other beneficial changes in eating physiology, behaviors, and attitudes. There is very little systematic research in this area. One study has compared outcomes of family therapy and individual therapy, both forms of treatment well-specified. (This project included some patients with bulimia nervosa, but there were many more patients with anorexia nervosa.) Family treatment was found to be superior for younger patients whose illness was not chronic, but older patients (irrespective of chronicity of illness) benefited more from individual treatment.

More than 10 years ago a well-known study was reported in which a very high success rate was achieved employing family treatment with a predominantly young group of patients whose illness was not chronic. This group of patients was highly selected in other respects, which probably favored a positive outcome. Nevertheless, putting together the results of two such different studies, each with a relatively large number of patients, suggests that family therapy is likely to be effective, or may even be the treatment of choice, with younger anorexic patients who have not been ill for too many years.

AUTHOR'S NOTE

For progress in treatment to be made there have to be patients who are willing to undergo the uncertainty, anxiety, and extra hassle attendant upon participation in the trial of a method with unproven benefit. Hundreds of such individuals participated in the studies reviewed above. In addition to the satisfaction of knowing that they contributed to others' well-being in the long run, I hope that each of these individuals received something from their participation that helped diminish their illness in some way. It is clear that many did benefit a great deal; some even with a total remission of their most troublesome symptoms by the end of their treatment study. The investigators involved spent a great deal of thought, time, and effort designing and executing these projects.

Note: Because of the excessive number of references that could be cited for this article, a customary list of references will not be found. Additionally, it seemed that to assign attribution to the studies mentioned in this article would have been to slight the far more numerous researchers whose labors were included in summaries of studies.

How to Find Treatment for an Eating Disorder

▼
▼
▼
▼

by Nancy Ellis-Ordway

WHY IS TREATMENT NECESSARY?

Most individuals with eating disorders need some sort of treatment in order to recover. While there are certainly some people who get better on their own, most people need to be under the care of specialized professionals. The longer treatment is delayed, the greater the risk of serious complications, and the more the illness may become entrenched. The sooner treatment is initiated, the sooner results will be seen. People who engage in treatment early in the course of the illness tend to get better more quickly and spend less time in treatment.

Once the decision has been made to enter treatment, the choice about where to go can seem enormous. Good treatment is much more available than it was a decade ago, but it still must be sought and found. Ideally, an individual will research all the options and make a calm, considered decision. More often, however, the decision is made in the midst of a crisis, or the person with the disorder is too overwhelmed to carry out the task of finding and inquiring about programs. An interested family member or friend can be of great help at this point by making phone calls and following up leads, when possible, to discover what options are available.

KINDS OF TREATMENT

Treatment can include individual psychotherapy, group therapy, family therapy, nutritional counseling, support groups, self-help groups, and classes. Most people need some combination of approaches at different points in recovery. All of these can be provided on an in-patient or out-patient basis. Professionals who treat individuals with eating disorders include psychiatrists and other physicians, psychologists, psychotherapists, social workers, dietitians, nurses, counselors, music therapists, art therapists, and pastoral counselors.

In-Patient Treatment (Hospitals and Special Eating Disorder Units)

There are advantages and disadvantages to both in-patient and out-patient treatment. In-patient treatment is, obviously, more disruptive to school, work, and family life, and it is also more expensive. On the other hand, a specialized in-patient unit can provide much more structure and safety for the person who is having a great deal of difficulty eating normally. In-patient treatment also provides a more intensive psychotherapeutic experience, in that therapy can continue on a 24-hour basis, as opposed to starting and stopping for an hour at a time once or twice a week. Some people also need the close medical monitoring that can only take place in the hospital.

There are several reasons to consider in-patient treatment. A person who is significantly underweight will have a very hard time eating enough to gain weight unless there is a great deal of structure around food intake. Because of metabolic abnormalities, such individuals usually require a huge number of calories to restore the metabolism to normal before they even begin to gain weight. For a person with a terror of food, this can be a seemingly impossible task. Additionally, there are some medical risks associated with weight gain that should be monitored. Malnutrition can cause depression, inability to concentrate, moodiness, and a decreased ability to think clearly. All of these make success in out-patient treatment very difficult. And, people of normal weight can even benefit from in-patient treatment if they are feeling out of control with food. It is possible to be malnourished even at a normal body weight.

Among the numerous medical reasons for in-patient treatment are to monitor, control, or prevent fainting, dizziness, abnormal electrolyte levels, dehydration, persistent muscle cramps, uncontrollable or spontaneous vomiting, vomiting of blood, and chest pain. Suicidal thoughts, plans, gestures, and attempts are also reasons for in-patient treatment.

Sometimes in-patient treatment for an adolescent can be helpful if the family is feeling overwhelmed and out of control. It can give family members time to calm down and reevaluate their roles in the problem. Adolescents who deny having eating disorders may need in-patient treatment to help them confront their problems.

People with eating disorders tend to get better faster on in-patient units that are specialized. Some units just treat people with anorexia and/or bulimia; some also treat compulsive overeating. Many hospitals treat eating disorders on a general unit, combining patients with diagnoses ranging from depression and stress to chemical abuse, mood disorders, and even psychosis. Some specialized treatment programs for problems such as stress and personality disorders see so many patients with eating disorders that they have developed treatment protocols especially for them. In other words, the title of the program may not tell you what you need to know.

Some questions to ask about an in-patient eating disorder program include:

- **How specialized is it?** How do you feel about being on a unit with people who are there for treatment of something other than an eating disorder? Will you have enough in common with them to benefit from group therapy?
- **What is the age range of the patients?** If all the patients have similar diagnoses, then a mix of adolescents and adults may do well. However, being the only adolescent on a general adult psychiatric unit or the only adult on a general adolescent unit may be quite difficult.
- **How individualized is the treatment?** Some people get better quickly; some get better slowly; some require more than one hospital stay. A program with a fixed number of days does not necessarily take this into account. A program that recognizes individual differences will be more likely to be flexible about length of stay.
- **How is food handled on the unit?** There are many ways to handle food but the goal should be to allow patients a sense of safety and structure until they are able to eat normally and then to allow them to gradually take more responsibility for making good decisions about food. The problem with many general psychiatric units is that they have food sitting out for snacks throughout the day. For someone with an eating disorder, this is terrifying and it makes it difficult to eat at all.
- **How much is the family involved?** Family involvement in treatment is often critical, especially with younger patients. Programs may offer treatment for the immediate or extended family, classes and educational programs, group family therapy involving members of several families, and/or support groups.

- **What kind of follow-up is available?** No one is cured when he or she leaves the hospital. After-care can include group, individual, and family therapy; ongoing nutritional counseling; weight monitoring; and partial hospitalization or "day treatment."
- **What is the training and experience of the staff?** There are now several ways that professionals can be involved in ongoing training in this field. Current research continues to provide new information about the problem as well as effective treatment approaches.
- **How long has the program been in existence?** If the program is very new, it is important to ask about the qualifications of specific staff members. Asking about "success rate" will not tell you very much. First of all, "success" is very difficult to define in the field of eating disorders; therefore any statistics quoted are suspicious. Second, a program that is widely known for excellent treatment tends to draw more patients who are very ill or have been involved in the illness for a long time, and thus is going to have poorer "success rates" than a program with less expertise.
- **May I have a tour of the unit?** In a sense, allowing tours of the unit is a violation of the privacy of the patients already there. For an individual considering admission, however, it is reasonable to want a "visual image" to go with the description. Most programs will not allow tours to students or interested onlookers, and may or may not allow tours to family members, depending on the circumstances.

When investigating any treatment program, it is reasonable to ask for an evaluation appointment. Sometimes this appointment will be free of charge, but it is worth paying for if it is not. If you tend to get flustered in this kind of a situation, make out a list of questions ahead of time and take it along. Make notes if you think you might forget something. You are entitled to have your questions answered before you make a decision. Other questions to ask at this point are, "Why are you recommending this kind of treatment? What are the alternatives?"

Out-Patient Treatment (Therapists and Programs)

Out-patient treatment can often provide help in a gradual recovery without interrupting day-to-day life. It can be offered through a well-organized, specialized program, but it is most often offered through individual psychotherapists.

Questions to ask include:

- **What background do you have in treating this specific problem?** An interest in the field doesn't mean much unless combined with training and expertise. One way many therapists develop expertise in this field is by being supervised by clinicians with extensive background. This greatly expands the availability of quality treatment.
- **Who provides nutritional counseling?** Psychotherapists and dietitians have very different kinds of training. Few people have a background in both. A team approach can be very helpful, especially for patients who use their preoccupation with food to obscure other issues.
- **How is weight monitoring handled, if necessary?** For a family member, responsibility for monitoring weight can be a huge burden unless it is specifically part of the family therapy and is frequently discussed. Otherwise, it can lead to battles at home over control and independence, just when the focus needs to be on improved communication. In most cases, however, weight does need to be monitored somewhere.
- **What happens if the patient needs to be hospitalized?** Sometimes eating problems and other symptoms such as depression actually get worse

in response to talking about difficult issues in therapy. Sometimes out-patient therapy can be helpful in dealing with the emotional issues, but the eating does not improve. An individual psychotherapist should have some kind of backup for these situations when in-patient treatment may be necessary. Ideally, they should have access to the in-patient unit chosen.

- **What other resources are available?** Can the therapist refer for family therapy? Individual therapy for other family members? Group therapy?

FINDING HELP

The first step in finding treatment often involves making lots of telephone calls. Call your family doctor, the local medical or psychological society, the library, and the mental health association. Look in the telephone book under dietitians, hospitals, eating disorders, anorexia, and bulimia for promising listings. Check the facilities listed in the directory section (Part 4) of this book. Try the counseling department at local colleges and high schools. Call women's organizations, parents clubs, and physician referral services. Check with the national organizations listed in Part 5 of this book, as well as the psychiatric departments of local hospitals. Ask each of them, "Where do you know of that provides treatment for eating disorders?" You will begin to hear the same names repeated and that will help you narrow your search. Set aside some time to gather information and take notes. Don't get discouraged because you keep getting referred elsewhere or you get transferred several times on one call. When you find someone who can answer your questions, make a note of the person's name and ask for a direct phone number.

While major cities have many programs and resources to choose from, small towns and rural areas will, of course, have fewer. It is important to evaluate options based on both geographic availability and quality of treatment. Driving farther in order to get better treatment will pay off in the long run. On the other hand, great distances can present obstacles to length of treatment as well as the family involvement. Sometimes, particularly when in-patient treatment is needed, a less specialized program close enough to provide aftercare and family therapy will work better than a more specialized program farther away. On the other hand, some patients who are very ill or having a hard time getting better may benefit from traveling farther to a better program.

Choosing treatment is an important decision. Spending some time and energy to evaluate all the options is well worth it. Good luck!

Assessment: Joining the Eating-Disordered Individual with the Right Professional

▼
▼
▼
▼

by John L. Levitt, Ph.D.

INTRODUCTION

The terms anorexia, bulimia, compulsive overeating, and eating disorders are commonly heard in schools and households and are regular features on television and radio. As public awareness is increasing, many individuals are beginning to recognize that food, weight, eating, and self-image have seriously interfered with the quality of their lives. For some of these people, these problems may even become life threatening.

Today, the number of people seeking help for problems associated with an eating disorder is reaching epidemic proportions. Eating disorder programs of all sorts as well as eating disorder therapists and counselors are abundant in many areas. For individuals who are feeling overwhelmed or out of control over food, weight, and many areas of their lives, initial contacts with eating disorder professionals are full of fear, dread, and a longing for understanding, support, and hope that the "monster" may be put to rest.

This chapter will briefly explore that aspect of the "joining" process that occurs between a client trying to obtain help for an eating disorder and the professional who will be providing those services.

THE RELATIONSHIP BETWEEN PROFESSIONAL AND CLIENT

As in any relationship, one of the first objectives is for people to get to know each other. Of course, depending upon the situation, people get to know each other in very different ways. When two people meet each other socially for the first time, for example, they both try to assess or find out about each other's likes and dislikes, interests and activities, and develop some "feeling" about their capability to join with each other as friends, acquaintances, or intimates. That is, they try to collect, sort, and evaluate information about each other to give them some direction for their relationship. When one visits a professional for help for a problem such as an eating disorder, this relationship is slightly different with a different set of expectations and interactions. What follows is a description of those first few contacts between therapist and client that lead to collecting, sorting, and analyzing information—the assessment.

What Is Assessment?

Assessment is a *process* that occurs between a client and a therapist which allows the professional to develop an awareness and understanding about the client as a person, the reason for seeking help, the client's goals and objectives, and the nature of the problem.

The assessment of a person who has an eating disorder is really an ongoing process that takes place over the length of the treatment relationship. In the beginning contacts there is a focus, however, on collecting and organizing information that is used to develop a therapeutic plan for the client's recovery. Generally, this assessment period takes place within the first five sessions. It is equally important to note that the client is also collecting and evaluating information in those first sessions.

The Phone Contact. Assessment often begins at the time of the first phone contact. Here the client is generally informing the therapist, or the intake person who will later inform the therapist, about what services he or she is seeking. For example, the client may be calling to obtain information about a program's or therapist's availability, the type of therapy, fees, or treatment options. The client might also obtain some information about the therapist: voice tone, style, and methods of helping. At the same time the therapist is learning from the client: name and other identifying information, the problem in general, and possibly deciding from the requests and tone of voice some of the client's most immediate needs.

During the phone contact the client may also be told what to bring to the first session. Some possible materials requested might include past physical or psychological test reports and records. If the relationship is to continue, the phone contact will result in the establishment of an appointment time, place, length of session, and method of payment.

The First Meeting. The first session is the time when the client and therapist first meet each other face to face. At that time the therapist begins to gather information about the client's immediate physical and emotional condition. Therapists usually try to be sensitive to the client's fears and anxieties at that first meeting because, while this is a regular experience for the therapist, it is often a time of considerable uncertainty for the client. Many clients feel ashamed or uncomfortable talking about their eating disorder and may feel physically ill as well. The therapist's first goal, therefore, is to collect information about the client's "presenting" condition while providing support and reassurance so that further information may be collected.

The first assessment task is to exchange general information. The therapist is particularly concerned with what caused the client to want help at that moment in time: Are you having physical problems? Feeling emotionally overwhelmed? Are family members bugging you? Are you planning to go to college or have a baby? The therapist wants to be familiar with not only the reasons for requesting treatment but also wants to have some sense of the client's personal goals.

Further Meetings. The characteristics of the eating disorder are the next areas to be evaluated. What is being explored is not only the specific features of the eating disorder but also its effects upon the client and his or her functioning. By understanding the eating disorder and how it fits into the client's life the therapist derives a great deal of information about the client as a person. Of course, all information is obtained through interaction and exchange with the client. The client, too, often benefits by sorting through and developing a realistic appraisal of his or her own disorder.

The areas of the eating disorder to be assessed include some of the following aspects. Certainly other areas unique to the client's situation will be examined as the assessment continues.

A. *History of the Eating Disorder.* When it began, what led to its onset, how the eating disorder has changed over time, what having an eating disorder means to the client.

B. *Weight*. Current, past, and goal weight; history of being overweight; meaning of weight to the client; appropriate weight for height and build.

C. *Eating behaviors*. Changes in eating styles, food selectivity, rituals, restrictions, quantity, locations, and meanings.

D. *Weight Control Methods*. Fasting, vomiting, purgatives, exercise.

E. *Physical Condition*. General physical condition; swollen glands; dental changes; changes in skin, hair, or nails; changes in menstrual cycle; experiences of chilling easily.

F. *Psychological Condition*. Difficulties with concentrating or memory, fatigue or lethargy, sleep disturbances, changes in sexual interest, anxiety or panic attacks, depression, body image distortion.

The therapist will likely spend at least one if not two sessions or more just exploring the eating disorder and its implications for the client's life. Quite soon, however, the therapist will make a recommendation (that is, an initial treatment plan) for further out-patient assessment, further medical evaluation, or possibly, if the physical/psychological/emotional condition is serious enough, assessment and stabilization in a hospital setting.

Additional assessment sessions will focus on understanding the client's unique way of coping with and functioning in the world. Some of those areas to be explored and characteristics of each area might include:

- *Thinking Styles*. Irrational thinking, which may include "mind reading," "black-and-white thinking," minimizing important information, denial, and so forth.
- *Body Image*. Satisfaction/dissatisfaction with various parts of the body and the ways the body appears and is experienced.
- *Self-Concept*. Experience of self and worthiness; perception of capacity for change.
- *Interpersonal Relationships*. Number and pattern of friendships; and the experience of trust, closeness, and feelings of competency within various relations.
- *Family History*. History of alcoholism, mental illness or physical illness; history of physical or sexual abuse; type and nature of relationships with family members; and ways important events in the client's life have been handled within the family.

Assessment Tools

These areas are the primary ones that the therapist will be examining during the face-to-face interviews. To aid in understanding clients, therapists may also ask them to take various tests, or instruments, that will give therapists additional, or even just supporting, information. The following is a brief list of some of the instruments and their purposes.

Assessment of Eating Disorder Symptoms. Many instruments have been developed to aid the therapist in assessing the symptoms of the eating disorders themselves. These tools are usually simple paper-and-pencil tests that give the therapist a numerical estimate of various symptom clusters. They inform the therapist of the type of symptom, its severity, and relationship to other symptoms. Some of the most well-known of these assessments were developed by Dr. David Garner and associates and are referred to as the Eating Attitudes Test (EAT) and the Eating Disorder Inventory (EDI) (Garner & Garfinkel, 1979; Garner, Olmsted, & Polivy, 1983).

Assessment of Specific Problematic Symptoms. There are, of course, specific areas associated with eating disorders that the therapist may want to examine. The therapist might feel that a specific area of concern needs to be evaluated. Two problem areas that the therapist might want to additionally examine are depression and anxiety. To some extent, aspects of these conditions will have been explored in the assessment interview(s) described above. If further information is deemed necessary, paper-and-pencil tests are generally used. Some of the most frequently used ones for depression and anxiety are the Beck Depression Inventory (BDI), developed by Beck and Beamesderfer in 1974, and the State-Trait Anxiety Inventory (STAI), developed by Spielberger, Gorsuch, and Lushene in 1970.

Assessment of Personality and Other Psychological Problems.

Frequently the therapist will want to obtain a broad-based understanding of the general personality characteristics of the client. These instruments give the therapist another method of understanding the clients' "inner world." In addition to developing awareness of the general personality characteristics, these measures may also provide a screening mechanism for other problems such as guilt, impulsivity, and social adjustment. Two of the most well-known tests are the Minnesota Multiphasic Personality Inventory (MMPI), developed by Hathaway and McKinley in 1951, and the Millon Clinical Multiaxial Inventory (MCMI), developed by Millon in 1982.

A Word about Diagnosis

More often than not clients wonder and are concerned about the diagnosis or label that the therapist applies to their condition. A diagnosis is a shorthand method for identifying and communicating to others about a group of symptoms experienced by a client. Clearly, a client is much more than a "group of symptoms," but by using this label, professionals can communicate to each other and more simply locate written material that may aid in treating the client. The sourcebook for diagnosing conditions is the third revised edition of the *Diagnostic and Statistical Manual* (*DSM-III-R*), of the American Psychiatric Association (1987).

In the area of eating disorders there are three general diagnoses that are frequently used. These are briefly summarized as follows:

Anorexia Nervosa. The primary characteristics are severe loss of weight, fear of becoming obese, disturbance in the ways one sees and/or experiences one's body, and an absence of menstrual cycles in females. Other possible characteristics are hyperactivity, concentration difficulties, mood changes, and a reduced capacity to tolerate cold.

Bulimia Nervosa. Features include eating large amounts of food (binging), use of purgatives (vomiting, laxatives, etc.), and an experience of loss of control. Other symptoms might include mood changes, secretiveness, impulsive behaviors, sleep difficulties, and obsession with food and exercise.

Eating Disorders not Otherwise Specified. This category is a catch-all for any combination of symptoms that doesn't neatly fall into one of the categories described above.

A well-known disorder that is not in the *DSM-III-R* but that requires some special consideration is *compulsive overeating*, characterized by a person consuming large amounts of food which are not needed, or which are more than can be comfortably consumed. The compulsive overeater will often feel out of control when eating and will turn to food as a way of managing stress or emotional discomfort. Other features may include secret eating, moodiness, depression, sleep difficulties, and the interference of food and eating in various areas of their lives.

The Client's Assessment

We began this chapter by talking about assessment as a mutual process that occurs between *both* a client and the therapist. It would seem appropriate to conclude the chapter with a brief discussion of the role of the client assessment.

As one can see in the descriptions above, assessment is an active process. This is true not only for the therapist but should also be true for the client as well. There are several areas the client would be wise to assess with the therapist. Some useful areas for a person with an eating disorder to explore with a therapist are:

A. What are the therapist's degree and clinical training?
B. What are the amount and type of experience and training the therapist has in assessing and treating people who have an eating disorder?
C. What are the therapist's philosophy and orientation about the development and course of an eating disorder?
D. What are the goals of treatment and how are they obtained?
E. What will be the costs involved?

In addition to the above, the client would benefit from evaluating whether the therapist is both comfortable and challenging, offers strength but flexibility, and listens but is also willing to help sort out misunderstandings and confusions. It is not uncommon for one to need the same two to five sessions as the therapist to decide whether the "mix" is advantageous for the client. The important thing to remember is that the client must be an active participant in all areas of both the assessment and treatment process.

REFERENCES

American Psychological Association. (1987). *Diagnostic and statistical manual of mental disorders* (3rd edition, revised). Washington, DC: American Psychiatric Association Press.

Beck, A.T. (1961). Depression inventory. *Archives of General Psychiatry, 4* 561-571.

Garner, D.M. & Garfinkel, P.E. (1979). The eating attitudes test: an index of the symptoms of anorexia nervosa. *Psychological Medicine, 9,* 273-279.

Garner, D.M., Olmsted, M.P., & Polivy, J. (1983). The eating disorder inventory: a measure of the cognitive/behavioral dimensions of anorexia nervosa and bulimia. In P.L. Darby, P.E. Garfinkel, D.M. Garner and D.V. Coscina (Eds.) *Anorexia nervosa: recent developments*. New York: Guilford Press, 173-184.

Hathaway, S., & McKinley, J. (1951). *MMPI manual, revised edition*. New York: The Psychological Corporation.

Millon, T. (1982). *Millon clinical multiaxial inventory* (2nd ed.). Minneapolis, MN: National Computer Systems.

Spielberger, C.D., and others. (1970). *State-trait anxiety inventory*. Palo Alto, CA: Consulting Psychologists Press.

Using Medications to Treat Anorexia Nervosa and Bulimia Nervosa

▼
▼
▼
▼

by Linda P. Bock, M.D.

Medications can be helpful in the treatment of anorexia nervosa and bulimia nervosa. However, while penicillin effectively treats a strep throat, there is no single medication that is effective for anorexia nervosa. Just as the common cold has no cure because there are no effective anti-viral drugs—but many "cold medications" help the symptoms and make the recovery easier—there similarly is no medicine to "cure" anorexia nervosa, but there are medications that can be helpful.

EATING DISORDER MANIFESTATIONS

Anorexia Nervosa and Obsessive Compulsive Disorder (OCD)

A significant number of anorexics develop obsessive compulsive disorders (OCD). An obsession is an irrational, unwanted intrusive thought such as a magic number or a concern about order or cleanliness. A compulsion is a repetitive action driven by an obsessive thought—such as chewing food 20 times because 20 is the "magic" number, or arranging shoes or closets or foods with rigid order or washing hands 10 or 20 times per day.

Only since 1990 have anti-obsessional drugs become available in the United States. Fluoxetine and clomipramine act by increasing brain serotonin, a naturally occurring brain transmitter.

This increase in serotonin eventually "cools down" the overactivity in the basal ganglia, a specific relay area in the brain. The result is that, though the obsessive and compulsive drives may continue, the intensity or pressure is reduced so that the individual can better resist the drive to count calories, or exercise ritualistically.

Anorexia Nervosa and Depression

Starvation and depression often occur together. It is difficult to sort out which came first, the depression or the malnutrition. For someone with anorexia nervosa, the first choice of an "antidepressant" is food. If after reestablishment of nutrition depressive symptoms continue, such as difficulty falling asleep, early morning awakening, loss of energy, moodiness, irritability, nervousness, suicidal thinking, inability to have "fun," lack of sex drive, poor concentration or poor memory, then antidepressant medications may be helpful and may be necessary. It is not always wise to use these medications when an individual is severely underweight, however, because there can be slowing of the heart and decrease in blood pressure from use of antidepressants. A psychiatrist who is familiar with anorexia nervosa can best judge when, how much, and how long to use medications.

Bulimia Nervosa and Depression

In the early 1980s, many researchers believed that bulimia was simply a variant of depression. Many bulimics were treated with antidepressants and had a genuine decrease in frequency of symptoms. In more recent times, however, most clinicians and researchers have come to agree that bulimia nervosa is a separate and distinct disease from depression.

Some tests that indicate depression include scales such as the Beck Depression Inventory (BDI) or the Hamilton Scales, and lab tests such as the dexamethasone suppression test (DSI) and thyroid releasing hormone stimulation test (TRH Stimulation Test). However, these tests are not definitive in identifying who will respond to antidepressant treatment. Bulimia nervosa patients without depressive symptoms had both normal and abnormal results on these tests, but bulimic patients *with* depressive symptoms also had both normal and abnormal results. Curiously, a high percentage (60 to 80 percent) of patients with bulimia nervosa improve on antidepressant medications, whether these objective tests are normal or not. Many clinicians will try antidepressant medications to help decrease the frequency of binging and purging—especially in the early phase of treatment, until greater success is achieved by other therapeutic modalities. This approach can make a significant impact on recovery.

Anxiety

Medications that decrease anxiety may be helpful for both anorexia nervosa and bulimia nervosa. Unfortunately, there are numerous side effects—for example, the major tranquilizers such as Thorazine are nonaddictive but very sedating, while the minor tranquilizers such as Valium, Librium or Xanax, are not so sedating but are addictive. Clearly these medications can be helpful at circumscribed specific times but always with the direction of a competent psychiatrist.

Sometimes stress and anxiety can become so intense, that they are overwhelming. When a person is overwhelmed for long periods of time, psychosis may result. In times of psychosis, the individual has difficulty sorting the real from the unreal. During such out-of-contact times, a person may seem dazed or frozen, have fixed distorted ideas, or become involved in self-mutilation. At such times, antipsychotic medication is very helpful. The person finds his or her "jumbled thinking" becomes calmer and clearer with medication.

USING PSYCHOTHERAPEUTIC DRUGS

By using antidepressants to treat "concomitant depression" (depression that may accompany the eating disorder), or antiobsessional agents to treat obsessive compulsive disorder, or antianxiety agents to treat anxiety, or other psychiatric medications to control psychosis, key stumbling blocks can be bypassed. Treatment for anorexia or bulimia is easier if the patient is not tired, irritable, or unable to concentrate, some symptoms of depression. Antidepressant drugs are widely prescribed and seem to be effective in decreasing binge-purge frequency even in nondepressed bulimics. Certainly some antidepressants (such as amitriptyline) and some antipsychotics (such as chlorpromazine or thioridazine) can cause some weight gain; many other antidepressants and antipsychotic agents do not affect appetite or weight.

Addiction and Medications

Attention to addiction is important because so many people with bulimia are vulnerable to other addictive disorders (such as drug, alcohol, sexual, gambling, and shoplifting addictions). The medications cited here (with the exception of some minor tranquilizers) are nonaddicting. However these are significant medications that require close supervision by a physician. Starting, continuing, and ending any of these medications must be at the direction of a physician.

There are often side effects which occur as one begins to use a psychiatric drug and reverse symptoms as the drug is decreased. This is not because of addiction but is only from adjustments of other chemical systems in the body. And, this is one reason why such medications should be taken only under the supervision of a psychiatrist or physician who knows about all the various systems involved during use of medication.

There are many, many symptoms present in the illnesses of anorexia nervosa and bulimia nervosa. By starting to cure one or many of these symptoms, a person can function more normally and move toward recovery more quickly than one would be able to do with the symptoms' interferences.

FOR ADDITIONAL READING

Franklin, J. (1987). *Molecules of the mind.* New York: Dell Publishing Company.

Rapoport, J.L. (1989). *The boy who couldn't stop washing.* New York: E. P. Dutton.

Using Individual Psychotherapy to Treat Anorexia Nervosa and Bulimia Nervosa

▼
▼
▼
▼
by Linda P. Bock, M.D.

The most frequently used treatment form for people with anorexia nervosa and bulimia nervosa is individual psychotherapy. Individual psychotherapy refers to the treatment of psychological disorders by a professional method that involves a professionally trained therapist who focuses on treating the individual alone, not, say, in a group setting.

THE STRUCTURE OF INDIVIDUAL PSYCHOTHERAPY

There are a wide variety of therapists. Therapists differ in their location, cost, personality, style, and training or background. Therapists from a medical background may have credentials in nursing or medicine. A nurse usually is licensed as an L.P.N. (licensed practical nurse) or R.N. (registered nurse), and a physician, such as a psychiatrist, has an M.D. degree. Other therapists come from nonmedical backgrounds and studied at graduate schools rather than at medical centers. These include social workers with a degree such as M.S.W. or A.C.S.W. and psychologists with a Ph.D. or Psy.D. degree. Because anorexia nervosa and bulimia nervosa are psychiatric illnesses with serious medical problems, an individual psychotherapist with affiliation in a system of medical care is critical.

There is a wide range of types of individual psychotherapy. Some labels include cognitive-behavioral psychotherapy, Gestalt therapy, rational-emotive therapy, supportive therapy, insight-oriented psychotherapy, and psychoanalytic psychotherapy. These types of treatment differ in the amount of activity of the therapist, the use of information and teaching, and the depth of emotional expressivity.

Therapists who specialize in the treatment of eating disorders often work with other colleagues with this same interest, are affiliated with a specialized treatment program, or attend national training conferences about eating disorders. Several national information clearing houses can assist with referral to a specialized therapist. (See Organizations in Part 5 of this book.)

After an evaluation wherein individual psychotherapy is prescribed the patient and the therapist need to agree on the fee, the appointment time, and goals of treatment. The frequency of appointments can vary from a rare appointment every two months to regular appointments once, twice, or more times per week. The frequency chosen depends on many factors. The interest and insight of the patient may be very high, so very frequent sessions of three or more times per week may be helpful. For active psychotherapy, it is common that sessions are held at least weekly. The sessions must be frequent enough so that the process stays alive and fresh for the patient and the therapist and yet not so frequently that the patient cannot manage to live his or her own life.

ROLES IN INSIGHT-ORIENTED INDIVIDUAL PSYCHOTHERAPY

In *insight-oriented* therapy (also called *psychodynamic* therapy), the therapist agrees to accept all that the patient wishes to discuss and agrees to keep private the content of their work. Contracts are often used to address problems such as low weight or binging or purging.

The patient's role is to talk freely to the therapist and to avoid censoring thoughts and ideas. In this way, the patient can experience his or her own emotional feelings, memories, and dreams.

Behaviors such as law breaking, drug abuse, low body weight, or severely uncontrolled eating can prompt hospitalization for protection from self-harm. A contract is therefore helpful to spell out which behaviors will be beyond the limits of out-patient psychotherapy as well as what the consequences for those behaviors will be.

COURSE OF THERAPY

Therapy can be depicted as having a beginning, a middle, and an end. In a complete course of treatment, a patient completes all three "parts," but many patients leave therapy before real completion.

Beginning Stages of Therapy

The main tasks in the initial phase of treatment are to establish trust in the therapist and to develop a language for emotions. This task of labeling affect (i.e., emotions) is very difficult because most people with eating disorders are poorly skilled at using words to express their emotions. The word to describe this state is *alexithymia*.

Trust is a major problem for patients with anorexia nervosa and bulimia. Often feeling closeness in a human relationship is experienced as dangerous with potential for rejection, rather than being warm and nurturing. Trust, therefore, is often difficult to establish. Another impediment to the development of trust is compliancy. People with eating disorders often use a defense of compliancy to protect themselves from rejection. Compliancy, or being "people-pleasing," clouds the individual's true self. With this "sham" self, genuineness and trust do not develop easily.

As trust and word skill become stronger there are often fewer and fewer symptoms in the patient's life. This marks the beginning of the middle phase of treatment.

Middle Stages of Therapy

During the middle phase, whatever tension that caused major problems in the patient's life becomes less problematic in the patient's "real" life and more operationally active in the "therapy" life, that is, in the relationship between the patient and the therapist. For example, a patient who is overdependent on her parents may become more appropriate with her parents, feel safer about growing up, but become more dependent on the therapist instead. As another example, a patient who is so involved in people-pleasing that she has no identity for herself may find herself trying to please the therapist in the session but more able to stand up for her own likes and dislikes outside of therapy.

Once the conflicts are compartmentalized within the therapeutic relationship, the conflicts can be observed in three areas or circles. These circles of tension observation are (1) the patient-therapist relationship, (2) relationships of the past, and (3) relationships of the patient's current life. As an example, a patient with conflict over dishonesty may find herself caught in a deceit by her boyfriend or husband. During treatment the patient and therapist would look for similar tensions or feeling states about deceit in her current life as well as times in her past (perhaps with parents or teachers) and also now in treatment with her therapist.

By using these three arenas of focus, the conflict(s) unravel and have a clear meaning. As the protective function of the symptoms are more clearly seen, patients can develop new skills to protect themselves. With new skills replacing the symptoms, the end phase of therapy is at hand because conflict is understood. Resolution occurs and the patient no longer needs old symptoms to manage a previously misunderstood conflict.

End Stages of Therapy

As termination is begun, it is common for some symptoms to return. In part these reappearing symptoms are a way to express the patient's terror of leaving. In part, the exacerbation of symptoms can allow the patient to go over his or her work in a synoptic or review manner.

Just as learning to trust the therapist was the challenge in the initial phase, learning to trust oneself is the challenge of termination of treatment.

CONFLICTS ADDRESSED IN THERAPY

Some commonly encountered conflicts that underlie an eating disorder are listed below as side-by-side tensions:

- Abandonment/Engulfment
- Dependence/Independence
- False Identity/Compliance

These poles are the extremes to which a person can feel drawn. The optimum or healthy position involves a comfortable ability with human relationships, with inderdependence, and with genuine identity, and thus health is a mid-zone between the two poles. Often there are problems in the process called *separation* and *individuation*. This nor-

mal developmental process usually is at a peak from six months to three years. Within adolescence, there is a reawakening of separation-individuation struggles. The task, within both age groups, is how well the child can manage as a separate person and yet relate safely and competently with the surrounding world of people.

Commonly, individuals with anorexia and/or bulimia have had problematic childhood or adolescent years. Often the families are dysfunctional with an emotionally overwhelming or emotionally unavailable parent. Parental alcoholism or "work-a-holism," child neglect, physical abuse, sexual abuse, date rape, or other major trauma are very common.

These overstimulating burdens make the usual tasks of separation and individuation impossible. An eating disorder with all its defensive protections serves to both provide safety from trauma and also to draw forth caretaking from the very people the child needs to leave.

AFTER THERAPY

If the termination phase allows adequate time, the patient leaves treatment with self-reliance and is able to continue the self-observing process—but without the therapist's presence.

The beginning, middle, and end phases of therapy can take equal amounts of time—for instance in an 18-month course of therapy, roughly 6 months may be spent in each phase. Other times, one treatment phase can be protracted due to a major crisis in one's current life; thus a death of a significant person (in the patient's childhood or current life) can make the termination phase richer and more time-consuming. Other times a patient may be highly word skilled or have ease in trusting so the initial phase may be quite brisk.

While many patients can and do successfully complete treatment, not all patients who stop therapy have "finished" their treatment. There are difficulties from incomplete or inadequate therapy. Some patients start with one therapist, work a while, and then leave, only to begin afresh at a later time. Often in the second course of treatment, with new skills acquired in the first therapy, treatment can progress more rapidly. Other people return to treatment, even after a full and successful therapy, when life's problems provoke distress and dysfunction. These new life stressors can reawaken old, forgotten defenses and dysfunctional patterns.

COMBINATION OF THERAPIES

Individual insight-oriented therapy is often augmented by nutritional counseling, cognitive-behavioral therapy, family therapy, and group therapy. Some patients may benefit greatly from one therapy in the earlier stages of recovery and from another therapy at another time. Thus at first family therapy may, for one patient, be helpful to conquer denial; however, later family therapy may be minimally significant when the patient is nearer the close of individual therapy.

The overall goal of therapy is to maximize the intensity of discovery, to minimize symptoms and acting out, and to maintain fullness of living.

Group Therapy for Bulimia Nervosa

▼
▼
▼
▼

by Lillie Weiss, Ph.D., Melanie Katzman, Ph.D., and Sharlene Wolchik, Ph.D.

Has your eating gotten out of control? Do you eat too much and then throw up? Do you get depressed and disgusted with yourself afterwards? Do you feel that you would simply die if anyone discovered your "secret"?

You Are Not Alone!

There are many other people in your situation who are experiencing the same problems. They binge regularly and follow that either by vomiting, taking laxatives or water pills, or by starving themselves afterwards. They feel guilty, embarrassed, and ashamed and think that they are all alone with their suffering. Actually, the binge-purge cycle or bulimia, as it is called, is fairly common. It is estimated that 8.3 percent of high school girls fill diagnostic criteria for bulimia (Johnson, Lewis, Love, Lewis, & Stuckey, 1984) and that one in five regularly engages in binge-eating (Levine, 1987).

Group therapy can be very helpful for bulimics, who often feel isolated, alone, and misunderstood. In a group setting, you can learn, change, and share your experience with other persons who have similar problems.

What Is Group Therapy?

Group therapy is when persons meet in a warm, supportive, and confidential setting to discuss their common concerns and learn to deal with their problems through mutual sharing, support, and feedback from other group members. Most groups meet on a weekly basis, usually for one and one-half to two hours, and are led by one or more therapists.

Why Is Group Therapy Helpful?

Group therapy helps, first of all, to let you know you are not alone. No longer do you have to feel isolated or that "nobody can understand." When you see others in your situation, you begin to make more personal connections that start you on the path of coping with problems by relying on people, not food. Many bulimics think that they are the only ones who binge and purge or have an extreme dislike for themselves and their bodies. They are often relieved to find that others have similar fears, preoccupations, and feelings. For teenagers in particular, it is such a relief to be able to finally express feelings of shame and hurt and be understood! The experience of sharing negative feelings and still being accepted by the group can help free them from these emotions.

Groups provide a "safe" place where you can express your concerns and not feel that you are going to be judged. You can learn to accept yourself and no longer feel ashamed or abnormal or that you would "die" if anyone found out. Instead, through your experience and the experiences of others, you can learn to understand the reasons behind your preoccupation with food and weight.

Group therapy also provides the support you need to make changes, which comes from knowing that others are coping with the same feelings and fears that you have. It is much easier to work on getting better when you have a whole team rooting for you and giving you encouragement along the way. Group members can help you through these rough times and be there for you when you need them. In some groups, members talk with each other at times other than in the group sessions. These relationships can provide support for the changes group members make.

Group therapy also gives you a chance to learn. By seeing how others solve similar problems, you can learn new ways of looking at and dealing with your problems. You can learn a great deal just by listening and vicariously sharing in the experiences of others. For example, listening to another group member's distorted view of her body may help you to recognize similar distortions in your perceptions of your body. Group members can also provide you with valuable feedback on your behavior, and you can use this information to make meaningful changes.

A group can also offer education about your eating problems and provide you with new tools to break out of old patterns. Group leaders can give information about bulimia and correct common myths and misconceptions about it. They can also teach you new coping skills to deal with your stresses.

Groups also give you a chance to practice what you have learned. Jamie, for example, learned that she ate uncontrollably whenever she disagreed with someone but didn't speak up. In the group, she was encouraged to express herself whenever she had an opinion. Being able to practice her assertiveness skills in a group helped her to do so outside the therapy situation. She started to learn that she didn't need to "eat" her feelings but that she could express them to others.

Probably one of the most important ways in which a group can be helpful is to offer you hope. When you see someone with a similar problem as yours making progress, it lets you know that you can change too. As many have told us, "If she (or he) can do it, I can do it!"

What Kinds of Groups Are Available?

There are several types of groups for persons with eating disorders. Some groups are *closed* groups, which means that the same group members meet every time and that the group is not open to new members. Closed groups are generally but not always short-term and meet for a certain number of sessions with a beginning and ending date. *Open* or ongoing groups are those that are open to new members. These tend to be generally longer-term and may go on indefinitely, with new members coming in and older ones dropping out. Sometimes a beginning group member may start out in a closed group of limited duration and may then join an open, long-term group for follow-up and maintenance.

Groups can also be *structured* or *unstructured*. Some groups have certain themes or topics for each week and follow a specified format. Generally, many short-term, closed groups tend to have a definite format or structure. Psychoeducational groups, or groups that combine psychotherapy and education, tend to be fairly structured and have planned teaching materials for each session. Group members can share their experiences and feelings within the context of that structure. Many long-term, open-ended groups tend to be unstructured, with no specific topic or agenda planned. In these groups, members discuss problems that came up since the last meeting and learn about how they deal with relationships by discussing the interactions that occur among the group members.

There are also *homogeneous* groups and *heterogeneous* groups. Homogeneous groups are only for persons with bulimia, whereas heterogeneous groups include individuals with all types of eating disorders and may include anorexics, bulimics, and overweight members. Although there are good arguments for mixing patients, it has been our experience that it is generally not useful for persons with different eating problems to be together in the same group. In particular, we feel that anorexic people should not be in the same groups as bulimic people because their dynamics differ (Weiss & Katzman, 1984).

When we speak of group therapy, we are generally referring to groups led by trained therapists. There are also peer support groups or *self-help* groups—groups that are organized and run by persons who have had eating disorders in the past. One function of these groups is ongoing support.

In addition to groups for the person with the eating problem, there are also support groups for family members. These groups can provide information, give support, and help your family give you the kinds of encouragement you need. Many families want to be helpful and may not know how. In addition, they may have received much misinformation about bulimia, and groups can help correct their misconceptions and provide them with accurate information.

What Can I Expect to Happen in Group Therapy?

In a typical group therapy session, a small number of people, usually between five and 12, discuss their eating habits and their feelings about themselves. They receive feedback from other group members and learn other ways of dealing with their feelings besides binging and purging.

In our groups (Weiss, Katzman, & Wolchik, 1985, 1986), we offer a combination of education and a chance for sharing of feelings and experiences. Topics include information about bulimia, its medical and psychological complications, and myths and misconceptions about it. In addition to discussing proper nutrition and eating in a healthy manner, we discuss how eating is often used as a coping strategy and provide

group members alternative ways of dealing with their stresses. Some of our sessions are devoted to perfectionism and handling anger, as many bulimics set unrealistically high standards for themselves and have a difficult time asserting themselves. We also talk about our feelings about our bodies and how there is so much societal pressure for women to be thin. We use reading materials, exercises, and homework for each session to address these topics, and group members practice what they learn outside the therapy session.

Is Group Therapy Enough or Do I Need Some Other Type of Help as Well?

Group therapy is not the only treatment for bulimia and does not preclude individual treatment. Group therapy is frequently most effective in conjunction with individual therapy. It can also be used for follow-up and maintenance after a person has been in individual therapy for some time and wants to continue to have ongoing support when therapy is completed.

Are All Groups Beneficial?

The answer to that question is, unfortunately, no. Although group therapy, conducted by properly trained professionals is for the most part, very helpful, there are "bad" groups that may have some negative consequences. These groups are frequently led by persons who are neither knowledgeable about eating disorders nor about group therapy. Make certain to check out the therapist's training and credentials before you join a group. It is important that the therapist be sufficiently familiar with eating disorders so that you can receive accurate information.

Although it is natural to feel uncomfortable at first when joining a new group, if you feel very ill at ease, belittled, or attacked, trust your instincts and find a group where you feel more comfortable. Although sometimes in a group you may hear feedback that is uncomfortable from the therapist, it should not be given in a disrespectful or humiliating manner. If you believe the therapist has done this, discuss it with him or her afterwards.

One unfortunate consequence of some groups is that the members may want to talk about new ways of purging rather than to learn other ways to cope with their feelings and problems. If you find that the main topic in the group is a comparison of the most effective vomiting techniques, this is clearly the wrong group for you. A good group will encourage you to *decrease* your binging and purging, not teach you new ways to promote your bad habits. A good group will also focus on feelings and the meaning of food, not just on what you ate.

Another feature of a "bad" group is pessimism. If you come out of a group feeling as though there is no hope, then you are probably getting a great deal of misinformation. In a good group, you will receive encouragement and hope and will be given healthy tools to help you break your habit. However, be aware that it may take several meetings to judge whether the group is right for you.

How Can I Find the Right Group for Me?

Contact your family physician, a school nurse or counselor, or the nearest university to get the names of some groups in your area. Remember, eating problems can be medically serious and psychologically draining, but you *can* change your eating habits and learn to have more control over them. Remember, *you are not alone!*

REFERENCES

Johnson, C.L., Lewis, C., Love, S., Lewis, L., & Stuckey, M. (1984). Incidence and correlates of bulimic behavior in a female high school population. *Journal of Youth and Adolescence, 13,* 15-26.

Levine, M.P. (1987). *How schools can help combat student eating disorders*. Washington, DC: National Education Association.

Weiss, L., & Katzman, M.K. (1984). Group treatment for bulimic women. *Arizona Medicine, 41*(2), 100-104.

Weiss, L., Katzman, M.K., & Wolchik, S.A. (1985). *Treating bulimia: a psychoeducational approach*. New York: Pergamon Press.

Weiss, L., Katzman, M.K., & Wolchik, S.A. (1986). *You can't have your cake and eat it too: a program for controlling bulimia*. Saratoga, CA: R & E Publishers.

Eating-Disordered Families: Issues between the Generations

▼
▼
▼
▼

by Bonnie L. Pelch

HAND ME DOWN HURT*

Hand me down hurt,
It's nothing new
As was done unto me now
I do unto you.

Like his daddy's daddy,
and his father's son,
over and over the same course is
run.

You're so damn stupid,
That's what you are
Thru generations those words
travel far.

Please break the cycle,
Help stop the pain
Don't keep repeating this
Sad, sad refrain.

This poem wasn't written by a family member of an eating-disordered victim but by a fiancé. Wise beyond his years, he realizes that unresolved issues in past relationships are revisited in new relationships and in new generations. Therapists and writers in the fields of psychiatry, social psychology, family therapy, and self-help talk about issues among generations in families in a variety of ways. Virginia Satir (*Peoplemaking*) refers to "scripting"; Judith Viorst (*Necessary Losses*) points out the need to grieve the loss of dreams as well as the loss of loved ones; Charles Whitfield (*Healing the Child Within*) addresses the dynamics of shame and low self-esteem; Harriet Goldhor Lerner (*The Dance of Intimacy*) explains that overfunctioners need as much understanding and attention as do chronic un-der-functioners. This author/therapist offers that you can't give what you didn't get.

In order to better understand multi-generational issues in eating-disordered families, a brief description of healthy families helps the reader to see that, in family therapy, the "patient" is the family, not the individual. Comments regarding the healthy family will provide specific signs and symptoms that distinguish healthier from less functional families. Common traits of eating-disordered families, which may be similar to other dysfunctional family systems, will be discussed. Finally, the role of the family in the recovery of the eating-disordered victim and the healing of the family as a whole will be explored through the eyes of a family therapist.

HEALTHY FAMILIES

Family systems share at least nine characteristics that provide a natural pulse to the progress of a family unit in its life cycle. Those characteristics are:

- Quality of parental relationships.
- Allocation of power.
- Problem-solving ability.
- Ability to discuss feelings.
- Commonality of values.
- Communication.
- Intimacy and autonomy.
- Closeness.
- Toleration of change.

*Copyright 1991 by Steve Finazzo. Used by permission.

If the primary goal of the family is to support the development of all of its members, then these nine characteristics must be monitored regularly.

For example, allocation of power in healthy families is democratically distributed; no one person dictates decisions and plans for the family or its individual members. Functional systems avoid dominant-submissive interactions. A healthier family has open communication, with members having the ability to discuss negative and positive feelings. Autonomy and intimacy are not privileges to the family adults only. Harriet Lerner (1989) clarifies intimacy as requiring "authenticity in the context of connectedness. Authenticity means we can be who we are in a relationship...it requires that we allow the other person to do the same."

Problem solving is a shared, joint task, negotiated by two or more in the family. The success of that task is not measured by a unanimous decision. Instead, asserting one's ideas and understanding other family members' points of view are the most important goals.

The ability to discuss one's feelings is critical to healthy individual and family development. The acceptance of emotions as valid, without assigning a negative or positive value to one's anger, sadness, or fear, is a priority task for the growth-conscious family.

For the purpose of this article, all nine family characteristics have not been examined. The section to follow will look at some characteristics as they relate to the psychosomatic or eating-disordered family.

DYSFUNCTIONAL FAMILIES: VICTIMS OF EATING DISORDERS

All families must pass through their own unique life cycles. If one views the system as traveling horizontally through time, the phases are as predictable as the stages of the individual. The stressors/phases are leaving home, marriage, birth of children, parenting, children exiting the nuclear family, and retirement. What complicates this picture is that the family also experiences a vertical/intergenerational dimension at the same time. Members of the family are pushed to change or reorganize at each phase (their horizontal task), while coping with whatever legacy has been passed down from previous generations (their vertical task). Attitudes about illness, money, sex, divorce, and death are a part of that legacy which may be more or less functional. The difference in healthy and less healthy families is in the management of these vertical and horizontal stressors. The dysfunctional family gets derailed or stuck in either the normal or the unexpected life crises.

Eating disorders do not thrive in a healthy environment. Be clear, however, that no parent sets out to have a child with an eating disorder. Although each family is different, common problems repeatedly surface. The family often mirrors the difficulties of the eating-disordered individual. In this case, common family themes are preoccupation with food, weight, and/or appearance; perfectionism; too much focus on success (particularly financial); family members who are hypersensitive to one another (not distinguishing where one member's problem ends and the other member's begins); poor skills to solve conflicts; and absence of flexibility regarding family rules or expectations.

The eating-disordered family has at least four vulnerable areas of family functioning that deserve some distinction. Those areas are:

- Perfectionism.
- Life in the extremes.
- Suppression of one or more inherent human emotions (sadness, anger, gladness, fear, or confusion).
- Conflict related to one's sexuality.

Perfectionism is a thread that may run from appearance to eating only "healthy" foods to being first at school or work to being the world's best daughter. The concept of being "good enough" is rarely acceptable to the success-driven individual or family. Even one's selective sport or recreation depends on having the perfect or best score/performance.

Life in the extremes (all or nothing thinking) can be a trap that fuels the eating disorder. Moderation is seen as boring, mediocre, or insignificant. Obsessions and compulsions are some extreme forms in action. Alcoholism is by far the best known compulsion/addiction, but the list of "-holic" states grows yearly: Some commonly recognized types seen in families are "workaholics," "rageholics," "sadaholics," "hypochondriaholics," etc.

A third area of vulnerability is disconnection from or suppression of one's emotions. The very response (fight or flight) that has preserved generations of humans as well as other life forms is discouraged in obvious and not so obvious ways within the dysfunctional family. A person's emotions instruct the individual in creativity, spontaneity, and genuineness. Being cut off from one's emotional self is a sure way to repeat the unresolved issues of the generations past.

How does the fourth area, conflicted sexuality, fit into this dysfunctional family picture? If the family environment is one in which communication related to sexual relations is considered shameful or inappropriate, one's body and sexual urges are perceived as bad or negative. Therapists of eating-disordered families have long noticed that the family and the individual with an eating disorder have a harder time than most in accepting adult sexuality.

FAMILY THERAPY OF THE EATING-DISORDERED FAMILY

The above paragraphs may paint a rather fatalistic picture for chances of recovery, but individuals and families need not be prisoners of their past. The author believes that families do the best they can do, and they truly *want* to have greater health and happiness compared with their families of origin. A primary goal of the family therapist is to assist families in becoming healthier and happier. Although the process of bringing unconscious, unsettled issues from the past is painful, the process frees the parent, spouse, or child to react in a more positive way. A family member may *want* to have a different kind of system than the one from which he or she came. However, without competent therapy, support, and education, the member may *need* to repeat old family patterns.

Oftentimes the overprotectiveness of a family member contributes to maintenance of the eating disorder. Love may be the original intent of the protectiveness, but overprotectiveness stunts the separation process that occurs in adolescence (the usual time when eating disorder symptoms surface in the physical patient of the eating-disordered family).

A dynamic in eating-disordered families that requires immediate attention is preoccupation with weight and appearance. If family members/significant others who reside with the victim of the eating disorder continue to focus on food, obsessive weighing of oneself, etc., any individual movement toward recovery is like to be sabotaged; throwing out the family scale is always a good first step.

In selecting a family therapist the decision should be tailored individually to the needs of the family. If the parents relate to the therapist and yet one or more children don't feel comfortable, find a different therapist (and vice versa). If one family member consistently finds fault with the therapist, the family may need to move on without that individual being in treatment. Start family therapy with the idea that the family has reasons for being in this place at this time. Let the family therapist accompany you into the new and scary places you will need to go to become healthy.

CONCLUSION

Family therapy plays a crucial role in the recovery of the eating-disordered family. When used in connection with individual treatment, chances for a full recovery are greatly improved. Rarely can eating-disordered family systems survive the collision of the dysfunctional vertical/intergenerational dimensions of family members with the normal family life cycle tasks (marriages, childbirths, launching of grown children, etc.) without professional therapy intervention. The goals of family therapy would be accepting family as good enough, moving away from perfectionistic thinking, see-ing guilt and self-doubt as a dead-end street, and recognizing that healthy traits as well as unhealthy ones are passed from generation to generation. With multi-therapy intervention, full recovery is possible.

REFERENCES

Lerner, H.G. (1989). *The dance of intimacy*. Harper & Row.

Satir, V. (1972). *Peoplemaking*. Palo Alto, CA: Science and Behavior Books, Inc.

Viorst, J. (1987). *Necessary losses*. New York: Ballantine Books.

Whitfield, C. (1987). *Healing the child within*. Deerfield Beach, FL: Health Communications, Inc.

Discovering, Re-Creating, and Healing the Self through Art and Dreams: Help for Persons with Eating Disorders

▼
▼
▼
▼

by Cappi Lang, Ph.D.

The expression of oneself through the arts provides another means of communicating in addition to talking or verbal therapy. As a person paints, draws, sculpts, moves his or her body, or participates in a drama or music, what is inside is projected outward and takes a form that can be looked at, discussed, reworked, and re-created.

Because what is expressed in the creative arts comes directly from inside the person it is a mirror of the true self of that person. Through the arts one has the opportunity to express feelings, thoughts, and ideas that otherwise might remain hidden or repressed. This is especially true of those feelings, traumas, and experiences pushed down into the unconscious.

Many times past experiences and the feelings connected with them are not allowed expression because of the fear or pain associated with them. They remain unconscious. If this happens the repressed material often causes us to become ill, to act in unhealthy and destructive ways. Because art provides a means to bypass the defenses that repress experiences and feelings, this material so long unknown to us becomes revealed. We can then re-experience it, deal with it, and begin to re-discover a clearer sense of self. This enables us to act in new, constructive ways.

Another way we receive messages from our unconscious, our true self and source of wisdom, is through the nightly drama of our dreams. It has been proven that everyone dreams and that dreams provide us with valuable information about living in healthy, meaningful ways. Dreams are related to the arts in that we dream in images and symbols. When we combine the use of the creative art therapies with dream analysis, a powerful means of expressing, discovering, transforming, and healing the self is provided.

Eating-disordered patients seem especially to be helped by art therapies and dream analysis because in many cases they have not been allowed to express feelings, have not been appreciated as unique individuals, have often been abused and neglected, and have often been put in the position of taking care of others at a very young age.

In the following pages, I will present the stories of four eating-disordered patients' work in art therapy and dream analysis.

CASE HISTORIES

Jane

During a group session I have asked the patients to do some dream work. They have been asked to sculpt in clay an image from a dream. Jane sculpts what appears to be an ape. Next, the patients are asked to do a drawing of their dream. Her drawing is of a large ape wearing a birthday hat. There are smaller apes surrounding the large ape.

In the left-hand corner is a small child crying in a crib. In the dream, Jane says she is surrounded by apes who she feels are going to hurt her. She is crying for help. Jane believes the dream was brought on by a party she attended when she was two where a man dressed as a giant ape entertained but also terrified her. She had had the dream several times as a child, and now it is re-occurring.

As we talk through the dream, decoding the symbols, Jane feels that the ape symbolizes the anorexia part of her, and the baby her small, undeveloped self. The message of the dream to Jane is that the anorexia is getting out of control, and her baby self is crying for help. She needs to accept this help if she is to heal. The crib Jane describes is a safe place that could also become lonely and confining. It is a place where one could isolate one's self. The disease, which has at first made her feel safe and in control, is now becoming out of control, and she is feeling confined, scared, and lonely.

I believe there is more to this dream. I ask her if she feels able to take it further. Would she feel comfortable if the group were to act out the dream? Jane agrees and chooses several other patients to be the different parts of the dream. She chooses to portray herself (the baby). As the apes approach the baby, Jane suddenly grabs her lower abdomen, stating she feels faint and does not want to go on. The group helps her to a chair where she sits for a few moments and then begins to cry.

Jane says she does not know why she is crying except that she feels scared and alone and her stomach hurts. She is unable to come up with anything more at this time.

To try to force what is not ready to come up can often cause a person to pull back and become blocked or stuck. I decided to hold off and to sit with Jane until she can regain her composure. The group provides a protective circle around her.

Two days later Jane asks for a private session to work on a dream she has had the previous night. She sculpts out of clay a teardrop. She then draws a man and child in a cellar. The man has chased the child into the cellar and has her pinned against the wall. The cellar is described as a smelly, damp, and scary place.

I ask her to feel the dream in her body. She sits for awhile with her body drawn up. In a whisper she tells me that someone in her family, a boy eight years her senior, chased her into the basement when she was six and sexually abused her. This abuse continued for four years.

Jane looks at the drawings of the apes and tells me she believes the boy came into her bedroom when she was much younger and molested her. She says she does not remember the molestation but feels it in her body. I ask her if she can do a drawing of how she would end this dream. She draws the child with an axe chopping off the boy's head. Jane says she has always wanted to chop off this person's head and has a feeling of satisfaction after being allowed to do it in the art.

Making this drawing is an example of how we can express powerful feelings in an acceptable and creative way. We cannot chop off a person's head in reality without experiencing severe, destructive consequences. But we can do it through art.

It is significant that the symbol of the apes represents both Jane's sexual abuse and her eating disorder. The two dreams show how a dream or series of dreams can bring up a trauma from the past that is acted out in a behavior (the eating disorder) in the present and connect the two. Jane is unable "to stomach" the abuse. She tries to purge it from her system. She attempts to purify herself through fasting and exercise, but art becomes a more constructive way of cleansing herself.

Sherre

Sherre has come to see me as a private patient. She has brought a number of dreams in her therapy sessions to explore. Two will be discussed here.

Dream 1: Sherre draws her dream. It is of a cottage, two people in front of a refrigerator, a cedar closet, roller skates, a fire, and four children. In the dream Sherre is at a cottage with an old boyfriend. It is his cottage. Sherre is putting on her roller skates, which have been in a very small cedar closet. Sherre and her boyfriend see a fire outside the window and feel compelled to go there.

Sherre describes the feel of the dream as being in a place that is not very nurturing (her boyfriend's house), feeling like a child (symbolized by the skates), and being drawn to something very exciting (the fire). Sherre defines the symbols as follows: her boyfriend as a father figure; the cedar closet as nurturing but too small; skates, as something fun for kids; fire, as shoplifting (an act for which she has recently been arrested)—something that can burn you.

As the dream is worked through Sherre comes up with several thoughts. One is that her boyfriend did not provide a very nurturing environment. Neither did her father, who was drunk most of the time. Her stepfather died when she was 11, leaving her and her mother alone. The cedar closet (nurturing), where the skates (child) are found, is extremely small in the drawing. There was not much nurturing at home. The fire (shoplifting) gives her a thrill for the moment but fire burns. It is dangerous, as is shoplifting. Sherre decides to re-create the image of the fire whenever she has the urge to shoplift.

Dream 2: This dream takes place three months later and is in two parts. In part one, Sherre is caught shoplifting by a security guard. We see her heart pounding in the drawing. Sherre feels this part of the dream is her anxiety over being caught shoplifting. I ask Sherre to describe what part of herself the two figures might represent. She says the security guard is the part that tells her she is bad and takes her to jail. The figure with the pounding heart is the part that feels she can only have nurturing if she steals it. She does this at great risk. The dream is a serious warning.

In the second part of the dream, Sherre's mother is stealing a pot. Sherre tries to stop her. Her mother minimizes her stealing. As we talk about her drawing of the dream, Sherre remembers that her mother also steals. "She taught me to shoplift," Sherre cries out in indignation. Sherre then recalls how many things she was denied as a child, including nurturing. One part of her wanted these things and felt deprived. The other part—"the good little Sherre"—felt guilty because her mother had to work and times were hard. The part Sherre repressed emerges as the brat who steals what she feels too guilty to give the little child within her. Sherre must learn to give to herself.

Again we see how feelings and memories repressed and forgotten come up in dreams and are given form through art. This information enables us to begin to make sense of why we behave in destructive ways. We are then able to go back and with help, reparent our wounded child, find our lost self, and heal and transform ourselves. In this case Sherre needs reparenting that provides both nurturing and boundaries.

Ann

I often ask patients to make a family collage. It is to include as much of the family as possible, going back at least as far as grandparents. These creations are important because they reveal the family atmosphere, which often leads to behavior that can be destructive to oneself and others. There may also be, however, much love and many positive feelings within the family. The collage allows the patient to sort out these experiences as well and decide which cycles to perpetuate and which cycles to attempt to break.

Ann's collage is divided in half. The two halves are connected by strips of red and black tissue, representing love (red) and pain (black). One half is her father's family. The other half is her mother's family. The collage reveals a theme of perfection and secrets. Beginning with her grandparents the message has been given that no matter what happens within the family, outsiders are only to see the family as perfect and nice.

In reality Ann's mother has a mental illness; her father drinks and has affairs and eventually divorces her mother. Ann becomes her mother's caretaker and perpetuates the image of perfection. She strives to keep everything in order, to be the perfect daughter in every way. Because everything is so out of control she strives for perfect control. In order to control her body she becomes bulimic. In order to maintain the perfect family image she represses her feelings and loses herself.

As Ann looks at the images she has created in the art work, she realizes that she has put love and pain together. She acknowledges that the two can coexist. She loves her family but there is much pain. She has expressed in the art what she has been unable until now to express in words. She also acknowledges how destructive secrets can be, yet struggles with revealing too much about the family, lest she betray them. She struggles to let go of the role of being her mother's mother. The work for Ann is just beginning.

Kate

Writing and illustrating a fairy tale can bring up important themes in a person's life. It is more than likely the story of that person's life. When acted out within the art therapy group, it is brought alive for the creator as well as the other members of the group, who always relate their own lives to the characters they are asked to play.

Kate writes a tale about a bird who falls from the nest at a very young age. She is the beautiful color of lapis blue. This color is most important to Kate and represents the spiritual and the feminine. A black cat finds the bird and takes her home to eat her for supper. However, the bird begins to sing, and the cat falls so in love with her voice that he is unable to destroy her. She sings for him every evening and they become close friends. The bird is allowed to fly wherever she chooses as long as she returns each night.

On one of her flights, she discovers a magic castle where a magician lives. Cat warns her that she may be in danger if she flies too close. But she is drawn to the castle by its magic. One day she flies too close and is captured by the magician. He puts her in a beautiful golden cage covered by pink rosebuds and demands she sing for him.

Cat dies of heartbreak and the blue bird is trapped and lonely.

One day a beautiful purple butterfly appears and becomes the bird's friend and confidante. This butterfly has a plan to release the bird. The bird will pretend to die. The bird does as instructed and the magician is devastated, thinking his beautiful treasure is gone. The butterfly suggests to the magician that he spin a chrysalis around the bird so that she may hang in view of everyone to be remembered and honored for the pleasure she has brought. The magician so orders.

But while the magician is mourning the death of his beautiful bird what actually happens is that the bird is transformed into a butterfly. As she emerges she takes on the color of brightest yellow. The purple butterfly tells her as she grows in experience she will take on all the colors of the rainbow. She begins her journey heading out into the fields towards a group of dancing princesses. The butterfly cautions her to head not for these perfect maids but for a group of young boys playing ball. "They will teach you about play and being a 'good sport,'" says the purple butterfly.

After Kate presents her story and it is dramatized by the group we identify several life themes which have meaning to Kate. She describes herself as being pushed out of the family nest too soon and having to grow up too soon. The cat she feels represents both her father and her husband, whom at times may devour her with their love and for whom she performs. They care for her but at the same time keep her prisoner in many ways. It is hard for her to separate from them.

However she is lured and seduced by the magical thinking represented by the magician, only to become even more trapped within the golden cage. (She remembers a book she has read called *The Golden Cage* about anorexia.) She feels magical thinking is an effort to escape the control of her father and husband and has led her to her eating disorder, which traps her even more. The purple butterfly she feels symbolizes the spiritual, all-knowing, mother part of her who assists her in freeing herself. As Kate (the bird transformed into butterfly) begins her journey she wishes to go towards the beautiful, perfect princesses. The part of herself which is all-knowing (the purple butterfly) cautions her. She must first learn to play and get dirty with the boys and learn their rugged games. In doing this she takes on the color yellow, representing to her personal power and uniqueness.

Kate's journey is just beginning. Her fairy tale gives her strong messages about her life in the past, her present striving, and her future work. Through her artistic expression in writing, art, and drama, the past, present, and future are brought together. I encouraged her to keep a journal of this work as I do all my patients. As time goes on new pieces are added to the puzzle. New information is gleaned as we continue to grow and develop and change.

CONCLUSION

The arts and dreams give us a powerful way of expressing what is inside, bringing it up into consciousness, giving it form in a constructive way, and showing us our strengths. In this way, we discover, heal, and transform our inner selves. What is past is brought into the present so that we may live in a more constructive and fulfilling way now and in the future.

FOR ADDITIONAL READING

If you are interested in further information on art and dream therapy (and/or eating disorders), here are some useful books and articles.

Bartenieff, I. (1980). *Body movement coping with the environment.* New York: Gordon and Breach Science Publications.

Bernstein, P. (1979). *Eight theoretical approaches in dance-movement therapy.* Dubuque, IA: Kendall/Hunt Publishing Co.

Bollas, C. (1987). *The shadow of the object.* New York: Columbia University Press.

Browning, N. (1985). Long term dynamic group therapy with bulimia patients. In S.W. Emmett (Ed.), *Theory and treatment of anorexia nervosa and bulimia.* New York: Brunner/Mazel.

Bruch, H. (1978). *The golden cage: the enigma of anorexia nervosa.* Cambridge, MA: Harvard University Press.

Crowl, M. (1980). Art Therapy with Patients Suffering from Anorexia Nervosa. *The Arts in Psychotherapy, 7,* 141-151.

Emmett, S.W. (1985). *Theory and treatment of anorexia nervosa and bulimia.* New York: Brunner/Mazel.

Freud, S. (1950). *The interpretation of dreams.* New York: Random House.

Geist, R.A. (1955). Therapeutic dilemmas in the treatment of anorexia nervosa: A self-psychological perspective. In S.W. Emmett (Ed.), *Theory and treatment of anorexia nervosa and bulimia*. New York: Brunner/Mazel.

Gendlin, E. (1986). *Let your body interpret your dreams*. Wilmette, IL: University of Chicago.

Giovacchini, P. (1986). *Developmental disorders*. New York: Jason Aronson Inc.

Horner, A. (1979). *Object relations and the developing ego*. New York: Jason Aronson Inc.

Kramer, E. (1972). *Art as therapy with children*. New York: Schocken Books.

Jung, C.G. (1964). *Man and his symbol*. New York: Doubleday and Co.

Jung, C.G. (1974). *Dreams*. Princeton, NJ: Princeton University Press.

Leonard, L. (1983). *The wounded woman*. Boston: Shambhala.

Levenkron, S. (1982). *Treating and overcoming anorexia nervosa*. New York: Warner Books, Inc.

Levenkron, S. (1985). Structuring a nurturant authoritative psychotherapeutic relationship with the anorexic patient. In S.W. Emmett (Ed.), *Theory and treatment of anorexia nervosa and bulimia*. New York: Brunner/Mazel.

Lowen, A. (1976). *Bioenergenetics*. New York: Simon and Schuster, Inc.

Mahler, M., Pine, F. & Bergman, A. (1975). *The psychological birth of the human infant*. New York: Basic Books, Inc.

Mahoney, F. (1966). *The meaning in dreams and dreaming*. New York: Citadel Press.

Mindell, A. (1985). *Working with the dreaming body*. Boston: Routledge and Kegan Paul.

Mitchell, D. (1981). Anorexia Nervosa. *The Arts in Psychotherapy*. 7, 53-60.

Rizzuto, A. (1985). Eating and monsters: A psychodynamic view of bulimarexia. In S.W. Emmett ed., *Theory and treatment of anorexia nervosa and bulimia*. New York: Brunner/Mazel.

Robbins, A. (1980). *Expressive therapies: A creative arts approach to depth oriented treatment*. New York: Human Sciences Press.

Sandel, S.L. (1982). The process of individuation in dance movement therapy with schizophrenic patients. *The Arts in Psychotherapy*. 9, 11-18.

Sanford, J. (1978) *Dreams and healing*. New York: Paulist Press.

Schwartz, D., Thompson, M. & Johnson, C. (1985). Anorexia nervosa and bulimia: the sociocultural context. In S.W. Emmett (Ed.), *Theory and treatment of anorexia nervosa and bulimia*. New York: Brunner/Mazel.

Spegnesi, A. (1983). *Starving women: a psychology of anorexia nervosa*. Dallas, TX: Spring Publications, Inc.

Weiss, L. (1986). *Dream analysis in psychotherapy*. New York: Pergamon Press.

Winnicott, D.W. (1971). *Playing and reality*. London: Tavestock Publications Limited.

Wolf, J.M. and others. (1985). The role of art in the therapy of anorexia nervosa. *International Journal of Eating Disorders*. 4, 185-200.

Woodman, M. (1980). *The owl was a baker's daughter*. Toronto: Inner City Books.

Woodman, M. (1982). *Addiction to perfection: the still unravished bride*. Toronto: Inner City Books.

Nutritional Counseling for Anorexic and Bulimic Patients

▼
▼
▼
▼

by Annika Kahm

Is there a need to educate eating-disordered patients about calories and nutritional balance? Don't most of them know it all?

There *is* a need even if the patients feel it's unnecessary. Very often their parents, relatives, or friends ask: "Can't you just tell her to eat normally, like everybody else does and at regular intervals?" We know, however, it's not that easy, and the patients know it too. Actually, they often *know* all about good eating habits; they just cannot *follow* them. We see this in hospitalized patients who have been forced to gain weight in order to "earn points" to be allowed to have visitors, exercise, or be discharged, but who have never taken the time to understand or learn how to get control over their food intake and body weight. They will usually repeat the old pattern of restriction and weight loss after being discharged because it's too scary to gain weight and to feel out of control.

That's partly why nutritional counseling, with education and motivation, is an important part of the teamwork necessary to help these patients achieve full recovery. The counseling described here is done on an out-patient basis, and most visits are weekly. Treatment is individualized and can vary in length from a few weeks to over a year, depending on the patient's needs.

THE BASICS OF NUTRITIONAL COUNSELING

At the initial office visit a thorough nutritional history is taken. The purpose of this is not only to find out about patients' eating habits, but also about their psychological growth and development as well as their families'. It's also important that patients understand the purpose of nutritional counseling and agree that the final goal is to be able to eat a meal when hungry, to stop when comfortably full, and to do so at least three to four times per day, without thinking or obsessing about food in between meals. It is also important that patients ultimately accept and like themselves at healthy body weights and trust that the scale won't go up after a meal (and will know why if it does). In other words, they should feel and have control over their food intake and weight.

Small, manageable steps should be presented to help the patient reach this long-term goal. A first step will be a low-calorie meal plan designed jointly by the patient and the nutritionist. It is important to have the patient involved in these decisions. At this initial visit it's also crucial that a relationship be formed—a warm, trusting, nonthreatening relationship so that the patient feels safe to express likes and/or dislikes.

The Minimum Caloric Need

Nutritional education, then, is introduced as an integral part of the motivation to improve eating behavior.

Only when patients can understand why and how the body responds to starvation, binging, and/or restriction can they dare to try to eat properly. Their metabolism, which has adapted to fasting by slowing down, will then speed up and function appropriately (Apfelbaum [1975]; Flatt, [1980]). If they can accept and trust that their metabolism has not been destroyed but has only been sluggish for as long as the eating disorder has been active, patients then have the greatest potential for normalizing their abnormal eating habits. Part of the education will be to learn not only how many calories the body needs on a daily basis but also why it needs them:

1. The basic metabolic rate is approximately 1200 kcal (calories)/day (for breathing, blood circulation, etc.).
2. For growth and maintenance, the body needs approximately 150-300 kcal/day (renewal of blood cells, hair, skin, etc.).
3. Digesting and absorbing food requires approximately 150 kcal/day.
4. For maintaining body temperature, hydration, and chemical concentration in cells, the body needs approximately 150 kcal/day.

This means that a human being who does not exercise needs at least 1650 kcal/day. With physical activity we can add 300-500 kcal/day. An individual who eats less than 1200 kcal/day is not getting enough calories to fulfill the above four tasks. Consequently, his or her metabolism will cope by lowering its rate and becoming sluggish. This means that eating will become more threatening than ever because weight gain will occur on fewer calories than before.

Most eating-disordered patients are trying to lose weight to feel better. Because most of them are eating or keeping down less than the minimum amount of food needed for their body functions, this is not possible. This is where the motivation to get out of this "trap" is so important. Only if they understand and trust the concept of metabolism and weight gain will patients be able to work through this frightening period of first eating the minimal amount of calories for an adult (1200–1500 cal/day) or teenager (1500 cal/day) in order to get their metabolic rates up to normal. Patients must be eating this amount for at least a few weeks in order for the metabolism to increase. Although patients may initially gain weight during this time, it will first be mostly water weight (two to seven pounds). By consistent good eating, weight gain will continue until normal body weight is reached. During this time, the metabolism in most cases has come up to normal. If so, the minimal amount of calories that caused the weight gain will cause a slow but slight weight loss, because more calories are now required to maintain body weight. This is a big moment for both patient and nutritionist: It means that the rate of metabolism is increased and all the calories are being used for bodily functions and not stored as excess fat, the biggest fear of all for anorexics and bulimics.

The Food Plan

It is important to check out how the patient experienced the first meeting and his or her understanding of the discussion. Misunderstandings are clarified, and the food plan is discussed again. Was the patient comfortable when we discussed and designed the plan on the first visit? Was it too much or too little to eat? No one can follow a food plan exactly, but it's important to choose and design one that patients feel motivated to try.

The plan should be balanced and include choices from the four food groups based on U.S.D.A. dietary guidelines. As discussed, the *minimum* caloric need to fulfill all bodily functions is approximately 1200-1500 calories daily for an adult and 1500 calories daily for a teenager, divided among these foods:

- Two servings of dairy (four servings for teens).
- Four to six ounces of protein (fish, chicken, or meat).
- Three fruits and two cups of vegetables.
- Six servings of starch (bread, cereal, pasta, rice, etc.) for women and 10 for men.
- Two servings of fat for women and five for men.

The need to eat a varied diet has to be emphasized frequently, and a booklet with samples from the different food groups is a frequently used handout.

Keeping a diet record helps patients see for themselves how they are able to meet the minimum requirement from each of the four food groups. It is also a helpful tool for the nutritionist to view how the patient is able to follow the meal plan. If used correctly, the diet record gives room for approval and praise. Because eating-disordered patients are likely to be perfectionists, they have a hard time dealing with not being able to follow the food plan exactly as it is outlined. By learning what their patients have written in their records, nutritionists have the opportunity to help them turn what has been a personal failure into a learning experience.

The meal plan always includes three meals, with or without snacks, depending on the patient's preference. Breakfast is usually the hardest part, because by eating it patients often think they will be hungrier for the rest of the day. After learning about hunger and that the body burns more calories spread out over three or more meals, breakfast can frequently become the most enjoyable meal for patients. They learn that hunger is a signal informing us that whatever we previously ate is used up—not stored—and it is now time to refuel again.

Frequently patients will experience some initial gastrointestinal discomfort after eating, but if that has been described and discussed beforehand, they will cope better and understand that this is normal and that their capacity and comfort with food will increase slowly ("Nutrition and Eating Disorders—Guidelines for the Patient with Anorexia Nervosa and Bulimia Nervosa," 1990). Also, it is helpful if the bulk content of meals is kept small because of the patient's sense of fullness or bloating.

ANOREXIA

Nutritional Assessment

For the anorexic, cessation of weight loss has to be the first goal, and to achieve this a nutritional assessment is usually helpful and motivational. It can be done in many different ways. One of the simplest involves measuring the tricep skinfold (upper arm fat-fold), the mid-arm circumference, and the hip fat-fold. Based on these figures we can estimate the patient's fat-fold, muscular mass, and percent body fat and compare this with others of the same age (Grant, 1979). If an individual is below the fifth percentile for upper arm fat-fold (which is a trend among the severely anorexic), then he or she has the minimum amount of fat and is undernourished. Only less than five percent of the population would have so little subcutaneous fat (50th percentile = normal, 95th percentile = overweight/obese). If the person's muscle-mass is also low, i.e., below the 10th percentile (50th percentile = normal), he or she can now realize that losing more weight is dangerous because it means loss of more muscular tissue (since there is no more fat to lose). This indicates potentially life-threatening weight loss in all muscular tissue, including such organs as the heart.

From these numbers we can also determine percent of body fat. When the female patient looks at the chart, she realizes that normal-thin means having 20–24 percent body fat. When she sees her own number is below 15–16 percent, she may begin to realize why her period has stopped—that the body has reversed developmentally and is now prepubertal. (The ovary has shrunk to the size of a plum instead of a pear.) The pubertal development takes about five years (ages 8-18) to complete; during this time girls gradually put on 50-60 pounds, and their body fat goes from 17 percent (a girl) to 23-28 percent (a woman). This happens whether we like it, want it, or not! The period itself may be something a patient can live without, but being normal and having a normally functioning body matters.

Trusting Their Hunger Signals

Anorexic patients usually complain of waking up early (four to six a.m. in the morning) but feeling very weak. Actually, they would like to sleep longer but their bodies will not allow it because they are too hungry. Of course these patients would like to eat. If they give in to eating so early in the day they are afraid the hunger will increase later on, and they won't be able to make it on the few hundred calories allowed (by their own rules) for the rest of the day. By discussing and clarifying physiological facts such as caloric needs, it is hoped that anorexic individuals will be able to listen to bodily signals and respond to them appropriately. In this situation it means that eating more allows the body to sleep longer (because it doesn't have to wake up early to search for food) and that hunger is a safe signal to eat. This seems to be one of the hardest facts for anorexics to accept and follow, because hunger is something they've always had to deny in order to stay thin. Hunger is our body's way of telling us that all the food we consumed earlier has been used up for bodily functions and energy; it is also a signal for us to eat. If we don't, after a while the body will compensate by reducing its metabolic rate and by making us crave and think about food in an obsessive way. "Well, what about if I

eat more than I need?" or "How do I know how much I need?" are some of the questions often asked by the worried patient. The answer still remains the same: "If you undereat, you'll be hungry sooner—maybe even within one hour! This, of course, is very scary. But if you eat an appropriate amount, there will be a while before you need to eat again. It's only the person who eats when *not* hungry who will put on excess weight. This is not only hard for eating-disordered patients to understand but also for the 60 million Americans dieting today."

What's so troublesome for anorexic patients is that they are always hungry, but they have become used to suffering and denying it. Therefore they identify their hunger state as being their normal condition. When they start to eat and acknowledge hunger, it can lead to their feeling overwhelmed because they then feel as if they could eat all day long with no bottom to their stomachs. Anorexic patients feel like ravenous animals—as they should—and we nutritionists are glad they do because it means that they can again listen to their hunger signals. The body is simply saying, "Please eat and make up for earlier starvation and deprivation." What is so hard to trust is that this ravenous hunger will eventually stop. The body will signal when it's had enough and when it's satisfied. It is hard for anorexics to believe this will happen *before* they put on excess weight.

Body Image and Weight Gain Expectations

All patients should be warned about the possibility of a rapid weight gain (two to seven pounds) when treatment begins. This results from retention of water through expansion of the extra-cellular compartment and increase in depleted liver and muscle glycogen associated with refeeding. If this isn't explained patients will usually stop eating because of fear that they will continue to gain at the same rate. They must be reassured that rehydration weight will resolve spontaneously if they continue to follow the prescribed diet.

Needless to say, in order to overcome their eating disorder, anorexic patients must gain weight. But how much? From the nutritional history and nutritional assessment we can determine a 10-pound weight range for the ideal body weight, a weight at which normal physiological functions, including menstruation, can be presumed to occur. Frequently this ideal weight range is unacceptable for the patient, and a lower weight is chosen as an initial goal, with reevaluation of the situation when that initial goal is achieved.

Usually these patients know that they are underweight and that they should gain weight, but they still see themselves as fat. This distorted body image has to be addressed frequently so that patients see themselves realistically and are thus motivated to eat. This is easier said than done. It is usually helpful to look at a picture of 10 different body outlines where 1 is emaciated, 2 underweight, 3 normal thin, 4 normal, 5 normal heavy, and so forth with 10 as obese. (See Figure 1.) Patients usually think they resemble 3, 4, or even 5 and would really like to look like 2. To do so they feel they would have to lose weight, which exemplifies their distorted body image because in reality they often represent a 1 or 2 and have to gain to become normal.

There is no set pattern for weight gain but ideally a gain of one to two pounds per week is expected, or caloric intake should be increased by 200 calories per week. This is usually hard to achieve because a person cannot be forced to eat. We frequently also have to allow for steps backwards. What is important is that patients try hard and slowly give up their old habits of denying hunger, which depresses the metabolic rate. When they reach the weight that is "normal" for their height, the ravenous hunger decreases. They can eat less (i.e., a normal amount), and the weight gain eventually stops. Now that their bodies are of "normal" weight and their metabolism is functioning "normally," they too will begin to lose weight. They should now be able to trust their bodies and feel a new sense of control. They can now eat in order to maintain weight and see clearly that it's possible to eat at least three times a day, when hungry, without gaining weight.

BULIMIA

Bulimia is characterized by the erratic eating of large amounts of food, which is followed by self-induced vomiting or abuse of laxatives and diuretics. Since restrictive eating patterns between binges are common, bulimic patients experience many of the anorexic characteristics already mentioned, along with feelings of shame and self-deprecation which negatively influence all aspects of their lives. Although most bulimics are not obese, they too misperceive themselves as being overweight and want to weigh less. Part of the treatment must address setting normal weight range goals and maintaining them until they are accepted by the patients so that they do not remain chronic yo-yo dieters.

Most bulimics have chaotic eating patterns characterized by cycles of fasting or severe dieting followed by bouts of compulsive overeating. For many, these patterns are so entrenched that the patients have no idea how to eat "normally." They are frightened that if they begin eating regular meals they will gain weight. Patients need to be reassured that establishing a pattern of regular eating is essential in gaining control over binge eating. Initially, eating must become "mechanical." There should be a predetermined and definite maintenance plan that minimizes decision making. Without such a plan, bulimic patients can easily slip back into a pattern of binging and purging, since lower weight is these patients' ultimate goal. They, as well as anorexics, have to be warned of possible water retention of two to seven

Figure 1. Body image illustrations.

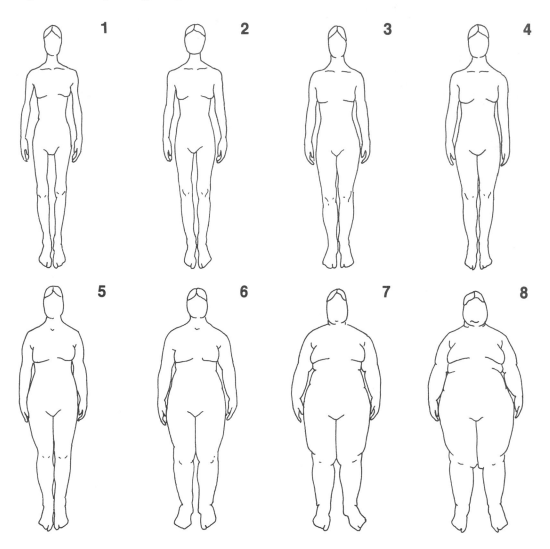

pounds, which is likely to happen when they decide to stop purging and try to eat normally. This can be a rapid weight gain (within a few days), experienced as bloatedness, which will subside.

Just like anorexics, bulimics can experience an initial weight gain followed by a weight loss. When they resume normal eating and have done so for a while (weeks or even months, depending on how long they have struggled with their eating disorder), their metabolisms will return to normal, and it is then that they are likely to lose weight if calories are kept at 1200–1500 per day.

Separating Feelings from Eating in Bulimia

I've talked about stopping the binge/purge cycle and resuming normal eating, but this will not happen overnight. If that were possible, patients would not have to seek help; they could simply do it on their own. They need support to practice prevention (to stop binging and/or purging) and to feel motivated. They need praise and encouragement to go through this painful part of breaking an old habit and to face and deal with their repressed emotions.

By prevention I mean helping themselves stop binging by:

- Realizing what triggered the overeating (feelings of anxiety, anger, etc.).
- Deciding on appropriate action.
- *Never* skipping a meal.

In order to realize what triggers overeating and how those triggers make them think and feel, it is critical that patients feel at ease and be able to talk about their experiences in an accepting, nonjudgmental atmosphere.

Bulimics need to learn how to separate their thoughts and feelings from eating. They have to know how to express themselves clearly. Frequently their communication is based on fear of what others will say, so anxiety builds and results in eating. By practicing expressing themselves directly in actual situations, that is, by saying "I feel... because...and therefore...," "I wish you would...," or "I will...," they are on their way to recovery (Faber and Mazlish, 1980).

When they realize what uncomfortable thoughts and/or feelings cause them to eat, they will understand that eating neither solves the problem nor takes away those feelings. Eating, however, temporarily allows them to feel better and saves them from having to focus on the problem. But, beneath all of the stuffed food remains unresolved emotions.

In order for the patient to recover fully, treatment should thus include therapy, individual as well as group. It can help them work through underlying thoughts and conflicts that have caused these patients to build up high levels of anxiety and low self-esteem, which in turn caused these disturbed eating patterns.

Most important for bulimics is learning to maintain their weight; when they reach their turning point (i.e., when their metabolisms return and when they start to lose weight while eating the minimum intake [1200–1500 cal/day]), the intake should then be increased, slowly, until maintenance is achieved for at least a month. Then they are able to trust and respond accurately to signals of hunger and satiety and can handle an occasional episode of overeating simply by waiting till hunger comes back—the safe signal that all the earlier consumed calories are used up.

After being able to maintain their weight for a month, bulimic patients will be allowed to lose weight if needed. They will not be allowed to eat less than the minimum intake for an adult (1200–1500 calories) because that would cause a decrease in metabolic rate. This time dieting is safe because they know how to maintain their weight after dieting. At this point patients frequently prefer not to lose weight because by eating "normally" they get more energy, are less obsessed, and, because of therapy, it is hoped, like and accept themselves better the way they are.

THINNER MEANS "HAPPIER"

Eating-disordered patients have a distorted image not only of their body size (and frame) but also of their happiness. They are convinced that only if they get thinner will they be happier. Actually it's the opposite—the more weight they lose the more they are likely to isolate themselves from friends and social activities. They become more miserable and more involved in stricter self-administered rules about eating. Typically exercise increases, sometimes to the point of exercising during the night when unable to sleep.

To reach their goal of trying to become thinner and happier, these eating disorder patients are being restrictive. Very little is eaten and most of it is quickly burned off (sometimes by immediate exercise). Energy and emotional tolerance levels are extremely low. That's one reason patients become frustrated by ever so small changes—perhaps a different food is served at home, or their schedule is changed, with less time for exercise. This can have devastating effects not just for themselves but also for significant others, reinforcing their vain belief: "If only I were thinner, things would be better!"

What is known is that the more patients can eat or keep down, the more energy they have. The more energy they have, the easier it is to deal with and accept an ideal body weight with less body image distortion. It is hoped that they are then more open to therapeutic work.

CONCLUSION

With all this knowledge and these tools, why is it so hard for people to stop hurting themselves when they suffer from eating disorders? There are probably as many answers as there are patients today, but two factors stand out:

1. An eating disorder is the symptom of underlying problems. These have to be admitted and dealt with, and the associated thoughts and feelings have to be separated from eating. Many times it is easier to avoid uncomfortable feelings by focusing on eating or restriction.
2. In today's society we certainly get enough messages telling us that "thin is in." If you're thin you'll be happy, marry the right upper-class person, get a better job, be able to

fit into the clothes the models advertise. Less than two percent of the population is *naturally* "model thin." The rest of us must learn to like ourselves because of who we are, not because of how thin we are.

REFERENCES

Apfelbaum, M. (1975). Influence of level of energy intake on energy expenditure in man: Effects of spontaneous intake experimental starvation, and experimental overeating. In G.A. Bray (ed.) *Obesity in perspective*. Washington, DC: U.S. Department of Health, Education and Welfare.

Faber, A., & Mazlish, E. (1980). *How to talk so kids will listen and listen so kids will talk*. New York: Avon Books.

Flatt, J.P. (1980). Energetics of intermediary metabolism. In Ross Conference Report No. 1 *Assessment of energy metabolism in health and disease*. Columbus, OH: Ross Laboratories.

Grant, A. (1979). Nutritional Assessment Guidelines. Anne Grant, Box 25057, Northgate Station, Seattle WA 98125.

Nutrition and Eating Disorders—Guidelines for the Patient with Anorexia Nervosa and Bulimia Nervosa. (1990). A Nutrition and the M.D. Publication. California: PM, Inc.

Suggested reading:

Siegel, M., Brisman, J., & Weinshel, M. (1988). *Surviving an eating disorder: strategies for family and friends*. New York: Harper and Row.

Eating Disorders and Behavior Change: How a Contract Can Help

▼
▼
▼
▼

by Margo Maine, Ph.D.

MEANING OF EATING DISORDER SYMPTOMS

Both the people suffering from eating disorders and the professionals who try to help them often come to the same conclusion: Changing one's eating behaviors and meeting one's physical needs can seem like an impossible task. Even when the patient really wants to change and regain health, the old habits can be very difficult to break. Often people whom I have treated have worked very hard in psychotherapy, addressing painful issues in their families and other relationships, being more open and honest about their own feelings and needs, connecting with others in a mutually satisfying way, confronting difficult situations rather than avoiding them, and finding ways to shed their perfectionism and accept themselves. Still, their behavior around food may not change at the same pace. Thus, for some people with eating disorders, psychological and personal changes alone do not result in a decrease or termination of the painful eating disorder symptoms.

For those of you with eating disorders, why is it so difficult to stop these painful behaviors surrounding your relationship with food and your body? For each of you, individual experiences and factors will affect how quickly you can change these behaviors. Giving up your symptoms can feel like a loss. Some of you had no other ways to comfort yourselves, so the symptoms are like a security blanket. Others may feel that, because your symptoms are so central to

your identity, to give them up is to give up a large part of yourself. Still others may feel that your families only see you as "bulimic" or "anorexic," so if you change, you may lose these relationships. (Family therapy can be very helpful in changing your family's perceptions and helping you to develop a fuller sense of who you are and how you are special.)

In addition to these unique factors, I believe that eating disorder symptoms can take on lives of their own. That is, the symptoms, although initially responses to stress, pain, anger, confusion, or other feelings, may simply become parts of your normal routine. You no longer are vomiting or exercising in response to difficult feelings or external stressors; you vomit or exercise because that's what you are used to doing. So, the symptoms may not necessarily function as a response to feelings, but may be spontaneous and independent. You may work very hard on issues in relationships and on your self-image, self-knowledge, and identity, but you still find yourself doing the same old things. You feel angry with yourself and frustrated as a result. These feelings may lead to hopelessness and then you may feel less able to try to overcome the symptoms.

In any of these cases, whether the eating disorder symptoms are mostly habitual or whether they remain very important to your sense of identity or security, you can still gain control of your behavior and make the changes that will lead you to greater happiness and stability. In our treatment program, we have developed behavioral contracts to assist our patients in symptom control. A "contract" may initially sound like a horrible idea, one where you give up control, rather than gain control, but this does not have to be the case. Contracts do not only help you decrease your symptoms and gradually regain your health, they can also help you feel in control and successful. Basically, the contract is an agreement about the pace of your recovery and the physical limitations that should be in place if you are having difficulty taking care of your body. A contract, if you view it as potentially constructive, can really help you gain control of your life.

HOW A BEHAVIORAL CONTRACT CAN HELP

Let us see how the contract can help you face some of the issues underlying your eating disorder, give you examples of contracts, and outline the steps to take to design your own contract. The focus will be on out-patient contracts—those you can develop individually to help yourself. In-patient contracts tend to be standard for all the patients on the unit and also tend to be more limiting since your condition has placed you at such risk that you need hospitalization. Out-patient contracts are designed for the individual, although the underlying principles and philosophy are the same for both in-patient and out-patient contracts.

It Gives You Structure

One of the important functions of the contract is that it provides predictability and structure to everyone involved in your recovery. For example, if you develop a contract with your out-patient therapist, doctor, dietitian, or nurse, it will spell out what limitations should occur if you are not doing well. You will know ahead of time what these limitations are, and life will be more predictable for you. The contract also helps the

persons working with you to react appropriately. Otherwise, your helpers might overreact and suggest you come into the hospital, or be at home on bedrest if you lose weight or have similar difficulties. Or your helpers might underreact, especially if you present to them that you can get back in control by yourself when, in fact, you are feeling out of control already. The contract gives sensible guidelines and helps the people who are helping you as much as it helps you.

The contract can also help your parents or significant others to avoid over- or underreacting. It makes you responsible for yourself—if you are not doing well, you have consequences. If you are doing well, your activities can expand. The contract takes your parents or loved ones out of the position of control they may have tried to take as you became ill, because it is basically an agreement between you and your clinicians. While your family may play a role in the contract by having some responsibilities and by agreeing to enforce the contract, their role is prescribed and defined so that they will be less apt to become overly involved.

It May Prevent Hospitalization

An out-patient contract also may help you avoid being hospitalized. By coming up with an agreement about how to regain your health and what gradual limitations should occur if you cannot control your symptoms, you may be able to follow the limitations and get back on track without being hospitalized. The contract also provides some of the security of the hospital, since it is very structured, predictable, and health-focused. This may be especially important to you if you have been hospitalized in the past and miss the structure and security of that environment. The contract is like a small piece of the hospital that you can take with you and use as you need it. In essence, the contract can return the control that your eating disorder has taken from you, if you collaborate with your therapist to develop one that works for you.

HOW A CONTRACT RELATES TO THE PROBLEMS UNDERLYING EATING DISORDERS

While you may accept the notion that a behavioral contract can help you gain symptom relief, you may not realize that the contract can also allow you to address some of the issues underlying your eating disorder. A contract can help you understand these deeper issues, but this is most likely to happen if you are involved in a whole treatment program, especially with individual therapy. If you still live with your parents, family therapy is also important, since the contract and the changes you begin to make will also have an impact on your relationship with your family.

Just changing your behavior without exploring and understanding why you developed an eating disorder is not enough. If you ignore the underlying issues you will have more problems. You may regress and become symptomatic again, or your conflicts will express themselves in some other way. Often, people with eating disorders develop substance abuse problems later if they have not learned new ways to cope. Families of eating-disordered patients, especially bulimic families, have a higher incidence of substance abuse. Whether the risk factors are learned, behavioral patterns of ineffective coping, genetic predispositions, or a combination of the two is not clear as yet. Regardless, people with eating disorders are at high risk for substance abuse. So, I caution you to stay in therapy even after your symptoms are under control—try to understand yourself and your eating problems within the larger context of your family and relationships and culture, so that you can develop new ways to handle the feelings these evoke.

The Struggles Faced When You Have an Eating Disorder

Although recovery takes place over a very long period of time and psychotherapy for eating disorders is also long-term, a behavioral contract can stimulate some important insights and changes related to the problems underlying the eating disorder. Here is a summary of some of the struggles represented by the eating disorder and how a behavioral contract might help you deal with each of these.

Control. Anorexia and bulimia are both attempts to gain control of your life. They often begin at a developmental point when an individual feels powerless. The symptoms—not eating, losing weight, exercising, binging, purging—give a false and temporary sense of mastery but lead you eventually to be very out of control, often to the point of endangering your health and even your life and requiring you to be hospitalized. Although you may see a contract as another threat to your autonomy, it actually gives you back control, bit by bit, in a step-wise fashion. Gradually, you will no longer need the contract, because you will be exerting a healthy form of self-determination. Your eating disorder has actually made you out of control of your life: A contract can put you back in control.

Autonomy. Anorexia and bulimia are also ways of defining yourself, taking a stand, being separate from your families or significant others. They are attempts at autonomous or self-directed living, but as with control the attempts backfire and you often end up very dependent once more on others because of your health. You are unable to make decisions for yourself because of your preoccupation with your body and food and the consequent interference in your thinking, concentration, and problem solving. If you see yourself as the architect of your contract and work with the clinical staff to redefine it over time, a contract can help you regain some autonomy and build in steps to greater independence. For example, after you have been stable for a certain length of time, you can change the contract to allow you alone to come up with consequences when you have difficulties in the future. See "Maintenance Contract Sample A" at the end of this article for an example of a contract to use after you have been doing well for several weeks. This type of contract might say that if your steps don't work after two weeks, you should return to your original contract, which provides more external guidelines. (See Samples B, C, D, and E for examples of contracts with more external guidelines.)

Self-Determination. As with control and autonomy, through your eating disorder you try to increase your ability to determine your own destiny. Again, your efforts will backfire. An eating disorder allows you more self-destruction than self-determination. Still you may be very wrapped up in thinking "you are what you eat" and nobody is going to make you eat and gain weight. You're right; nobody can make you do this, and a contract can't make you do it either. If you eat or avoid purging, it is *you* doing this; you are actively choosing health, and the contract can't do it for you. So, don't confuse things: It is you, not the contract, who is choosing your destiny.

Dependency. Most people with anorexia and bulimia have also struggled with dependency. Often your families have given you too much and overprotected you, making you very dependent on them. For others, your families may have given you too little structure, so you had to be totally independent. Some of you have played the role of parent in your family and haven't been able to depend on others. Regardless of the dynamic, you can develop a contract to help with this. Basically, you can pre-

scribe how others can help you. This is especially important for teenagers or individuals still living with their parents. The contract can include a section called "Parents' Responsibilities." (This can be adapted to a spouse if you are married.) The "Parents' Responsibilities" section can be very detailed in its description of how they can help and can specifically instruct parents to leave you alone in certain areas related to your eating disorder. (See Out-Patient Contract Sample B.)

Meeting Your Body's Physical Needs. You really need help in this area. Most of you have spent your lives so focused on other people's needs that you cannot read and respond to your own needs, even very essential physical ones. The contract can help you with this. Basically, the contract balances energy input with energy output. If you're taking care of your health, you can do more because you are getting enough fuel to compensate for your energy expenditure. When you aren't taking in enough food, you need to limit your output. It is very simple. Over time you will internalize this system and be able to recognize and meet your own needs but the contract provides the initial external structure for this. This is especially important for people who have exercised excessively or for patients who have been athletes in the past. The contract can help you get back "in shape." Out-patient Contract Sample B is a contract designed for a high school athlete after discharge from the hospital.

Struggle between Life and Death. Many of you have been so depressed and cut off from others, have had so many losses, and feel so helpless about recovery that you may vacillate between wanting to live and wanting to die. Developing a contract is the beginning of an alliance with the part of you that wants to live. It also builds in activities that you may enjoy and therefore you may find that "life is worth living."

Developmental Pressures.

If you are a young person, you may have felt unable to handle the pressures as you left childhood, became an adolescent, and now proceed (or have proceeded) toward adulthood. That old feeling, "I can't face this"/"I can't handle this," may be very familiar to you. As you approach the time in your life where more and more responsibilities come your way, you may have become increasingly frightened. This fear can get you stuck in your eating disorder. You may know you're not ready for a boyfriend or a full social life so you may feel the need to stay sick. The contract can help you recover and face these developmental pressures gradually, instead of all at once. For example the contract can limit your time with friends at first so that you don't have to completely structure this yourself, although you would still choose which friends you see. Or the contract can say when you should begin taking driver's lessons, get your license, have fuller access to the car, or go away to school. It can slow down all these developmental pressures to a pace you can handle. Out-Patient Contract Sample C is an example of a contract written for a high school student whose severe bulimia was interfering with her school attendance and performance. It helped her to regain control of her behavior slowly and then expanded her privileges and independence. It helped her parents know how to respond to her problems. Having predetermined consequences allowed the whole family to be more stable emotionally.

Denial.

Be honest. You're probably an expert at denying your feelings and at ignoring your eating disorder and its effects on your life. The contract makes you face your symptoms—it defines them and the parameters for reasonable change. The contract may also bring up family dynamics that have been denied. For example, if your parents do not communicate about the contract or cannot follow their responsibilities, you can discuss this in family therapy. You might become more aware of the ways family members have disappointed you and, through therapy, be able to work with them to improve your relationships. Sample B illustrates how the responsibilities can include issues related to parents' communication and the interactions between you and your parents.

Self-Esteem.

Your eating disorder is probably an attempt to feel good about yourself. Most people with eating disorders cannot see their personal values and strengths. Although your eating disorder in some ways enhances your self-esteem, it also limits it because you may begin to feel that you have failed or disappointed others. A contract can help you rebuild your self-esteem as you see your progress toward recovery. You may develop a sense of mastery or control as you advance on your contract and eventually take more responsibility for yourself.

Dichotomous Thinking.

You are probably used to seeing yourself and your world in all-or-nothing or black-and-white terms. You are either a great success because of your control over your body or a worthless failure. You are either completely healthy or very sick. When you have more trouble controlling your symptoms, you feel like you've never made any progress. With this way of looking at yourself, it's easy to feel depressed and defeated. Since no one can recover perfectly, you are bound to feel like a failure if you can only see black and white. The contract, with its gradual steps toward recovery, can help you find the shades of gray between severe symptoms and complete recovery. This may help you avoid the tendency to catastrophize and give up when you are having more trouble controlling your symptoms.

Inconsistent Relationships.

You may have suffered many disappointments in relationships. Some of you have had major losses of important people in your lives. Others have been victimized and abused. You have not been able to consistently rely on people to recognize and meet your needs and you have had difficulty articulating these. Consequently you find relationships often unpredictable and unsatisfying. You can't trust people to react fairly to you or to be there for you. The contract can make relationships more predictable for you. It gives your family guidelines to help you, and it tells you that your therapist is going to make recommendations to you based on your health and the terms of the contract. You won't walk into the therapist's office and hear him or her suddenly say, "You're going into the hospital." However, you will know that this recommendation is coming if you have not been able to meet the expectations of your contract and if your condition has deteriorated. The contract therefore provides some predictability in your relationships, at least with your therapist and, it is hoped, with your family.

HOW TO DEVELOP A CONTRACT

A contract is basically an agreement with yourself that you are going to try to get better. It is also, however, a statement that you need help and structure from others—that you can't do it all by yourself. That is probably a big step for you. Developing a contract can be a way of letting others help you and a way to end your loneliness and isolation. So, the first step is to decide to use an external structure to help you, not to only rely on yourself. Once you have made that decision, you are ready to take the other steps.

Along the way, however, you may have to remind yourself frequently that everyone needs help from others and that the discomfort of all the changes you'll be making in your relationships (to food, to your body, to yourself, and to others) will gradually go away, and you will in fact, feel very good someday. Find ways to remind yourself of this—sometimes developing a saying that you can repeat to yourself when you're anxious can be helpful. For example, a patient of mine was having difficulty eating more because she felt so full. (She had eaten so little for so long, her body wasn't used to feeling full.) She was struggling with severe loneliness and inner emptiness; her illness had really interrupted her life. She had not had fun in years but was starting to want to experience new things. I suggested that whenever that full feeling came, she repeat to herself "I have to feel full now to have a full life later." You need to come up with the cognition that will work for you and, as always, I advise that you work with a therapist on this. This leads to one of the first decisions you have to make in the steps of developing a contract.

Who Should Be Involved

Whom will you allow to help you? Who will your reliable allies be, both therapist and health professional (a dietitian or a nurse), who can also work with your doctor? They all represent important sources of the guidance you will need to get better. It is easiest if these professionals are members of a "team" who confer regularly and are familiar with eating disorders. Although this is the optimal situation, it may not be available. Some people with eating disorders have been able to avoid hospitalization because they have had access to an interdisciplinary out-patient eating disorder service. Others may require hospitalization mainly because out-patient services are not available.

If you are still living with your parents or if you are married, these family members will also be involved with your contract. The contract can tell them what to do (and what not to do!) to help you. They should also be involved with you in therapy, as your recovery will both require and cause changes in those relationships. So, add a family therapist to the list of people you may need to help you. If on the other hand you are an adult living alone, a contract such as Sample D, designed for an adult with restricting anorexia, might be a helpful guide.

What Do You Need to Change?

With the help of your therapist, set priorities for the behaviors you need to address. The first step is usually to normalize your eating by developing meals and trying to increase your caloric intake. This usually requires what we call "self-monitoring," where you record what you eat and sometimes the feelings or circumstances when you eat. For those of you who purge, you may need to target those behaviors and work toward decreasing the frequency and developing other stress-reducing activities that can be built into your contract. Therefore, list enjoyable activities and make them part of your day. Build in rewards for yourself also as you gain control of your symptoms. Sometimes a contract needs to address issues such as school attendance, taking medication, the use of drugs or alcohol, or other self-destructive behaviors. (See Sample E.)

How Quickly Can You Change?

This is very important: You want success instantly or else you feel that you're a failure, right? However, you need to build your contract around the concept of slow change and not push yourself to face new challenges too soon. For example, a vacation, eating in restaurants, or staying at a friend's house overnight may strain your control of your eating. With your therapist, identify the tasks that will endanger your recovery and build in a realistic approach to these. For example, if you want to join friends who are renting a cottage at a beach for a week but antici-

pate you'll have greater difficulty eating there, go for one or two nights. Don't endanger your recovery because you want to do it all and have instant success. Having a contract to which to refer when new things like vacations come up may help you decide how to handle these unusual situations. Although the contract can't prescribe everything you should do, it can remind you to think and plan rather than act impulsively. Usually our contracts have steps or periods of time that need to elapse before you move to the next level. Because your illness has endangered your health, it is very important to change your eating and exercise routines slowly so that you do not cause any physical damage or undue psychological stress.

What Rewards or Limitations Will Help You Change?

A contract won't help unless it has some built-in motivators that will make you want to continue trying to change even when you're discouraged, tired, or ambivalent about recovery. Use your therapist to help find activities that will motivate you to become or stay healthy. Many people include driving a car as one of these. This makes sense—although driving gives a sense of independence and accomplishment and freedom, you shouldn't drive if your health is impaired because of the risks to you and others. Teenagers often work curfews into their contract: When they're doing well, they have fuller privileges; when they're less healthy, they have to conserve energy and get more rest. If you are living independently, you can still use these kinds of restrictions on your contract—except *you* will enforce them— you will be your own parent. It can also be helpful to have both short-term and long-term rewards.

When Does the Contract Need to Be Revised?

The contract should be a "working document." You and your therapist (and family and family therapist if appropriate) need to talk about the contract regularly to see if it really is helping and to change it if necessary. Don't look at the contract as cast in stone; talk about it and improve it. On most contracts I have co-written, we include that if the patient goes down levels (that is, has increasing difficulties), we need to look at the contract and see if it needs to be changed or if the patient needs hospitalization. Similarly, when a patient has been at the top levels of the contract for a period of time, we then reevaluate and move to what we call maintenance: Basically you have no restrictions as long as you do well; after two weeks of not doing well, some restrictions or reinstituting of the old contract would occur.

SUMMARY

Behavioral contracting can help you to gain control of your eating disorder. A contract or behavior change alone, however, without working through the many factors that contributed to your problems with food and your body and finding new coping mechanisms, will probably only provide temporary relief. You may revert to your eating disorder, become depressed, or engage in some other self-destructive behavior if you stop short of understanding your problems and developing your identity more fully. I hope this article has given you ideas that you can use in your recovery and I urge you to share these ideas with your therapist.

Maintenance Contract (Sample A)

Maintenance goes into effect after you have been at top level of your out-patient contract for six consecutive weeks. You will have full privileges as long as:

- Weight is in range.
- Other eating disorder symptoms are absent.
- Health and nutritional guidelines are followed.
- Laboratory studies (blood work), done as recommended by physician, are within normal limits.

The first week that you do not meet above criteria, no restrictions will be imposed by the Team. Use your own self-knowledge and ask for help from therapist, dietitian, or nurse to get back "on track."

The second week of difficulty you will reduce formal exercise. Staff will help you guide this.

The third week, make further reductions on exercise and on extracurricular activities.

The fourth week, consider further reductions on above or a return to your out-patient contract. Work with the Team on this decision.

Out-Patient Contract (Sample B)

Purpose:

1. To assist you in making transition to living at home.
2. To provide clear guidelines and limits between parents and children.
3. To assist you in stabilizing your health and your behaviors on an out-patient basis and to help you feel in charge of yourself.

Patient's Responsibilities:

1. Maintain weight in target range.
2. Follow nutritional and health related-responsibilities. Take in recommended calories.
3. Discuss problems with contract and food-related issues with clinical staff.
4. Express feelings verbally.
5. Develop a list of safe meals to prepare for yourself when other meals are not available. ("Safe meals" are meals that can be prepared easily by the patient and are easy to eat. The ingredients are kept in the house at all times.)
6. Have option of eating meals alone.
7. Spend at least 20 minutes each day relaxing.
8. Attend all weekly appointments.

Parents' Responsibilities:

1. Enforce the privileges or restriction of phase.
2. Make sure ingredients for safe meals are available at home.
3. Express feelings verbally.
4. Discuss problems with the contract and food-related issues in family therapy. Don't argue or nag about food.
5. Prepare all family meals except safe meals.
6. Clear table after meals. Avoid leaving food around kitchen or other areas of house.
7. Remember that weight and nutritional intake are _____'s responsibilities. Hospital staff will advise you if you need to become more involved.

Out-Patient Contract (Sample B) (continued)

Levels of Conditions and Consequences

Level	Conditions	Daily Activities
1	Binge or vomit or inadequate nutritional intake daily.	No exercise. No use of car.
2	Binge or vomit or inadequate intake (4-6 days per week).	1/4 hour stretching or nonaerobic exercise, no team involvement. Use car for appointments only
3	Binge or vomit or inadequate intake (2-3 days per week).	1/2 hour stretching or nonaerobic exercise. 1/2 hour walk or practice with team. No phys. ed. Use car for appointments, school, and work.
4	Binge or vomit or inadequate intake (1 day per week).	May choose: 1 hour exercise—stretching or aerobics. *or* Full team practice or participation in game. *or* Phys. ed. participation. Full use of car.
5	No binging or vomiting. Adequate nutritional intake.	May choose 2 of above activities (1 hour exercise, full practice or game, phys. ed.). Full use of car.
6	4 consecutive weeks at level 5.	Reevaluation and possibly graduate to new contract.

Out-Patient Contract (Sample C)

Purpose:

To promote _____'s health and well-being.

Provide opportunities for _____ to demonstrate responsible behavior.

To help parents feel appropriately in charge of family and _____ to feel in charge of herself.

To help _____ to move toward more adult relationships with parents and to establish individual relationships with each parent.

_____'s **Responsibilities:**

Follow nutritional and health-related recommendations made by clinical staff (calorie counts, self-monitoring, exercise, etc.).

No binging or vomiting.

Attend school each day.

Take responsibility for initiating contact with each parent each day.

Follow family rules regarding weekend activities.

Continue individual therapy.

Discuss contract with parents and clinical staff. Support changes that might be helpful to you.

Parents' Responsibilities:

Encourage and support _____'s efforts to promote her health.

Provide the foods _____ needs.

Enforce expectations and consequences of the contract.

Discuss concerns about _____'s food intake and eating disorder in family therapy. Avoid nagging about this. Talk about other concerns instead.

Discuss possible modifications of the contract between each other first, to be shared in family therapy.

Work on having an individual parent-child relationship with _____. Spend some time getting to know her/him alone.

This contract will have five phases of behaviors and consequences. _____'s phase will be established during her/his clinic visit with the nurse. _____ will be encouraged to suggest an appropriate consequence in situations which require additional limitations. This will be discussed in weekly family therapy and modified if necessary.

Out-Patient Contract (Sample C) (continued)

Phase	Behaviors	Activities/Privileges
1	Skipping 3 or more classes. Daily episodes of binging or vomiting.	Loss of evening weekend activities.
2	Skipping 1-2 classes	Weekend activities limited to one evening—midnight curfew.
3	Attendance at all classes. 2 days without binging or vomiting.	Weekend activities with permission. No extensions of midnight curfew. No overnights.
4	Attendance at all classes. 3 days without binging or vomiting.	Weekend activities with permission. Extension of curfew with permission. Prearranged overnights permitted. Initiate involvement at health spa after 2 consecutive weeks on Phase 4 and with Team approval.
5	Attendance at all classes. 4 or more days without binging or vomiting.	All of the above. May increase fitness (spa involvement) after 2 consecutive weeks on Phase 5 and with Team approval. Make arrangements for Driver's Ed.

Out-Patient Contract (Sample D)

Primary Responsibilities:

- Weight gain of one pound per week until reaching maintenance range.
- Remaining in target range upon reaching it.
- Maintaining daily calorie intake as recommended.
- Daily logging of intake and activities.
- Following other Team recommendations regarding health and nutrition.

When meeting these responsibilities, you will have no restrictions imposed on your activity level. When unable to meet these criteria, or when weight is below the target for each week, you will restrict activities for the following week in order to balance input and output of energy. You will work with your nurse to establish appropriate restrictions.

Out-Patient Contract (Sample E)

Goal: To help you to be healthy and safe.

1. If binges over 1,000 calories, report to therapist and nurse.

2. Stay within weight range.

   If over maximum of weight range, discuss with staff.

   If under, 2 weeks to get back to weight range following which there will be limitations of bedrest except for school or job; all meals will be eaten at home, alone; and only passive leisure activities such as TV and reading will be allowed until you reach your weight range.

3. If vomiting or using laxatives, report to staff and will need to eat all meals with another person, one week minimum.

4. Medication must be taken as prescribed, or discontinued.

5. No drug or alcohol abuse.

6. No self-destructive gestures.

If numbers 5 and 6 occur, mother and father will be notified and safety plan devised. This may include hospitalization.

More than Anorexia: An Example of an Integrated Treatment Approach for Adolescents

▼
▼
▼
▼

by Alexandra O. Eliot, Ph.D.

Eating disorders such as anorexia and bulimia nervosa and compulsive overeating have received a great deal of attention and notoriety in the past two decades. A policy paper recently developed for the American College of Physicians (Snyder, 1989) states that eating disorders are among the nine most serious problems facing the youth of this country. Providing care to adolescents that is acceptable *to* them as well as good *for* them is a challenge. Their immediate health problems must be addresssed and efforts to influence their health habits and lifestyle choices must be made because both will have far-reaching consequences throughout adulthood. Thousands of women and some men in all the industrialized nations of the world where food is in abundance are battling with anorexia and bulimia, and still there is a lack of agreement about many aspects of theory and treatment. One notable point of agreement is that the most common time for abnormal patterns of eating and body weight regulation to become problems is during adolescence, that is, between 12 and 21 years of age.

An eating disorders clinic at a hospital in Boston will be described here. It represents an effort to deliver specialized and comprehensive treatment to young people with eating disorders within the framework of their general care as developing adults. This out-patient clinic was started in 1981 as part of a collaborative effort between the division of adolescent/young adult medicine and the department of psychiatry. To date, more than 750 patients and their families have been involved in the clinic.

The major phases of the clinic process include telephone intake, medical evaluation, psychosocial assessment of the family, psychiatric and nutritional consultation, team coordination, recommendations for treatment, and implementation of these plans. Since the clinic draws patients from distances that may prohibit frequent visits, a network of clinicians has been established throughout the New England area with whom the core team can collaborate. The patient's treatment plan is highly individualized and may include any or all of eight kinds of interventions. These include individual, group, and family therapy; self-help/support groups; nutritional counseling; cognitive/behavioral techniques; psychopharmacology; and emergent or elective in-patient admission, all delivered under the category of the primary adolescent care facility. It should be noted that this hospital has a great number of specialized out-patient clinics that tend to categorize patients by disease entity and to meet at specific times. Indeed, most of the treatment centers for eating disorders continue to focus upon the narrow aspects of these illnesses. Thus, eating-disordered adolescents become "anorexics" and "bulimics" and are not treated in an holistic manner. By contract, adolescents who are seen in the out-patient eating disorders clinic can come anytime when the division of adolescent medicine is in session and are not differentiated from others who are there for routine health care or other medical problems. This format is based on the idea that although adolescents may be ambivalent about changing attitudes and behaviors regarding eating and body image, they are still highly preoccupied with all aspects of their bodily functions.

The clinic was started for two reasons: (1) to meet the needs of an increasing number of adolescents presenting with symptoms of self-starvation and the binge/purge syndrome and (2) to complement the treatment already provided by the in-patient services within the hospital. Attention was given to the working hypothesis that treatment on an out-patient basis might reduce the need for emotionally disruptive in-patient care, again considering the developmental needs of adolescents.

THE INITIAL EVALUATION

Admission to the clinic begins with an intake process designed to be as simple and friendly as possible to the anxious caller, usually a parent who is calling at the suggestion of another clinician or concerned party. Appointments can often be given within two weeks. Patients begin the evaluation process by being weighed and measured, having blood pressure monitored, and taking an eye test, all administered by a nursing assistant. While the parents meet with the physician to give a developmental history, the patient's attention is focused on filling out a standardized questionnaire. This includes the Beck Depression Inventory (Beck, 1967) adapted for adolescents, "anorexia" questions developed at The Children's Hospital in Boston by Rollins and Piazza (1978), and the Eating Attitudes Test (Garner and Garfinkel, 1979). The patient then sees the physician to tell his or her own story without parental interference, and to have a complete physical exam. Concerns often range far afield from the eating disorder. The physician is at least board-qualified in pediatrics or internal medicine and is specializing

in the treatment of adolescents. The medical examination is similar to that administered in other clinics of this kind.

While the patient is with the doctor, the family is seen by a social worker for psychosocial assessment. Active collaboration by parents in the diagnostic and treatment process is strongly encouraged. However, since the Boston area has such a large number of college students whose families do not reside locally, patients may be seen independently, especially if they are between 18 and 21 years, in which case contact with the family is established and maintained by telephone. Parents may also be requested to come in person as needed.

For the young person with anorexia, remaining very thin is of enormous value. Interference in this process can be so threatening that the patient wishes only to withdraw from treatment altogether. The initial task of the physician, therefore, is to "help the patient become a patient" (Crisp, 1986); that is, to introduce the idea that there is something wrong that needs to be changed. All members of the team convey to patient and family alike that uncontrolled caloric abstinence and binge/purge behavior are incompatible with life. With adolescents, this at least implies a commitment to "negotiated moderation" (Levenkron, 1985). By the same token, incremental rather than abrupt changes are fostered in order to minimize anxiety.

Although individual treatment plans are tailored to each adolescent's needs and wishes, there are three main goals for everyone. These include (1) remediation of physical complications such as dehydration, unstable blood pressure, heart rate, and unstable electrolytes; (2) weight stabilization and restoration; and (3) change in distorted mental attitudes. The adolescent specialist remains the primary coordinator and medical treater, providing an important resource for patients who are especially resistant to dealing with the psychiatric aspects of their illness.

After the initial evaluation phase, which may take several weeks and comprises a number of clinic visits for medical, psychiatric, and nutritional assessment, patients and families are seen according to individual need and recommended for services mentioned earlier, when deemed both tolerable and appropriate. One of these services, the family crisis group, deserves particular mention, since it is an unusual and effective treatment model.

FAMILY CRISIS GROUP

The family crisis group was started in 1983 as an adjunctive component of the out-patient clinic that had begun one and one-half years earlier. It is a noncontractual multifamily group open to relatives, friends, and partners; anyone, in fact, *except* the so-called identified patient. It shares some common attributes with other groups in that it is a hybrid of psychoeducation, group and family psychotherapy, support, and self-help models. It also has some unique features of its own, chiefly embodied in its co-leadership (Eliot, 1990), which is shared by this author and the parents of a recovered anorexic girl who had sustained a three-year course of both in- and out-patient treatment. These parents had highly ambivalent feelings about their experiences with hospital staff, and it was speculated that their negative energy might be transformed into something positive for them and for other families if they were recast from the role of patients into the role of facilitators.

The co-leader parents are easily able to make connections with, rather than distinguish themselves from, other group members as the latter negotiate the crisis stages of their adolescents' illness. This negotiation demands accompanying coping strategies on the part of the parents. The co-leader father is comfortable with aggressive and confrontive behavior and is able to stay with members' intense feelings of anger toward their child's illness as well as toward the people charged with his or her care. This helps the open expression of ambivalence and strong emotion, thus defusing these feelings and making them more manageable and compatible with the positive feelings that are required to care optimally for a sick child. The model also requires disempowerment of the traditional therapist's role and relocation of the power base from the therapist to the family, in order to strengthen the capacity for self-correction and competence promotion (Maluccio, 1981).

THE DISRUPTION OF ADOLESCENT DEVELOPMENT

The continued effectiveness of this clinic gives evidence that it is helpful to treat adolescents in a setting where their other medical and psychosocial concerns can be dealt with and where their treaters understand the complex issues unique not just to their illnesses but to their age. It is important that clinicians be aware of the psychobiological regression and/or arrest in normal adolescent development which occurs as part of the natural course of eating disorders. They need to be able to relate to patients whose intellectual and emotional view of the world is not commensurate with their chronological age. If this process is interrupted by a psychosomatic illness such as anorexia or bulimia nervosa, relatives, as well as clinicians, must be prepared for the fact that the patient will need to master the tasks of adolescence according to a slower and different timetable. Treatment centers where staff understand human timetables as well as eating disorders offer the best chance to adolescents for meaningful recovery.

REFERENCES

Beck, A. (1967). *Depression: clinical, experimental, and theoretical aspects.* New York: Harper and Row Publishers.

Crisp, A. (1986). *Prevention of eating disorders.* Proceedings of the Second International Conference on Eating Disorders. New York, NY, April 1986.

Eliot, A. (1990). Group coleadership: a new role for parents of adolescents with anorexia and bulimia nervosa. *International Journal of Group Psychotherapy, 40*(3), 339-351.

Garner, D., & Garfinkel, P. (1979). The eating attitudes test: an index of the symptoms of anorexia nervosa. *Psychological Medicine, 9,* 273-279.

Levenkron, S. (1985). Structuring a nurturant/authoritative psychotherapeutic relationship. In S. Emmett, (Ed.), *Theory and treatment of anorexia nervosa and bulimia,* pp. 234-245. New York: Brunner/Mazel.

Maluccio, A. (1981). *Promoting competence in clients.* New York: Free Press.

Rollins, N. & Piazza, E. (1978). Diagnosis of anorexia nervosa: a critical reappraisal. *Journal of the American Academy of Child Psychiatry, 17,* 126-137.

Snyder, L. (1989). Health care needs of the adolescent: position paper. *Annals of Internal Medicine, 110*(11), 930-935.

Eating Disorders: A Holistic Approach to Treatment

▼
▼
▼
▼

by Marie C. Shafe, Ed.D. and James M. Parsons, M.D.

Eating disorders shatter relationships, families, and personal lives. Eating disorders are a complex structure of psychological issues, family dynamics, biochemical interactions, nutritional components, social systems, spiritual deprivation, and medical aspects. The study and treatment of eating disorders have shifted over the past few years from a purely biological, medical orientation to a more comprehensive approach. Various researchers and authors have promoted the benefits of considering social, emotional, and family issues, while others have focused more on biological factors (Bruch, 1973; Bradshaw, 1988; Stuart and Orr, 1987; and Johnson, 1987).

THE COMPONENTS OF THE HOLISTIC SYSTEM OF TREATMENT

Each individual is a complex being of emotional, social, physical, and spiritual dimensions. A holistic treatment means caring for the whole person and all of his or her parts. The holistic treatment presented here uses psychotherapy, as well as the 12-step, addictions model, and it involves family systems, wellness issues, medical/physiological aspects, and nutritional dimensions, which rely on knowledge from recent studies about the biological and behavioral impact of certain food substances and combinations of substances.

The holistic model of treatment is based on the belief that eating disorders are caused by multiple factors; this is evidenced in the diversity of research literature (Baird and Sights, 1986; Brownell and Foreyt, 1986; Bradshaw, 1988; Hall, 1990). This model contains six distinct dimensions: (1) a personal/self system, (2) a family system, (3) a 12-step, addictions model, (4) wellness, (5) nutrition, and (6) medical/physiological issues. Each of these parts will be discussed in relation to the treatment of eating disorders. Most eating disorder programs do not include all of these dimensions in the treatment patients receive. In holistic treatment these components are implemented in a program as follows:

A. Psychotherapy
   1. Individual
   2. Group — In-patient, Day patient, Out-patient, and Aftercare
   3. Family
B. Psychoeducational Groups (allows one to learn new information experimentally)
   1. Sexuality and Relationships
   2. Family Issues
   3. Communication Patterns
   4. Spirituality
   5. 12-Step Work
   6. Art Therapy
C. Educational Groups
   1. Medical/Physiological Aspects
   2. Nutrition
   3. Wellness
D. Medical Assessments and Monitoring

E. Therapeutic Assessment and Monitoring
F. Physical Fitness Assessment and Planning
G. Therapeutic Outings
H. Support Groups
  1. 12-Step
  2. Continuing Care Follow-up
I. Renewal Workshops

Personal/Self System

Compulsive and addictive behaviors are often a search for personhood—a desire to have a self that is significant, worthwhile, and lovable. Eating-disordered individuals seem to be medicating, through misuse of food, negative feelings such as shame, abandonment, depression, rejection, and anger. There is a fear that one must prevent others from knowing one's faults. Individuals who feel shame at their core will believe they are "defective," "a mistake," and "not as good as others." They strive to perform, to keep others at a distance, to control, and to achieve. There is an intense conflict—the individual wanting desperately to have close relationships while afraid to have others get too close and risk knowing "how bad and defective I really am." These individuals carry shame that rightly belongs to someone else, in the sense that someone else has imposed it. The process is to separate the shaming events from the person's being and significance. When one constantly hears "You never get anything right," "Who gave you the right to think for yourself?" "Why can't you be more like _____?," or "Don't feel that way," these shaming experiences begin to feel "normal." Being pressured to be someone other than oneself or given messages not to talk, think, or feel is shaming. Living with shame is not "normal" or "okay." It is a sign the patient needs to discover his or her own needs, thoughts, feelings, and behaviors.

Authors in the eating disorders field have identified shame as well as low self-esteem, depression, lack of boundaries, control, and fear as present in the eating-disordered individual (Bradshaw, 1988; Holleran, Pascale and Fraley, 1988; Orbach, 1978; Chernin, 1985). Shame, fears, abandonment, unmet needs, and fantasized parental bonds are the core emotional issues to be explored in treatment. Shame may have been experienced in the form of sexual abuse, family secrets, rigid religious beliefs and rituals, overly critical comments, or other controlling behaviors. The control-release cycle created by shame may include such controlling, compulsive behaviors as too much dieting, working, helping others, rigidity, and exercising. These behaviors may be accompanied by such personal traits as being self-righteous, overly critical, blaming, and overly concerned with pleasing others. When the release comes, it may be in the form of abusing food, sex, alcohol, other people, money, or self. One may self-mutilate by inflicting pain with cuts, burns, bruises, and the like. Issues of physical, emotional, and sexual abuse may also be present.

It is important to recognize that when people live fear-based lives, they will set up conditions to make that fear become reality. For example, if they fear rejection, they may (1) reject others before they have the chance to reject them, (2) exhibit offensive behaviors that distance others from them, (3) present excessively pleasing, dependent, or clinging behaviors which actually result in distancing others, (4) tend to wait for others to initiate any interactions, or (5) keep relationships on a superficial level, not allowing intimate relationships to develop so as "not to get hurt." Intimacy is defined as the sharing of our innermost thoughts, beliefs, feelings, fears, and aspirations with another. Being intimate means being vulnerable, taking risks, and allowing oneself to experience the rewards of discovering inner potentials. It is difficult to let others know how one feels and thinks when one's self-esteem is low, identity confused, needs unknown, and boundaries nonexistent. Intimacy is a process never taught or allowed to develop in far too many families.

Treatment involves teaching these individuals to identify their needs, get in touch with and express their feelings, and learn new ways to get needs met. Identification of needs begins with an awareness that it is okay to have needs. Every individual has five basic needs:

1. Belonging—to feel included and connected with others.
2. Love and affection—to love and to be loved.
3. Nurturance—to have one's well-being taken care of; to receive care when sick, exhausted, or stressed.
4. Separateness—to feel important and worthwhile because of *being oneself* rather than *doing*.
5. Spirituality—to know a higher power exists that is greater than oneself alone—this may be God, nature, a group, meditation, or such.

It is important to discuss and experience "pressed down" and "denied" feelings along with the experiences and messages patients use to keep themselves hurting and victims. These experiences and messages may be years old, yet are kept alive and seen as "truths" by the patient who replays them in his or her thoughts and emotions. Early childhood trauma needs to be addressed to allow the individual to experience the pain and overcome it. As long as the pain is denied or suppressed, the individual cannot move out of the pain towards healthy growth.

Letting one's emotions out and learning new behaviors allow the patient to replace self-defeating messages and experiences with positive views of self and new life skills. Individuals can learn to accept and value themselves. They can begin to take responsibility for their own thoughts and actions.

Boundary setting is a necessary part of treatment of the personal system. There are three types of boundaries: social, physical, and psychological (personal). Individuals need to learn they have a right to their feelings, beliefs, and needs as well as a right to express them. Stating a boundary means expressing what one will share, how far one will go, what one will and will not accept, and having the right to say "no." One patient in treatment, upon a discussion of social boundaries, remarked, "I never knew I had a right to decide whom I could have in my life." A social boundary indicates the kind of people with whom one wishes to be associated. A physical boundary states where and how one wishes to be touched and how far/close others are to come. A psychological boundary includes the expression of needs and feelings. Individuals really do have a right to talk, to think, to feel, and to be who they are—not just what other people want them to be. People can be trusting and loving without allowing others to use or abuse them.

Family System

What happens in the family strongly affects how a person sees him- or herself. An open, healthy family system encourages individual growth, ideas, boundaries, feelings, and needs. Individuals are encouraged to develop their own sense of identity, taught to express and negotiate for need fulfillment, and assisted to develop boundaries. Family rules are used to help teach caring, set limits, and teach what is normal as one develops. Healthy families do not have persons feeling "crazy," or normal only when there is chaos, fighting, or abuse.

Within a dysfunctional family system rules are rigid, secrets are guarded, shame abounds, and individual growth is prohibited (Mason and Fossum, 1988; McFarland and Baker-Baum, 1988; Forward, 1989). John Bradshaw (1987) has written about the fears, delusions, shame, secrets, lack of boundaries, sacrificed needs, and harmful communication in unhealthy families. Often a family is unaware of how unhealthy its system really is. That which is unhealthy becomes the norm over a period of time. The family needs to be treated in order to teach new skills and ways of talking with each other, to help members learn how to be supportive of each other, and to develop a process of healing.

Treatment must explore the messages one has received while growing up. To what experience were these messages connected? What happened when one wanted to have emotions—feel angry, sad, hurt, happy? What happened when one had opinions to express or decisions upon which to act? What happens in the family when there is conflict or disagreement? What fantasy bonds are present? (Fantasy bonds are unrealistic expectations of how relationships with family members should be or will be *"if only...."*)

Treating the family system allows individual patients to talk about the myths, secrets, and fantasy bonds that keep them in their eating disorders. Should the rest of the family choose to stay in the dysfunction, the individual can make changes for him- or herself. The patient learns the types of roles family members play. There are therapy groups to discuss family rules, issues, and relationships; learn how to communicate with one another; learn to listen to ourselves and others; and learn that other families have the same issues and conflicts. Family therapy sessions allow each family member the chance to explore communication patterns, rules, and conflicts. Helping the family work towards a more open, flexible system which allows for individual growth, sharing, and boundaries is the goal.

In addition to an individual therapist, there may also be a family therapist assigned to each patient. The family therapist may conduct family therapy sessions in person or via conference telephone calls, educational groups about family issues, multi-family groups, and a family day filled with new information, recreational fun, and multi-family supportiveness.

The family system is the first social system in which one tests needs, feelings, and boundaries. When these needs are unmet, individuals begin to disown a part or all of themselves, deny they have needs, and view themselves as "bad" should any of these needs present themselves. In the family, the patient needs to hear "I'm glad you're here," "I love you," "I may not like your behaviors, but I love you and will be here to support you," "I'll take care of you; you don't have to fix this family," and "It's okay for you to have your feelings and thoughts." Treating the family system is not designed to affix blame. It is designed to show the patient that one cannot achieve wholeness if his or her family system was lacking. Individuals do the best they know how to do at any moment in time. Family therapy focuses upon developing new skills and patterns of communicating to offer each family member the option of healthy functioning.

12-Step, Addictions Model

The 12-step, addictions model is a social structure that provides a support and instruction system to decrease isolation and increase belonging. Individuals become socialized within the context of persons who accept and care regardless of past behaviors, feelings, or experiences because they have had similar ones themselves. The 12 steps provide a structure for relearning and new behavior experimentation.

The 12 steps introduce the person to the freedom of recovery, growth, and acceptance. The ongoing support of the 12-step groups focuses on the responsibility of the eating-disordered individual. However, individuals are assisted in taking responsibility for themselves rather than focusing upon other people, places, or things to control their lives.

The addictions model introduces the disease concept as one approach to eating disorders. With this model it is believed that an eating disorder can be seen as an addiction because food is used as a mood-altering substance and use or control of food has life-damaging effects. The treatment approach here is to develop a baseline of behavior without antidepressants. It is believed that often when individuals are detoxed from sugar and high-fat and high-caloric food substances, and discharge repressed emotional issues, the depression lifts without the use of medications.

Wellness

In the holistic model of treatment, wellness takes on a broad perspective. It includes spirituality, physical fitness, social wellness, and psychological wellness. Explored are such issues as: What is spirituality? How does one develop one's own concept of spirituality? How does one use a higher power to empower oneself? How does one take care of oneself? What is connectedness with others?

Individuals need to explore which dimensions of their lives need attention beyond just the specific eating disorder and how to provide what is needed. Wellness means balancing the psychological, social, spiritual, work, physical, and fun elements of one's life. One learns to be well by addressing each of these dimensions in small increments of time and content. This process may involve artistic expression, use of leisure time, giving and receiving honest feedback, learning to be alone, expressing one's sexuality, making choices, discovering one's self, or a multitude of other options. One dimension of expressing wellness is fulfilling one's own needs while being open to the needs of others.

Nutrition

Within the holistic model of treatment of eating disorders, the biochemical impact of certain food substances is considered. Patients are educated about healthy and unhealthy food substances and food substance combinations. Trigger foods are identified. These are foods that are individual to each person and tend to trigger a binge/purge cycle. Caloric intent and weight goals are set.

Medical/Physiological Aspects

Physiologic and medical aspects of eating disorders are best seen through an understanding of the autonomic nervous system.

Patients need to know that they have a vegetative (cholinergic) system and an adrenergic ("fight or flight") system which are mutually exclusive of each other. Fear, caffeine, and stimulant drugs can activate the adrenergic system which "turns off" the vegetative system.

The adrenergic system is mediated through adrenalin which, in a state of great fear, can provoke chills, elevated blood pressure, increased heart rate, cold hands and feet, dilated pupils, and a rise in blood sugar by the conversion of liver glycogen into glucose. Salivation is stopped, as well as secretion of bile and digestive juices. Conversely, when in the rest state of vegetation, the cholinergic system actively promotes salivation, secretion of hydrochloric acid and pepsin in the stomach, and bile and pancreatic enzymes in the duodenum. Throughout the gastrointestinal tract, a rhythmic movement called peristalsis aids the progress of digestion and elimination.

Because of the chronic fear that often exists in eating disorders, patients may be under adrenergic influence much of the time. Their vegetative system is inactivated, leading to lack of peristalsis and constipation. Patients eat when they are not hungry in the sense that the digestive tract is not prepared to process food in the normal manner. Patients pick at their food, or else force it via binging. Often patients vomit what they have eaten. That their digestive tract was not prepared for the food is reflected in patients' vague explanations of their vomiting such as, "I don't like how it feels inside me." Eating disorder patients are also especially affected by cortisol, the stress hormone, and all types of stress are mediated in the body through cortisol. Cortisol is energizing, anti-allergic, anti-inflammatory, and immunosuppressive, but it may also divert people with eating disorders from eating. Often anorexics and bulimics describe their energized cortisol-stimulated state as, "I'm running on my glands." Parents and loved ones are dismayed at the truth of the patient's statement, "I get more done if I don't eat than if I do eat." Compulsive exercise or sports activity often results.

Eating disorder patients also have a change in body chemistry due to accompanying depression. A change in nutritional intake, however, and emotional release from underlying psychological issues often result in the depression lifting without the use of antidepressant medications.

There are many health risks that the eating-disordered individual should know about. Some of these include, but are not limited to: kidney damage or failure; heart failure; suicide; digestive problems; electrolyte imbalance, which may lead to irregular heartbeat, heart failure, and kidney damage; stomach or throat rupture; dental problems; gallbladder disease; diabetes; high blood pressure; and high cholesterol.

CONCLUSION

The holistic model of the treatment of eating disorders works. Eating disorders are complex and have a diversity of origins. Individuals are complex beings and thus require an approach that recognizes all of the person—not just part of him or her. One patient came into treatment with more than a dozen medications for medical conditions and depression, a breathing machine, and feelings and experiences repressed by years of practice with food and control. The holistic model of treatment was used to allow her to no longer need the

breathing machine and only minimal medications in less than three weeks. This is not to say that her physical symptoms weren't real previously. However, once a system of treating the wholeness of body was applied, these conditions were reduced or disappeared altogether. Individuals are made up of many parts, and each must be acknowledged along with honoring needs, boundaries, and feelings.

The underlying psychological issues in the personal/self system and the family system receive the greatest emphasis in this holistic model, although each of the six dimensions is addressed.

REFERENCES

Baird, P., & Sights, J. (1986) Low self-esteem as a treatment issue in the psychotherapy of anorexia and bulimia. *Journal of Counseling and Development, 64*, 449-451.

Bradshaw, J. (1987) *Bradshaw: on the family*. Deerfield Beach, FL: Health Communications.

Bradshaw, J. (1988) *Healing the shame that binds you*. Deerfield Beach, FL: Health Communications.

Brownell, K., & Foreyt, J. (1986) *Handbook of eating disorders*. New York: Basic Books.

Bruch, H. (1973) *Eating disorders: obesity, anorexia, and the person within*. New York: Basic Books.

Chernin, K. (1985) *The hungry self: women, eating and identity*. New York: Harper and Row.

Forward, S. (1989) *Toxic parents*. New York: Bantam Books.

Hall, R. (1990) *Clinical diagnosis and management of eating disorders*. Longwood, FL: Ryandic Publishing.

Holleran, P., Pascale, J., & Fraley, J. (1988) Personality correlates of college age bulimics. *Journal of Counseling and Development, 66*, 378-381.

Johnson, C. (1987) Initial consultation for patients with bulimia and anorexia nervosa. In D. Garner and P. Garfinkel (Eds.), *Handbook of psychotherapy for anorexia nervosa and bulimia*. New York: Guilford Press.

Mason, M., & Fossum, R. (1988) *Facing shame: families in recovery*. New York: W. W. Norton.

McFarland, B., & Baker-Baum, L. (1988) *Feeding the empty heart*. Center City, MN: Hazelden.

Orbach, S. (1978) *Fat is a feminist issue*. New York: Berkley Books.

Stuart, M., & Orr, L. (1987) *Otherwise perfect*. Deerfield Beach, FL: Health Communications.

Self-Help Groups in the Treatment of Eating Disorders

▼
▼
▼
▼

by Jeanne Phillips

WHY SELF-HELP?

The major goal of a self-help group for those with eating disorders is to provide support to and communication between individuals who are at different stages of recovery, create self-awareness and insight, and give members the opportunity to increase communication and problem-solving skills. For teenagers and young adults, self-help group meetings allow for a safe format in which members can express an opinion oftentimes opposite to that expressed within their peer group and culture and still remain a part of that culture. As members become comfortable with one another and more self-assured in expressing feelings and concerns that do not necessarily support the cultural preoccupation with thinness and perfectionism as the ideal, they are practicing skills of independence and autonomy, possibly for the first time in their lives.

Growing up—the teen years and early twenties—is a frightening, confusing time in the face of tremendous cultural pressures that dictate how young people must look and feel about themselves. Each group member is encouraged to respond to his or her real feelings, rather than be the perfect person one feels he or she must be in order to gain acceptance. A support group allows members to take an opposite stand without fear of rejection or abandonment.

When a support group becomes cohesive and participants begin sharing and bonding, they are able to let go of some of the shame and guilt that goes along with an eating disorder. Sharing one's experiences and being supportive to others who are going through similar experiences is an important part of the group. The group provides a safe environment to feel close to someone; take risks; and talk about feelings in terms of home life, emancipation, relationships, intimacy, sexuality, and family expectations. Unique relationships can develop through a self-help group.

WHAT TO EXPECT

The group is usually led by an individual who has recovered from an eating disorder. This differs from group therapy, which is led by a professional. Usually structured on a "no cost" basis, donations are accepted to support group functions. The self-help group can be attended as needed because it is ongoing, with participants not having to make a commitment to join in the way that formal group therapy requires. In this informal fashion, the group provides individuals the opportunity to share when they feel comfortable, identify with someone who has gone through similar experiences, and see that an eating disorder need not be a lifelong affliction, and that, indeed, recovery is possible.

It is essential for the group leader to be honest and open with the group, sharing his or her own recovery, giving direct feedback, letting members know that recovery is indeed a process and will take time and, most important, that trying to do "it" (recover) perfectly is a set-up for failure.

For most people, coming to a group for the first time is a major step in recovery. Usually open only to individuals who have eating disorders, this membership protects the anonymity of others and also provides a safe place for people to begin taking responsibility for their own recovery. Individuals with eating disorders often have a strong desire to be taken care of and yet are yearning to grow up and be independent; still, they are afraid to do so or don't know how. By being able to come to group and talk about their own feelings, instead of having friends or parents interject, their independence is fostered, paramount to the recovery process.

Joining a group can create feelings of anxiety and apprehension. Individuals inquiring about the group may ask if they have to talk or if one is permitted to just listen during the meeting. In many groups, it is explained that all one must do is give his or her name and sign a sign-up sheet. Often during the meeting, the individual will hear what other people are going through and will be able to identify with other group members. At the end of the group the individual may be asked by the group leader how it felt to be in the group. Often the response is, "What was discussed were many of the things I am going through or have gone through. It feels good knowing I'm not so alone," or, "I thought I was the only one who had those feelings."

Some individuals come to group expecting to attend just a few times and then recover from their eating disorder. This type of thinking is common for someone with an eating disorder. What one learns from other group members is that recovery is a process and takes time. One doesn't develop an eating disorder overnight so one should not expect to recover overnight. Some folks may believe that all one has to do is just stop the behavior (restricting or binging and purging) and everything will be okay. This myth is dispelled by feedback from other group members. People with eating disorders have a tremendous need for control and perfectionism and think in black-and-white terms. In group, people learn through others to be patient with themselves and that recovery cannot be done perfectly. The length of time spent in a self-help group depends primarily on the individual with the eating disorder and how willing he or she is to take the risks that are necessary to change his or her behavior.

Often, people come to a group meeting believing that their problem is only with food and fear of weight gain, and they just need to learn how to eat normally. It is important, however, to shift the focus from food and weight to feelings. Discussion topics in a self-help group include issues surrounding poor self-esteem, perfectionism, people-pleasing behavior, setting realistic goals and expectations, the desire to be special, control issues, the desire to be accepted and loved by everyone, the purpose and function of food and weight rituals, the meaning of thinness and fatness, fear of intimacy and sexuality, fear of inadequacy, fear of anger, emancipation and separation from family, fear of rejection and abandonment, feelings of guilt and shame, and cultural attitudes toward fatness and thinness.

When a person finds someone who shares feelings and fears and has gone through similar experiences and emotions, that person often experiences a tremendous sense of relief. When group members together identify what triggers their eating disorder behavior (e.g., anger, shame, guilt, loneliness, boredom), they usually begin to identify with each other, thus enhancing their sense of camaraderie.

The group provides a safe place to do role modeling, risk-taking and honestly share feelings, as well as give and receive feedback about their and others' recovery. One can expect anonymity, a networking and support system, and to not feel so alone or different.

SUPPORT GROUPS BASED ON THE 12-STEP MODEL

Some support groups are based on the Alcoholics Anonymous (AA) 12-Step Model, such as Overeaters Anonymous. The AA concept is one that deals with a progressive, lifelong illness that must be controlled by abstinence from the substance to which the individual is "addicted." This model views someone with an eating disorder as having a disease rather than a behavior disorder. Eating-disordered individuals are seen as suffering from a compulsive illness that cannot be cured, but only arrested.

In these groups members admit—as a first "step"—to being powerless over food, with emphasis being placed on control rather than normalizing intake. This model does not try to explain the behavior but defines it with the terms "compulsive" or "addiction." Members are encouraged to find a sponsor whom they can call when they need help abstaining from overeating, binging, or purging. The sponsor is someone who is at a later stage of recovery and available to those first entering the program.

A PERSONAL NOTE

It is the opinion of this author that one can recover completely from an eating disorder. It is my belief that an eating disorder is not a disease but a behavior that is learned and can be unlearned; that people are not powerless over food per se, but have become powerless over their feelings. People with eating disorders must learn to take responsibility for their feelings and behaviors; begin realistic goal-setting; be willing to take risks without being absolutely certain of the outcomes; ask others for help and support; take the words "should" and "can't" out of their vocabulary; realize that recovery is a process and cannot be done perfectly; avoid isolating and withdrawing; not assume what other people are thinking; not gauge their feelings of specialness on external symbols of success (e.g., how pretty or thin they are; what size clothes they wear; or how much they weigh); and begin to establish an identity apart from being someone who is bulimic or anorexic.

Whether an individual can recover from an eating disorder solely by attending a self-help group depends on the particular individual, as each case is unique. There are a number of issues which must be addressed and resolved in order for one to completely recover. Most support groups are run by a lay person who has recovered from an eating disorder, not by a professional therapist. It is my belief that a self-help group is *not* intended to take the place of individual or family therapy but rather serve as a support system during one's recovery.

SELF-HELP GROUPS NOT FOR EVERYONE

Support groups are not usually recommended for individuals who are severely restricting their food intake and unable to relate well enough to others to benefit from the interaction. These individuals are also often intensely competitive to be the thinnest, and they are unable to experience the good feelings one gets after sharing problems, nor are they able to feel the mutual support, trust, and respect that occurs in this kind of setting.

FINDING SUPPORT

Information about support groups may be found through local telephone directories, community information and referral services, mental health facilities, newspapers, county social service departments, or self-help hotlines.

In Section 5 of this book, the reader will find a directory of national organizations that provide information about support groups, referrals to therapists, and other kinds of information about eating disorders.

PART 4
Facilities and Programs

Directory of Facilities and Programs

▼
▼
▼
▼

This directory lists 200 facilities and programs for which questionnaires have been returned or phone surveys have been answered from August to November 1991. All information has been supplied by personnel from the program or facility. This is not a comprehensive list of all eating disorder programs, nor is it a list of recommended facilities. It is meant to provide a starting point. Check with a therapist or other local health professional who is knowledgeable about eating disorders for further recommendations. Also check with the national organizations listed in "Organizations" in Part 5 of this book. Some of them can provide referral lists of programs and professionals.

See "Locating a Therapist or Treatment Program," beginning on page vii of this book, and "How to Find Treatment for an Eating Disorder," beginning on page 83, for more information.

▼ ▼ ▼ ▼

ALABAMA

Birmingham

1. University of Alabama Department of Psychiatry
School of Medicine, Jefferson Tower N-275, Birmingham, AL 35294
(205) 934-6054
CONTACT: Dr Hal Thurstin, Prog Dir
FAX: (205) 975-6559
DATE ESTABLISHED: 1983
EATING DISORDERS TREATED: Anorexia nervosa; Bulimia nervosa; Compulsive overeating/obesity
TREATMENT/THERAPY: Psychological; Group; Individual; Family; Cognitive-behavioral; Out-patient education; In-patient available on per-case basis
SETTING: In-patient; Out-patient
PROGRAM LENGTH: Out-patient varies depending on response; In-patient, 2-4 wks
NO. OF PATIENTS PROGRAM CAN SERVE: Out-patient, 25; In-patient, 5; NO. TREATED PREVIOUS YEAR: 50-75
FOLLOW-UP EVALUATIONS: 3-6 mos; Progress review; Current dietary patterns per individual basis; Stability of patterns; Symptom patterns

Phenix City

2. The Rader Institute at Phenix Medical Park Hospital
PO Box 190, 1707 21 Ave, Phenix City, AL 36867
(205) 291-8600
CONTACT: Vernelle Sapp, RN
EATING DISORDERS TREATED: Anorexia nervosa; Bulimia nervosa; Compulsive overeating/obesity

ARIZONA

Scottsdale

3. Eating Disorders Center of Greater Phoenix
3337 N Miller Rd, Ste 105, Scottsdale, AZ 85251
(602) 994-9773
CONTACT: Ray Lemberg, PhD
DATE ESTABLISHED: 1982
EATING DISORDERS TREATED: Anorexia nervosa; Bulimia nervosa; Compulsive overeating/obesity
TREATMENT/THERAPY: Psychological; Group; Individual; Family; Adolescent; Holistic model; Out-patient education; Nutrition program
SETTING: Out-patient
PROGRAM LENGTH: Varies
NO. OF PATIENTS PROGRAM CAN SERVE: 25/wk; NO. TREATED PREVIOUS YEAR: 100

4. Scottsdale Camelback Hospital
7575 E Earll Dr, Scottsdale, AZ 85251
(602) 941-7500
CONTACT: Deborah Desprois, Adult Service
Line Mgr
CONTACT TELEPHONE: (602) 941-7510
HOTLINE: (800) 253-1334
FAX: (602) 994-5558
DATE ESTABLISHED: 1983
EATING DISORDERS TREATED: Anorexia
nervosa; Bulimia nervosa; Compulsive
overeating/obesity
TREATMENT/THERAPY: Addiction;
Psychological; Group; Individual; Family;
Adolescent; 12-step; Creative arts; Out-
patient education; Exercise; Body image;
Psychodrama
SETTING: Hospital; In-patient; Out-patient
PROGRAM LENGTH: Varies
NO. OF PATIENTS PROGRAM CAN SERVE: 8-10; NO.
TREATED PREVIOUS YEAR: 50-60
FOLLOW-UP EVALUATIONS: Ongoing aftercare
program for 1 yr after discharge

5. Willow Creek Hospital and Treatment Center
8435 E McDowell Rd, Scottsdale, AZ 85257
(602) 945-2330
CONTACT: Terri Andersen
CONTACT TELEPHONE: (602) 945-2330
HOTLINE: (800) 228-5328
FAX: (602) 945-0322
DATE ESTABLISHED: 1990
EATING DISORDERS TREATED: Anorexia
nervosa; Bulimia nervosa; Compulsive
overeating/obesity; Affective disorders
TREATMENT/THERAPY: Psychological; Group;
Individual; Family; Adolescent; Level
system; Creative arts; Out-patient
education; Exercise; Body image; Self-
enhancement
SETTING: Hospital; In-patient; Out-patient;
Full-day hospitalization; Partial
hospitalization
PROGRAM LENGTH: 10-day minimum
NO. OF PATIENTS PROGRAM CAN SERVE: 17 in-
patients; NO. TREATED PREVIOUS YEAR: 119
FOLLOW-UP EVALUATIONS: 6 mos; 12 mos;
Annually; Phone interview; Weekly
aftercare groups; Alumni quarterly
meetings

Tucson

6. Sahuaro Vista Ranch
7501 N Wade Rd, Tucson, AZ 85743
(602) 744-1999
CONTACT: Anita Bussiere
HOTLINE: (800) 825-2624
FAX: (602) 744-1669
DATE ESTABLISHED: 1985

EATING DISORDERS TREATED: Anorexia
nervosa; Bulimia nervosa; Compulsive
overeating/obesity
TREATMENT/THERAPY: Addiction;
Psychological; Group; Individual; Family;
Holistic model; 12-step; Body image;
Females only
SETTING: Free-standing residential
PROGRAM LENGTH: 28-42 days
NO. OF PATIENTS PROGRAM CAN SERVE: 35
FOLLOW-UP EVALUATIONS: Every 4-6 wks for 1
yr by phone

7. Sierra Tucson
16500 N Lago del Oro, Tucson, AZ 85737
CONTACT: Elaine Alexander, Exec Dir
CONTACT TELEPHONE: (602) 792-2323
DATE ESTABLISHED: 1990
EATING DISORDERS TREATED: Anorexia
nervosa; Bulimia nervosa; Compulsive
overeating/obesity
TREATMENT/THERAPY: Addiction;
Psychological; Group; Individual; Family;
Separate adolescent treatment (9/91);
Holistic model; 12-step; Creative arts;
Exercise; Body image
SETTING: Hospital; In-patient
PROGRAM LENGTH: 42 days (6 wks minimum)
NO. OF PATIENTS PROGRAM CAN SERVE: 70; NO.
TREATED PREVIOUS YEAR: 45
FOLLOW-UP EVALUATIONS: 6 mos; 12 mos;
Phone contact at 30 days

8. Sonora Desert Hospital—Women's Resource and Treatment Center
1920 W Rudasill, Tucson, AZ 85704
(602) 297-5500
HOTLINE: (602) 297-5500; ask for RESPOND
DATE ESTABLISHED: 1989
EATING DISORDERS TREATED: Anorexia
nervosa; Bulimia nervosa
TREATMENT/THERAPY: Psychological; Group;
Family; Adolescent; Adult-women-only
unit; Adult men/women (adult psychiatric
unit); Creative arts
SETTING: Hospital; In-patient; Out-patient;
Out-patient treatment affiliated with
University of Arizona Family and
Community Medicine; Day treatment
available
PROGRAM LENGTH: Varies

9. University of Arizona Health Sciences Center, Department of Family and Community Medicine
Eating Disorders Program, Tucson, AZ 85724
(602) 626-7863
CONTACT: Catherine M Shisslak, PhD
FAX: (602) 321-7745
DATE ESTABLISHED: 1982

EATING DISORDERS TREATED: Anorexia
nervosa; Bulimia nervosa; Compulsive
overeating/obesity
TREATMENT/THERAPY: Psychological; Group;
Individual; Family; Adolescent; Exercise
SETTING: Hospital; In-patient; Out-patient
PROGRAM LENGTH: Varies
NO. OF PATIENTS PROGRAM CAN SERVE: No
limit; NO. TREATED PREVIOUS YEAR: 100-150
FOLLOW-UP EVALUATIONS: 6 mos

Wickenburg

10. Remuda Ranch
Jack Burden Rd, PO Box 21333, Wickenburg,
AZ 85358
(602) 684-3913
CONTACT: Roxie Glover
HOTLINE: (800) 445-1900
FAX: (602) 684-7903
DATE ESTABLISHED: 1990
EATING DISORDERS TREATED: Anorexia
nervosa; Bulimia nervosa
TREATMENT/THERAPY: Psychological; Group;
Individual; Family; Adolescent; Creative
arts; Body image; Females only
SETTING: Hospital; In-patient
PROGRAM LENGTH: 45 days average
NO. OF PATIENTS PROGRAM CAN SERVE: 25-bed
facility; NO. TREATED PREVIOUS YEAR: 120
FOLLOW-UP EVALUATIONS: 1 wk; 6 mos; 12
mos; Telephone and written evaluations

ARKANSAS

Little Rock

11. St Vincent Infirmary—Restore
2 St Vincent Cr, Little Rock, AR 72205-5499
(800) 225-1112
CONTACT TELEPHONE: (501) 376-1200
HOTLINE: (800) 225-1112
FAX: (501) 662-2FAX
DATE ESTABLISHED: 1983
EATING DISORDERS TREATED: Anorexia
nervosa; Bulimia nervosa; Compulsive
overeating/obesity; Noncompensatory
bulimia
TREATMENT/THERAPY: Addiction; Group;
Individual; Family; Adolescent; Older
adolescents only (14 and up); 12-step;
Creative arts; Out-patient education;
Exercise; Body image
SETTING: Hospital; Residential treatment
PROGRAM LENGTH: Varies
NO. OF PATIENTS PROGRAM CAN SERVE: 20; NO.
TREATED PREVIOUS YEAR: 300+
FOLLOW-UP EVALUATIONS: 6 mos; 12 mos;
Written evaluations; Ongoing alumni
group meets weekly; Annual alumni
reunion

CALIFORNIA

Belmont

12. CPC Belmont Hills Hospital
1301 Ralston Ave, Belmont, CA 94002
(415) 593-2143
CONTACT: Linda Burge, Eating Disorders
Coord
CONTACT TELEPHONE: (415) 593-0857
HOTLINE: (800) 675-5599
FAX: (415) 595-8922
DATE ESTABLISHED: 1983
EATING DISORDERS TREATED: Anorexia
nervosa; Bulimia nervosa; Compulsive
overeating/obesity
TREATMENT/THERAPY: Group; Individual;
Family; Adolescent; Weekend workshops;
Cognitive-behavioral; Free community
support group for eating disorders; 12-step;
Creative arts; Out-patient education;
Exercise; Body image; Individualized
nutrition counseling; Support groups for
significant others
SETTING: Hospital; In-patient; Out-patient;
Day treatment and evening treatment
programs
PROGRAM LENGTH: Varies
NO. OF PATIENTS PROGRAM CAN SERVE: 20
adults; 10 adolescents; 5 children; NO.
TREATED PREVIOUS YEAR: Approx 180 in-
patients
FOLLOW-UP EVALUATIONS: Ongoing eating
disorders support groups and self-help
groups

Dana Point

13. Capistrano by the Sea Hospital
34000 Capistrano by the Sea Dr, Dana Point,
CA 92629
(714) 496-5702
CONTACT: Beverly Wright
HOTLINE: (800) 237-9506
DATE ESTABLISHED: 1980
EATING DISORDERS TREATED: Anorexia
nervosa; Bulimia nervosa; Compulsive
overeating/obesity
TREATMENT/THERAPY: Addiction;
Psychological; Group; Individual; Family;
Adolescent; 12-step; Creative arts; Out-
patient education; Exercise; Body image
SETTING: Hospital; In-patient
PROGRAM LENGTH: Varies
NO. OF PATIENTS PROGRAM CAN SERVE: 20; NO.
TREATED PREVIOUS YEAR: 47
FOLLOW-UP EVALUATIONS: 1-yr aftercare

La Mesa

14. Alvarado Parkway Institute

7050 Parkway Dr, La Mesa, CA 91942-2352
(619) 465-4411
CONTACT: Karen Dunford, MA
HOTLINE: (619) 465-1000, (800) THERAPY
FAX: (619) 465-5015
DATE ESTABLISHED: 1982
EATING DISORDERS TREATED: Anorexia
nervosa; Bulimia nervosa; Compulsive
overeating/obesity
TREATMENT/THERAPY: Group; Family;
Adolescent; Available programs: in-patient
adults (men and women); Separate
adolescent in-patient units; Out-patient
adult program; Creative arts; Out-patient
education; Body image; Nutrition program;
Co-dependency issues; Assertion; Cognitive
restructuring; Body image workshops;
Education groups; Multifamily groups
SETTING: Hospital; In-patient; Out-patient
PROGRAM LENGTH: 3 wks in-patient; 6 wks
out-patient
NO. OF PATIENTS PROGRAM CAN SERVE: 24 in-
patient; 15 out-patient; NO. TREATED
PREVIOUS YEAR: Several hundred
FOLLOW-UP EVALUATIONS: 6 mos; Phone call
back-up with follow-up form

Lemon Grove

15. New Attitudes Recovery Center

1852 Sonoma Ln, Lemon Grove, CA 91945
(619) 469-6771
CONTACT: Linda Santangelo, Dir
CONTACT TELEPHONE: (619) 969-0458
DATE ESTABLISHED: 1986
EATING DISORDERS TREATED: Anorexia
nervosa; Bulimia nervosa; Compulsive
overeating/obesity
TREATMENT/THERAPY: Addiction; Group;
Individual; Family; Workshops; 12-step;
Out-patient education; Body image;
Females only (in-patient)
SETTING: In-patient; Out-patient; Counseling
center; Individual and groups
PROGRAM LENGTH: 6-12 mos, in-patient; 8
wks, out-patient
NO. OF PATIENTS PROGRAM CAN SERVE: 8 in-
patient; 4 out-patient, plus counseling
center; NO. TREATED PREVIOUS YEAR: 100
FOLLOW-UP EVALUATIONS: Aftercare program

Long Beach

16. Charter Hospital of Long Beach

6060 Paramount Blvd, Long Beach, CA
90805
(213) 220-1000
HOTLINE: (800) 262-1414
FAX: (213) 408-1894
DATE ESTABLISHED: 1980
EATING DISORDERS TREATED: Bulimia nervosa;
Compulsive overeating/obesity
TREATMENT/THERAPY: Addiction;
Psychological; Group; Individual; Family;
Adolescent; 12-step; Creative arts;
Exercise; Body image; Females only
SETTING: Hospital
PROGRAM LENGTH: Varies
NO. OF PATIENTS PROGRAM CAN SERVE: 14 beds;
NO. TREATED PREVIOUS YEAR: 131
FOLLOW-UP EVALUATIONS: 6 mos; Social
worker

Los Angeles

17. The Rader Institute—Los Angeles

1663 Sawtelle Blvd, Los Angeles, CA 90025
(213) 478-8238
CONTACT: Toni Luppino
CONTACT TELEPHONE: (213) 478-8238
HOTLINE: (800) 255-1818
FAX: (213) 477-7822
DATE ESTABLISHED: 1984
EATING DISORDERS TREATED: Anorexia
nervosa; Bulimia nervosa; Compulsive
overeating/obesity
TREATMENT/THERAPY: Addiction;
Psychological; Group; Individual; Family;
Holistic model; 12-step; Creative arts; Out-
patient education; Exercise; Body image
SETTING: Hospital; In-patient; Out-patient
PROGRAM LENGTH: Individualized
NO. OF PATIENTS PROGRAM CAN SERVE: 18
locations/average unit is 15 patients
FOLLOW-UP EVALUATIONS: 6 mos; 12 mos; 2-yr;
5-yr; Database and satisfaction orientation

18. UCLA Neuropsychiatric Institute & Hospital—Adolescent Eating Disorders Program

760 Westwood Plaza, Los Angeles, CA 90024-
1759
(213) 825-0051
CONTACT: Michael Strober, PhD
CONTACT TELEPHONE: (213) 825-5730
DATE ESTABLISHED: 1965
EATING DISORDERS TREATED: Anorexia
nervosa; Bulimia nervosa
TREATMENT/THERAPY: Psychological; Group;
Individual; Family; Adolescent; Programs
and treatment are for adolescents and

families only; Nutrition program; Out-patient and in-patient programs; Multiple family groups
SETTING: Hospital; In-patient; Out-patient
PROGRAM LENGTH: As needed

19. UCLA Neuropsychiatric Institute & Hospital—Adult Eating Disorders Program

760 Westwood Plaza, Los Angeles, CA 90024-1759
(213) 825-0478
CONTACT: Dr Mary Neal
CONTACT TELEPHONE: (213) 825-0764
DATE ESTABLISHED: 1982
EATING DISORDERS TREATED: Anorexia nervosa; Bulimia nervosa
TREATMENT/THERAPY: Psychological; Group; Individual; Family; Programs and treatments for adults only; Intensive out-patient program; Out-patient education; Body image; Females only; Meals included during program hours
SETTING: Hospital; Out-patient
PROGRAM LENGTH: Unlimited
NO. OF PATIENTS PROGRAM CAN SERVE: 10-15; NO. TREATED PREVIOUS YEAR: 20
FOLLOW-UP EVALUATIONS: Beginning a follow-up program

North Hollywood

20. The Rader Institute at Medical Center of North Hollywood

12629 Riverside Dr, North Hollywood, CA 91607
(818) 766-9410
HOTLINE: (800) 255-1818
FAX: (818) 753-2239
DATE ESTABLISHED: 1984
EATING DISORDERS TREATED: Anorexia nervosa; Bulimia nervosa; Compulsive overeating/obesity
TREATMENT/THERAPY: Addiction; Psychological; Group; Individual; Family; Adolescent; 12-step; Out-patient education; Exercise; Body image
SETTING: Hospital; In-patient; Out-patient; Day treatment
PROGRAM LENGTH: Varies
NO. OF PATIENTS PROGRAM CAN SERVE: 13 in-patients; No limit on day treatment and out-patients; NO. TREATED PREVIOUS YEAR: 130
FOLLOW-UP EVALUATIONS: 6 mos; Following each in-patient/day treatment/out-patient stay there is a 3-mo continuing care program

Northridge

21. Northridge Hospital Medical Center—Eating Disorders Program

18300 Roscoe Blvd, Northridge, CA 91328
(818) 885-5450; (800) 233-5450
CONTACT: Marilyn G Leaf, LCSW, Prog Dir
CONTACT TELEPHONE: (818) 885-5352
HOTLINE: (818) 885-5450
FAX: (818) 885-8905
DATE ESTABLISHED: 1983
EATING DISORDERS TREATED: Anorexia nervosa; Bulimia nervosa; Compulsive overeating/obesity (evening program, out-patient only)
TREATMENT/THERAPY: Psychological; Group; Individual; Family; Adolescent; Multiple family group, in-patient only; Creative arts; Out-patient education; Exercise; Body image; Cognitive, behavioral, dynamic orientation; Full and partial hospitalization out-patient component available; Supervised supermarket shopping; Meal preparation; Lunches out; Mall outings for further body image work
SETTING: Hospital; Out-patient; In-patient (med/psych unit)
PROGRAM LENGTH: Individualized
NO. OF PATIENTS PROGRAM CAN SERVE: 9 in-patients; 17-20 day treatment; 8-10 evening compulsive overeating program; NO. TREATED PREVIOUS YEAR: Approx 150 in-patients and out-patients
FOLLOW-UP EVALUATIONS: 6 mos; 12 mos; Weekly support group (ANAD) meetings and monthly alumni group; In-person interview and questionnaires

Palo Alto

22. Lucile Packard Children's Hospital at Stanford

725 Welch Rd, Palo Alto, CA 94304
(415) 497-8000
CONTACT: Tom McPherson
CONTACT TELEPHONE: (415) 723-5511
DATE ESTABLISHED: 1978
EATING DISORDERS TREATED: Anorexia nervosa; Bulimia nervosa; Compulsive overeating/obesity; Full range of psychiatric and medically related eating problems
TREATMENT/THERAPY: Group; Individual; Family; Adolescent; Out-patient education; Nutrition program
SETTING: Hospital; In-patient; Out-patient
PROGRAM LENGTH: Varies
NO. OF PATIENTS PROGRAM CAN SERVE: No limit; NO. TREATED PREVIOUS YEAR: 50

Lucile Packard Children's Hospital at Stanford *(continued)*

FOLLOW-UP EVALUATIONS: 6 mos; 12 mos; 4 yrs; 8 yrs; Phone contacts; Questionnaires; Interviews

Port Hueneme

23. Anacapa Hospital
307 E Clara St, Port Hueneme, CA 93044
(805) 488-3661
CONTACT: Juli Hayes, RD
HOTLINE: (800) 827-8377
FAX: (805) 488-0533
DATE ESTABLISHED: 1991
EATING DISORDERS TREATED: Anorexia nervosa; Bulimia nervosa; Compulsive overeating/obesity
TREATMENT/THERAPY: Addiction; Psychological; Group; Individual; Family; Adolescent; Holistic model; 12-step; Creative arts; Exercise; Body image; Outdoor adventure; Restaurant outings; Nutrition program; Food/body issues group
SETTING: Hospital; In-patient
PROGRAM LENGTH: Depends on patient and facility—no set length
NO. OF PATIENTS PROGRAM CAN SERVE: 24; NO. TREATED PREVIOUS YEAR: 5
FOLLOW-UP EVALUATIONS: 6 mos; 12 mos; Telephone follow-up—structured questionnaire

24. STEPS Residential Treatment Facility
PO Box 428, 224 E Clara St, Port Hueneme, CA 93044
(805) 488-6424
CONTACT: Denee Jordan
HOTLINE: (800) 827-8377
FAX: (805) 488-6717
DATE ESTABLISHED: 1990
EATING DISORDERS TREATED: Anorexia nervosa; Bulimia nervosa; Compulsive overeating/obesity
TREATMENT/THERAPY: Addiction; Psychological; Group; Individual; Family; Adolescent; Holistic model; 12-step; Creative arts; Exercise; Body image; Outdoor adventure; Restaurant outings; Nutrition program; Food/body issues group
SETTING: Residential facility
PROGRAM LENGTH: Depends on patient and facility—no set length
NO. OF PATIENTS PROGRAM CAN SERVE: 20; NO. TREATED PREVIOUS YEAR: 12

Redondo Beach

25. The Rader Institute at South Bay Hospital
514 N Prospect Ave, Redondo Beach, CA 90277
(213) 318-4702
CONTACT: Jonathan Rader
HOTLINE: (800) 255-1818
DATE ESTABLISHED: 1984
EATING DISORDERS TREATED: Anorexia nervosa; Bulimia nervosa; Compulsive overeating/obesity
TREATMENT/THERAPY: Addiction; Psychological; Group; Individual; Family; Adolescent; 12-step; Creative arts; Out-patient education; Exercise; Body image; Nutrition program
SETTING: Hospital; In-patient; Out-patient
PROGRAM LENGTH: 30-42 days in-patient; 12 wk follow-up
NO. OF PATIENTS PROGRAM CAN SERVE: 24
FOLLOW-UP EVALUATIONS: 6 mos; Free alumni group 1/wk

Sacramento

26. University of California at Davis Medical School, University Psychiatry Center
4430 V St, Sacramento, CA 95818
(916) 734-3574
CONTACT: Intake coordinator
EATING DISORDERS TREATED: Anorexia nervosa; Bulimia nervosa
TREATMENT/THERAPY: Psychological; Group; Individual; Psychodynamic approach
SETTING: Out-patient
PROGRAM LENGTH: Ongoing
NO. OF PATIENTS PROGRAM CAN SERVE: 15
FOLLOW-UP EVALUATIONS: Treatment modality is ongoing

San Diego

27. The Rader Institute at Sharp Cabrillo Hospital
3475 Kenyon St, San Diego, CA 92075
(619) 221-3485
CONTACT: Ruthann Allison
FAX: (619) 221-3482
DATE ESTABLISHED: 1984
EATING DISORDERS TREATED: Anorexia nervosa; Bulimia nervosa; Compulsive overeating/obesity
TREATMENT/THERAPY: Addiction; Psychological; Group; Individual; Family; Adolescent; 12-step; Creative arts; Out-patient education; Exercise; Body image; Lunches out; Food issues group; Peer group; Body image group

SETTING: Hospital; In-patient; Day treatment
PROGRAM LENGTH: Individually designed
program—varies
NO. OF PATIENTS PROGRAM CAN SERVE: In-
patient, 12 beds
FOLLOW-UP EVALUATIONS: 6 mos;
Questionnaire; Therapeutic follow-up;
Weekly alumni group

Stanford

28. Stanford University Behavioral Medicine Clinic, Department of Psychiatry and Behavioral Sciences
Stanford University School of Medicine, Stanford, CA 94305
(415) 723-5868
CONTACT: Dr Bruce Arnow, Prog Dir
CONTACT TELEPHONE: (415) 723-5868
FAX: (415) 723-9807
DATE ESTABLISHED: 1975
EATING DISORDERS TREATED: Anorexia
nervosa; Bulimia nervosa; Compulsive
overeating/obesity
TREATMENT/THERAPY: Psychological; Group;
Individual; Family; Medication; Nutrition
program
SETTING: In-patient; Out-patient
PROGRAM LENGTH: Varies
NO. OF PATIENTS PROGRAM CAN SERVE: 12 in-
patients; Out-patient varies according to
therapist's time
FOLLOW-UP EVALUATIONS: Aftercare

COLORADO

Boulder

29. Boulder Community Hospital, Women's Recovery Program
PO Box 9130, 311 Mapleton Ave, Boulder, CO 80301
(303) 441-0594
CONTACT: Kimberly Johnson, Prog Dir
CONTACT TELEPHONE: (303) 441-0563
FAX: (303) 441-0465
DATE ESTABLISHED: 1982
EATING DISORDERS TREATED: Anorexia
nervosa; Bulimia nervosa; Compulsive
overeating/obesity
TREATMENT/THERAPY: Addiction;
Psychological; Group; Individual; Family;
Holistic model; 12-step; Creative arts; Out-
patient education; Exercise; Body image;
Females only
SETTING: Hospital; In-patient; Out-patient
PROGRAM LENGTH: Individualized for in-
patients and partial patients; Intensive out-
patient program is a minimum of 8 wks
and 12 wks of continuous care

NO. OF PATIENTS PROGRAM CAN SERVE: 14 in-
patients; 10 partial patients; 20 intensive
out-patients; NO. TREATED PREVIOUS YEAR:
110
FOLLOW-UP EVALUATIONS: 6 mos; 12 mos;
Verbal and written

Colorado Springs

30. Cedar Springs Psychiatric Hospital
2135 Southgate Rd, Colorado Springs, CO 80906
(719) 633-4114
CONTACT: Cindy Silvis, PsyD, Prog Dir
CONTACT TELEPHONE: (719) 633-4114 ext 1214
FAX: (719) 578-0857
DATE ESTABLISHED: 1986
EATING DISORDERS TREATED: Anorexia
nervosa; Bulimia nervosa; Compulsive
overeating/obesity; Binge eating disorder
TREATMENT/THERAPY: Psychological; Group;
Individual; Family; Adolescent; Creative
arts; Out-patient education; Exercise; Body
image
SETTING: Hospital; In-patient; Out-patient;
Partial hospitalization
PROGRAM LENGTH: 1-3 mos; 9 hrs/wk for day
treatment; 2 hrs/wk for out-patient
NO. OF PATIENTS PROGRAM CAN SERVE: 17
FOLLOW-UP EVALUATIONS: 6 wks; 3 mos

Denver

31. Porter Memorial Hospital
2525 S Downing St, Denver, CO 80210
(303) 778-5774
CONTACT: Marlene Swift, Coord
DATE ESTABLISHED: 1985
EATING DISORDERS TREATED: Anorexia
nervosa; Bulimia nervosa; Compulsive
overeating/obesity
TREATMENT/THERAPY: Addiction;
Psychological; Group; Individual; Family;
Adolescent; Out-patient education; Body
image
SETTING: Out-patient
PROGRAM LENGTH: 6-12 mos, 1-2 times/wk NO.
TREATED PREVIOUS YEAR: 50
FOLLOW-UP EVALUATIONS: Aftercare

32. Presbyterian/St Luke's Medical Center
Center for Eating Management, 601 E 19th Ave, Denver, CO 80401
(303) 869-2533
CONTACT: Melissa Kendrick
DATE ESTABLISHED: 1986
EATING DISORDERS TREATED: Anorexia
nervosa; Bulimia nervosa; Compulsive
overeating/obesity

Presbyterian/St Luke's Medical Center
(continued)

TREATMENT/THERAPY: Addiction;
  Psychological; Group; Individual; Family;
  12-step; Out-patient education; Exercise;
  Body image

Fort Collins

33. Fort Collins Eating Disorders Program
318 E Oak, Fort Collins, CO 80524
(303) 484-6913
CONTACT: Judy Vernon-Chandler, Prog Dir
FAX: (303) 493-1419
DATE ESTABLISHED: 1985
EATING DISORDERS TREATED: Anorexia
  nervosa; Bulimia nervosa; Compulsive
  overeating/obesity
TREATMENT/THERAPY: Out-patient education;
  Body image; Females only
SETTING: Out-patient
PROGRAM LENGTH: 6 wk intensive then 1
  group/wk
NO. OF PATIENTS PROGRAM CAN SERVE: 40
FOLLOW-UP EVALUATIONS: 6 mos; 12 mos

Littleton

34. Columbine—Eating Treatment Center
8565 S Poplar Way, Littleton, CO 80126
(303) 470-9500; (800) 942-2734
CONTACT: Kathleen Reeves
HOTLINE: (800) 942-2734
FAX: (303) 470-0607
DATE ESTABLISHED: 1988
EATING DISORDERS TREATED: Anorexia
  nervosa; Bulimia nervosa; Compulsive
  overeating/obesity
TREATMENT/THERAPY: Psychological; Group;
  Individual; Family; Adolescent; Nutrition
  program; 12-step; Creative arts; Out-
  patient education; Body image
SETTING: Hospital; In-patient; Out-patient
PROGRAM LENGTH: Varies, average is 21-24
  days
NO. OF PATIENTS PROGRAM CAN SERVE: 10 at a
  time; NO. TREATED PREVIOUS YEAR: 73
FOLLOW-UP EVALUATIONS: 6 mos; 12 mos;
  Every year; Questionnaire

CONNECTICUT

Greenwich

35. Wilkins Center for Eating Disorders
7 Riverside Rd, Greenwich, CT 06831
(203) 531-1909
CONTACT: Diane Mickley, MD
FAX: (203) 531-8326
DATE ESTABLISHED: 1982
EATING DISORDERS TREATED: Anorexia
  nervosa; Bulimia nervosa; Compulsive
  overeating/obesity
TREATMENT/THERAPY: Psychological; Group;
  Individual; Family; Adolescent; Short-term
  summer college group; High school, young
  adult, and adult groups; Overweight
  psychotherapy group; Out-patient
  education; Nutrition program; Medical
  care; Medication
SETTING: Out-patient
PROGRAM LENGTH: Open-ended
NO. OF PATIENTS PROGRAM CAN SERVE: No
  limit; NO. TREATED PREVIOUS YEAR: More
  than 200
FOLLOW-UP EVALUATIONS: Ongoing,
  individualized

New Canaan

36. Behavioral Medicine Institute
885 Oenoke Ridge Rd, New Canaan, CT
06840
(203) 966-8060
CONTACT: Nancy J Kolodny, MA, MSW, Dir
FAX: (203) 966-9807
DATE ESTABLISHED: 1983
EATING DISORDERS TREATED: Anorexia
  nervosa; Bulimia nervosa; Compulsive
  overeating/obesity; Eating disorders not
  otherwise specified
TREATMENT/THERAPY: Psychological; Group;
  Individual; Family; Adolescent; Out-
  patient education; Body image;
  Bibliotherapy in conjunction with
  cognitive/behavioral work; Nutritional
  evaluations in conjunction with local
  hospitals on a referral basis
SETTING: Out-patient
PROGRAM LENGTH: 4-6 mos NO. TREATED
  PREVIOUS YEAR: 40-50
FOLLOW-UP EVALUATIONS: Monthly for 6 mos,
  then every 6 mos

New Haven

37. Yale-New Haven Hospital Out-patient Psychiatry Clinic

20 York St, CB 2046, New Haven, CT 06504
(203) 785-4628
CONTACT: Dr Claudia Bemis
CONTACT TELEPHONE: (203) 785-4628
FAX: (203) 737-2221
DATE ESTABLISHED: 1990
EATING DISORDERS TREATED: Anorexia
    nervosa; Bulimia nervosa
TREATMENT/THERAPY: Psychological; Group;
    Individual; Family; Medication
SETTING: Out-patient
PROGRAM LENGTH: No limit
NO. OF PATIENTS PROGRAM CAN SERVE: No
    limits currently; NO. TREATED PREVIOUS
    YEAR: Approx 45—however, this was prior
    to our current expanded services and
    capacity
FOLLOW-UP EVALUATIONS: Follow-up
    evaluations are being considered

Newington

38. Newington Children's Hospital

181 E Cedar St, Newington, CT 06111
(203) 667-5350
CONTACT: Steven Broyde
FAX: (203) 667-5284
DATE ESTABLISHED: 1980
EATING DISORDERS TREATED: Anorexia
    nervosa; Bulimia nervosa
TREATMENT/THERAPY: Psychological;
    Individual; Family; Adolescent;
    Multidisciplinary; Pediatric setting
SETTING: Hospital; In-patient; Out-patient
PROGRAM LENGTH: 6-8 wks
NO. OF PATIENTS PROGRAM CAN SERVE: 62
FOLLOW-UP EVALUATIONS: Aftercare

DISTRICT OF COLUMBIA

Washington

39. Children's National Medical Center

111 Michigan Ave NW, Washington, DC
20010
(202) 745-3067
CONTACT: Darlene M Atkins, PhD
CONTACT TELEPHONE: (202) 745-2178
FAX: (202) 939-4492
DATE ESTABLISHED: 1970
EATING DISORDERS TREATED: Anorexia
    nervosa; Bulimia nervosa; Compulsive
    overeating/obesity; Diabetes protocol;
    Swallowing phobias
TREATMENT/THERAPY: Psychological; Group;
    Individual; Family; Adolescent; Nutrition
    counseling; Pharmacotherapy; In-patient

school program; Holistic model; Out-
    patient education; Exercise; Body image;
    Multidisciplinary team; In-patient medical
    unit (not psychiatric)
SETTING: Hospital; In-patient; Out-patient;
    Suburban satellite clinics
PROGRAM LENGTH: 4 wks bulimia; 6 wks
    anorexia nervosa
NO. OF PATIENTS PROGRAM CAN SERVE: 8 in-
    patients; Unlimited out-patients; NO.
    TREATED PREVIOUS YEAR: 50-75
FOLLOW-UP EVALUATIONS: Ongoing
    psychological and medical; Structured
    interviews; Nutritional and medical
    parameters

40. Georgetown University Diet Management and Eating Disorders Program

L L Gorman Bldg, 3800 Reservoir Rd,
Washington, DC 20007
(202) 687-8128
CONTACT: Sheila Ramsey, MA
DATE ESTABLISHED: 1974
EATING DISORDERS TREATED: Anorexia
    nervosa; Bulimia nervosa; Compulsive
    overeating/obesity
TREATMENT/THERAPY: Psychological; Group;
    Individual; Family; Adolescent; Body
    image; Multidisciplinary treatment team:
    physicians, therapists, dieticians, health
    educator
SETTING: Out-patient
PROGRAM LENGTH: Individualized
NO. OF PATIENTS PROGRAM CAN SERVE: 100/wk;
    80 individuals, 20 groups; NO. TREATED
    PREVIOUS YEAR: 120
FOLLOW-UP EVALUATIONS: 6 mos; 12 mos;
    Scheduled aftercare follow-up sessions

41. Psychiatric Institute of Washington DC, Minirth-Meier-Byrd Unit

4118 Wisconsin Ave NW, Washington, DC
20015
(202) 965-8228
CONTACT: Jeannette Williams
DATE ESTABLISHED: 1990
EATING DISORDERS TREATED: Anorexia
    nervosa; Bulimia nervosa; Compulsive
    overeating/obesity
TREATMENT/THERAPY: Addiction;
    Psychological; Group; Individual; Family;
    Holistic model; 12-step; Creative arts;
    Body image; Biblical base of all therapy
SETTING: Hospital; In-patient
PROGRAM LENGTH: 3-6 wks
NO. OF PATIENTS PROGRAM CAN SERVE: 8; NO.
    TREATED PREVIOUS YEAR: Approx 50
FOLLOW-UP EVALUATIONS: Out-patient follow-
    up for all

42. Washington Hospital Center
110 Irving St NW, Washington, DC 20010
(202) 829-2026
EATING DISORDERS TREATED: Anorexia
nervosa; Bulimia nervosa

FLORIDA

Altamonte Springs

43. Renaissance Counseling Center
370 Whooping Loop, Ste 1154, Altamonte
Springs, FL 32701
(407) 260-5451
CONTACT: Trish Rose
DATE ESTABLISHED: 1987
EATING DISORDERS TREATED: Anorexia
nervosa; Bulimia nervosa; Compulsive
overeating/obesity
TREATMENT/THERAPY: Psychological; Group;
Individual; Family; Adolescent; Holistic
model; 12-step; Creative arts; Out-patient
education; Exercise; Body image

Coconut Creek

44. Renfrew Center
7700 Renfrew Ln, Coconut Creek, FL 33073
(305) 698-9222
CONTACT: Adrienne Ressler
CONTACT TELEPHONE: 1990
HOTLINE: (800) 332-8415
FAX: (305) 698-9007
DATE ESTABLISHED: 1990
EATING DISORDERS TREATED: Anorexia
nervosa; Bulimia nervosa; Compulsive
overeating/obesity
TREATMENT/THERAPY: Psychological; Group;
Individual; Family; Adolescent; Creative
arts; Exercise; Body image
SETTING: In-patient; Out-patient; Residential
treatment facility
PROGRAM LENGTH: 7-9 wks
NO. OF PATIENTS PROGRAM CAN SERVE: 40; NO.
TREATED PREVIOUS YEAR: 300
FOLLOW-UP EVALUATIONS: Aftercare

Coral Gables

**45. Anorexia and Bulimia Resource
Center**
255 Alhambra Cr, No. 321, Coral Gables, FL
33134
(305) 444-3731
CONTACT: Paula Levine, PhD
DATE ESTABLISHED: 1983
EATING DISORDERS TREATED: Anorexia
nervosa; Bulimia nervosa; Compulsive
overeating/obesity

TREATMENT/THERAPY: Psychological; Group;
Individual; Family; Adolescent; Couples;
Out-patient education; Body image
SETTING: Out-patient
PROGRAM LENGTH: 3 mos-3 yrs; 12-wk
freedom from bulimia group workshop
NO. OF PATIENTS PROGRAM CAN SERVE: 100/wk;
NO. TREATED PREVIOUS YEAR: 500-600
FOLLOW-UP EVALUATIONS: 6 mos; Phone calls

Hialeah

46. Glenbeigh Hospital of Miami
4425 W 20th Ave, Hialeah, FL 33012
(305) 558-9999
CONTACT: Lesly Schermer
CONTACT TELEPHONE: (305) 558-9999 ext 186
HOTLINE: (800) 234-9990
FAX: (305) 828-3297
DATE ESTABLISHED: 1987
EATING DISORDERS TREATED: Anorexia
nervosa; Bulimia nervosa; Compulsive
overeating/obesity
TREATMENT/THERAPY: Addiction;
Psychological; Group; Individual; Family;
12-step; Creative arts; Out-patient
education; Exercise; Body image; Aftercare
education
SETTING: In-patient
PROGRAM LENGTH: 28 days
NO. OF PATIENTS PROGRAM CAN SERVE: 20
FOLLOW-UP EVALUATIONS: 6 mos; 12 mos;
Recharges; Aftercare

Hollywood

**47. The Rader Institute at Hollywood
Medical Center**
3600 Washington St, Hollywood, FL 33021
(305) 985-6292
FAX: (305) 985-6245
DATE ESTABLISHED: 1986
EATING DISORDERS TREATED: Anorexia
nervosa; Bulimia nervosa; Compulsive
overeating/obesity
TREATMENT/THERAPY: Psychological; Group;
Individual; Family; Adolescent; 12-step;
Creative arts; Out-patient education;
Exercise; Body image
SETTING: Hospital; In-patient; Out-patient
NO. OF PATIENTS PROGRAM CAN SERVE: 12-18
in-patients; NO. TREATED PREVIOUS YEAR:
Over 100
FOLLOW-UP EVALUATIONS: 6 mos; 12 mos;
Each yr; Status of patient

Kissimmee

48. Charter Hospital Orlando
206 Park Place Dr, Kissimmee, FL 34741
(800) 877-5863
CONTACT: Marie Shafe
CONTACT TELEPHONE: (407) 646-2390
EATING DISORDERS TREATED: Anorexia
nervosa; Bulimia nervosa; Compulsive
overeating/obesity
TREATMENT/THERAPY: Addiction;
Psychological; Group; Individual; Family;
Adolescent; Holistic model; 12-step;
Creative arts; Out-patient education;
Exercise; Body image
SETTING: Hospital; In-patient; Out-patient
PROGRAM LENGTH: Usually 28 days in-patient;
Out-patient varies, 3-6 mos average
FOLLOW-UP EVALUATIONS: Aftercare groups

Naples

49. The Willough at Naples
9001 Tamiami Trail E, Naples, FL 33962
(813) 775-4500
CONTACT: Christie Jones
CONTACT TELEPHONE: (813) 775-4500
HOTLINE: (800) 722-0100
FAX: (813) 793-0534
DATE ESTABLISHED: 1984
EATING DISORDERS TREATED: Anorexia
nervosa; Bulimia nervosa
TREATMENT/THERAPY: Addiction;
Psychological; Group; Individual; Family;
Experiential; Holistic model; 12-step;
Exercise; Body image; Nutrition program
SETTING: Hospital; In-patient
PROGRAM LENGTH: Varies
NO. OF PATIENTS PROGRAM CAN SERVE: 64; NO.
TREATED PREVIOUS YEAR: 420
FOLLOW-UP EVALUATIONS: 6 mos; 12 mos;
Alumni groups weekly; Aftercare; Cator
outcome studies (independent evaluator, St
Paul, MN)

North Miami Beach

50. Jewish Family Services Eating Disorders Program
18999 Biscayne Blvd, Ste 200, North Miami
Beach, FL 33162
(305) 933-9820
EATING DISORDERS TREATED: Anorexia
nervosa; Bulimia nervosa; Compulsive
overeating/obesity

Ocala

51. Charter Springs Hospital, Psychiatric Unit
3130 SW 27th Ave, Ocala, FL 32674
(800) 334-1455
CONTACT: Joe Melocchi, Prog Admin
EATING DISORDERS TREATED: Anorexia
nervosa; Bulimia nervosa; Compulsive
overeating/obesity
TREATMENT/THERAPY: Psychological; Group;
Individual; Family; Adolescent; Creative
arts; Out-patient education; Exercise; Body
image; Nutrition program; Relaxation
SETTING: Hospital; In-patient; Out-patient
PROGRAM LENGTH: Varies
FOLLOW-UP EVALUATIONS: Aftercare

Orlando

52. Florida Hospital—Eating/Affective Disorders Unit
601 E Rollins St, Orlando, FL 32803
(407) 897-1801
CONTACT: Richard C W Hall, MD, Prog Dir
CONTACT TELEPHONE: (407) 897-1801
HOTLINE: (407) 897-1800
FAX: (407) 897-5778
DATE ESTABLISHED: 1984
EATING DISORDERS TREATED: Anorexia
nervosa; Bulimia nervosa; Compulsive
overeating/obesity
TREATMENT/THERAPY: Psychological; Group;
Individual; Family; Adolescent; Creative
arts; Out-patient education; Exercise; Body
image; Out-patient psychotherapy
SETTING: Hospital; In-patient; Out-patient
PROGRAM LENGTH: Individualized
NO. OF PATIENTS PROGRAM CAN SERVE: 16; NO.
TREATED PREVIOUS YEAR: 80
FOLLOW-UP EVALUATIONS: Follow-up
evaluations as necessary; Weekly aftercare
group; 3-mo evaluation

53. Janet Greeson's A Place for Us
PO Box 720895, Orlando, FL 32872-0895
(800) 543-3662
CONTACT: Beatrice Cohen, PR Dir
CONTACT TELEPHONE: (800) 633-6268
HOTLINE: (800) 633-6268
FAX: (407) 339-0725
DATE ESTABLISHED: 1985
EATING DISORDERS TREATED: Anorexia
nervosa; Bulimia nervosa; Compulsive
overeating/obesity
TREATMENT/THERAPY: Group; Individual;
Family; Psychotherapy; Holistic model; 12-
step; Exercise; Body image
SETTING: Hospital; In-patient
PROGRAM LENGTH: 16-28 days

Janet Greeson's A Place for Us
(continued)

NO. OF PATIENTS PROGRAM CAN SERVE: 180; NO.
  TREATED PREVIOUS YEAR: 2200
FOLLOW-UP EVALUATIONS: 5 yrs; Alumni,
  critique, questionnaires

Ormond Beach

**54. Peninsula Medical Center Eating
Disorders Program**
264 S Atlantic Ave, Ormond Beach, FL
32176
(904) 672-4161; (800) 288-5856
CONTACT: Rosemary Rogers, Prog Dir
DATE ESTABLISHED: 1985
EATING DISORDERS TREATED: Anorexia
  nervosa; Bulimia nervosa; Compulsive
  overeating/obesity
TREATMENT/THERAPY: Psychological; Group;
  Individual; Family; 12-step; Creative arts;
  Body image; Stress management; Dual
  diagnosis
SETTING: Hospital; In-patient; Out-patient
PROGRAM LENGTH: 1-3 wks

Pensacola

55. Baptist Hospital
PO Box 17500, 1101 W Moreno St,
Pensacola, FL 32522
(904) 434-4866
CONTACT: Dr Szmurlo, Prog Dir
EATING DISORDERS TREATED: Anorexia
  nervosa; Bulimia nervosa; Compulsive
  overeating/obesity
TREATMENT/THERAPY: Addiction; Group;
  Individual; Family; Adolescent; 12-step;
  Creative arts; Out-patient education; Body
  image
SETTING: Hospital; In-patient; Out-patient
PROGRAM LENGTH: 3-4 wks
FOLLOW-UP EVALUATIONS: Aftercare

Seminole

**56. The Rader Institute at Women's
Medical Center**
9675 Seminole Blvd, Seminole, FL 34642
(813) 398-3350
CONTACT: Anne McWeeney
FAX: (813) 398-3305
DATE ESTABLISHED: 1988
EATING DISORDERS TREATED: Anorexia
  nervosa; Bulimia nervosa; Compulsive
  overeating/obesity
TREATMENT/THERAPY: Addiction;
  Psychological; Group; Individual; Family;
  Holistic model; 12-step; Out-patient

education; Exercise; Body image; Extensive
  family therapy program; Long-term
  aftercare
SETTING: Hospital; In-patient; Out-patient;
  Partial hospitalization
PROGRAM LENGTH: 30-40 days
NO. OF PATIENTS PROGRAM CAN SERVE: 14; NO.
  TREATED PREVIOUS YEAR: 150
FOLLOW-UP EVALUATIONS: 6 mos; 12 mos

Tampa

**57. Glenbeigh Hospital of Tampa Food
Addiction Unit**
3102 E 138th Ave, Tampa, FL 33613
(813) 971-5000
CONTACT: Martha Simmons
CONTACT TELEPHONE: (800) 444-4434
HOTLINE: (800) 444-4434
FAX: (813) 971-6210
DATE ESTABLISHED: 1986
EATING DISORDERS TREATED: Anorexia
  nervosa; Bulimia nervosa; Compulsive
  overeating/obesity
TREATMENT/THERAPY: Addiction; Group;
  Individual; Family; Adolescent; Holistic
  model; 12-step; Out-patient education;
  Exercise; Body image; Dual diagnosis
SETTING: Hospital; In-patient; Partial
  hospitalization
PROGRAM LENGTH: Individualized
NO. OF PATIENTS PROGRAM CAN SERVE: 50; NO.
  TREATED PREVIOUS YEAR: 360
FOLLOW-UP EVALUATIONS: Recharge weeks and
  weekends; Liaison with therapists for 6
  mos after discharge, if appropriate

58. Turning Point of Tampa
6301 Memorial Hwy, Ste 202/203, Tampa,
FL 33615
(813) 882-3003
CONTACT: Barbara Bollenback, Dir
CONTACT TELEPHONE: (813) 882-3003
FAX: (813) 885-6974
DATE ESTABLISHED: 1989
EATING DISORDERS TREATED: Anorexia
  nervosa; Bulimia nervosa; Compulsive
  overeating/obesity; Any accompanying
  sexual trauma, chemical dependency, or
  co-dependency
TREATMENT/THERAPY: Addiction;
  Psychological; Group; Individual; Menu
  planning; Grocery shopping; Basic cooking;
  12-step; Out-patient education; Exercise
  Individual fitness assessment and fitness
  treatment plan; Body image; Day care
  program, Level I; Work or school, Level II
SETTING: Extended residential treatment: Day
  care, Level I, halfway house, Level II;
  Maintain contact with the referring facility
  with monthly progress reports

PROGRAM LENGTH: 3, 6, 12 mos
NO. OF PATIENTS PROGRAM CAN SERVE: 25; NO.
TREATED PREVIOUS YEAR: 100
FOLLOW-UP EVALUATIONS: Aftercare; Monthly
follow-up phone calls

59. University of South Florida College of Medicine, Eating Disorders Clinic

3515 E Fletcher, Tampa, FL 33613
(813) 974-2201
CONTACT: Dr Pauline Power
EATING DISORDERS TREATED: Anorexia
nervosa; Bulimia nervosa; Compulsive
overeating/obesity
TREATMENT/THERAPY: Group; Individual;
Family; Adolescent; Holistic model; Body
image
SETTING: In-patient; Out-patient
PROGRAM LENGTH: Varies, 30-60 days

West Palm Beach

60. Glenbeigh Hospital of the Palm Beaches

4700 N Congress Ave, West Palm Beach, FL
33407
(407) 848-5500
CONTACT: Linda C Casey, Dir of Nursing
CONTACT TELEPHONE: (407) 848-5500 ext 138
HOTLINE: (800) 926-9355
FAX: (407) 863-8077
DATE ESTABLISHED: 1988
EATING DISORDERS TREATED: Anorexia
nervosa; Bulimia nervosa; Compulsive
overeating/obesity; Food addiction
TREATMENT/THERAPY: Addiction;
Psychological; Group; Individual; Family;
Adolescent; Family co-dependent week;
Holistic model; 12-step; Creative arts; Out-
patient education; Exercise; Body image
SETTING: Hospital
PROGRAM LENGTH: 30 days and out-patient
aftercare
NO. OF PATIENTS PROGRAM CAN SERVE: 15
adolescents, 15 adults
FOLLOW-UP EVALUATIONS: Written

Winter Haven

61. Rader Institute Eating Disorders Unit—Winterhaven Hosptial at Regency Medical Center

101 Ave "O," SE, Winter Haven, FL 33880
(813) 294-7010
CONTACT: Josie Sullivan, Intake Coord
CONTACT TELEPHONE: (800) 274-7015
HOTLINE: (800) 255-1818
EATING DISORDERS TREATED: Anorexia
nervosa; Bulimia nervosa; Compulsive
overeating/obesity

TREATMENT/THERAPY: Addiction;
Psychological; Group; Individual; Family;
Adolescent; 12-step; Out-patient education;
Exercise; Body image
SETTING: Hospital; In-patient; Partial
hospitalization/day treatment
NO. OF PATIENTS PROGRAM CAN SERVE: 14; NO.
TREATED PREVIOUS YEAR: 125
FOLLOW-UP EVALUATIONS: Continuing care;
Alumni program

GEORGIA

Atlanta

62. Advance

4200 Northside Pkwy, No. 2, Atlanta, GA
30327
(404) 231-3906
CONTACT: Carole Anderson, Prog Dir
EATING DISORDERS TREATED: Anorexia
nervosa; Bulimia nervosa; Compulsive
overeating/obesity
TREATMENT/THERAPY: Psychological; Group;
Individual; Family; Holistic model; 12-
step; Creative arts; Out-patient education;
Exercise; Body image; Family systems
model; Nutrition program
SETTING: Hospital; In-patient; Out-patient
PROGRAM LENGTH: 30 day in-patient
minimum
NO. OF PATIENTS PROGRAM CAN SERVE: 12
FOLLOW-UP EVALUATIONS: Extended care
program

63. Northside Hospital Education Center

1000 Johnson Ferry Rd NE, Atlanta, GA
30342
(404) 851-8741, 851-8954
CONTACT: Lucia Martin
CONTACT TELEPHONE: (404) 851-8954
DATE ESTABLISHED: 1990
EATING DISORDERS TREATED: Anorexia
nervosa; Bulimia nervosa; Compulsive
overeating/obesity
TREATMENT/THERAPY: Psychological; Group;
Individual; 12-step; Creative arts; Out-
patient education; Body image; Food
journals
SETTING: Hospital; In-patient; Out-patient
PROGRAM LENGTH: Varies, though generally 8
wks
NO. OF PATIENTS PROGRAM CAN SERVE: 6-8
people
FOLLOW-UP EVALUATIONS: Aftercare

Clayton

64. Woodridge Hospital

PO Box 1764, Clayton, GA 30525
(404) 782-3100
CONTACT: Dr Don Cornelius, Clinical Dir
HOTLINE: (800) 235-7759
DATE ESTABLISHED: 1984
EATING DISORDERS TREATED: Anorexia
nervosa; Bulimia nervosa; Compulsive
overeating/obesity
TREATMENT/THERAPY: Addiction;
Psychological; Group; Individual; Family;
Adolescent; 12-step; Creative arts;
Exercise; Body image
SETTING: Hospital; In-patient
PROGRAM LENGTH: 15-30 days
NO. OF PATIENTS PROGRAM CAN SERVE: 34
FOLLOW-UP EVALUATIONS: Aftercare for 2 yrs

Decatur

65. Decatur Hospital Eating Disorders Program

450 N Chandler St, Decatur, GA 30030
(404) 377-0221
CONTACT: Diane Harris
CONTACT TELEPHONE: (404) 377-5768
HOTLINE: (800) 783-7318
FAX: (404) 371-0930
DATE ESTABLISHED: 1983
EATING DISORDERS TREATED: Anorexia
nervosa; Bulimia nervosa; Compulsive
overeating/obesity
TREATMENT/THERAPY: Addiction; Group;
Individual; Family; 12-step; Out-patient
education; Exercise; Body image
SETTING: Hospital; In-patient; Out-patient
PROGRAM LENGTH: 28 days in-patients; 5 wks
out-patients
NO. OF PATIENTS PROGRAM CAN SERVE: 10
eating disorder in-patients/mo; 22 alcohol
and drug in-patients/mo; 50 out-patients/
mo; NO. TREATED PREVIOUS YEAR: Approx
500
FOLLOW-UP EVALUATIONS: Continuing care up
to 2 yrs

Savannah

66. The Clark Center, Memorial Medical Center

5002 Waters Ave, Savannah, GA 31403
(912) 351-5600
CONTACT: Julie DeLettre, Prog Coord
HOTLINE: (800) 548-8169
DATE ESTABLISHED: 1987
EATING DISORDERS TREATED: Anorexia
nervosa; Bulimia nervosa; Compulsive
overeating/obesity

TREATMENT/THERAPY: Addiction;
Psychological; Group; Individual; Family;
Adolescent; Aftercare group; Holistic
model; 12-step; Creative arts; Out-patient
education; Exercise; Body image
SETTING: Hospital; In-patient; Out-patient
PROGRAM LENGTH: Individualized; Out-patient
program, approx 8 wks
NO. OF PATIENTS PROGRAM CAN SERVE: 10-15
in-patient/out-patient; Up to 30 aftercare;
NO. TREATED PREVIOUS YEAR: Approx 100
FOLLOW-UP EVALUATIONS: Weekly aftercare
group

Smyrna

67. Smyrna Hospital Advance

3949 S Cobb Dr, Smyrna, GA 30081
(404) 436-3162
CONTACT: Carol Anderson
CONTACT TELEPHONE: (404) 438-5218
EATING DISORDERS TREATED: Anorexia
nervosa; Bulimia nervosa; Compulsive
overeating/obesity
TREATMENT/THERAPY: Addiction; Group;
Individual; Family; Holistic model; 12-
step; Creative arts; Out-patient education;
Exercise; Body image; Nutrition program
SETTING: Hospital; In-patient; Out-patient
PROGRAM LENGTH: In-patient, 30 days
NO. OF PATIENTS PROGRAM CAN SERVE: In-
patients, 10
FOLLOW-UP EVALUATIONS: Extended care
program

HAWAII

Ewa Beach

68. Kahi Mohala Hospital

91-2301 Fort Weaver Rd, Ewa Beach, HI
96706
(808) 671-8511; (800) 999-9889
CONTACT: Kristen Lindsey-Dudley, Coord
EATING DISORDERS TREATED: Anorexia
nervosa; Bulimia nervosa; Compulsive
overeating/obesity
TREATMENT/THERAPY: Psychological; Group;
Individual; Family; Adolescent; Body
image; Recreational
SETTING: Hospital; In-patient; Out-patient
PROGRAM LENGTH: Varies

IDAHO

Boise

69. Intermountain Hospital Psychiatric Unit
303 Allumbaugh, Boise, ID 83704
(208) 377-8400
EATING DISORDERS TREATED: Anorexia
  nervosa; Bulimia nervosa
TREATMENT/THERAPY: Addiction;
  Psychological; Individual; Adolescent; 12-
  step; Dual diagnosis
SETTING: Hospital; In-patient

ILLINOIS

Aurora

70. Mercy Center for Health Care Services
1325 N Highland Ave, Aurora, IL 60506
(708) 801-2777
CONTACT: Patricia Santucci, MD
FAX: (708) 801-2687
DATE ESTABLISHED: 1989
EATING DISORDERS TREATED: Anorexia
  nervosa; Bulimia nervosa
TREATMENT/THERAPY: Psychological; Group;
  Individual; Family; Adolescent; Holistic
  model; Creative arts; Out-patient
  education; Exercise; Body image; Females
  only Nutrition program; Medication
  management; Support group (ANAD)
SETTING: Hospital; In-patient; Out-patient;
  Partial hospitalization
PROGRAM LENGTH: Varies
NO. OF PATIENTS PROGRAM CAN SERVE: 8; NO.
  TREATED PREVIOUS YEAR: 60-70
FOLLOW-UP EVALUATIONS: Aftercare available

Chicago

71. Northwestern Medical Faculty Foundation Eating Disorders Program— Northwestern Memorial Hospital
446 E Ontario, 8th Fl, Chicago, IL 60611
(312) 908-7850
CONTACT: Dr Dan Kirschenbaum, Dir
EATING DISORDERS TREATED: Anorexia
  nervosa; Bulimia nervosa; Compulsive
  overeating/obesity
TREATMENT/THERAPY: Psychological; Group;
  Individual; Family; Adolescent; Creative
  arts; Out-patient education; Body image
SETTING: Hospital; In-patient; Out-patient
PROGRAM LENGTH: Varies
FOLLOW-UP EVALUATIONS: Aftercare

72. The Rader Institute at Belmont Community Hospital
4058 W Melrose Ave, Chicago, IL 60641
(312) 736-8693
CONTACT: Laureeann E Lerner
CONTACT TELEPHONE: (312) 736-8693
HOTLINE: (800) 437-HEAL
FAX: (312) 202-4366
DATE ESTABLISHED: 1988
EATING DISORDERS TREATED: Anorexia
  nervosa; Bulimia nervosa; Compulsive
  overeating/obesity; Depression concurrent
  with eating disorder
TREATMENT/THERAPY: Addiction;
  Psychological; Group; Individual; Family;
  Adolescent; Holistic model; 12-step; Out-
  patient education; Exercise; Body image
SETTING: Hospital; In-patient; Out-patient
  Day hospital
PROGRAM LENGTH: 6 wks in-patient, plus 12
  wks aftercare; Out-patient, 6 mos
NO. OF PATIENTS PROGRAM CAN SERVE: 30 in-
  patients; 10 day patients; 20 out-patients;
  NO. TREATED PREVIOUS YEAR: 144
FOLLOW-UP EVALUATIONS: Alumni group
  weekly; Patient self-survey

73. University of Chicago Medical Center, Department of Psychiatry Eating Disorders Program
5841 S Maryland Ave, Chicago, IL 60637
(312) 947-1000
CONTACT: Dr Regina Casper
CONTACT TELEPHONE: (312) 702-5844
EATING DISORDERS TREATED: Anorexia
  nervosa; Bulimia nervosa; Compulsive
  overeating/obesity
TREATMENT/THERAPY: Psychological; Group;
  Individual; Family; Creative arts; Out-
  patient education; Exercise; Body image
SETTING: Hospital; In-patient; Out-patient
PROGRAM LENGTH: Varies
NO. OF PATIENTS PROGRAM CAN SERVE: 6-8
  people
FOLLOW-UP EVALUATIONS: 8-10 yrs of patient
  evaluation studies

Des Plaines

74. Forest Hospital
555 Wilson Ln, Des Plaines, IL 60016
(708) 635-4100
CONTACT: Paulette Trumm, MD, Prog Dir
CONTACT TELEPHONE: (708) 612-5477
HOTLINE: (800) 866-9600
FAX: (708) 827-0368
DATE ESTABLISHED: 1985
EATING DISORDERS TREATED: Anorexia
  nervosa; Bulimia nervosa; Compulsive
  overeating/obesity

Forest Hospital *(continued)*

TREATMENT/THERAPY: Psychological; Group;
Individual; Adolescent; 12-step; Creative
arts; Out-patient education; Exercise; Body
image
SETTING: Hospital; In-patient; Out-patient
PROGRAM LENGTH: Varies
NO. OF PATIENTS PROGRAM CAN SERVE: 10-12
in-patients; NO. TREATED PREVIOUS YEAR: 60
FOLLOW-UP EVALUATIONS: Weekly aftercare for
compulsive overeating; Aftercare program

**75. HELP—Healthy Eating Lifestyle
Program**
1695 Elk Blvd, Des Plaines, IL 60016
(708) 298-HELP
CONTACT: John L Levitt, PhD
HOTLINE: (800) 437-SAFE
DATE ESTABLISHED: 1983
EATING DISORDERS TREATED: Anorexia
nervosa; Bulimia nervosa; Compulsive
overeating/obesity
TREATMENT/THERAPY: Addiction;
Psychological; Group; Individual; Family;
Adolescent; 12-step; Creative arts; Out-
patient education; Exercise; Body image
SETTING: Hospital; In-patient; Out-patient
PROGRAM LENGTH: Varies
FOLLOW-UP EVALUATIONS: Aftercare; Partial
hospitalization, day treatment; Client-
family education/support

Highland Park

**76. Highland Park Hospital—The
Center on 3-East**
718 Glenview, Highland Park, IL 60035
(708) 432-8000 ext 1397
CONTACT: Jean Montrimas, RN; Vivian
Meehan, RN
CONTACT TELEPHONE: (708) 480-3990; 480-
3961
DATE ESTABLISHED: 1985
EATING DISORDERS TREATED: Anorexia
nervosa; Bulimia nervosa; Compulsive
overeating/obesity
TREATMENT/THERAPY: Psychological; Group;
Individual; Family; Adolescent; Multidimensional; Psychodynamic; Creative
arts; Out-patient education; Exercise; Body
image; Nutrition counseling
SETTING: Hospital; In-patient; Out-patient
PROGRAM LENGTH: Varies—preferred stay, 4-6
wks on work with individual capabilities
NO. OF PATIENTS PROGRAM CAN SERVE: In-
patient, 6; Out-patient, 6; Family therapy,
unlimited
FOLLOW-UP EVALUATIONS: Ongoing therapy,
individual and family

Hoffman Estates

77. HCA Woodland Hospital
1650 Moon Lake Blvd, Hoffman Estates, IL
60194
(708) 882-1600
CONTACT: Janet Behrens, RN
HOTLINE: (800) 342-0469
FAX: (708) 843-6557
DATE ESTABLISHED: 1990
EATING DISORDERS TREATED: Anorexia
nervosa; Bulimia nervosa; Compulsive
overeating/obesity
TREATMENT/THERAPY: Psychological; Group;
Individual; Family; Adolescent; Underlying
sexual trauma; 12-step; Creative arts; Out-
patient education; Exercise; Body image;
Females only
SETTING: Hospital; In-patient; Out-patient
PROGRAM LENGTH: 2-6 wks
NO. OF PATIENTS PROGRAM CAN SERVE: 22; NO.
TREATED PREVIOUS YEAR: 21
FOLLOW-UP EVALUATIONS: As determined by
therapist

Park Ridge

78. Parkside Lutheran Hospital
1700 Luther Ln, Park Ridge, IL 60068
(708) 696-6050
CONTACT: Debbie Costabilo; Nancy Scovill
CONTACT TELEPHONE: (708) 696-5653
HOTLINE: (800) PARKSIDE
FAX: (708) 698-4068
DATE ESTABLISHED: 1982
EATING DISORDERS TREATED: Anorexia
nervosa; Bulimia nervosa; Compulsive
overeating/obesity
TREATMENT/THERAPY: Addiction; Group;
Individual; Family; Holistic model; 12-
step; Out-patient education; Exercise; Body
image
SETTING: Hospital; In-patient; Out-patient
PROGRAM LENGTH: Approx 6 wks in-patient;
6-8 wks out-patient
NO. OF PATIENTS PROGRAM CAN SERVE: 20-25
in-patient; 10 out-patient
FOLLOW-UP EVALUATIONS: 6 mos; 12 mos

79. Parkside Medical Services Corp
205 W Touhy, Park Ridge, IL 60068
(708) 698-4778
CONTACT: Gina Priestley
FAX: (708) 318-0966
DATE ESTABLISHED: 1982
EATING DISORDERS TREATED: Anorexia
nervosa; Bulimia nervosa; Compulsive
overeating/obesity
TREATMENT/THERAPY: Addiction;
Psychological; Group; Individual; Family;
Adolescent; Daily living skills; Holistic

model; 12-step; Creative arts; Out-patient education; Exercise; Body image; 6 to 9 mos independent living program after primary treatment, if needed
SETTING: Hospital; In-patient; Out-patient
PROGRAM LENGTH: Individualized
FOLLOW-UP EVALUATIONS: 6 mos; 12 mos; Weekly continuing care groups up to 2 yrs; Questionnaires

INDIANA

Indianapolis

80. Charter Hospital of Indianapolis Eating Disorders Program
5602 Caito Dr, Indianapolis, IN 46226
(317) 545-2111
HOTLINE: (800) 843-9299
FAX: (317) 549-0838
EATING DISORDERS TREATED: Anorexia nervosa; Bulimia nervosa; Compulsive overeating/obesity
TREATMENT/THERAPY: Addiction; Psychological; Group; Individual; Family; Adolescent; 12-step; Out-patient education; Exercise; Body image; Dual diagnosis
SETTING: Hospital; In-patient; Out-patient
PROGRAM LENGTH: In-patient: Adult 2-4 wks; Adolescent 4-6 wks

81. Indiana University Hospital Eating Disorders Program
926 W Michigan St, Indianapolis, IN 46223
(317) 274-8928
CONTACT: Sue Rhee, Dietitian
EATING DISORDERS TREATED: Anorexia nervosa; Bulimia nervosa; Compulsive overeating/obesity
TREATMENT/THERAPY: Psychological; Group; Individual; Family; Adolescent; Out-patient education
SETTING: Hospital; In-patient; Out-patient
PROGRAM LENGTH: 6 wks

82. Winoma Memorial Hospital Corp
3232 N Meridian St, Indianapolis, IN 46208
(317) 924-3392
CONTACT: Denise Bush, Prog Mgr
DATE ESTABLISHED: 1984
EATING DISORDERS TREATED: Anorexia nervosa; Bulimia nervosa; Compulsive overeating/obesity
TREATMENT/THERAPY: Psychological; Group; Individual; Family; Adolescent; Creative arts; Out-patient education; Exercise; Body image
SETTING: Hospital; In-patient; Out-patient
PROGRAM LENGTH: Varies, 14 days average
NO. OF PATIENTS PROGRAM CAN SERVE: 16
FOLLOW-UP EVALUATIONS: Aftercare

IOWA

Des Moines

83. Iowa Lutheran Hospital—Eating Disorders Treatment Center
University and Penn St, Des Moines, IA 50316
(515) 263-5612
CONTACT: Paula McManus, RN, CC, MS
CONTACT TELEPHONE: (515) 263-5672
HOTLINE: (515) 263-5672 (call collect)
FAX: (515) 263-5164
DATE ESTABLISHED: 1985
EATING DISORDERS TREATED: Anorexia nervosa; Bulimia nervosa; Obese bingers
TREATMENT/THERAPY: Psychological; Group; Individual; Family; Adolescent; Out-patient education; Exercise; Body image
SETTING: Hospital
PROGRAM LENGTH: Varies
NO. OF PATIENTS PROGRAM CAN SERVE: 10 in-patients and partial hospitalization; 10-20 out-patients/wk; NO. TREATED PREVIOUS YEAR: 150-200
FOLLOW-UP EVALUATIONS: 1 yr aftercare provided

84. Mercy Hospital Eating Disorder Unit
6th and University, Des Moines, IA 50314
(515) 247-3020
CONTACT: Pat Millin, Mgr
FAX: (515) 247-8498
DATE ESTABLISHED: 1984
EATING DISORDERS TREATED: Anorexia nervosa; Bulimia nervosa
TREATMENT/THERAPY: Psychological; Group; Individual; Family; Adolescent; Cognitive-behavioral; Out-patient education; Exercise; Body image
SETTING: Hospital; In-patient; Out-patient; Intensive day program
PROGRAM LENGTH: 4-6 wks
NO. OF PATIENTS PROGRAM CAN SERVE: 10-15/wk; NO. TREATED PREVIOUS YEAR: 50
FOLLOW-UP EVALUATIONS: 1 mo; 3 mos; 6 mos; 12 mos; Weekly aftercare meetings

Iowa City

85. University of Iowa, Department of Psychiatry
500 Newton Rd, Iowa City, IA 52242
(319) 356-1354
FAX: (319) 356-2487
DATE ESTABLISHED: 1975
EATING DISORDERS TREATED: Anorexia nervosa; Bulimia nervosa; Compulsive overeating/obesity

University of Iowa, Department of Psychiatry *(continued)*

TREATMENT/THERAPY: Psychological; Group; Individual; Family; Adolescent; Body image; Program for males is available; Chronically ill
SETTING: Hospital; In-patient; Out-patient; Diagnostic clinic
PROGRAM LENGTH: Varies
NO. OF PATIENTS PROGRAM CAN SERVE: 8; NO. TREATED PREVIOUS YEAR: 30
FOLLOW-UP EVALUATIONS: 1-5 yrs; Multimodal

Sioux City

86. St Luke's Gordon Recovery Centers
Box 2000, 2700 Pierce St, Sioux City, IA 51104
(712) 279-3960
CONTACT: Ann Jons, Dir, Adult In-patient Services
CONTACT TELEPHONE: (712) 279-3940
HOTLINE: (712) 279-3941
DATE ESTABLISHED: 1985
EATING DISORDERS TREATED: Anorexia nervosa; Bulimia nervosa; Compulsive overeating/obesity
TREATMENT/THERAPY: Addiction; Group; Individual; Family; Adolescent; In-patient and out-patient/day or evening treatment; Holistic model; 12-step; Out-patient education; Body image
SETTING: Hospital; In-patient; Out-patient; Adolescents in residential setting
PROGRAM LENGTH: Adult, 2-6 wks; Adolescents, 30-90 days
NO. OF PATIENTS PROGRAM CAN SERVE: 20 adult in-patients, 60 adult out-patients; 35 adolescent in-patients, 20 adolescent out-patients
FOLLOW-UP EVALUATIONS: 6 mos; 12 mos; Telephone call

KANSAS

Topeka

87. Menninger Clinic
PO Box 829, 5600 SW 6th Ave, Topeka, KS 66601
(913) 273-7500
EATING DISORDERS TREATED: Anorexia nervosa; Bulimia nervosa; Compulsive overeating/obesity
TREATMENT/THERAPY: Psychological; Individual; Family; Adolescent; Out-patient education; Exercise; Body image; Dual diagnosis
SETTING: Hospital; In-patient; Out-patient

NO. OF PATIENTS PROGRAM CAN SERVE: In-patient 18
FOLLOW-UP EVALUATIONS: Ongoing

KENTUCKY

Louisville

88. Norton Psychiatric Clinic, Eating Disorders Program
PO Box 35070, 200 E Chestnut, Louisville, KY 40232
(502) 629-8850
EATING DISORDERS TREATED: Anorexia nervosa; Bulimia nervosa
TREATMENT/THERAPY: Psychological; Group; Individual; Family; Adolescent; Body image
SETTING: Hospital; In-patient; Out-patient; Day hospital
PROGRAM LENGTH: Average 6 wks in-patient
NO. OF PATIENTS PROGRAM CAN SERVE: 6; NO. TREATED PREVIOUS YEAR: 36-40

LOUISIANA

Baton Rouge

89. The Rader Institute at Woman's Hospital
PO Box 95009, 9050 Airline Hwy, Baton Rouge, LA 70895-9009
(504) 924-8302
CONTACT: Rachelle Dupre, MS, LPC, MSW
CONTACT TELEPHONE: (504) 924-8302
HOTLINE: (800) 255-1818
FAX: (504) 924-8647
EATING DISORDERS TREATED: Anorexia nervosa; Bulimia nervosa; Compulsive overeating/obesity
TREATMENT/THERAPY: Addiction; Psychological; Group; Individual; Family; Adolescent; Holistic model; 12-step; Creative arts; Out-patient education; Exercise; Body image; Females only; Continuing care; Aftercare; Structured alumni program
SETTING: Hospital; In-patient; Out-patient
PROGRAM LENGTH: 30-42 days
NO. OF PATIENTS PROGRAM CAN SERVE: 13
FOLLOW-UP EVALUATIONS: They are tracked for 5 yrs

Lafayette

90. Cypress Hospital

302 Dulles Dr, Lafayette, LA 70506
(318) 233-9024
CONTACT: Beth Brooks, Prog Dir
EATING DISORDERS TREATED: Anorexia
nervosa; Bulimia nervosa; Compulsive
overeating/obesity
TREATMENT/THERAPY: Addiction;
Psychological; Group; Individual; Family;
Adolescent; 12-step; Creative arts
SETTING: Hospital; In-patient
PROGRAM LENGTH: 3-4 wks
NO. OF PATIENTS PROGRAM CAN SERVE: 36-40
FOLLOW-UP EVALUATIONS: Aftercare for
adolescent; Referral for general aftercare

New Orleans

91. Coliseum Medical Center Eating Disorders Program

3601 Coliseum, New Orleans, LA 70115
(504) 897-9700
EATING DISORDERS TREATED: Anorexia
nervosa; Bulimia nervosa; Compulsive
overeating/obesity
TREATMENT/THERAPY: Psychological; Group;
Individual; Adolescent
SETTING: Hospital; In-patient; Out-patient
PROGRAM LENGTH: Varies, 30 days average

92. Ochsner Clinic, Addictive Behavior Unit

1516 Jefferson Hwy, New Orleans, LA 70121
(504) 838-4000
EATING DISORDERS TREATED: Anorexia
nervosa; Bulimia nervosa
TREATMENT/THERAPY: Group; Individual;
Family; 12-step; Out-patient education;
Stress management
SETTING: In-patient; Out-patient
FOLLOW-UP EVALUATIONS: Aftercare for 1 yr

93. Tulane Medical Center

1415 Tulane Ave, New Orleans, LA 70112
(504) 587-2155
CONTACT: Susan G Willard, MSW
CONTACT TELEPHONE: (504) 587-2155
DATE ESTABLISHED: 1982
EATING DISORDERS TREATED: Anorexia
nervosa; Bulimia nervosa; Compulsive
overeating/obesity; Psychogenic vomiting
TREATMENT/THERAPY: Psychological; Group;
Individual; Family; Adolescent; Nutrition
program
SETTING: Out-patient

MARYLAND

Baltimore

94. The Johns Hopkins Eating and Weight Disorders Program

Meyer 101, 600 N Wolfe St, Baltimore, MD
21205
(301) 955-3863 (out-patient), 955-9333 (in-
patient)
CONTACT: James Wirth, MD, PhD
FAX: (301) 955-0946
DATE ESTABLISHED: 1976
EATING DISORDERS TREATED: Anorexia
nervosa; Bulimia nervosa; Compulsive
overeating/obesity
TREATMENT/THERAPY: Psychological; Group;
Individual; Family; Creative arts; Out-
patient education; Exercise; Body image;
Behavioral model; Relaxation therapy;
Assertiveness training
SETTING: Hospital; In-patient; Out-patient
PROGRAM LENGTH: 30 days
NO. OF PATIENTS PROGRAM CAN SERVE: 10 in-
patients; NO. TREATED PREVIOUS YEAR:
Approx 85
FOLLOW-UP EVALUATIONS: 1 mo; 6 mos; 12
mos; 18 mos

95. Mercy Hospital Eating Disorder Unit

301 St Paul Pl, Baltimore, MD 51202
(301) 332-9000
CONTACT: Dr Harry Brandt
CONTACT TELEPHONE: (301) 332-9800
EATING DISORDERS TREATED: Anorexia
nervosa; Bulimia nervosa; Compulsive
overeating/obesity
TREATMENT/THERAPY: Psychological; Group;
Individual; Family; Adolescent; Body
image; Nutrition program
SETTING: Hospital; In-patient; Out-patient;
Day treatment
PROGRAM LENGTH: Usually 3-4 wks in-patient

96. Sheppard-Pratt Hospital Eating Disorders Program

6501 N Charles St, Baltimore, MD 21209
(301) 938-3000 ext 4219
CONTACT: David Roth, PhD
CONTACT TELEPHONE: (301) 938-3000 ext 4219
HOTLINE: (301) 938-5000
DATE ESTABLISHED: 1982
EATING DISORDERS TREATED: Anorexia
nervosa; Bulimia nervosa; Compulsive
overeating/obesity
TREATMENT/THERAPY: Psychological; Group;
Individual; Family; Adolescent; Nutrition
program; Activity therapy; Movement
therapy; Pharmacotherapy; Holistic model;
Creative arts; Out-patient education;
Exercise; Body image

Sheppard-Pratt Hospital Eating Disorders Program *(continued)*

SETTING: Hospital; In-patient; Out-patient; Intensive out-patient
PROGRAM LENGTH: 4-12 wks
NO. OF PATIENTS PROGRAM CAN SERVE: 10+ in-patient; NO. TREATED PREVIOUS YEAR: 75 in-patient

Bethesda

97. National Institutes of Mental Health, Unit on Eating Disorders
9000 Rockville Pike, Bldg 10, Rm 3S, 231, Bethesda, MD 20014
(301) 496-3421
CONTACT: Dr Margaret Altemus
FAX: (301) 402-0188
DATE ESTABLISHED: 1975
EATING DISORDERS TREATED: Anorexia nervosa; Bulimia nervosa; Compulsive overeating/obesity; Depends on current research studies
TREATMENT/THERAPY: Depends on research study in progress
PROGRAM LENGTH: Varies
NO. OF PATIENTS PROGRAM CAN SERVE: Varies; NO. TREATED PREVIOUS YEAR: 60 out-patients; 20 in-patients
FOLLOW-UP EVALUATIONS: Depends on research study

MASSACHUSETTS

Belmont

98. McLean Hospital
115 Mill St, Belmont, MA 02178
(617) 855-2564
CONTACT: Dr Philip Levendusky, Prog Dir
EATING DISORDERS TREATED: Anorexia nervosa; Bulimia nervosa; Compulsive overeating/obesity
TREATMENT/THERAPY: Psychological; Group; Individual; Family; Adolescent; Body image
SETTING: Hospital; In-patient
PROGRAM LENGTH: Varies, 2-3 wks

Boston

99. Children's Hospital, Division of Adolescent/Young Adult Medicine, Out-Patient Eating Disorders Clinic
300 Longwood Ave, Boston, MA 02115
(617) 735-7178
CONTACT: Dr Alexandra Eliot, Co-Dir
CONTACT TELEPHONE: (617) 735-7178
FAX: (617) 735-7429
DATE ESTABLISHED: 1981

EATING DISORDERS TREATED: Anorexia nervosa; Bulimia nervosa; Compulsive overeating/obesity
TREATMENT/THERAPY: Group; Individual; Family; Adolescent; Holistic model; Out-patient education; Exercise; Medical psychological model; Diagnostic evaluations
SETTING: Hospital; Out-patient
PROGRAM LENGTH: Varies
NO. OF PATIENTS PROGRAM CAN SERVE: Varies; NO. TREATED PREVIOUS YEAR: 100+
FOLLOW-UP EVALUATIONS: 6 mos; 12 mos; 2 yrs; Aftercare referral

100. Hahnemann Hospital, Eating Disorders Service
1515 Commonwealth Ave, Boston, MA 02135
(617) 254-1100
CONTACT: Marilyn Weller, Coord
CONTACT TELEPHONE: (617) 254-1100 ext 606
FAX: (617) 783-1813
DATE ESTABLISHED: 1986
EATING DISORDERS TREATED: Anorexia nervosa; Bulimia nervosa; Enteric feeding program; Medical monitoring
TREATMENT/THERAPY: Psychological; Group; Individual; Family; Adolescent; Out-patient education; Body image; Skill building; Strategies to manage disorder; Development of strong out-patient supports
SETTING: Hospital; In-patient; Out-patient; Comprehensive evaluation and treatment plan
PROGRAM LENGTH: Individually determined
NO. OF PATIENTS PROGRAM CAN SERVE: 10 in-patients; NO. TREATED PREVIOUS YEAR: 65
FOLLOW-UP EVALUATIONS: Transition group, 4 meetings; Monthly informational support group

101. Massachusetts General Hospital
55 Fruit St, Boston, MA 02114
(617) 726-2000
CONTACT: Dr David Herzog, Dir
CONTACT TELEPHONE: (617) 726-2724
DATE ESTABLISHED: 1980
EATING DISORDERS TREATED: Anorexia nervosa; Bulimia nervosa; Compulsive overeating/obesity
TREATMENT/THERAPY: Psychological; Group; Individual; Family; Adolescent; Holistic model; Out-patient education; Nutrition program
SETTING: Hospital; In-patient; Out-patient
PROGRAM LENGTH: Varies
NO. OF PATIENTS PROGRAM CAN SERVE: 3-4 beds
FOLLOW-UP EVALUATIONS: Aftercare

102. New England Medical Center Hospitals
750 Washington St, Boston, MA 02146
(617) 956-5273
CONTACT: Marcia English, Coord
CONTACT TELEPHONE: (617) 956-5732
DATE ESTABLISHED: 1988
EATING DISORDERS TREATED: Anorexia nervosa; Bulimia nervosa; Compulsive overeating/obesity
TREATMENT/THERAPY: Psychological; Group; Individual; Family; Adolescent; Out-patient education; No age limits or time limits
SETTING: Out-patient
PROGRAM LENGTH: Varies
NO. OF PATIENTS PROGRAM CAN SERVE: No limit; NO. TREATED PREVIOUS YEAR: Approx 30
FOLLOW-UP EVALUATIONS: Review team every 4-8 wks for each patient

Cambridge

103. Cambridge Hospital Eating Disorders Program
1493 Cambridge St, Cambridge, MA 02139
(617) 498-1150
CONTACT: Dr Deborah Hulihan, Prog Dir
EATING DISORDERS TREATED: Anorexia nervosa; Bulimia nervosa; Compulsive overeating/obesity
TREATMENT/THERAPY: Psychological; Group; Individual; Adolescent; Out-patient education; Body image
SETTING: Hospital; Out-patient

104. Massachusetts Institute of Technology
25 Carleton, Cambridge, MA 02139
(617) 253-2916
CONTACT: Dr Margaret Ross
DATE ESTABLISHED: 1978
EATING DISORDERS TREATED: Anorexia nervosa; Bulimia nervosa; Compulsive overeating/obesity
TREATMENT/THERAPY: Individual; Adolescent; Nutrition program; Life style
SETTING: Out-patient

105. Mt Auburn Hospital Out-patient Psychiatry Center
330 Mount Auburn, Cambridge, MA 02238
(617) 499-5054
CONTACT: Joan Kraus
EATING DISORDERS TREATED: Anorexia nervosa; Bulimia nervosa; Compulsive overeating/obesity
TREATMENT/THERAPY: Psychological; Individual

New Bedford

106. Parkwood Hospital
4499 Acushnet Ave, New Bedford, MA 02745
(508) 995-4400
CONTACT: Pauline Mased
DATE ESTABLISHED: 1990
EATING DISORDERS TREATED: Anorexia nervosa; Bulimia nervosa; Compulsive overeating/obesity
TREATMENT/THERAPY: Psychological; Group; Individual; Family; Adolescent; Holistic model; 12-step; Creative arts; Body image; Relaxation
SETTING: Out-patient
PROGRAM LENGTH: 8 wks, 2 hrs 2 times/wk
FOLLOW-UP EVALUATIONS: Maintenance group ongoing 1 time/wk

Newton

107. Wellesley Hospital
2014 Washington St, Newton, MA 02162
(617) 243-6000
CONTACT: Perry L Belfer
CONTACT TELEPHONE: (617) 243-6157
DATE ESTABLISHED: 1984
EATING DISORDERS TREATED: Bulimia nervosa; Compulsive overeating/obesity
TREATMENT/THERAPY: Psychological; Group; Individual; Family; 12-step; Out-patient education; Exercise; Body image; Nutrition program
SETTING: Out-patient
PROGRAM LENGTH: Varies
NO. OF PATIENTS PROGRAM CAN SERVE: Unlimited; NO. TREATED PREVIOUS YEAR: 200-300/yr

Salem

108. North Shore Children's Hospital, Eating Disorders Program, Mental Health Center
57 Highland Ave, Salem, MA 01970
(508) 745-2100 ext 286
CONTACT: Susan Sorrentino, PhD
CONTACT TELEPHONE: (508) 745-2100 ext 286
FAX: (508) 745-5954
DATE ESTABLISHED: Early 1970s
EATING DISORDERS TREATED: Anorexia nervosa; Bulimia nervosa; Compulsive overeating/obesity
TREATMENT/THERAPY: Psychological; Group; Individual; Family; Adolescent; Psychopharmacological evaluation; Adolescent medical clinic; Nutrition program; Long-term psychotherapy is predominant model with cognitive behavioral interventions integrated into treatment plans

North Shore Children's Hospital, Eating Disorders Program, Mental Health Center (continued)

SETTING: Hospital; Out-patient
PROGRAM LENGTH: Open-ended
NO. OF PATIENTS PROGRAM CAN SERVE: 50; NO. TREATED PREVIOUS YEAR: Approximately 1400 clinical hrs
FOLLOW-UP EVALUATIONS: As needed or requested by patients

Worchester

109. University of Massachusetts Medical Center
55 Lake Ave N, Worchester, MA 01655
(508) 856-0011
CONTACT: Dr Russell Barkley
CONTACT TELEPHONE: (508) 856-3260
EATING DISORDERS TREATED: Anorexia nervosa; Bulimia nervosa; Compulsive overeating/obesity
TREATMENT/THERAPY: Psychological; Individual; Evaluation
SETTING: Out-patient
PROGRAM LENGTH: Varies
FOLLOW-UP EVALUATIONS: Support groups

MICHIGAN

Ann Arbor

110. University of Michigan Eating Disorders Program
Box 0116, 1500 E Medical Center Dr, Ann Arbor, MI 48109
(313) 936-4861
CONTACT: Ken Castagna
CONTACT TELEPHONE: (313) 936-4861
FAX: (313) 936-9761
DATE ESTABLISHED: 1983
EATING DISORDERS TREATED: Anorexia nervosa; Bulimia nervosa; Comorbid diagnosis such as depression, anxiety, alcohol and drug abuse
TREATMENT/THERAPY: Psychological; Group; Individual; Family; Nutrition program; Out-patient education; Body image
SETTING: Hospital; In-patient; Out-patient; Partial hospitalization
PROGRAM LENGTH: In-patient, 2-3 wks; Partial hospitalization, 6-8 wks; Out-patient, open-ended NO. TREATED PREVIOUS YEAR: 200+
FOLLOW-UP EVALUATIONS: 6 mos; 12 mos; Questionnaire or phone call

Battle Creek

111. Battle Creek Adventist Hospital
165 N Washington Ave, Battle Creek, MI 49016
(616) 964-7121
CONTACT: Dr Nancy Zielke
CONTACT TELEPHONE: (616) 349-2777
EATING DISORDERS TREATED: Anorexia nervosa; Bulimia nervosa; Compulsive overeating/obesity
TREATMENT/THERAPY: Psychological; Group; Individual; Family; Adolescent; Out-patient education; Exercise; Body image
SETTING: Hospital; In-patient; Out-patient
PROGRAM LENGTH: Varies
FOLLOW-UP EVALUATIONS: Continuing care; Support groups

Livonia

112. St Mary Hospital—Eating Disorders Recovery Center (EDRC)
36475 W Five Mile Rd, Livonia, MI 48154
(313) 591-2936
CONTACT: Suzanne Cullen
CONTACT TELEPHONE: (313) 591-2936
FAX: (313) 591-2992
DATE ESTABLISHED: 1986
EATING DISORDERS TREATED: Anorexia nervosa; Bulimia nervosa; Compulsive overeating/obesity
TREATMENT/THERAPY: Addiction; Group; Individual; Family; Adolescent; Exercise; Food planning; Creative arts; Out-patient education; Exercise; Body image
SETTING: Hospital; Out-patient
PROGRAM LENGTH: Varies by individual need
NO. OF PATIENTS PROGRAM CAN SERVE: No limit; NO. TREATED PREVIOUS YEAR: 60 new patients
FOLLOW-UP EVALUATIONS: Telephone; Follow-up questionnaires

MINNESOTA

Duluth

113. St Luke's Hospital Eating Disorder Treatment Center
915 E 1st St, Duluth, MN 55805
(218) 726-5506
CONTACT: Yvonne M Prettner, Prog Supv
CONTACT TELEPHONE: (218) 726-5514
HOTLINE: (218) 728-5126
FAX: (218) 726-5180
DATE ESTABLISHED: 1987
EATING DISORDERS TREATED: Anorexia nervosa; Bulimia nervosa; Compulsive overeating/obesity

TREATMENT/THERAPY: Addiction;
Psychological; Group; Individual; Family;
Adolescents assessed, treated individually
or referred; Holistic model; 12-step;
Creative arts; Out-patient education;
Exercise; Body image; Females only; Males
assessed, treated individually or referred
SETTING: Hospital; Out-patient; In-patient
stays for physiological stability only
PROGRAM LENGTH: 3 days/wk for 8 wks
NO. OF PATIENTS PROGRAM CAN SERVE: 10 in
treatment program; NO. TREATED PREVIOUS
YEAR: 35 in treatment program, many more
served in groups and individually
FOLLOW-UP EVALUATIONS: 12 mos; 24 mos pre-
and post-discharge; EDI; POI; Wooley
body chart; Quality of life questionnaire;
Program evaluation questionnaire;
Aftercare for 1 yr

Minneapolis

114. Metropolitan Clinic of Counseling Inc
1010 S 7th St, Ste 650, Minneapolis, MN
55415
(612) 333-1410 ext 329
CONTACT: Susan Bu sing
FAX: (612) 333-5706
DATE ESTABLISHED: 1980
EATING DISORDERS TREATED: Anorexia
nervosa; Bulimia nervosa; Eating disorders
not otherwise specified
TREATMENT/THERAPY: Psychological; Group;
Individual; Family; Adolescent; Out-
patient education; Nutrition program
SETTING: Out-patient
PROGRAM LENGTH: 12 wks
NO. OF PATIENTS PROGRAM CAN SERVE: 8/group;
NO. TREATED PREVIOUS YEAR: 100+

115. University of Min esota Hospital & Clinic, Department of Psychiatry, Eating Disorders
Box 301 Mayo, 420 Delaware St SE,
Minneapolis, MN 55455
(612) 626-6188, 626-3463
CONTACT: Jean Grable
DATE ESTABLISHED: 1978
EATING DISORDERS TREATED: Anorexia
nervosa; Bulimia nervosa
TREATMENT/THERAPY: Psychological; Group;
Individual; Family; Body image;
Medication management
SETTING: In-patient; Out-patient
PROGRAM LENGTH: 4-6 wks for in-patient; 3
mos minimum for out-patient
NO. OF PATIENTS PROGRAM CAN SERVE: 125 out-
patient
FOLLOW-UP EVALUATIONS: 6 mos; 12 mos

Rochester

116. Mayo Clinic
200 1st St SW, Baldwin Bldg, Rochester,
MN 55905
(507) 284-4500
CONTACT: Carol Cunningham, Coord
CONTACT TELEPHONE: (507) 284-5387
DATE ESTABLISHED: 1986
EATING DISORDERS TREATED: Anorexia
nervosa; Bulimia nervosa
TREATMENT/THERAPY: Group; Individual;
Family; Adolescent; Creative arts; Out-
patient education; Exercise; Body image;
Multimodality
SETTING: In-patient; Out-patient; Day hospital
PROGRAM LENGTH: Varies, 6-8 wks average
NO. OF PATIENTS PROGRAM CAN SERVE: 16 in-
patient
FOLLOW-UP EVALUATIONS: Aftercare
maintenance

St Louis Park

117. Eating Disorders Institute
6490 Excelsior Blvd, Meadowbrook Medical
Bldg, Ste 315E, St Louis Park, MN 55426
(612) 932-6200
CONTACT: Linda Barnhart, RN, Nurse Mgr
CONTACT TELEPHONE: (612) 932-6200
FAX: (612) 932-5936
DATE ESTABLISHED: 1987
EATING DISORDERS TREATED: Anorexia
nervosa; Bulimia nervosa; Compulsive
overeating/obesity
TREATMENT/THERAPY: Psychological; Group;
Individual; Family; Adolescent; Out-
patient education; Exercise; Body image;
Medical stabilization; Food/cooking
groups; Parenting groups
SETTING: Hospital; In-patient; Out-patient
PROGRAM LENGTH: Individualized
NO. OF PATIENTS PROGRAM CAN SERVE: 12 in-
patients; No limit for out-patients; NO.
TREATED PREVIOUS YEAR: 200
FOLLOW-UP EVALUATIONS: 6 mos; 12 mos;
Groups

MISSISSIPPI

Jackson

118. University of Mississippi Medical Center
2500 N State St, Jackson, MS 39126-4505
(601) 984-5805
CONTACT: William Johnson, PhD, Dir
FAX: (601) 984-1262
EATING DISORDERS TREATED: Anorexia
nervosa; Bulimia nervosa; Compulsive
overeating/obesity

University of Mississippi Medical Center
(continued)

TREATMENT/THERAPY: Psychological; Group; Individual; Family; Adolescent; Out-patient education; Exercise; Body image
SETTING: In-patient; Out-patient
PROGRAM LENGTH: 20 days in-patient
NO. OF PATIENTS PROGRAM CAN SERVE: Varies
FOLLOW-UP EVALUATIONS: Aftercare

MISSOURI

Poplar Bluff

119. Lucy Lee Hospital Eating Disorders Program
2620 N Westwood Blvd, Poplar Bluff, MO 63901
(314) 785-7721
CONTACT: Dr Jane Niskey, Clinical Dir
EATING DISORDERS TREATED: Anorexia nervosa; Bulimia nervosa; Compulsive overeating/obesity
TREATMENT/THERAPY: Addiction; Psychological; Group; Adolescent; 12-step
SETTING: Hospital; In-patient
PROGRAM LENGTH: 2-4 wks

St Louis

120. Eating Disorder Clinic
11709 Old Ballas, Ste 103, St Louis, MO 63141
(314) 993-8950, 837-7980, 481-8090
CONTACT: Irshad Khan
EATING DISORDERS TREATED: Anorexia nervosa; Bulimia nervosa; Compulsive overeating/obesity
TREATMENT/THERAPY: Psychological; Group; Individual; Family; Adolescent; 24-hr emergency care
SETTING: Out-patient
FOLLOW-UP EVALUATIONS: Ongoing free support group

121. Lutheran Medical Center
2639 Miami St, St Louis, MO 63118
(314) 772-1456
EATING DISORDERS TREATED: Anorexia nervosa; Bulimia nervosa; Compulsive overeating/obesity
TREATMENT/THERAPY: Addiction; Psychological; Group; Family; Adolescent; 12-step; Out-patient education; Exercise
SETTING: Hospital; In-patient; Out-patient
PROGRAM LENGTH: 4-6 wks, in-patient; 3 times/wk for 4 mos, out-patient
FOLLOW-UP EVALUATIONS: Continuing care

122. St Anthony's Psychiatric Center
10016 Kennerly Rd, St Louis, MO 63128
(314) 525-1816, 525-4400
EATING DISORDERS TREATED: Anorexia nervosa; Bulimia nervosa; Compulsive overeating/obesity
TREATMENT/THERAPY: Psychological; Group; Family; Adolescent; 12-step
SETTING: Hospital; In-patient; Out-patient
PROGRAM LENGTH: Usually 2 wks in-patient
FOLLOW-UP EVALUATIONS: Approx 20 wks aftercare

123. St John's Mercy Medical Center, Anorexia-Bulimia Treatment and Education Center (ABTEC)
615 S New Ballas Rd, St Louis, MO 63141
(314) 569-6898; (800) 22-ABTEC
CONTACT: Nancy Ellis-Ordway
FAX: (314) 569-6910 ext 6898
DATE ESTABLISHED: 1981
EATING DISORDERS TREATED: Anorexia nervosa; Bulimia nervosa
TREATMENT/THERAPY: Psychological; Group; Individual; Family; Adolescent; Creative arts; Out-patient education; Exercise; Body image
SETTING: Hospital; In-patient; Out-patient; Partial hospitalization
PROGRAM LENGTH: Varies, 3-6 wks
NO. OF PATIENTS PROGRAM CAN SERVE: 15 in-patient; NO. TREATED PREVIOUS YEAR: 150 in-patient
FOLLOW-UP EVALUATIONS: Aftercare; free support groups

MONTANA

Grass Range

124. Red Canyon Ranch
PO Box 27, Grass Range, MT 59032
(406) 428-2224
CONTACT: Pegge McCluey
HOTLINE: (800) 521-6572
FAX: (406) 428-2436
DATE ESTABLISHED: 1990
EATING DISORDERS TREATED: Bulimia nervosa; Compulsive overeating/obesity
TREATMENT/THERAPY: Addiction; Psychological; Group; Individual; Family; Adolescent; 12-step; Creative arts; Body image; Females only; Therapeutic horse riding
SETTING: In-patient
PROGRAM LENGTH: Minimum: 42 days
NO. OF PATIENTS PROGRAM CAN SERVE: 8; NO. TREATED PREVIOUS YEAR: 60
FOLLOW-UP EVALUATIONS: 3-mo evaluation with continuing care counselor; 6 mos; 12 mos; Question/answer assessment

Great Falls

125. Rocky Mountain Treatment Center
920 Fourth Avenue N, Great Falls, MT 59401
(406) 727-8832
CONTACT: Pegge McCluey
HOTLINE: (800) 521-6572
FAX: (406) 727-8172
EATING DISORDERS TREATED: Bulimia nervosa;
  Compulsive overeating/obesity
TREATMENT/THERAPY: Addiction;
  Psychological; Group; Individual; Family;
  Adolescent; Holistic model; 12-step; Out-
  patient education; Exercise; Body image
SETTING: In-patient; Out-patient
PROGRAM LENGTH: Minimum: 28 days/adults;
  42 days/adolescents
NO. OF PATIENTS PROGRAM CAN SERVE: 24
FOLLOW-UP EVALUATIONS: 3-mo evaluation
  with continuing care counselor; 6 mos; 12
  mos

Missoula

126. St Patrick Hospital Addiction Treatment Program
PO Box 4587, 500 W Broadway, Missoula,
MT 59806
(406) 543-7271
CONTACT: Dorothy Lescantz
HOTLINE: (800) 822-7271
DATE ESTABLISHED: 1982
EATING DISORDERS TREATED: Anorexia
  nervosa; Bulimia nervosa; Compulsive
  overeating/obesity
TREATMENT/THERAPY: Addiction;
  Psychological; Group; Individual; Family;
  Holistic model; 12-step; Creative arts;
  Exercise; Body image; Meditation
SETTING: Hospital; In-patient; Out-patient
PROGRAM LENGTH: 21 days
NO. OF PATIENTS PROGRAM CAN SERVE: 21
FOLLOW-UP EVALUATIONS: 3 mos; Aftercare for
  1 yr

NEBRASKA

Omaha

127. University of Nebraska Medical Center Eating Disorders Program
600 S 42nd St, Omaha, NE 68198
(402) 559-4000
CONTACT: Dr James Madison, Dir
EATING DISORDERS TREATED: Anorexia
  nervosa; Bulimia nervosa
TREATMENT/THERAPY: Psychological; Group;
  Individual; Family; Adolescent; Creative
  arts; Out-patient education; Exercise; Body
  image

SETTING: Hospital; In-patient; Out-patient
PROGRAM LENGTH: Varies
FOLLOW-UP EVALUATIONS: Aftercare

NEVADA

Las Vegas

128. HCA Montevista Hospital
6000 W Rochelle Ave, Las Vegas, NV 89102
(702) 364-1111
CONTACT: Deborah Martz, Prog Dir
EATING DISORDERS TREATED: Anorexia
  nervosa; Bulimia nervosa; Compulsive
  overeating/obesity
TREATMENT/THERAPY: Psychological; Group;
  Individual; Family; Adolescent; Body
  image
SETTING: Hospital; In-patient

NEW JERSEY

Belle Mead

129. Carrier Foundation
PO Box 147, Belle Mead, NJ 08502
(908) 281-1000
CONTACT: Dr William Postal
HOTLINE: (800) 872-4991 (NJ)
EATING DISORDERS TREATED: Anorexia
  nervosa; Bulimia nervosa; Compulsive
  overeating/obesity
TREATMENT/THERAPY: Psychological; Group;
  Individual; Family; Adolescent; Creative
  arts; Out-patient education; Body image;
  Behavior modification
SETTING: Hospital; In-patient; Out-patient;
  Day hospital program
PROGRAM LENGTH: 6-8 wks; Varies with
  individual
NO. OF PATIENTS PROGRAM CAN SERVE: 16 in-
  patient
FOLLOW-UP EVALUATIONS: Aftercare

Rancocas

130. Hamptom Hospital
PO Box 7000, Rancocas Rd, Rancocas, NJ
08073
(609) 267-7000
DATE ESTABLISHED: 1986
EATING DISORDERS TREATED: Anorexia
  nervosa; Bulimia nervosa
TREATMENT/THERAPY: Psychological; Group;
  Individual; Adolescent; 12-step; Creative
  arts; Exercise; Body image
SETTING: Hospital; In-patient
NO. OF PATIENTS PROGRAM CAN SERVE: 30
FOLLOW-UP EVALUATIONS: Aftercare referral

NEW YORK

Amityville

131. South Oaks Hospital Eating Disorders Unit
400 Sunrise Hwy, Amityville, NY 11701
(516) 264-4000
CONTACT: Carol Flood, Dir
CONTACT TELEPHONE: (516) 264-5126
EATING DISORDERS TREATED: Anorexia nervosa; Bulimia nervosa; Compulsive overeating/obesity
TREATMENT/THERAPY: Addiction; Psychological; Group; Individual; Family; Adolescent; 12-step; Creative arts; Out-patient education; Body image
SETTING: Hospital; In-patient; Out-patient
NO. OF PATIENTS PROGRAM CAN SERVE: 33 in-patient
FOLLOW-UP EVALUATIONS: Aftercare

Brooklyn

132. Brooklyn Heights Center for Counseling
142 Joralemon St, Ste 3E, Brooklyn, NY 11201
(718) 935-9313
CONTACT: Dr Leslie Morrison Faerstein
DATE ESTABLISHED: 1987
EATING DISORDERS TREATED: Anorexia nervosa; Bulimia nervosa; Compulsive overeating/obesity
TREATMENT/THERAPY: Psychological; Group; Individual; Family; Adolescent; Out-patient education; Body image; Non-diet, feminist approach
SETTING: Out-patient
PROGRAM LENGTH: Individual and group psychotherapy ongoing
NO. OF PATIENTS PROGRAM CAN SERVE: No limit; NO. TREATED PREVIOUS YEAR: 1610 cases

133. New York Center for Eating Disorders
490 3rd St, Brooklyn, NY 11215
(718) 788-6986
CONTACT: Mary Ann Cohen
DATE ESTABLISHED: 1984
EATING DISORDERS TREATED: Anorexia nervosa; Bulimia nervosa
TREATMENT/THERAPY: Addiction; Psychological; Group; Individual; Family; Adolescent; Holistic model; 12-step; Exercise; Body image
SETTING: Out-patient; Self-help tapes
PROGRAM LENGTH: Varies
NO. OF PATIENTS PROGRAM CAN SERVE: 75; NO. TREATED PREVIOUS YEAR: 100

Harrison

134. St Vincent's Hospital Eating Disorders Programs
240 North St, Harrison, NY 10528
(914) 967-6500
CONTACT: Dr Samuel Langer, Dir
DATE ESTABLISHED: 1983
EATING DISORDERS TREATED: Anorexia nervosa; Bulimia nervosa
TREATMENT/THERAPY: Psychological; Group; Individual; Family; Adolescent; Nutrition program
SETTING: Hospital; In-patient; Out-patient
PROGRAM LENGTH: 1-3 mos
NO. OF PATIENTS PROGRAM CAN SERVE: 13
FOLLOW-UP EVALUATIONS: May see physician afterwards

Katonah

135. Four Winds Hospital Eating Disorders Service
800 Cross River Rd, Katonah, NY 10536
(914) 763-8151
CONTACT: Kathleen Perrin
EATING DISORDERS TREATED: Anorexia nervosa; Bulimia nervosa
TREATMENT/THERAPY: Psychological; Group; Individual; Family; Adolescent; Exercise; Body image
SETTING: Hospital; In-patient
PROGRAM LENGTH: Varies
NO. OF PATIENTS PROGRAM CAN SERVE: 30
FOLLOW-UP EVALUATIONS: Aftercare; Day treatment; Follow patients' progress for several yrs

New York

136. Bulimia Treatment Associates
88 University Pl, Ste 505, New York, NY 10003
(212) 989-3987
CONTACT: Dr Judith Brisman
DATE ESTABLISHED: 1984
EATING DISORDERS TREATED: Anorexia nervosa; Bulimia nervosa; Compulsive overeating/obesity
TREATMENT/THERAPY: Psychological; Group; Individual; Family; Adolescent; 12-step; Out-patient education
SETTING: Out-patient
PROGRAM LENGTH: 6 wks ongoing
NO. OF PATIENTS PROGRAM CAN SERVE: 100 patients/wk

137. Center for the Study of Anorexia & Bulimia
1 W 91st St, New York, NY 10024
(212) 595-3449
DATE ESTABLISHED: 1979
EATING DISORDERS TREATED: Anorexia
   nervosa; Bulimia nervosa; Compulsive
   overeating/obesity
TREATMENT/THERAPY: Group; Individual;
   Family; Adolescent; Out-patient education;
   Body image
SETTING: Out-patient
PROGRAM LENGTH: Varies, usually 1-3 times/
   wk for a minimum of 1 yr

138. Columbia Presbyterian Medical Center/New York State Psychiatric Institute
722 W 168th St, New York, NY 10032
(212) 960-5746
CONTACT: Katharine Leob; Juli Goldfein
EATING DISORDERS TREATED: Anorexia
   nervosa; Bulimia nervosa
TREATMENT/THERAPY: Psychological;
   Individual; Females only
SETTING: In-patient; Out-patient
PROGRAM LENGTH: Varies
NO. OF PATIENTS PROGRAM CAN SERVE: Varies;
   NO. TREATED PREVIOUS YEAR: 75

139. Gracie Square Hospital Eating Disorder Program
420 E 76th St, New York, NY 10021
(212) 988-4400
CONTACT: Donna Gajda
CONTACT TELEPHONE: (212) 222-2832
HOTLINE: (800) 382-2832
FAX: (212) 879-8249
DATE ESTABLISHED: 1985
EATING DISORDERS TREATED: Anorexia
   nervosa; Bulimia nervosa; Compulsive
   overeating/obesity
TREATMENT/THERAPY: Psychological; Group;
   Individual; Family; Creative arts; Exercise;
   Body image

140. River Center Inc
20 Waterside Plaza, New York, NY 10010
(212) 481-4111
CONTACT: Deirdre Flannery, Intake Coord
EATING DISORDERS TREATED: Anorexia
   nervosa; Bulimia nervosa; Compulsive
   overeating/obesity
TREATMENT/THERAPY: Psychological; Group;
   Individual; Family; Adolescent; 12-step;
   Creative arts; Out-patient education; Body
   image
SETTING: Out-patient
FOLLOW-UP EVALUATIONS: Aftercare groups

141. St Luke's Roosevelt Hospital Center
428 W 59th St, New York, NY 10019
(212) 523-6714
CONTACT: Dr Schiff Mayer, Prog Dir
EATING DISORDERS TREATED: Anorexia
   nervosa; Bulimia nervosa
TREATMENT/THERAPY: Psychological
SETTING: Hospital; In-patient

142. Women's Therapy Center Institute
80 E 11th St, Rm 101, New York, NY 10003
(212) 420-1974
CONTACT: Margery Rosenthal
DATE ESTABLISHED: 1981
EATING DISORDERS TREATED: Anorexia
   nervosa; Bulimia nervosa; Compulsive
   overeating/obesity
TREATMENT/THERAPY: Psychological; Group;
   Individual; Adolescent; Holistic model;
   Creative arts; Out-patient education; Body
   image
SETTING: Out-patient
PROGRAM LENGTH: Varies
FOLLOW-UP EVALUATIONS: Immediately after
   workshop or group; Written questionnaires

Rochester

143. University of Rochester Medical Center, Department of Psychiatry & Adult Eating Disorders Program
300 Crittenden Blvd, Rochester, NY 14642
(716) 275-2121
CONTACT: Denise Plane, Coord
CONTACT TELEPHONE: (716) 275-3582
EATING DISORDERS TREATED: Anorexia
   nervosa; Bulimia nervosa
TREATMENT/THERAPY: Psychological; Group;
   Individual; Family; Creative arts; Out-
   patient education; Exercise; Body image
SETTING: In-patient
PROGRAM LENGTH: Varies, usually 3-4 wks
NO. OF PATIENTS PROGRAM CAN SERVE: 5-6
   people

Saratoga Springs

144. Four Winds Hospital—Saratoga
30 Crescent Ave, Saratoga Springs, NY 12866
(800) 888-5448
CONTACT: Frank Arcangelo, PhD
EATING DISORDERS TREATED: Anorexia
   nervosa; Bulimia nervosa
TREATMENT/THERAPY: Group; Individual;
   Family; Adolescent; 12-step; Dual
   diagnosis
SETTING: Hospital; In-patient; Out-patient
NO. OF PATIENTS PROGRAM CAN SERVE: 75
FOLLOW-UP EVALUATIONS: Follow-up groups

White Plains

145. New York Hospital—Cornell Medical Center

21 Bloomingdale Rd, White Plains, NY 10605
(914) 997-5875
CONTACT: Katherine Halmi, MD
FAX: (914) 997-5958
EATING DISORDERS TREATED: Anorexia nervosa; Bulimia nervosa
TREATMENT/THERAPY: Psychological; Group; Individual; Family; Creative arts; Outpatient education; Exercise; Body image
SETTING: Hospital; In-patient; Out-patient
PROGRAM LENGTH: Varies
NO. OF PATIENTS PROGRAM CAN SERVE: 18 inpatients

NORTH CAROLINA

Durham

146. Anorexia Nervosa/Bulimia Treatment Program

PO Box 3245, Duke University Medical Center, Durham, NC 27710
(919) 684-3073
CONTACT: Dr Kenneth Rockwell
FAX: (919) 684-8666
DATE ESTABLISHED: 1979
EATING DISORDERS TREATED: Anorexia nervosa; Bulimia nervosa; Compulsive overeating/obesity
TREATMENT/THERAPY: Psychological; Group; Individual; Family; Adolescent; Assertiveness training; Relaxation therapy; Activity therapy and program
SETTING: In-patient; Out-patient
PROGRAM LENGTH: Varies
NO. OF PATIENTS PROGRAM CAN SERVE: Maximum 10 in-patient

OHIO

Brecksville

147. Associates in Adult Adolescent and Child Psychotherapy Inc

8221 Brecksville Rd, One Brecksville Commons, Ste 201, Brecksville, OH 44141
(216) 526-4426
CONTACT: Dr Linda Pendleton
DATE ESTABLISHED: 1985 (relocated from Cleveland Metro General Hospital)
EATING DISORDERS TREATED: Anorexia nervosa; Bulimia nervosa; Compulsive overeating/obesity; Childhood eating problems

TREATMENT/THERAPY: Psychological; Group; Individual; Family; Adolescent; Outpatient education; Body image; Referral for nutritional counseling available
SETTING: Out-patient
PROGRAM LENGTH: 1 yr +
NO. OF PATIENTS PROGRAM CAN SERVE: Approx 50-75/yr; NO. TREATED PREVIOUS YEAR: Approx 50
FOLLOW-UP EVALUATIONS: Aftercare support group

Chagrin Falls

148. Windsor Hospital

115 E Summit St, Chagrin Falls, OH 44022
(800) 542-5432
CONTACT: Ron Colonna, Prog Dir
DATE ESTABLISHED: 1985
EATING DISORDERS TREATED: Anorexia nervosa; Bulimia nervosa
TREATMENT/THERAPY: Psychological; Group; Individual; Family; Adolescent; Creative arts; Exercise; Body image; Nutrition program; Pet therapy
SETTING: Hospital; In-patient; Out-patient; Day treatment
PROGRAM LENGTH: 3-4 wks usually; Shortterm acute care facilities
NO. OF PATIENTS PROGRAM CAN SERVE: 8; NO. TREATED PREVIOUS YEAR: 200-300
FOLLOW-UP EVALUATIONS: Aftercare

Cincinnati

149. The Christ Hospital Eating Disorders Unit

2139 Auburn Ave, Cincinnati, OH 45220
(513) 369-2626
CONTACT: Kay Atkins, Head Nurse
HOTLINE: (513) 369-2626
DATE ESTABLISHED: 1984
EATING DISORDERS TREATED: Anorexia nervosa; Bulimia nervosa
TREATMENT/THERAPY: Psychological; Group; Individual; Family; Adolescent; Creative arts; Out-patient education; Exercise; Body image; Nutrition program
SETTING: Hospital; In-patient; Out-patient; Day treatment
PROGRAM LENGTH: Varies
NO. OF PATIENTS PROGRAM CAN SERVE: 20 inpatient
FOLLOW-UP EVALUATIONS: Aftercare

150. **University of Cincinnati Eating Disorders Center**
UC Medical Center, Department of
Psychiatry, Cincinnati, OH 45267-0559
(513) 558-5118
CONTACT: Marsha Basquette, Prog Coord;
Susan C Wooley, PhD, Dir
FAX: (513) 558-4805
DATE ESTABLISHED: 1974; Intensive treatment
program established 1983
EATING DISORDERS TREATED: Anorexia
nervosa; Bulimia nervosa; Compulsive
overeating/obesity
TREATMENT/THERAPY: Psychological; Group;
Individual; Family; Creative arts; Body
image; Females only treated in intensive
treatment program. We treat men who live
locally on an out-patient basis.
SETTING: Out-patient; Patients reside in
nearby apartments and receive 6-8 hrs of
structured psychotherapy each weekday
PROGRAM LENGTH: Program is run in 4-wk
sessions, 6-8 women per session
NO. OF PATIENTS PROGRAM CAN SERVE: 8 per 4-
wk session (7 sessions/hr); NO. TREATED
PREVIOUS YEAR: 56 in intensive treatment
program; 300+ in out-patient work
FOLLOW-UP EVALUATIONS: 12 mos; Follow-up
questionnaire, plus inventories of eating
disorder symptomology, body image, and
general psychological functioning. Each
patient completes the same measure pre-
and post-treatment.

Cleveland

151. **Case Western Reserve University
School of Medicine, Behavior Therapy
Clinic, University Hospitals of Cleveland**
2074 Abington Rd, Cleveland, OH 44106
(216) 844-8550
EATING DISORDERS TREATED: Anorexia
nervosa; Bulimia nervosa; Compulsive
overeating/obesity
TREATMENT/THERAPY: Psychological;
Individual; Adolescent
SETTING: Out-patient

152. **Cleveland Clinic Foundation,
Department of Psychiatry**
9500 Euclid Ave, Cleveland, OH 44195
(216) 444-2200
CONTACT: Judy Goldman, LCSW
EATING DISORDERS TREATED: Anorexia
nervosa; Bulimia nervosa; Compulsive
overeating/obesity
TREATMENT/THERAPY: Addiction;
Psychological; Group; Individual;
Adolescent; 12-step; Out-patient education;
Body image
SETTING: Hospital; In-patient; Out-patient

153. **St Vincent Charity Hospital**
2351 E 22nd St, Cleveland, OH 44115
(216) 861-6200, 363-2570
EATING DISORDERS TREATED: Anorexia
nervosa; Bulimia nervosa
TREATMENT/THERAPY: Psychological; Group;
Individual; Family; Adolescent; Creative
arts; Exercise; Occupational
SETTING: Hospital; In-patient
PROGRAM LENGTH: Varies
NO. OF PATIENTS PROGRAM CAN SERVE: 25 beds
FOLLOW-UP EVALUATIONS: Aftercare bimonthly
support group

Columbus

154. **Center for the Treatment of
Eating Disorders**
1925 E Dublin-Granville Rd, Columbus, OH
43229
(614) 436-1112
CONTACT: Barbara Reardon, PhD
HOTLINE: (614) 436-1112
FAX: (614) 848-5460
DATE ESTABLISHED: 1980
EATING DISORDERS TREATED: Anorexia
nervosa; Bulimia nervosa; Compulsive
overeating/obesity; Eating disorders not
otherwise specified
TREATMENT/THERAPY: Psychological; Group;
Individual; Family; Adolescent; Medical;
Nutrition program; Intensive out-patient;
Creative arts; Out-patient education;
Exercise; Body image
SETTING: Hospital; In-patient; Out-patient
PROGRAM LENGTH: Individualized; Depends
on client need
NO. OF PATIENTS PROGRAM CAN SERVE: 100+;
NO. TREATED PREVIOUS YEAR: 179
FOLLOW-UP EVALUATIONS: 6 mos; A two-page
form evaluates type of treatment, setting,
therapist, etc; Free support groups

OKLAHOMA

Tulsa

155. **The Rader Institute at Tulsa
Regional Medical Center**
744 W 9th St, Tulsa, OK 74127
(918) 599-5755
CONTACT: Veronica Jeffus, MEd, LPC
CONTACT TELEPHONE: (918) 599-5755
FAX: (918) 599-5829
DATE ESTABLISHED: 1986
EATING DISORDERS TREATED: Anorexia
nervosa; Bulimia nervosa; Compulsive
overeating/obesity; Major depression;
Eating disorders not otherwise specified

The Rader Institute at Tulsa Regional Medical Center *(continued)*

TREATMENT/THERAPY: Addiction; Psychological; Group; Individual; Family; Adolescent; Holistic model; 12-step; Creative arts; Out-patient education; Exercise; Body image; Out-patient treatment program
SETTING: Hospital; In-patient; Out-patient; Day hospital
PROGRAM LENGTH: Varies
NO. OF PATIENTS PROGRAM CAN SERVE: 20; NO. TREATED PREVIOUS YEAR: 150
FOLLOW-UP EVALUATIONS: Every 6 mos; Questionnaire

OREGON

Eugene

156. Sacred Heart General Hospital, Department of Psychiatry
PO Box 10905, 1255 Hilyard St, Eugene, OR 97440
(503) 686-7372
CONTACT: Elise Curry, Coord
FAX: (503) 686-7391
DATE ESTABLISHED: 1985
EATING DISORDERS TREATED: Anorexia nervosa; Bulimia nervosa
TREATMENT/THERAPY: Psychological; Group; Family; Out-patient education; Body image; Multidimensional model
SETTING: Hospital; In-patient; Out-patient
PROGRAM LENGTH: 20 wks for out-patient; Varies for in-patient
NO. OF PATIENTS PROGRAM CAN SERVE: 20 out-patient; NO. TREATED PREVIOUS YEAR: 20
FOLLOW-UP EVALUATIONS: 6 mos; 12 mos; 2 yrs; Free support group

Portland

157. Portland Adventist Medical Center
10123 SE Market St, Portland, OR 97216
(503) 251-6101
CONTACT TELEPHONE: (503) 257-2500 ext 4200
DATE ESTABLISHED: 1983
EATING DISORDERS TREATED: Anorexia nervosa; Bulimia nervosa; Compulsive overeating/obesity
TREATMENT/THERAPY: Addiction; Psychological; Group; Individual; Family; Holistic model; 12-step; Creative arts; Out-patient education; Exercise; Body image
SETTING: Hospital; In-patient; Out-patient; Day treatment for anorexia nervosa, bulimia nervosa, and compulsive overeaters
PROGRAM LENGTH: 4-6 wks average

NO. OF PATIENTS PROGRAM CAN SERVE: 5 in-patient; NO. TREATED PREVIOUS YEAR: 50-60 in-patient
FOLLOW-UP EVALUATIONS: Aftercare

158. St Vincent's Hospital
9205 SW Barnes Rd, Portland, OR 97225
(503) 297-4411
CONTACT TELEPHONE: (503) 291-3594
EATING DISORDERS TREATED: Anorexia nervosa; Bulimia nervosa
TREATMENT/THERAPY: Psychological; Group; Individual; Family; Adolescent
SETTING: Hospital; In-patient; Out-patient; Day hospital

PENNSYLVANIA

Hershey

159. Penn State University Hospital, The Milton S Hershey Medical Center, Department of Psychiatry
PO Box 850, Hershey, PA 17033
(717) 531-8515
CONTACT: John R Horn
CONTACT TELEPHONE: (717) 531-6771
HOTLINE: (800) 243-1455
FAX: (717) 531-6491
DATE ESTABLISHED: 1972
EATING DISORDERS TREATED: Anorexia nervosa; Bulimia nervosa; Compulsive overeating/obesity
TREATMENT/THERAPY: Addiction; Psychological; Group; Individual; Family; Adolescent; Child therapy; Cognitive-behavioral; Holistic model; Creative arts; Out-patient education; Exercise; Body image; Milieu; Nutrition program; Assertiveness training; Biofeedback; Stress management; Lifestyle changes; Supplemented fasting
SETTING: Hospital; In-patient; Out-patient
PROGRAM LENGTH: Minimum 2 wks
NO. OF PATIENTS PROGRAM CAN SERVE: 45; NO. TREATED PREVIOUS YEAR: 150
FOLLOW-UP EVALUATIONS: Alumni group weekly

Huntingdon

160. J C Blair Memorial Hospital Counseling Services
Warm Springs Ave, Huntingdon, PA 16652
(814) 643-8880
CONTACT: Roseann Mollica, Dir
DATE ESTABLISHED: 1981
EATING DISORDERS TREATED: Anorexia nervosa; Bulimia nervosa; Compulsive overeating/obesity

TREATMENT/THERAPY: Psychological;
Individual; Family; Adolescent; 12-step;
Out-patient education; Body image
SETTING: Out-patient
PROGRAM LENGTH: Varies NO. TREATED
PREVIOUS YEAR: 6-10

Philadelphia

161. Graduate Hospital
1740 South St, Philadelphia, PA 19146
(215) 893-7000
CONTACT: Michael Pertschuk, MD
HOTLINE: (800) 654-GRAD
FAX: (215) 955-2253
DATE ESTABLISHED: 1982
EATING DISORDERS TREATED: Anorexia
nervosa; Bulimia nervosa; Compulsive
overeating/obesity
TREATMENT/THERAPY: Psychological; Group;
Individual; Family; Adolescent; Creative
arts; Exercise; Body image
SETTING: Residential; Day treatment; Out-
patient
PROGRAM LENGTH: 30 days usually
FOLLOW-UP EVALUATIONS: 3 mos; Out-patient
aftercare

162. Institute of Pennsylvania Hospital
111 N 49th St, Philadelphia, PA 19139
(215) 471-2479
CONTACT: Cathy Dingfelder, MSW
DATE ESTABLISHED: 1984
EATING DISORDERS TREATED: Anorexia
nervosa; Bulimia nervosa
TREATMENT/THERAPY: Psychological; Group;
Individual; Family; Adolescent; Holistic
model; Creative arts; Out-patient
education; Exercise; Body image
SETTING: Hospital; In-patient
PROGRAM LENGTH: Average 30-90 days
NO. OF PATIENTS PROGRAM CAN SERVE: 8; NO.
TREATED PREVIOUS YEAR: Approx 40
FOLLOW-UP EVALUATIONS: Informal in an
ongoing out-patient service

163. Jefferson Medical College
1015 Walnut St, No. 327G, Philadelphia, PA
19107
(215) 955-6104
CONTACT: Harvey Schwartz, MD
FAX: (215) 923-9706
DATE ESTABLISHED: 1982
EATING DISORDERS TREATED: Anorexia
nervosa; Bulimia nervosa; Compulsive
overeating/obesity
TREATMENT/THERAPY: Psychological;
Individual; Family; Adolescent;
Psychoanalysis
SETTING: Out-patient

164. Philadelphia Child Guidance Center
34th St and Civic Center Blvd, Philadelphia,
PA 19104
(215) 243-2830
CONTACT: John Sargent, MD
FAX: (215) 243-2847
DATE ESTABLISHED: 1967
EATING DISORDERS TREATED: Anorexia
nervosa; Bulimia nervosa; Food refusal in
preadolescents
TREATMENT/THERAPY: Psychological; Group;
Individual; Family; Adolescent; Medical
monitoring; Nutrition program
SETTING: In-patient; Out-patient
PROGRAM LENGTH: 3-5 wks
NO. OF PATIENTS PROGRAM CAN SERVE: 7 in-
patient; NO. TREATED PREVIOUS YEAR: 50 in-
patient; 150 out-patient
FOLLOW-UP EVALUATIONS: Aftercare; Support
group

165. Philadelphia Psychiatric Center
Ford Rd and Monument Ave, Philadelphia,
PA 19131
(215) 581-5489
CONTACT: Candance Herrman, MSS, Prog Dir
CONTACT TELEPHONE: (215) 581-5489
FAX: (215) 581-3803
DATE ESTABLISHED: 1985
EATING DISORDERS TREATED: Anorexia
nervosa; Bulimia nervosa; Compulsive
overeating/obesity
TREATMENT/THERAPY: Psychological; Group;
Individual; Family; Adolescent; Holistic
model; Creative arts; Out-patient
education; Exercise; Body image
SETTING: Hospital; In-patient; Out-patient
PROGRAM LENGTH: 10-day minimum
NO. OF PATIENTS PROGRAM CAN SERVE: 14; NO.
TREATED PREVIOUS YEAR: 128

166. Renfrew Center
475 Spring Ln, Philadelphia, PA 19128
(215) 482-5353
CONTACT: Judy Gadstein, Admin Dir
HOTLINE: (800) 334-8415
DATE ESTABLISHED: 1985
EATING DISORDERS TREATED: Anorexia
nervosa; Bulimia nervosa
TREATMENT/THERAPY: Psychological; Group;
Individual; Family; Adolescent age 15 and
older; Creative arts; Exercise; Body image;
Females only in-patient
SETTING: In-patient; Out-patient
PROGRAM LENGTH: 7-9 wks; may extend on
case basis
NO. OF PATIENTS PROGRAM CAN SERVE: 40
FOLLOW-UP EVALUATIONS: Aftercare

167. University of Pennsylvania Hospital, Psychiatric Unit
3400 Spruce St, Philadelphia, PA 19104
(215) 662-4000
CONTACT: Dr John Paul Brady
CONTACT TELEPHONE: (215) 662-2825
FAX: (215) 662-7200
EATING DISORDERS TREATED: Anorexia nervosa; Bulimia nervosa
TREATMENT/THERAPY: Psychological; Individual; Family
SETTING: Hospital; In-patient; Out-patient

Pittsburgh

168. Center for Overcoming Problem Eating, Western Psychiatric Institute and Clinic
3811 O'Hara St, Pittsburgh, PA 15101
(412) 624-0227, 624-3507
CONTACT: Ginny Stevens, RN
CONTACT TELEPHONE: (412) 624-0227
FAX: (412) 624-0223
DATE ESTABLISHED: 1987
EATING DISORDERS TREATED: Anorexia nervosa; Bulimia nervosa
TREATMENT/THERAPY: Psychological; Group; Individual; Family; Adolescent; Holistic model; Out-patient education; Exercise; Body image; Cognitive-behavioral; Relapse prevention groups; Meal planning; Shopping and cooking groups
SETTING: Hospital; In-patient; Out-patient; Out-patient partial hospitalization program
PROGRAM LENGTH: 30-90 days in-patient
NO. OF PATIENTS PROGRAM CAN SERVE: 11 beds in-patient; NO. TREATED PREVIOUS YEAR: Approx 100 in-patients
FOLLOW-UP EVALUATIONS: 6 mos; 12 mos; Interview with psychiatrist; Biweekly community support group

TENNESSEE

Madison

169. Tennessee Christian Medical Center
500 Hospital Dr, Madison, TN 37115
(615) 865-2727
CONTACT: Ken Graham, Dir
CONTACT TELEPHONE: (615) 865-2727
FAX: (615) 865-0300 ext 2857
DATE ESTABLISHED: 1984
EATING DISORDERS TREATED: Anorexia nervosa; Bulimia nervosa; Compulsive overeating/obesity

TREATMENT/THERAPY: Addiction; Group; Individual; Family; Adolescent age 14 and over only; Nutrition program; Holistic model; 12-step; Creative arts; Out-patient education; Exercise; Body image
SETTING: In-patient; Out-patient
PROGRAM LENGTH: 4 wks generally
NO. OF PATIENTS PROGRAM CAN SERVE: 8
FOLLOW-UP EVALUATIONS: Out-patient aftercare

Maryville

170. Blount Memorial Hospital
907 E Lamar Alexander Pkwy, Maryville, TN 37801
(615) 977-5645
CONTACT: Dr Robert Booher, Prog Dir
HOTLINE: (800) 222-5822
DATE ESTABLISHED: 1987
EATING DISORDERS TREATED: Anorexia nervosa; Bulimia nervosa; Compulsive overeating/obesity
TREATMENT/THERAPY: Addiction; 12-step; Creative arts; Exercise; Body image
SETTING: In-patient; Eating disorders halfway house
PROGRAM LENGTH: 28-32 days
NO. OF PATIENTS PROGRAM CAN SERVE: 23-25
FOLLOW-UP EVALUATIONS: Aftercare

Memphis

171. Methodist Hospital of Memphis
1265 Union Ave, Memphis, TN 38104
(901) 726-7878
CONTACT: Carmen Hamilton, Admin
DATE ESTABLISHED: 1986
EATING DISORDERS TREATED: Anorexia nervosa; Bulimia nervosa; Compulsive overeating/obesity
TREATMENT/THERAPY: Addiction; Psychological; Group; Individual; Family; 12-step; Creative arts; Exercise; Body image
SETTING: Hospital; In-patient; Partial hospitalization
PROGRAM LENGTH: 30 days
NO. OF PATIENTS PROGRAM CAN SERVE: 16
FOLLOW-UP EVALUATIONS: Monthly for 6 mos; 6 mos; 12 mos; Aftercare 2 times/wk for first 3 mos then 1 time/wk for next 3 mos

172. University of Tennessee Weight Control Center
956 Court Ave, Ste E222, Department of Surgery, Memphis, TN 38163
(901) 528-5723
CONTACT: Dr George Cowan
DATE ESTABLISHED: 1983

EATING DISORDERS TREATED: Compulsive
overeating/obesity; Problems with previous
obesity surgery
TREATMENT/THERAPY: Psychological; Group;
Individual; Family; Postoperative; Out-
patient education; Body image; Also have
support groups for bariatric surgery
patients and their families; Hypnotherapy
SETTING: Hospital; In-patient; Out-patient
PROGRAM LENGTH: Wks to yrs
NO. OF PATIENTS PROGRAM CAN SERVE: 200+;
NO. TREATED PREVIOUS YEAR: 200+
FOLLOW-UP EVALUATIONS: Weekly and
monthly as required; 6 mos; 12 mos;
Evaluations include dietary, exercise,
biochemical, physiological, medical history
and exam, psychiatric as required, and
behavioral

TEXAS

Austin

**173. St David's Medical Center Eating
Disorders Program (EDP)**
PO Box 4039, 919 E 32nd St, Austin, TX
78765
(512) 476-7111
CONTACT: Jeff Lutes, Prog Dir
HOTLINE: (512) 397-4023
DATE ESTABLISHED: 1987
EATING DISORDERS TREATED: Anorexia
nervosa; Bulimia nervosa; Compulsive
overeating/obesity
TREATMENT/THERAPY: Psychological; Group;
Individual; Family; 12-step; Creative arts;
Out-patient education; Exercise; Body
image; Psychodynamic 12-step blend
SETTING: Hospital; In-patient; Out-patient
PROGRAM LENGTH: Varies
NO. OF PATIENTS PROGRAM CAN SERVE: 10 in-
patient; 8 day hospital; NO. TREATED
PREVIOUS YEAR: 120 in-patient; 60 day
hospital
FOLLOW-UP EVALUATIONS: 12 mos; Aftercare 1
time/wk

Corpus Christi

**174. Bayview Hospital Eating
Disorders Program**
6629 Wooldridge, Corpus Christi, TX 78414
(512) 993-9700
EATING DISORDERS TREATED: Anorexia
nervosa; Bulimia nervosa; Compulsive
overeating/obesity
TREATMENT/THERAPY: Psychological; Group;
Individual; Family; Adolescent; Holistic
model; 12-step; Exercise
SETTING: Hospital; In-patient; Out-patient;
Day hospital

PROGRAM LENGTH: Varies
FOLLOW-UP EVALUATIONS: Aftercare

Dallas

**175. University of Texas Southwestern
Eating Disorders Program**
5323 Harry Hines Blvd, Dallas, TX 75235
(214) 688-2218
CONTACT: Dr David Waller
CONTACT TELEPHONE: (214) 688-3898
DATE ESTABLISHED: 1983
EATING DISORDERS TREATED: Anorexia
nervosa; Bulimia nervosa
TREATMENT/THERAPY: Holistic model
SETTING: Hospital; In-patient; Out-patient
PROGRAM LENGTH: Varies

Grand Prairie

**176. The Rader Institute at Fort Worth
Medical Center**
2709 Hospital Blvd, Grand Prairie, TX 75051
(214) 641-5200
CONTACT: Phyllis Peake, Dir
CONTACT TELEPHONE: (214) 641-5301
DATE ESTABLISHED: 1989
EATING DISORDERS TREATED: Anorexia
nervosa; Bulimia nervosa; Compulsive
overeating/obesity
TREATMENT/THERAPY: Addiction;
Psychological; Group; Individual; Family;
Adolescent; Relaxation therapy; Gentle
eating; Holistic model; 12-step; Creative
arts; Out-patient education; Exercise; Body
image
SETTING: Hospital; In-patient; Out-patient
PROGRAM LENGTH: 4-6 wks
NO. OF PATIENTS PROGRAM CAN SERVE: 12
FOLLOW-UP EVALUATIONS: 6 mos; 12 mos;
Alumni group weekly

Houston

177. Nutrition Health Services
9660 Hillcroft, No. 437, Houston, TX 77096
(713) 721-7755
CONTACT: Karen Siegel, MPH, RD, LD
CONTACT TELEPHONE: (713) 721-7755
FAX: (713) 723-8065
DATE ESTABLISHED: 1989
EATING DISORDERS TREATED: Anorexia
nervosa; Bulimia nervosa; Compulsive
overeating/obesity
TREATMENT/THERAPY: Nutrition program
SETTING: In-patient; Private practice
dietitians
PROGRAM LENGTH: Ongoing/as needed
NO. OF PATIENTS PROGRAM CAN SERVE: As
needed; NO. TREATED PREVIOUS YEAR: 75

Nutrition Health Services *(continued)*

FOLLOW-UP EVALUATIONS: 6 mos; 12 mos;
Phone call; Office visit

178. Psychological Associates of Clear Lake

16815 Royal Crest, Ste B-3, Houston, TX 77058
(713) 280-8230
CONTACT: Lesli Zinn, PhD
DATE ESTABLISHED: 1990
EATING DISORDERS TREATED: Anorexia nervosa; Bulimia nervosa; Compulsive overeating/obesity
TREATMENT/THERAPY: Psychological; Group; Individual; Family; Adolescent; Psychodrama; 12-step; Creative arts; Body image
SETTING: Hospital; In-patient; Out-patient; Partial hospitalization
PROGRAM LENGTH: 28-30 days
NO. OF PATIENTS PROGRAM CAN SERVE: 20 in-patient
FOLLOW-UP EVALUATIONS: Aftercare

179. Spring Branch Memorial Hospital

PO Box 55227, 8850 Longpoint, Houston, TX 77055
(713) 467-6555
CONTACT: Edith Moore, Intake Coord
EATING DISORDERS TREATED: Anorexia nervosa; Bulimia nervosa; Compulsive overeating/obesity
TREATMENT/THERAPY: Psychological; Group; Individual; Family; Adolescent; 12-step; Creative arts; Exercise; Body image
SETTING: Hospital; In-patient; Out-patient
PROGRAM LENGTH: Varies
FOLLOW-UP EVALUATIONS: Continuing care

180. West Oaks Hospital Eating Disorders

6500 Hornwood, Houston, TX 77074
(713) 995-0909
CONTACT: Elaine Rose
DATE ESTABLISHED: 1986
EATING DISORDERS TREATED: Anorexia nervosa; Bulimia nervosa; Compulsive overeating/obesity
TREATMENT/THERAPY: Addiction; Psychological; Group; Individual; Family; Adolescent; 12-step; Creative arts; Out-patient education; Exercise; Body image; Nutrition program
SETTING: Hospital; In-patient; Out-patient; Partial hospitalization
PROGRAM LENGTH: Varies, 2-3 wks managed care
FOLLOW-UP EVALUATIONS: Aftercare; Free ongoing support group

Lubbock

181. Charter Plains Hospital

801 N Quaker, Lubbock, TX 79416
(806) 744-5505
CONTACT: Marcia Abbott, PhD
HOTLINE: (800) 692-4606 (TX); (800) 872-1433 (US)
EATING DISORDERS TREATED: Anorexia nervosa; Bulimia nervosa
TREATMENT/THERAPY: Psychological; Group; Individual; Family; Adolescent; Creative arts; Out-patient education; Exercise; Body image
SETTING: Hospital; In-patient; Out-patient; Day treatment
PROGRAM LENGTH: Varies, 30 days average
FOLLOW-UP EVALUATIONS: Free weekly aftercare

Plano

182. HCA Willow Park Hospital

1620 Coit Rd, Plano, TX 75075
(214) 867-8670
CONTACT: Gary Bourland, Prog Dir
EATING DISORDERS TREATED: Anorexia nervosa; Bulimia nervosa; Compulsive overeating/obesity
TREATMENT/THERAPY: Addiction; Psychological; Group; Individual; Family; Adolescent; Holistic model; 12-step; Creative arts; Out-patient education; Exercise; Body image
SETTING: Hospital; In-patient; Out-patient; Day hospital
PROGRAM LENGTH: Varies
NO. OF PATIENTS PROGRAM CAN SERVE: 38+
FOLLOW-UP EVALUATIONS: 30-, 60-, 90-day and 1-yr aftercare; Questionnaire

San Antonio

183. Hill Country Hospital

8205 Palisades Dr, San Antonio, TX 78233
(512) 659-9000
HOTLINE: (800) 468-5252
DATE ESTABLISHED: 1986
EATING DISORDERS TREATED: Anorexia nervosa; Bulimia nervosa
TREATMENT/THERAPY: Psychological; Group; Individual; Family; 12-step; Creative arts; Exercise; Body image
SETTING: Hospital; In-patient
PROGRAM LENGTH: 28 days average
FOLLOW-UP EVALUATIONS: Aftercare referral

184. Shin Oak Clinic Inc
8600 Wurzbach Rd, Ste 601, San Antonio, TX 78240
(512) 692-9741
CONTACT: John C Ramsay, MD
FAX: (512) 692-9749
DATE ESTABLISHED: 1989
EATING DISORDERS TREATED: Anorexia nervosa; Bulimia nervosa; Compulsive overeating/obesity
TREATMENT/THERAPY: Psychological; Group; Individual; Family
SETTING: Out-patient

185. Villa Rosa Hospital
5115 Medical Dr, San Antonio, TX 78229-4899
(512) 692-2656
CONTACT: Arturita Ruffin, Prog Dir
CONTACT TELEPHONE: (512) 692-2671
HOTLINE: (512) 692-2700
EATING DISORDERS TREATED: Anorexia nervosa; Bulimia nervosa; Binge eating disorders; Nonpurging bulimia
TREATMENT/THERAPY: Psychological; Group; Individual; Family; Adolescent; 12-step Optional; Creative arts; Out-patient education; Exercise; Body image; Psychodrama; Cognitive; Insight therapy; Nutrition program
SETTING: Hospital; In-patient; Out-patient; Day hospital
PROGRAM LENGTH: Varies, 3 wks in-patient
NO. OF PATIENTS PROGRAM CAN SERVE: 10 in-patient; NO. TREATED PREVIOUS YEAR: Not in existence last year
FOLLOW-UP EVALUATIONS: 6 mos aftercare groups free; Multifamily groups

VIRGINIA

Falls Church

186. Dominion Hospital
2960 Sleepy Hollow Rd, Falls Church, VA 22044
(703) 536-2000
CONTACT: Cheryl Collins, Dir
FAX: (703) 536-6139
EATING DISORDERS TREATED: Anorexia nervosa; Bulimia nervosa
TREATMENT/THERAPY: Addiction; Psychological; Group; Individual; Family; Adolescent; 12-step; Creative arts; Exercise; Body image; Nutrition program
SETTING: Hospital; In-patient; Hospital day treatment after in-patient
PROGRAM LENGTH: 4 wks generally
NO. OF PATIENTS PROGRAM CAN SERVE: 8-12
FOLLOW-UP EVALUATIONS: Day program after in-patient

Norfolk

187. Sentara Norfolk General Hospital
600 Gresham Dr, Norfolk, VA 23607
(804) 628-2027
CONTACT: Vicki Horne, Prog Dir
HOTLINE: (800) 541-3733 (VA); (800) 336-3733 (US)
DATE ESTABLISHED: 1984
EATING DISORDERS TREATED: Anorexia nervosa; Bulimia nervosa; Compulsive overeating/obesity
TREATMENT/THERAPY: Addiction; Family; 12-step; Creative arts; Exercise; Body image
SETTING: Hospital; In-patient; Out-patient; Partial day
PROGRAM LENGTH: Varies, 4-6 wks average
NO. OF PATIENTS PROGRAM CAN SERVE: 16 in-patient; 8 day; NO. TREATED PREVIOUS YEAR: 800 since 1984
FOLLOW-UP EVALUATIONS: 3 mos; 6 mos; 12 mos; 12-wk aftercare group; Support groups

188. York Street Center
142 W York St, Ste 710, Norfolk, VA 23510
(804) 624-9011
CONTACT: Dr Bert Newfield
FAX: (804) 627-1015
EATING DISORDERS TREATED: Anorexia nervosa; Bulimia nervosa; Compulsive overeating/obesity
TREATMENT/THERAPY: Psychological; Group; Individual; Family; Adolescent; 12-step; Out-patient education; Exercise; Body image; Behavior management
SETTING: In-patient; Out-patient; Intensive out-patient
PROGRAM LENGTH: Varies, 3 wks in-patient
FOLLOW-UP EVALUATIONS: Ongoing groups; Individual support

WASHINGTON

Auburn

189. The Rader Institute at Auburn General Hospital
200 2nd St, Auburn, WA 98002
(206) 833-7711
CONTACT: Paula Frederick, Dir
CONTACT TELEPHONE: (206) 833-6508
HOTLINE: (800) 255-1818
DATE ESTABLISHED: 1987
EATING DISORDERS TREATED: Anorexia nervosa; Bulimia nervosa; Compulsive overeating/obesity
TREATMENT/THERAPY: Psychological; Group; Family; Adolescent; 12-step; Creative arts; Out-patient education; Exercise; Body image

The Rader Institute at Auburn General Hospital *(continued)*

SETTING: Hospital; In-patient; Out-patient; Intensive day treatment
PROGRAM LENGTH: 30-42 days
NO. OF PATIENTS PROGRAM CAN SERVE: 20
FOLLOW-UP EVALUATIONS: Continuing care, then alumni support groups

Seattle

190. Ballard Community Hospital Eating Disorders Unit
PO Box C-70707, Seattle, WA 98107
(206) 789-9345
CONTACT: Kathleen Campbell, Prog Mgr
FAX: (206) 789-4642
DATE ESTABLISHED: 1986
EATING DISORDERS TREATED: Anorexia nervosa; Bulimia nervosa; Compulsive overeating/obesity
TREATMENT/THERAPY: Psychological; Group; Individual; Family; Adolescent; Movement therapy; Hunger/satiety issues; Relapse prevention; Abuse; Sexuality; Holistic model; 12-step; Creative arts; Out-patient education; Exercise; Body image
SETTING: Hospital; In-patient; Out-patient; Day treatment (partial hospitalization)
PROGRAM LENGTH: Varies
NO. OF PATIENTS PROGRAM CAN SERVE: 18 in-patients; NO. TREATED PREVIOUS YEAR: 200
FOLLOW-UP EVALUATIONS: 4 mos; 12 wks aftercare

191. The Rader Institute at Riverton Hospital
12844 Military Rd S, Seattle, WA 98168
(206) 244-0180
CONTACT: Chris Colman, Prog Dir
HOTLINE: (800) 255-1818
DATE ESTABLISHED: 1987
EATING DISORDERS TREATED: Anorexia nervosa; Bulimia nervosa; Compulsive overeating/obesity
TREATMENT/THERAPY: Addiction; Psychological; Group; Individual; Family; Adolescent; Holistic model; 12-step; Creative arts; Out-patient education; Exercise; Body image; Multidisciplinary
SETTING: Hospital; In-patient; Out-patient; Day patient
PROGRAM LENGTH: 42 days average
NO. OF PATIENTS PROGRAM CAN SERVE: 12-15; NO. TREATED PREVIOUS YEAR: 300
FOLLOW-UP EVALUATIONS: 2 yrs; 5 yrs; 3 mos continuing care, then lifetime alumni

Tacoma

192. St Joseph Hospital Center for Personal & Family Development
PO Box 2197, 1718 S "I" St, Tacoma, WA 98401-2197
(206) 591-6671
CONTACT: Renee Schenck, Prog Mgr
CONTACT TELEPHONE: (206) 591-6671
DATE ESTABLISHED: 1985
EATING DISORDERS TREATED: Anorexia nervosa; Bulimia nervosa; Compulsive overeating/obesity; Survivors of sexual abuse; Depression
TREATMENT/THERAPY: Psychological; Group; Individual; Family; Adolescent; Creative arts; Out-patient education; Body image; Nutrition program; Psychoeducational seminars
SETTING: Hospital; Out-patient
PROGRAM LENGTH: 9-wk intensive out-patient; Weekly individual and group sessions
FOLLOW-UP EVALUATIONS: Support group 2 times/mo

WISCONSIN

Madison

193. Physicians Plus Medical Group, Nutrition Center
345 W Washington Ave, Madison, WI 53703
(608) 252-8663
CONTACT: Deborah B Roussos, RD, MS
CONTACT TELEPHONE: (608) 252-8663
FAX: (608) 282-8422
DATE ESTABLISHED: 1984
EATING DISORDERS TREATED: Anorexia nervosa; Bulimia nervosa; Compulsive overeating/obesity
TREATMENT/THERAPY: Out-patient education; Body image; Focused eating exercises and imagery; Fashion illusion
SETTING: Out-patient
PROGRAM LENGTH: Group, 10 sessions; Individual, as needed
NO. OF PATIENTS PROGRAM CAN SERVE: No limit; NO. TREATED PREVIOUS YEAR: 125
FOLLOW-UP EVALUATIONS: 6 mos; 12 mos; Written tests; Bimonthly support group

194. University Hospital Eating Disorders Program
722 Hill St, Madison, WI 53705-3517
(608) 263-4760
CONTACT: Donald Fullerton, MD, Prog Dir
CONTACT TELEPHONE: (608) 263-4760
FAX: (608) 263-0908
DATE ESTABLISHED: 1972
EATING DISORDERS TREATED: Anorexia nervosa; Bulimia nervosa; Compulsive overeating/obesity

TREATMENT/THERAPY: Psychological; Group; Individual; Family; Adolescent; Out-patient education; Psychiatric treatment
SETTING: Hospital; In-patient; Out-patient
PROGRAM LENGTH: Varies with individual
NO. OF PATIENTS PROGRAM CAN SERVE: No limit; NO. TREATED PREVIOUS YEAR: 300 new patients; 7700-7800 visits
FOLLOW-UP EVALUATIONS: Re-evaluations of current program if needed; Re-evaluations of patients if they have left the program for more than 3 mos

Milwaukee

195. DePaul Hospital Out-patient Clinic
4143 S 13th St, Milwaukee, WI 53211
(414) 281-4407
CONTACT: Dr David VandeVusse
HOTLINE: (800) 472-8770 (WI); (800) 423-6028 (US)
FAX: (414) 281-6484
DATE ESTABLISHED: 1985
EATING DISORDERS TREATED: Anorexia nervosa; Bulimia nervosa; Compulsive overeating/obesity
TREATMENT/THERAPY: Addiction; Psychological; Group; Individual; 12-step; Out-patient education
SETTING: Out-patient
PROGRAM LENGTH: 5 mos intensive 2 times/wk
NO. OF PATIENTS PROGRAM CAN SERVE: 26

196. Milwaukee County Medical Complex, Behavior and Evaluation Treatment Unit
8700 W Wisconsin Ave, Milwaukee, WI 53132
(414) 257-5284
CONTACT: Harold H Harsch, MD
FAX: (414) 257-5241
DATE ESTABLISHED: 1984
EATING DISORDERS TREATED: Anorexia nervosa; Bulimia nervosa; Compulsive overeating/obesity
TREATMENT/THERAPY: Psychological; Group; Individual; Family; Body image
SETTING: Hospital; In-patient
PROGRAM LENGTH: Individualized
NO. OF PATIENTS PROGRAM CAN SERVE: Maximum 10; NO. TREATED PREVIOUS YEAR: 20
FOLLOW-UP EVALUATIONS: Individual followup with psychiatrist and/or therapist as needed

197. St Mary's Hill Hospital Eating Disorder Program
2350 N Lake Dr, Milwaukee, WI 53211
(414) 271-5555
CONTACT: Joy Kline, MD
CONTACT TELEPHONE: (414) 271-5555
DATE ESTABLISHED: 1983
EATING DISORDERS TREATED: Anorexia nervosa; Bulimia nervosa; Compulsive overeating/obesity
TREATMENT/THERAPY: Psychological; Group; Individual; Family; Adolescent; Creative arts; Out-patient education; Exercise; Body image; Cognitive
SETTING: In-patient; Out-patient; In-patient eating disorders program; Intensive evening out-patient program for eating disorders; Day hospital treatment
PROGRAM LENGTH: Varies
NO. OF PATIENTS PROGRAM CAN SERVE: Varies; NO. TREATED PREVIOUS YEAR: 50-60
FOLLOW-UP EVALUATIONS: 6 mos

Oconomowoc

198. Rogers Memorial Hospital Eating Disorders Unit
34700 Valley Rd, Oconomowoc, WI 53066
(800) 767-4411
CONTACT: Dr Jim Miller
DATE ESTABLISHED: 1984
EATING DISORDERS TREATED: Anorexia nervosa; Bulimia nervosa; Compulsive overeating/obesity
TREATMENT/THERAPY: Addiction; Psychological; Group; Individual; Family; Adolescent; 12-step; Creative arts; Exercise; Body image
SETTING: Hospital; In-patient
PROGRAM LENGTH: 30 days average
NO. OF PATIENTS PROGRAM CAN SERVE: 25; NO. TREATED PREVIOUS YEAR: 250-300
FOLLOW-UP EVALUATIONS: 1 mo; 6 mos; 12 mos

Wauwatosa

199. Milwaukee Psychiatric Hospital
1220 Dewey Ave, Wauwatosa, WI 53213
(414) 258-2600
CONTACT: Kate Connelly, MSW
CONTACT TELEPHONE: (414) 258-2032
DATE ESTABLISHED: 1984
EATING DISORDERS TREATED: Anorexia nervosa; Bulimia nervosa; Compulsive overeating/obesity
TREATMENT/THERAPY: Group; Individual; Family; Adolescent; Biopsycho Social Model; Cognitive-behavioral; Out-patient education; Body image
SETTING: Hospital; In-patient; Out-patient

Milwaukee Psychiatric Hospital
(continued)

PROGRAM LENGTH: Individualized in-patient and out-patient treatment
FOLLOW-UP EVALUATIONS: 6 mos; Patient survey

WYOMING

Lander

200. Pine Ridge Hospital Eating Disorders Program
150 Wyoming, Lander, WY 82520
(307) 332-5700
CONTACT: Teresa Alfertig, Intake Coord
CONTACT TELEPHONE: (800) 443-5700

EATING DISORDERS TREATED: Anorexia nervosa; Bulimia nervosa; Compulsive overeating/obesity
TREATMENT/THERAPY: Addiction; Psychological; Group; Individual; Family; Adolescent; 12-step; Creative arts; Exercise; Body image
SETTING: Hospital; In-patient
PROGRAM LENGTH: Varies
FOLLOW-UP EVALUATIONS: Aftercare

List of Facilities

▼
▼
▼
▼

To find the facilities listed here, turn first in the "Directory of Facilities and Programs" to the state given, then to the city, then to the facility. All facilities are listed in the directory alphabetically by state, then city, then name.

▼ ▼ ▼ ▼

Alvarado Parkway Institute, La Mesa, CA

Anacapa Hospital, Port Hueneme, CA

Anorexia and Bulimia Resource Center, Coral Gables, FL

Anorexia Nervosa/Bulimia Treatment Program, Durham, NC

Associates in Adult Adolescent and Child Psychotherapy Inc, Brecksville, OH

Ballard Community Hospital Eating Disorders Unit, Seattle, WA

Baptist Hospital, Pensacola, FL

Battle Creek Adventist Hospital, Battle Creek, MI

Bayview Hospital Eating Disorders Program, Corpus Christi, TX

Behavioral Medicine Institute, New Canaan, CT

J C Blair Memorial Hospital Counseling Services, Huntingdon, PA

Blount Memorial Hospital, Maryville, TN

Boulder Community Hospital, Women's Recovery Program, Boulder, CO

Brooklyn Heights Center for Counseling, Brooklyn, NY

Bulimia Treatment Associates, New York, NY

Cambridge Hospital Eating Disorders Program, Cambridge, MA

Capistrano by the Sea Hospital, Dana Point, CA

Carrier Foundation, Belle Mead, NJ

Case Western Reserve University School of Medicine, Behavior Therapy Clinic, University Hospitals of Cleveland, Cleveland, OH

Cedar Springs Psychiatric Hospital, Colorado Springs, CO

Center for Overcoming Problem Eating, Western Psychiatric Institute and Clinic, Pittsburgh, PA

Center for the Study of Anorexia & Bulimia, New York, NY

Center for the Treatment of Eating Disorders, Columbus, OH

Charter Hospital of Indianapolis Eating Disorders Program, Indianapolis, IN

Charter Hospital of Long Beach, Long Beach, CA

Charter Hospital Orlando, Kissimmee, FL

Charter Plains Hospital, Lubbock, TX

Charter Springs Hospital, Psychiatric Unit, Ocala, FL

Children's Hospital, Division of Adolescent/ Young Adult Medicine, Out-Patient Eating Disorders Clinic, Boston, MA

Children's National Medical Center, Washington, DC

The Christ Hospital Eating Disorders Unit, Cincinnati, OH

The Clark Center, Memorial Medical Center, Savannah, GA

Cleveland Clinic Foundation, Department of Psychiatry, Cleveland, OH

Coliseum Medical Center Eating Disorders Program, New Orleans, LA

Columbia Presbyterian Medical Center/New York State Psychiatric Institute, New York, NY

Columbine—Eating Treatment Center, Littleton, CO

CPC Belmont Hills Hospital, Belmont, CA

Cypress Hospital, Lafayette, LA

Decatur Hospital Eating Disorders Program, Decatur, GA

DePaul Hospital Out-patient Clinic, Milwaukee, WI

Dominion Hospital, Falls Church, VA

Eating Disorder Clinic, St Louis, MO

Eating Disorders Center of Greater Phoenix, Scottsdale, AZ

Eating Disorders Institute, St Louis Park, MN

Florida Hospital—Eating/Affective Disorders Unit, Orlando, FL

Forest Hospital, Des Plaines, IL

Fort Collins Eating Disorders Program, Fort Collins, CO

Four Winds Hospital Eating Disorders Service, Katonah, NY

Four Winds Hospital—Saratoga, Saratoga Springs, NY

Georgetown University Diet Management and Eating Disorders Program, Washington, DC

Glenbeigh Hospital of Miami, Hialeah, FL

Glenbeigh Hospital of Tampa Food Addiction Unit, Tampa, FL

Glenbeigh Hospital of the Palm Beaches, West Palm Beach, FL

Gracie Square Hospital Eating Disorder Program, New York, NY

Graduate Hospital, Philadelphia, PA

Janet Greeson's A Place for Us, Orlando, FL

Hahnemann Hospital, Eating Disorders Service, Boston, MA

Hamptom Hospital, Rancocas, NJ

HCA Montevista Hospital, Las Vegas, NV

HCA Willow Park Hospital, Plano, TX

HCA Woodland Hospital, Hoffman Estates, IL

HELP—Healthy Eating Lifestyle Program, Des Plaines, IL

Highland Park Hospital—The Center on 3-East, Highland Park, IL

Hill Country Hospital, San Antonio, TX

The Johns Hopkins Eating and Weight Disorders Program, Baltimore, MD

Indiana University Hospital Eating Disorders Program, Indianapolis, IN

Institute of Pennsylvania Hospital, Philadelphia, PA

Intermountain Hospital Psychiatric Unit, Boise, ID

Iowa Lutheran Hospital—Eating Disorders Treatment Center, Des Moines, IA

Jefferson Medical College, Philadelphia, PA

Jewish Family Services Eating Disorders Program, North Miami Beach, FL

Kahi Mohala Hospital, Ewa Beach, HI

Lucy Lee Hospital Eating Disorders Program, Poplar Bluff, MO

Lutheran Medical Center, St Louis, MO

Massachusetts General Hospital, Boston, MA

Massachusetts Institute of Technology, Cambridge, MA

Mayo Clinic, Rochester, MN

McLean Hospital, Belmont, MA

Menninger Clinic, Topeka, KS

Mercy Center for Health Care Services, Aurora, IL

Mercy Hospital Eating Disorder Unit, Baltimore, MD

Mercy Hospital Eating Disorder Unit, Des Moines, IA

Methodist Hospital of Memphis, Memphis, TN

Metropolitan Clinic of Counseling Inc, Minneapolis, MN

Milwaukee County Medical Complex, Behavior and Evaluation Treatment Unit, Milwaukee, WI

Milwaukee Psychiatric Hospital, Wauwatosa, WI

Mt Auburn Hospital Out-patient Psychiatry Center, Cambridge, MA

National Institutes of Mental Health, Unit on Eating Disorders, Bethesda, MD

New Attitudes Recovery Center, Lemon Grove, CA

New England Medical Center Hospitals, Boston, MA

New York Center for Eating Disorders, Brooklyn, NY

New York Hospital—Cornell Medical Center, White Plains, NY

Newington Children's Hospital, Newington, CT

North Shore Children's Hospital, Eating Disorders Program, Mental Health Center, Salem, MA

Northridge Hospital Medical Center—Eating Disorders Program, Northridge, CA

Northside Hospital Education Center, Atlanta, GA

Northwestern Medical Faculty Foundation Eating Disorders Program—Northwestern Memorial Hospital, Chicago, IL

Norton Psychiatric Clinic, Eating Disorders Program, Louisville, KY

Nutrition Health Services, Houston, TX

Ochsner Clinic, Addictive Behavior Unit, New Orleans, LA

Lucile Packard Children's Hospital at Stanford, Palo Alto, CA

Parkside Lutheran Hospital, Park Ridge, IL

Parkside Medical Services Corp, Park Ridge, IL

Parkwood Hospital, New Bedford, MA

Peninsula Medical Center Eating Disorders Program, Ormond Beach, FL

Penn State University Hospital, The Milton S Hershey Medical Center, Department of Psychiatry, Hershey, PA

Philadelphia Child Guidance Center, Philadelphia, PA

Philadelphia Psychiatric Center, Philadelphia, PA

Physicians Plus Medical Group, Nutrition Center, Madison, WI

Pine Ridge Hospital Eating Disorders Program, Lander, WY

Porter Memorial Hospital, Denver, CO

Portland Adventist Medical Center, Portland, OR

Presbyterian/St Luke's Medical Center, Denver, CO

Psychiatric Institute of Washington DC, Minirth-Meier-Byrd Unit, Washington, DC

Psychological Associates of Clear Lake, Houston, TX

The Rader Institute at Auburn General Hospital, Auburn, WA

The Rader Institute at Belmont Community Hospital, Chicago, IL

The Rader Institute at Fort Worth Medical Center, Grand Prairie, TX

The Rader Institute at Hollywood Medical Center, Hollywood, FL

The Rader Institute at Medical Center of North Hollywood, North Hollywood, CA

The Rader Institute at Phenix Medical Park Hospital, Phenix City, AL

The Rader Institute at Riverton Hospital, Seattle, WA

The Rader Institute at Sharp Cabrillo Hospital, San Diego, CA

The Rader Institute at South Bay Hospital, Redondo Beach, CA

The Rader Institute at Tulsa Regional Medical Center, Tulsa, OK

The Rader Institute at Woman's Hospital, Baton Rouge, LA

The Rader Institute at Women's Medical Center, Seminole, FL

Rader Institute Eating Disorders Unit— Winterhaven Hosptial at Regency Medical Center, Winter Haven, FL

The Rader Institute—Los Angeles, Los Angeles, CA

Red Canyon Ranch, Grass Range, MT

Remuda Ranch, Wickenburg, AZ

Renaissance Counseling Center, Altamonte Springs, FL

Renfrew Center, Coconut Creek, FL

Renfrew Center, Philadelphia, PA

River Center Inc, New York, NY

Rocky Mountain Treatment Center, Great Falls, MT

Rogers Memorial Hospital Eating Disorders Unit, Oconomowoc, WI

Sacred Heart General Hospital, Department of Psychiatry, Eugene, OR

Sahuaro Vista Ranch, Tucson, AZ

St Anthony's Psychiatric Center, St Louis, MO

St David's Medical Center Eating Disorders Program (EDP), Austin, TX

St John's Mercy Medical Center, Anorexia-Bulimia Treatment and Education Center (ABTEC), St Louis, MO

St Joseph Hospital Center for Personal & Family Development, Tacoma, WA

St Luke's Gordon Recovery Centers, Sioux City, IA

St Luke's Hospital Eating Disorder Treatment Center, Duluth, MN

St Luke's Roosevelt Hospital Center, New York, NY

St Mary Hospital—Eating Disorders Recovery Center (EDRC), Livonia, MI

St Mary's Hill Hospital Eating Disorder Program, Milwaukee, WI

St Patrick Hospital Addiction Treatment Program, Missoula, MT

St Vincent Charity Hospital, Cleveland, OH

St Vincent Infirmary—Restore, Little Rock, AR

St Vincent's Hospital, Portland, OR

St Vincent's Hospital Eating Disorders Programs, Harrison, NY

Scottsdale Camelback Hospital, Scottsdale, AZ

Sentara Norfolk General Hospital, Norfolk, VA

Sheppard-Pratt Hospital Eating Disorders Program, Baltimore, MD

Shin Oak Clinic Inc, San Antonio, TX

Sierra Tucson, Tucson, AZ

Smyrna Hospital Advance, Smyrna, GA

Sonora Desert Hospital—Women's Resource and Treatment Center, Tucson, AZ

South Oaks Hospital Eating Disorders Unit, Amityville, NY

Spring Branch Memorial Hospital, Houston, TX

Stanford University Behavioral Medicine Clinic, Department of Psychiatry and Behavioral Sciences, Stanford, CA

STEPS Residential Treatment Facility, Port Hueneme, CA

Tennessee Christian Medical Center, Madison, TN

Tulane Medical Center, New Orleans, LA

Turning Point of Tampa, Tampa, FL

UCLA Neuropsychiatric Institute & Hospital—Adolescent Eating Disorders Program, Los Angeles, CA

UCLA Neuropsychiatric Institute & Hospital—Adult Eating Disorders Program, Los Angeles, CA

University Hospital Eating Disorders Program, Madison, WI

University of Alabama Department of Psychiatry, Birmingham, AL

University of Arizona Health Sciences Center, Department of Family and Community Medicine, Tucson, AZ

University of California at Davis Medical School, University Psychiatry Center, Sacramento, CA

University of Chicago Medical Center, Department of Psychiatry Eating Disorders Program, Chicago, IL

University of Cincinnati Eating Disorders Center, Cincinnati, OH

University of Iowa, Department of Psychiatry, Iowa City, IA

University of Massachusetts Medical Center, Worchester, MA

University of Michigan Eating Disorders Program, Ann Arbor, MI

University of Minnesota Hospital & Clinic, Department of Psychiatry, Eating Disorders, Minneapolis, MN

University of Mississippi Medical Center, Jackson, MS

University of Nebraska Medical Center Eating Disorders Program, Omaha, NE

University of Pennsylvania Hospital, Psychiatric Unit, Philadelphia, PA

University of Rochester Medical Center, Department of Psychiatry & Adult Eating Disorders Program, Rochester, NY

University of South Florida College of Medicine, Eating Disorders Clinic, Tampa, FL

University of Tennessee Weight Control Center, Memphis, TN

University of Texas Southwestern Eating Disorders Program, Dallas, TX

Villa Rosa Hospital, San Antonio, TX

Washington Hospital Center, Washington, DC

Wellesley Hospital, Newton, MA

West Oaks Hospital Eating Disorders, Houston, TX

Wilkins Center for Eating Disorders, Greenwich, CT

The Willough at Naples, Naples, FL

Willow Creek Hospital and Treatment Center, Scottsdale, AZ

Windsor Hospital, Chagrin Falls, OH

Winoma Memorial Hospital Corp, Indianapolis, IN

Women's Therapy Center Institute, New York, NY

Woodridge Hospital, Clayton, GA

Yale-New Haven Hospital Out-patient Psychiatry Clinic, New Haven, CT

York Street Center, Norfolk, VA

PART 5
Selected Resources

Articles, Books, and Audiovisual Resources

▼
▼
▼
▼

Listed below are over 400 recent articles, books, and audiovisual sources that deal with eating disorders. These resources are arranged under four topics:

- Anorexia Nervosa and/or Bulimia Nervosa
- Compulsive Overeating/Obesity
- Eating Disorders (General)
- Issues Relating to Eating Disorders (e.g., body image, children and eating problems, etc.)

Each topic alphabetically lists first, articles, then books, then audiovisuals (if any) on the subject. Articles listed are recent, with most of them published between 1988 and 1991. Books included span a wider publication date range, but most of them have been published in the last four years.

Some of the resources listed are for the lay audience (that is, for people with eating disorders, their families, and friends), some are written for the professional caring for the person with the disorder, and some are for both audiences. Please note that articles from the *International Journal of Eating Disorders* and other periodicals focusing on eating disorders have been omitted here for space reasons only. These journals are excellent sources for the professional (and may be of use to the interested layperson). For more information about them, see "Journals, Indexes, and Other Sources."

▼ ▼ ▼ ▼

ANOREXIA NERVOSA AND/OR BULIMIA NERVOSA

Articles

Alderson, J.W. The Thin Binge. *Harper's Bazaar.* 124 (July 1991): 73ff.

Anorexia in the Elderly. *The Edell Health Letter.* 8 (March 1989): 7.

Anorexia in the Elderly: Take Prompt Action. *Medical Abstracts Newsletter.* 11(2) (Feb 1991): 6.

Anorexia Nervosa: Link to Personality Features. *Medical Abstracts Newsletter.* 10(6) (Jun 1990): 5.

Anorexia Nervosa: Obsession with Thinness. *Mayo Clinic Nutrition Letter.* 2 (Apr 1989): 2ff.

Anorexia Nervosa: Promising Long-Term Outcomes. *Medical Abstracts Newsletter.* 10(2) (Feb 1990): 5.

Arnow, Bruce. Psychologic Treatment for Binge Eating. *Healthline.* (May 1990): 2-4.

Attie, I., & J. Brooks-Gunn. Development of Eating Problems in Adolescent Girls: A Longitudinal Study. *Developmental Psychology.* 25(1) (1989): 70-79.

Bachrach, Laura K., David Guido, Debra Katzman, Iris F. Litt, & Robert Marcus. Decreased Bone Density in Adolescent Girls with Anorexia Nervosa. *Pediatrics.* 86 (Sept 1990): 440ff.

Barth, F.D. The Treatment of Bulimia from a Self Psychological Perspective. *Clinical Social Work Journal.* 16(3) (1988): 270-281.

Bauer, Barbara G., & Wayne P. Anderson. Bulimic Beliefs: Food for Thought. *Journal of Counseling and Development.* 67 (Mar 1989): 416ff.

Bowen-Woodward, Kathryn, & Leonard S Levitz. Impact of the College Environment on Bulimic Women. *Journal of College Student Psychotherapy.* 3(2-4) (1988-89): 181-190.

Brody, Jane E. Bulimia and Anorexia, Insidious Eating Disorders that Are Best Treated When Detected Early. *The New York Times.* 139 (Feb 22, 1990): B9.

Brody, Jane E. For Men and Boys, Anorexia and Bulimia Pose Special Problems. *The New York Times.* 139 (Aug 16, 1990): B7-B13.

Brody, Robert. Update on Anorexia/Bulimia. *Cosmopolitan.* 210(1) (Jan 1991): 80, 86, 88, 100.

Bulimia: Which Treatment Is Most Effective? *Medical Abstracts Newsletter.* 10(5) (May 1990): 5.

Cornelius, Coleman. Portraits of Hope: For Women with Eating Disorders, Recovery Can Be a Long and Arduous Journey. *Shape.* 10(8) (Apr 1991): 80-86, 98, 100, 103, 105-106.

Depressive Symptoms and Substance Abuse among Adolescent Binge Eaters and Purgers. *American Journal of Public Health.* 77(12) (1987) 1539-1541.

Dolan, Bridget M., Chris Evans, & J. Hubert Lacey. Family Composition and Social Class in Bulimia: A Catchment Area Study of a Clinical and a Comparison Group. *Journal of Nervous and Mental Disease.* 177 (May 1989): 267.

Drewnowski, A., D.K. Yee, & D.D. Krahm. Bulimia in College Women: Incidence and Recovery Rates. *American Journal of Psychiatry.* 145(6) (1988): 753-755.

Durham, Donald R. Eating Disorders: Today, Anorexia Is Much Less a Respector of Race or Socioeconomic Status...about One Percent of the Women between 18 and 25 have Anorexia. *Total Health.* 13 (June 1991): 37ff.

Edelstein, Carole K., Paul Haskew, & Janet P. Kramer. Early Clues to Anorexia and Bulilmia. *Patient Care.* 23 (August 1988): 155.

Eller, Daryn. Liquid Diets and Bulimia. *Self.* 12(8) (Aug 1990): 50.

An Evaluation of Family Therapy in Anorexia Nervosa and Bulimia Nervosa. *Archives of General Psychiatry.* 44(12) (December 1987): 1047-1056.

Friedrichs, Mary. The Dependent Solution: Anorexia and Bulimia as Defenses against Danger. *Women and Therapy.* 7(4) (1988): 53-73.

Giannini, James, Michael Newman, & Mark Gold. Anorexia and Bulimia. *American Family Physician.* 41 (Apr 1990): 1169ff.

Greene, Geoffrey W., Cheryl Achterberg, Jeffrey Crumbaugh, & Jan Soper. Dietary Intake and Dieting Practices of Bulimic and Non-bulimic Female College Students. *Journal of the American Dietetic Association.* 90 (Apr 1990): 576ff.

Harris, Robert. Anorexia Nervosa and Bulimia Nervosa in Female Adolescence. *Nutrition Today.* 26(2) (Apr 1991): 30-34.

Henderson, Richard. Bone Health in Adolescence: Anorexia and Athletic Amenorrhea. *Nutrition Today.* 26(2) (Apr 1991): 25-29.

Howat, Paula M., Lisa M. Varner, & Richard L. Wampold. The Effectiveness of a Dental/Dietitian Team in the Assessment of Bulimic Dental Health. *Journal of the American Dietetic Association.* 90 (Aug 1990): 1099ff.

Is Bulimia Inherited? *The Edell Health Letter.* 9(9) (Oct 1990): 4-5.

Jansen, Anita, Marcel van den Hout, & Eric Griez. Clinical and Non-clinical Binges. *Behaviour Research and Therapy.* 28 (Sept-Oct 1990): 439ff.

Jenkins, M.E. An Outcome Study of Anorexia Nervosa in an Adolescent Unit. *Journal of Adolescence.* 10(1) (1987): 71-81.

Johnson, Nancy S., & Elizabeth L. Holloway. Conceptual Complexity and Obssessionality in Bulimic College Women. *Journal of Counseling Psychology.* 35(3) (1988): 251-257.

Kassett, J.A., H.E. Gwertsman, W.H. Kaye, H.A. Brandt, & D.C. Jimerson. Pattern of Onset of Bulimic Symptoms in Anorexia Nervosa. *The American Journal of Psychiatry.* 145(10) (1988): 1287-1288.

King, Pamela. Turning Around Bulimia with Therapy. *Psychology Today.* 23 (Sept 1989): 14.

Lamb, Lawrence E. Bulimia: Hormones at Fault? *Muscle & Fitness.* 51 (Sept 1990): 43.

McCormack, Sheila, & Roderick S. Carman. Eating Motivations and Bulimic Behavior among College Women. *Psychological Reports.* 64(3) (1989): 1163-1166.

McGlynn, Thomas J., & Dorris E. Tinker. Anorexia Nervosa in Adulthood. *American Family Physician.* 39 (Jan 1989): 173ff.

Nine Attitude Adjustments that Banish Binges. *Lose Weight Naturally.* 4(6) (Jun 1990): 6-7.

Outcome in Anorexia Nervosa and Bulimia Nervosa: A Review of the Literature. *Journal of Nervous Mental Disorders.* 176(3) (1988): 131-143.

Position of the American Diabetic Association: Nutrition Intervention in the Treatment of Anorexia Nervosa and Bulimia Nervosa. *Journal of American Diabetic Association.* 88(1) (January 1988): 68-71.

Predictors of Binge Eating. *The Addiction Letter.* 7 (May 1991): 5.

Santucci, Patricia. Whoever Said,"You Can Never Be Too Thin?" What to Do When Your Child Has an Eating Disorder. *PTA Today.* 16(3) (Mar 1991): 268-78.

Silverstein, Brett, Lauren Perdue, Cordulla Wolf, & Cecelia Pizzolo. Bingeing, Purging, and Estimates of Parental Attitudes Regarding Female Achievement. *Sex Roles.* 19 (11-12) (1988): 723-733.

Steiner-Adair, Catherine. Developing the Voice of the Wise Woman: College Students and Bulimia. *Journal of College Student Psychotherapy.* 3(2-4) (1988-89): 151-165.

Suplee, Curt. Girls' Anorexia, Bulimia Linked to Mothers' Criticism. *The Washington Post.* 114 (Apr 30, 1991): A3.

Szekeley, Eva. Reflections on the Body in the Anorexia Discourse. *Resources for Feminist Research.* 17(4) (1988): 8-11.

Tolstoi, Linda G. The Role of Pharmacotherapy in Anorexia Nervosa and Bulimia. *Journal of the American Dietetic Association.* 89 (Nov 1989): 1640ff.

Warner-Berley, J. "Perfect Bodies to Die For. *McCalls.* 117 (May 1990): 64-65.

Warsen, J. Pretty Princess: A Teenager's Five-Year Struggle with Anorexia and Bulimia. *American Health.* 10(6) (Jul-Aug 1991): 38-40, 42-43.

Weiss, Rick. Bulimia's Binges Linked to Hormone. *Science News.* 134 (September 1988): 182.

Wierman, Victoria. A Feminist Interpretation of College Student Bulimia. *Journal of College Student Psychotherapy.* 3(2-4) (1988-89): 167-180.

Williamson, D.A., C.J. Davis, A.J. Goreczny, & D.C. Blovin. Body-image Disturbances in Bulimia Nervosa: Influences of Actual Body Size. *Journal of Abnormal Psychology.* 98(1) (1989): 97-99.

Woodside, D.B., & P.E. Garfinkel. An Overview of the Eating Disorders Anorexia Nervosa and Bulimia Nervosa. *Nutrition Today.* 24 (June 1989): 27.

Wooley, Susan Clark, & Karen Gail Lewis. The Missing Woman: Intensive Family-oriented Treatment of Bulimia. *Journal of Feminist Family Therapy.* 1(1) (1988): 61-83.

Books

Andersen, Arnold E. *Practical Comprehensive Treatment of Anorexia Nervosa and Bulimia.* Baltimore, MD: Johns Hopkins University Press, 1985, 207p.

Arenson, Gloria. *Binge Eating: How to Stop It Forever.* New York: Rawson Associates, 1984, 245p.

Bauer, Barbara G., Wayne P. Anderson, & Robert A. Hyatt. *Bulimia: Book for Therapist and Client.* Muncie, IN: Accelerated Development, 1986, 210p.

Bell, Rudolph M. *Holy Anorexia.* Chicago: University of Chicago Press, 1985, 248p.

Bhanji, S., & D. Mattingly. *Medical Aspects of Anorexia Nervosa.* Boston: Wright, 1988, 140p.

Boskind-White, Marlene, & William C. White, Jr. *Bulimarexia, the Binge/Purge Cycle.* 2nd Edition. New York: W.W. Norton & Co., 1987, 210p.

Bruch, Hilde. *The Golden Cage: The Enigma of Anorexia Nervosa.* Cambridge, MA: Harvard University Press, 1978, 159p.

Bruch, Hilde. *Conversations with Anorexics.* New York: Basic Books, 1988, 216p.

Brumberg, Joan Jacobs. *Fasting Girls: The Emergence of Anorexia Nervosa as a Modern Disease.* Cambridge, MA: Harvard University Press, 1988, 366p.

Burrows, G. D., P.J. Beumont, & R.C. Casper, eds. *Handbook of Eating Disorders, Pt. I: Anorexia Nervosa and Bulimia.* New York: Elsevier Science Publishing, 1987, 400p.

Byrne, Katherine. *A Parent's Guide to Anorexia and Bulimia: Understanding and Helping Self-Starvers and Binge/Purgers.* New York: Holt, Henry & Co., 1989, 167p.

Cauwels, Janice M. *Bulimia: The Binge-Purge Compulsion.* New York: Doubleday and Co., 1983, 249p.

Cohen, Ronald Jay. *Binge! It's Not a State of Hunger...It's a State of Mind.* New York: Macmillan, 1979.

Crisp, A. H. *Anorexia Nervosa: Let Me Be.* New York: Grune & Scratton, 1980.

Czyzewski, Danita, & Melanie Smith, eds. *Conversations with Anorexics: Hilde Bruch.* New York: Basic Books, 1988, 240p.

Dana, Mura, & Marilyn Laurence. *Women's Secret Disorder: A New Understanding of Bulimia.* London: Grafton Books, 1988.

Darby, P. L. et al. *Anorexia Nervosa: Recent Developments in Research.* New York: Alan R. Liss Inc., 1983.

Duker, Marilyn, & Roger Slade. *Anorexia Nervosa and Bulimia: How to Help.* New York: Taylor & Francis, Inc., 1988, 229p.

Emmett, Steven Wiley. *Theory and Treatment of Anorexia Nervosa and Bulimia: Biomedical, Sociocultural, and Psychological Perspectives.* New York: Brunner/Mazel, 1985, 332p.

Epling, W. Frank, & W. David Pierce. *Solving the Anorexia Puzzle: A Scientific Approach.* Lewiston, NY: Hogrefe and Huber, 1991, 229p.

Erichsen, Ann. *Anorexia Nervosa: The Broken Circle.* Boston: Faber and Faber, 1985, 220p.

Erlanger, Ellen. *Eating Disorders: A Question and Answer Book About Anorexia Nervosa and Bulimia Nervosa.* Minneapolis, MN: Lerner Publications Co., 1988, 64p. (Juvenile).

French, Barbara. *Coping with Bulimia: The Binge-Purge Syndrome.* San Bernardino, CA: Borgo Press, 1987, 160p.

Garfield, Johanna. *The Life of a Real Girl.* New York: St. Martin's Press, 1986.

Garfinkel, Paul E., & David M. Garner. *Anorexia Nervosa: A Multidimensional Perspective.* New York: Brunner/Mazel, 1982, 379p.

Garner, David M., & Paul E. Garfinkel. *Handbook of Psychotherapy for Anorexia Nervosa and Bulimia.* New York: Guilford Press, 1985, 592p.

Garner, David M., & Paul E. Garfinkel, eds. *Diagnostic Issues in Anorexia Nervosa and Bulimia Nervosa.* New York: Brunner/Mazel, 1988, 228p.

Gordon, Richard A. *Anorexia and Bulimia: Anatomy of a Social Epidemic.* Cambridge, MA: B. Blackwell, 1990, 174p.

Hall, Lindsey, & Leigh Cohn. *Bulimia: A Guide to Recovery: Understanding and Overcoming the Binge-Purge Syndrome.* Carlsbad, CA: Gürze Books, 1986, 160p.

Hall, Lindsey, & Leigh Cohn. *Understanding and Overcoming Bulimia: A Self-Help Guide.* Carlsbad, CA: Gürze Books, 1982.

Heater, Sandra H. *Am I Still Visible? A Woman's Triumph Over Anorexia Nervosa.* White Hall, VA: White Hall Books, 1983, 140p.

Hudson, James I., & Harrison G. Pope, Jr., eds. *The Psychobiology of Bulimia.* Washington, DC: American Psychiatric Press, 1987, 249p.

Johnson, Craig L., ed. *Psychodynamic Treatment of Anorexia Nervosa and Bulimia.* New York: Guilford Press, 1990, 404p.

Johnson, Craig, & Mary E. Connors. *The Etiology and Treatment of Bulimia Nervosa: A Biopsychosocial Perspective.* New York: Basic Books, 1987, 335p.

Johnson, William G., ed. *Bulimia Nervosa: Perspectives on Clinical Research and Therapy.* Greenwich, CT: JAI Press Inc., 1989, 281p.

Josephs, R. *Early Disorder.* New York: Farrar, Strauss & Giroux, 1980, 180p.

Kapoor, Sandra. *Bulimia: A Program for Friends and Family Members.* Springfield, IL: Thomas, 1988.

Kaye, Walter H., & Harry E. Gwirtsman, eds. *A Comprehensive Approach to the Treatment of Normal Weight Bulimia.* New York: Guilford Press, 1985.

Kinoy, Barbara P., & Estelle B. Miller, eds. *When Will We Laugh Again? Living and Dealing with Anorexia Nervosa and Bulimia.* New York: Columbia University Press, 1984.

Landau, Elaine. *Why Are They Starving Themselves? Understanding Anorexia Nervosa and Bulimia.* New York: Julian Messner, 1983, 110p.

Latimer, Jane E. *Living Binge-Free: A Personal Guide to Victory over Compulsive Eating.* Boulder, CO: LivingQuest, 1988, 138p.

Lawrence, Marilyn. *The Anorexic Experience.* London: Women's Press, 1984, 142p.

Levenkron, Steven. *The Best Little Girl in the World.* Chicago: Contemporary Books, 1978, 196p.

Levenkron, Steven. *Treating and Overcoming Anorexia Nervosa.* New York: Charles Scribner's Sons, 1982, 205p.

MacLeod, Sheila. *The Art of Starvation*. New York: Schocken Books, 1983, 181p.

Messinger, Lisa. *Biting the Hand that Feeds Me: Days of Binging, Purging and Recovery*. Novato, CA: Arena Press, 1986, 206p.

Miller, Caroline. *My Name Is Caroline*. New York: Doubleday, 1988, 278p.

Minuchin, Salvatore, B. L. Rosman, & L. Baker. *Psychosomatic Families: Anorexia Nervosa in Context*. Cambridge, MA: Harvard University Press, 1978, 351p.

Mitchell, James E. *Bulimia Nervosa*. Minneapolis, MN: University of Minnesota Press, 1990, 174p.

Neuman, Patricia A., & Patricia A. Halvorson. *Anorexia Nervosa and Bulimia: A Handbook for Counselors and Therapists*. New York: Van Nostrand Reinhold, 1983, 253p.

O'Neill, Cherry Boone. *Starving for Attention*. New York: Dell Publishing, 1983, 240p.

Orbach, Susie. *Hunger Strike: The Anorectic's Struggle as a Metaphor for Our Age*. New York: Avon Books, 1988, 259p.

Palazzoli, Maria Selvini. *Self-Starvation*. Northvale, NJ: Jason Aronson, 1978, 295p.

Palmer, R. L. *Anorexia Nervosa: A Guide for Sufferers and Their Families*. New York: Penguin Books, 1980, 156p.

Patterson, Catherine M. *Nutrition and Eating Disorders: Guidelines for the Patient with Anorexia Nervosa and Bulimia Nervosa*. Van Nuys, CA: PM, Inc., 1989, 34p.

Piran, Niva, & Allan S Kaplan, eds. *A Day Hospital Group Treatment Program for Anorexia Nervosa and Bulimia Nervosa*. New York: Brunner/Mazel, 1990, 158p.

Pope, Harrison G., Jr., & James Hudson. *New Hope for Binge Eaters: Advances in the Understanding and Treatment of Bulimia*. New York: HarperCollins Publishers, Inc., 1985, 256p.

Powers, Pauline S., & Robert C. Fernandez, eds. *Current Treatment of Anorexia Nervosa and Bulimia*. New York: S. Karger, 1984.

Reid, Larry D., ed. *Opioids, Bulimia, and Alcohol Abuse and Alcoholism*. New York: Springer-Verlag, 1990.

Remschmidt, Helmut, & Martin H. Schmidt, eds. *Anorexia Nervosa*. Lewiston, NY: Hogrefe and Huber, 1990, 179p.

Root, Maria P., Patricia Fallon, & William N. Friedrich. *Bulimia: A Systems Approach to Treatment*. New York: W. W. Norton and Co., 1986, 329p.

Ruckman, I. *The Hunger Scream*. New York: Walker & Co Inc., 1983, 188p.

Rumney, Avis. *Dying to Please: Anorexia and Its Cure*. Jefferson, NC: MacFarland, 1983, 116p.

Sacker, Ira M. *Dying to Be Thin*. New York: Warner Books, 266p.

Sandbek, Terence J. *The Deadly Diet: Recovering from Anorexia and Bulimia*. Oakland, CA: New Harbinger Publications, 1986, 264p.

Schwartz, Harvey J., ed. *Bulimia: Psychoanalytic Treatment and Theory*. Madison, CT: International Universities Press, 1988, 549p.

Scott, Derek, ed. *Anorexia and Bulimia Nervosa: Practical Approaches*. New York: New York University Press, 1988, 214p.

Sherman, Roberta Trattner. *Bulimia: A Guide for Family and Friends*. Lexington, MA: Lexington Books, 1990.

Slade, Roger. *The Anorexia Nervosa Reference Book*. New York: Harper & Row, 1984.

Sours, John. *Starving to Death in a Sea of Objects: The Anorexia Nervosa Syndrome*. Northvale, NJ: Jason Aronson, 1980, 443p.

Spignesi, Angelyn. *Starving Women: A Psychology of Anorexia Nervosa*. Dallas, TX: Spring Publications, 1983, 138p.

Squire, S. *The Slender Balance: Causes & Cures for Bulimia, Anorexia and the Weight-Loss/Weight-Gain Seesaw*. New York: Putnam, 1983, 248p.

Stein, Patricia M., & Barbara C. Unell. *Anorexia Nervosa: Finding the Life Line*. Minneapolis, MN: CompCare Publishers, 1986, 95p.

Stierlin, Helm, & Gunthard Weber. *Unlocking the Family Door: A Systemic Approach to the Understanding and Treatment of Anorexia Nervosa*. New York: Brunner/Mazel, 1989, 244p.

Valette, Brett Edouard. *A Parent's Guide to Eating Disorders: Prevention and Treatment of Anorexia Nervosa and*

Bulimia. New York: Walker Publishing, 1988, 190p.

Vandereycken, Walter, Elly Kog, & Johan Vanderlinden, eds. *The Family Approach to Eating Disorders: Assessment and Treatment of Anorexia Nervosa and Bulimia.* Costa Mesa, CA: PMA Publishing, 1989, 392p.

Vigersky, Robert. *Anorexia Nervosa.* New York: Raven Press, 1977, 392p.

Vredevelt, Pam, & Joyce Whitman. *Walking a Thin Line: Anorexia and Bulimia, The Battle Can Be Won.* Portland, OR: Multnomah Press, 1985.

Weiss, Lillie, Melanie Katzman, & Sharlene Wolchik. *You Can't Have Your Cake and Eat It Too: A Program for Controlling Bulimia.* Saratoga, CA: R & E Publishers, 1986, 103p.

Weiss, Lillie, Melanie Katzman, & Sharlene Wolchik. *Treating Bulimia: A Psychoeducational Approach.* New York: Pergamon Press, 1985, 111p.

Welbourne, Jill, & Joan Purgold. *The Eating Sickness: Anorexia, Bulimia, and the Myth of Suicide by Slimming.* Brighton, Sussex, England: Harvester Press, 1984, 163p.

Willard, S. *Anorexia and Bulimia: The Potential Devastation of Dieting.* Plainfield, NJ: Patient Education Press, 1990.

Wilson, C. Philip, Charles Hogan, & Ira Mintz. *The Fear of Being Fat: The Treatment of Anorexia Nervosa and Bulimia.* Northvale, NJ: Jason Aronson, 1983, 366p.

Audiovisuals

Anorexia & Bulimia: The Silent Struggle. Video. 29 mins. Eating Awareness Services & Education (EASE), PO Box 27268, Philadelphia, PA 19118. (215) 242-3358.

Anorexia Nervosa. Video. 10 mins. 1988. Professional Research, 930 Pitner Ave, Evanston, IL 60202. (800) 421-2363.

Anorexia Nervosa. Video. 50 mins. 1981. Social Psychiatry Research Institute, 150 E. 69th St, New York, NY 10021. (212) 628-4800.

Binge. Video. 28 mins. 1987. Video Out, 1102 Homer St, Vancouver, BC, Canada V68 2X6. (604) 688-4336.

Breaking out of a Binge: How to See Yourself Through. Audiocassette. 1984. The New York Center for Eating Disorders. 490 3rd St., Brooklyn, NY 11215. (718) 788-6986.

Bulimia. Video. 24 mins. 1986. Center for Media Communication. Available from East Carolina University, Greenville, NC 27858-4354. (919) 757-2472.

Bulimia and the Road to Recovery. Video. 27 mins. 1988. Women Make Movies, 225 Lafayette St, New York, NY 10012. (212) 925-0606.

Bulimia: Out of Control Eating. Video. 23 mins. 1986. Video Out, 1102 Homer St, Vancouver, BC, Canada V68 2X6. (604) 688-4336.

Bulimia: The Binge/Purge Syndrome. Video. 20 mins. 1988. Hospital Satelite Network. Avail. from: AIMS Media Inc., 9710 DeSoto Ave, Chatsworth, CA 91311-4409. (800) 367-2467.

Bulimia: The Binge-Purge Obsession. Video. 25 mins. 1986. Carle Medical Communications, 110 W Main St, Urbana, IL 61801-2700. (217) 384-4838.

Dark Secrets: Bright Victory: One Woman's Recovery from Bulimia. Video. 13 mins. 1987. Carle Medical Communications, 110 W Main St, Urbana, IL 61801-2700. (217) 384-4838.

The Enigma of Anorexia Nervosa. Part 1: Delusion and Discord. Part 2: Clinical Intervention and Rehabilitation. Part 3: The Battle of Wills. 3 videos. Pt 1, 18 mins; Pt 2, 16 mins; Pt 3, 24 mins. 1985. Carle Medical Communications. 110 W Main St, Urbana, IL 61801-2700. (217) 384-4838.

Faces of Recovery. Video. 35 mins. Available through Gürze Books, PO Box 2238, Carlsbad, CA 92018. (800) 756-7533 or (619) 434-7533.

I Don't Have to Hide: A Film about Anorexia and Bulimia. Video. 28 mins. 1982. Fanlight Productions. 47 Halifax, St., Boston, MA 02130. (617) 524-0980.

Portraits of Anorexia. Video. 28 mins. 1987. Churchill Films, 12210 Nebraska Ave, Los Angeles, CA 90025. (31) 207-6600.

Thin Dreams. Video. 21 mins. 1986. Carle Medical Communications. 110 W Main St, Urbana, IL 61801-2700. (217) 384-4838.

Understanding Bulimia. Audiocassette. 55 mins. Available from Gurze Books, PO Box 2238, Carlsbad, CA 92018. (800) 756-7533 or (619) 434-7533.

Wasting Away: Identifying Anorexia Nervosa and Bulimia. Video. 24 mins. Public Relations Office, Newington Children's Hospital, 181 E Cedar St, Newington, CT 06111. (203) 667-5387.

COMPULSIVE OVEREATING/ OBESITY

Articles

Czarjka-Narins, Dorice, & Ellen Parham. Fear of Fat: Attitudes toward Obesity. *Nutrition Today.* 25(1) (Feb 1990): 26-32.

Dieting Doesn't Ruin Your Metabolism. *Food and Nutrition Letter.* 4(12) (Dec 1990): 3.

Forget the "Freshman 10". *Tufts University Diet and Nutrition Letter.* 8(10) (Dec 1990): 2.

Frankl, Elizabeth. Fat's Still a Feminist Issue. *East West.* 20 (Apr 1990): 26ff.

Health Risks of Overweight. *Consumer Reports Health Letter.* 2(2) (Feb 1990): 11.

Kelly, Marguerite. Diagnosing Overeating. *The Washington Post.* 114 (Feb 28, 1991): D5.

Obesity Conference Research May Lead to Physical Cures for the Overweight. *Lose Weight Naturally.* 4(1) (Jan 1990): 1, 4.

Obesity: More Proof that It's an Inherited Trait. *Medical Abstracts Newsletter.* 10(6) (Jun 1990): 1.

Overblown Fear of Flab. *US News & World Report.* 108 (Feb 19, 1990): 70.

Papazian, Ruth. Infant Overeaters? *Health.* 22(9) (Oct 1990): 22.

Powers, Retha. Fat Is a Black Women's Issue. *Essence Magazine.* 20 (Oct 1989): 75ff.

Salk, Lee. Fear of Fat: How Young Can It Start? *McCall's.* 117(11) (Aug 1990): 65.

Segal, Marian. A Sometime Solution to a Weighty Problem. *FDA Consumer.* 24(3) (Apr 1990): 11-15.

Springer, Ilene. Family Ties. *Weight Watchers Magazine.* 24 (Mar 1991): 62ff.

Study Confirms Importance of Attacking Obesity Early. *Parents' Pediatric Report.* 7(10) (Dec 1990): 74.

Stunkard, Albert J., & Thomas A. Wadden. Restrained Eating and Human Obesity. *Nutrition Reviews.* 48 (Feb 1990): 78ff.

Vigorous Feeding Style: Linked to Later Obesity. *Medical Abstracts Newsletter.* 10(6) (Jun 1990): 4.

Willard, Mervyn D. Obesity: Types and Treatments. *American Family Physician.* 43 (June 1991): 2099ff.

Wise, Erica. Feeling Fat: Focusing on Your Body Is Often a Way of Ignoring What's Really Bothering You. *Shape.* 9 (July 1990): 20ff.

Wooley, S.C., & D.M. Garner. Obesity Treatment: The High Cost of False Hope. *Journal of the American Dietetic Association.* 91(10) (1991): 1248-1251.

Zarrow, Susan. New Treatment Breaks the Compulsive Eating Habit. *Lose Weight Naturally.* 4(3) (Mar 1990): 9.

Books

Altschul, Aaron M., ed. *Weight Control: A Guide for Counselors and Therapists.* New York: Praeger, 1987, 292p.

"B," Bill. *Compulsive Overeater.* Minneapolis, MN: CompCare Publishers, 1981, 287p.

"B," Bill. *Maintenance for Compulsive Overeaters: The Twelve-Step Way to Ongoing Recovery.* Minneapolis, MN: CompCare Publishers, 1986, 372p.

Bennett, W., & J. Gurin. *The Dieter's Dilemma: Eating Less and Weighing More.* New York: Basic Books, 1982, 329p.

Bilich, Marion. *Weight Loss from the Inside Out: Help for the Compulsive Eater.* New York: Seabury Press, 1983, 197p.

Bray, G. A., J. LeBlanc, S. Inove, & M . Suzuki, eds. *Diet and Obesity.* Farmington, CT: S. Karger Publishers, Inc., 1988, 248p.

Burrows, G. D., P. J. Beumont, & R. C. Casper, eds. *Handbook of Eating Disorders, Pt. 2: Obesity.* New York: Elsevier Science Publishing, 1988, 316p.

Ciliska, Donna. *Beyond Dieting: Psychoeducational Interventions for Chronically Obese Women—A Non-Dieting Approach.* New York: Brunner/Mazel, 1990, 176p.

Ebbitt, Joan. *Spinning: Thought Patterns of Compulsive Eaters.* Park Ridge, IL: Parkside Publishing.

Hirschmann, Jane R., & Carol H. Munter. *Overcoming Overeating.* New York: Fawcett Book Group, 1989, 259p.

Hollis, Judi. *Fat Is a Family Affair.* Center City, MN: Hazelden Foundation, 1985, 171p.

Johnson, William G., ed. *Treating and Preventing Obesity.* Greenwich, CT: JAI Press Inc., 1987.

"L," Elisabeth. *Listen to the Hunger: Why We Overeat.* San Francisco, CA: Harper, 1988, 85p.

Matsakis, Aphrodite. *Compulsive Eaters and Relationships: Ending the Isolation.* New York: Ballantine Books Inc., 1990.

Orbach, Susie. *Fat Is a Feminist Issue: The Anti-Diet Guide to Permanent Weight Loss.* New York: Berkley Books, 1982, 171p.

Roth, Geneen. *Breaking Free from Compulsive Eating.* New York: NAL/Dutton, 1986.

Roth, Geneen. *Why Weight? A Guide to Ending Compulsive Eating.* New York: NAL/Dutton, 1989.

Roth, Geneen. *Feeding the Hungry Heart: The Experience of Compulsive Eating.* New York: NAL/Dutton, 1989, 224p.

Schwartz, Hillel. *Never Satisfied: A Cultural History of Diets, Fantasies, and Fat.* New York: Free Press, 1986, 468p.

Slochower, Joyce Anne. *Excessive Eating: The Role of Emotions and Environment.* New York: Human Sciences Press, 1983, 112p.

Starlie, Jean, & Henry A. Jordan, eds. *Behavioral Management of Obesity.* New York: SP Medical & Scientific Books, 1984, 157p.

Ward, Susan. *Beyond Feast or Famine: Daily Affirmations for Compulsive Eaters.* Deerfield Beach, FL: Health Communications Inc., 1990, 366p.

Audiovisuals

Heavy Load. Video. 36 mins. 1988. Carle Medical Communications. 110 W Main St, Urbana, IL 61801-2700. (217) 384-4838.

Overweight: How Did I Get this Way? Video. 15 mins. 1979. Milner Fenwick, 2125 Greenspring Dr, Timonium, MD 21093. (800) 638-8652.

EATING DISORDERS (GENERAL)

Articles

Adapting the Twelve Step Model for Eating Disorders. *The Addiction Letter.* 6 (Nov 1990): 1ff.

Andron, Vicki. Overeating, Undereating Can Signal Emotional Disorder. *Diabetes in the News.* 10 (May-June 1991): 38ff.

Andronis, Paul T., & Robert F. Kushner. Orderly Dieting and Disordered Eating: A Case Report. *Nutrition Reviews.* 49 (Jan 1991): 16ff.

At What Price the Quest for Thinness? *Tufts University Diet and Nutrition Letter.* 9(6) (Aug 1991): 3-6.

Bankhead, Charles D. Myths Fueling Widespread Abuse of OTC Laxatives. *Medical World News.* 31 (Jan 8, 1990): 19.

Barron, Joan M. Compulsive Disorders: How to Help When Your Patient Has Lost Control. *Nursing.* 20 (Oct 1990): 83ff.

Beating Eating Disorders. *Diabetes Forecast.* 44 (Aug 1991): 62ff.

Berg, Kathleen M. The Prevalence of Eating Disorders in Co-ed Versus Single-sex Residence Halls. *Journal of College Student Development.* 29(2) (1988): 125-131.

Body Shape, Eating Disorders: Boys Worry, Too. *Medical Abstracts Newsletter.* 10(7) (July 1990): 4.

Button, Eric. Self-Esteem in Girls Aged 11-12: Baseline Findings from a Planned Prospecive Study of Vulnerability in Eating Disorders. *Journal of Adolescence.* 13(4) (Dec 1990): 407-414.

Cantrell, Peggy J., & Jon B. Ellis. Gender Role and Risk Patterns for Eating Disorders in Men and Women. *Journal of Clinical Psychology.* 47 (Jan 1991): 53ff.

Children's Eating Disorders, Parental Responsibility. *Vibrant Life.* 6(5) (Sep-Oct 1990): 8.

Clark, Nancy. How to Handle Eating Disorders among Athletes. *Scholastic Coach.* 58 (May-June 1989): 27.

Collier, Susan N., Sarah F. Stallings, Patricia Giblin Wolman, & Robert W. Cullen. Assessment of Attitudes about Weight and Dieting among College-aged Individuals. *Journal of the American Dietetic Association.* 90 (Feb 1990): 276ff.

Collins, M. Elizabeth. Education for Healthy Body Weight: Helping Adolescents Balance the Cultural Pressure for Thinness. *Journal of School Health.* 58 (Aug 1988): 227ff.

Connolly, Cynthia, & Patricia Corbett-Dick. Eating Disorders: A Framework for School Nursing Initiatives. *Journal of School Health.* 60 (Oct 1990): 401ff.

Connor-Greene, Patricia Anne. Gender Differences in Body Weight Perception and Weight-Loss Strategies of College Students. *Women and Health.* 14(2) (1988): 27-42.

Crim, Marilyn. Is An Eating Disorder Developing in Your Family? (Questions asked of Marilyn Crim of Children's Hospital of San Francisco). *Tufts University Diet and Nutrition Letter.* 7 (May 1989): 3.

Dawson, Marie. Why Women Get Addicted to Food. *Ladies Home Journal.* 58(9) (Sep 1990): 132, 134, 136.

Does My Daughter Have an Eating Disorder? *Patient Care.* 22(5) (1988): 125, 129.

Eating Disorders also Harm Fertility. *Edell Health Letter.* 10(3) (Mar 1991): 3.

Eating Disorders in Dieters. *Nutrition Research Newsletter.* 10 (Feb 1991): 16.

Eating Disorders Linked to Control Issues. *The Addiction Letter.* 6 (Dec 1990): 7.

Ebbitt, Joan. Understanding Food Addiction. *Alcoholism & Addiction Magazine.* 8 (June 1988): 42.

Elkind, David. Eating Disorders. *Parents' Magazine.* 63 (Apr 1988): 190.

Fairburn, Christopher, & Robert Peveler. Eating Disorders and Diabetes. *Diabetes Forecast.* 42 (May 1989): 32ff.

Farmer, Nancy. Chronic Dieting: The Cure or the Problem? *Addiction and Recovery.* 10 (5-6) (Dec 1990): 33-36.

Favazza, Armando R., Lori DeRosear, & Karen Conterio. Self-mutilation and Eating Disorders. *Suicide and Life-Threatening Behavior.* 19 (Winter 1989): 352ff.

Fear of Fat. *Pediatrics for Parents.* 10 (Apr 1989): 8.

Feineman, Neil. Striking a Balance. *AFAA's American Fitness.* 7 (Nov-Dec 1989): 14ff.

Flodin, Kim. Bitter Pills: Teens and Appetite Suppressants. *American Health.* 10(6) (Jul-Aug 1991): 64-67.

Food Addictions Treatment: The Difference that Makes the Difference. *The Addiction Letter Annual.* 7 (1990): 17ff.

Garfinkel, P.E., & D.M. Garner. The Eating Attitudes Test: An Index of the Symptoms of Anorexia Nervosa. *Psychological Medicine.* 9 (1979): 273-279.

Goleman, Daniel. New Drug Treatments May Help Some with Eating Disorders (Brain Disorders Seem to Perpetuate Symptoms of Anorexia, Bulimia). *The New York Times.* 139 (Nov 9, 1989): B8-B23.

Gross, J., J.C. Rosen, H.E. Leitenberg, & M.E. Wilmuth. Validity of the Eating Attitides Test and the Eating Disorders Inventory in Bulimia Nervosa. *Journal of Consulting and Clinical Psychology.* 54 (1986): 875-876.

Hahn, Cindy. Why Eating Disorders Pervade Women's Tennis. *Tennis.* 26 (Dec 1990): 19.

Hesse-Biber, Sharlene. Eating Patterns and Disorders in a College Population: Are College Women's Eating Problems a New Phenomenon? *Sex Roles.* 20(1-2) (1989): 71-89.

Heyman, Betsy. Food for Thought. *Women's Sports & Fitness.* 13 (May-June 1991): 18.

Hillard, Paula Adams. Eating Disorders and Pregnancy. *Parents Magazine.* 64 (Nov 1989): 202ff.

Horosko, Marian. Overeating. *Dance Magazine.* 64 (Sept 1990): 54-55.

Infertility: May Be Linked to Eating Disorders. *Medical Abstracts Newsletter.* 11(1) (Jan 1991): 4.

Jenish, D'Arcy. A Tragic Obsession: Eating Disorders Can Sometimes Be Fatal. *Maclean's.* 102 (Oct 9, 1989): 52-54.

Jonas, Jeffrey M. Eating Disorders and Alcohol and Other Drug Abuse; Is There an Association? *Alcohol Health & Research World.* 13 (Summer 1989): 267ff.

Karlsberg, Elizabeth. The Big Fat Lie; When Thin Does You In. *Teen Magazine.* 33 (July 1989): 28-29ff.

Katzman, Melanie A., Lillie Weiss, & Sharlene A. Wolchik. Speak, Don't Eat! Teaching Women to Express Their Feelings. *Women and Therapy.* 5 (1986): 143-157.

Kearney-Cooke, Ann. Group Treatment of Sexual Abuse among Women with Eating Disorders. *Women and Therapy.* 7(1) (1988): 5-21.

Kent, Debra. Sex and Eating Disorders. *Seventeen.* 49 (Sept 1990): 64ff.

Klemchuk, Helen P., et al. Body Dissatisfaction and Eating-Related Problems on the College Campus: Usefulness of the Eating Disorder Inventory with a Nonclinical Population. *Journal of Counseling Psychology* 37(3) (Jul 1990): 297-305

Koch, Jennifer J. Eating Disorders. *Shape.* 8 (June 1989): 18ff.

Krey, Susanna H., Karin Palmer, & Karen A. Porcelli. Eating Disorders: The Clinical Dietitian's Changing Role. *Journal of the American Dietetic Association.* 89 (January 1989): 41.

Kurtzman, Felice D., Joel Yager, John Landsverk, Edward Wiesmeier, & Diane C. Bodurka. Eating Disorders among Selected Female Student Populations at UCLA. *Journal of the American Dietetic Association.* 89 (Jan 1989): 45ff.

Lehman, Adam K, & Judith Rodin. Styles of Self-nurturance and Disordered Eating. *Journal of Consulting and Clinical Psychology.* 57 (February 1989): 117.

Lenihan, Genie, & William G. Kirk. Using Student Paraprofessionals in the Treatment of Eating Disorders. *Journal of Counseling and Development.* 68 (Jan-Feb 1990): 332ff.

Livermore, Beth. Caffeine Boosts Eating Disorders. *Health.* 23(5) (Jun 1991): 16.

Mallick, M. Joan, Thomas W. Whipple, & Enrique Huerta. Behavioral and Psychological Traits of Weight-Conscious Teenagers: A Comparison of Eating-Disordered Patients and High- and Low-Risk Group. *Adolescence.* 22 (1987): 156-168.

Membreno, Maria G. Overeating, Undereating Can Upset Your Management Plan. *Diabetes in the News.* 9 (May-June 1990): 55ff.

Meyer, Roberta. Food Addiction: A Family Illness. *Alcoholism & Addiction Magazine.* 8 (June 1988): 9.

Mintz, Laurie B., & Nancy E. Betz. Prevalence and Correlates of Eating Disordered Behaviors among Undergraduate Women. *Journal of Counseling Psychology.* 35(4) (1988): 463-471.

Model for the Group Treatment of Education. *International Journal of Group Psychotherapy.* 37(4) (October 1987): 189-602.

Morgan, Leslie. Why Are Girls Obsessed with Their Weight? *Seventeen.* 48 (Nov 1989): 118-19ff.

Neff, Craig. A Hidden Epidemic. *Sports Illustrated.* 71 (Aug 14, 1989): 16ff.

Pike, Kathleen M., & Judith Rodin. Mothers, Daughters, and Disordered Eating. *Journal of Abnormal Psychology.* 100 (May 1991): 198ff.

Pill, Roisin, & Odette Parry. Making Changes—Women, Food and Families. *Health Education Journal.* 48(2) (1989): 51-54.

Ross, Rita. Beyond the Body Beautiful (Eating Disorders). *Weight Watchers Magazine.* 21 (May 1988): 14.

Rowand, Linda D. Nutrition, Self-image and Control; Adolescents Have Special Issues which May Affect Their Reaction to Treatment. *Alcoholism & Addiction Magazine.* 9 (Nov 1989): 31ff.

Silverstein, Brett, & Lauren Perdue. The Relationship between Role Concerns, Preferences for Slimness and Symptoms of Eating Problems among College Women. *Sex Roles.* 18 (1988): 101-106.

Simonson, Maria. What's Your Fat Personality? *Shape.* 8 (Mar 1989): 74ff.

Sperry, Shirley Lorenzani. Dangerous Eating Disorders. *Let's Live.* 57 (October 1989): 34.

Stacey, Michelle. No More Bad Diets: The Line between Dieting and Eating Disorders Keeps Getting Thinner and Thinner. *Mademoiselle.* 97 (July 1991): 118ff.

Stallings, Sarah, & Patricia Wolman. Are You an Over-Restrained Eater? *Shape.* 9(8) (Apr 1990): 87-88.

Szekeley, Eva A. From Eating Disorders to Women's Situations: Extending the Boundaries of Psychological Inquiry. *Counselling Psychology Quarterly.* 2(2) (1989): 167-184.

Thornton, James S. Feast or Famine: Eating Disorders in Athletes. *The Physician and Sportsmedicine.* 18 (Apr 1990): 116ff.

Use of the Eating Attitudes Test and Eating Disorder Inventory in Adolescents. *Journal of Adolescent Health Care.* 8(3) (May 1987): 266-272.

Waldrop, H. Learning to Love the Woman Inside. *McCalls.* 118 (Feb 1991): 59-60ff.

When Growing Pains Hurt Too Much: Teens at Risk. *Tufts University Diet and Nutrition Letter.* 9(4) (Jun 1991): 3-6.

Williams, Katy. Eating Disorders among Women Can Devastate More than Athletic Performances. *Women's Sports & Fitness.* 13 (Nov-Dec 1991): 22-23.

Books

Abraham, Suzanne A., & Derek Llewellyn-Jones. *Eating Disorders: The Facts.* 2nd Edition. Oxford: New York: Oxford University Press, 1987, 162p.

Agras, W. Stewart. *Eating Disorders: Management of Obesity, Bulimia, and Anorexia Nervosa.* New York: Pergamon Press, 1987, 136p.

Andersen, Arnold E., ed. *Males with Eating Disorders.* New York: Brunner/Mazel, 1990, 264p.

Anding, Robert et al. *Clinical Diagnosis and Management of Eating Disorders.* Longwood, FL: Ryandic Publishing Inc., 1990, 334p.

Anonymous. *Inner Harvest.* San Francisco, CA: Harper, 1990, 371p.

Arenson, Gloria. *A Substance Called Food: How to Understand, Control and Recover from Addictive Eating.* Blue Ridge Summit, PA: TAB Books, 1989, 286p.

Bemporad, Jules R., & David B. Herzog, eds. *Psychoanalysis and Eating Disorders.* New York: Guilford Press, 1989, 171p.

Berry, Joy Wilt. *Good Answers to Tough Questions about Weight Problems and Eating Disorders.* Chicago: Children's Press, 1990, 48p.

Black, David R., ed. *Eating Disorders among Athletes: Theory, Issues, and Research.* Reston, VA: National Association for Girls and Women in Sports Publications, 1991.

Blinder, Barton J., Barry F. Chaitin, & Renee S. Goldstein, eds. *The Eating Disorders: Medical and Psychological Bases of Diagnosis and Treatment.* New York: PMA Publications Corp, 1988, 500p.

Boakes, Robert A., David A. Popplewell, & Michael J. Burton, eds. *Eating Habits: Food Physiology, and Learned Behaviour.* Chichester, NY: Wiley, 1987, 225p.

Brownell, Kelly D., & John P. Foreyt, eds. *Handbook of Eating Disorders: Physiology, Psychology, and Treatment of Obesity, Anorexia and Bulimia.* New York: Basic Books, 1986, 529p.

Bruch, Hilde. *Eating Disorders: Obesity, Anorexia Nervosa, and the Person within.* New York: Basic Books, 1979, 396p.

Carruba, Michele O., & John E. Blundell, eds. *Pharmacology of Eating Disorders: Theoretical and Clinical Developments.* New York: Raven Press, 1986, 178p.

Chernin, Kim. *The Hungry Self: Women, Eating, and Identity.* New York: Times Books, 1985, 213p.

Clark, Kristine L., Richard B. Parr, & William P. Castelli, eds. *Evaluation and Management of Eating Disorders: Anorexia, Bulimia, and Obesity.* Champaign, IL: Life Enhancement Publications, 1988, 349p.

Claypool, Jane, & Cheryl Diane Nelson. *Food Trips and Traps: Coping with Eating Disorders.* Minneapolis, MN: CompCare Publishers, 1989, 90p.

Eagles, Douglas A. *Nutritional Diseases.* New York: Watts, 1987, 96p. (Juvenile).

Ebbitt, Joan. *Tomorrow, Monday, or New Year's Day: Emerging Issues in Eating Disorder Recovery.* Park Ridge, IL: Parkside Publishing, 1989, 104p.

Ebbitt, Joan. *The Eating Illness Workbook.* Park Ridge, IL: Parkside Publishing, 1987, 61p.

Edelstein, E. L. *Anorexia Nervosa and Other Dyscontrol Syndromes.* New York: Springer-Verlag, 1989, 117p.

Fairchild, Thomas N., ed. *Crisis Intervention Strategies for School-Based Helpers.* Springfield, IL: C.C. Thomas, 1986, 549p.

Ferrari, E., & F. Brambilla, eds. *Disorders of Eating Behaviour: A Psychoneuroendocrine Approach: Proceedings of the International Symposium Held in Pavia, Italy, September 1985.* New York: Pergamon Press, 1986, 404p.

Field, Howard L., & Barbara B. Domangue, eds. *Eating Disorders throughout the Lifespan.* New York: Praeger, 1987, 164p.

Garfinkel, Paul E., & David M. Garner, eds. *The Role of Drug Treatments for Eating Disorders.* New York: Brunner/Mazel, 1987, 192p.

Gibson, Diane, ed. *The Evaluation and Treatment of Eating Disorders.* New York: Haworth Press Inc., 1986.

Gilbert, Sara. *Pathology of Eating: Psychology and Treatment.* New York: Routledge & Kegan Paul, 1986, 246p.

Greeson, Janet. *It's Not What You're Eating, It's What's Eating You.* New York: Pocket Books, 1990, 306p.

Hampshire, Elizabeth. *Freedom from Food: The Secret Lives of Dieters and Compulsive Eaters.* Englewood Cliffs, NJ: Prentice-Hall, 1990.

Hansen, James C. *Family Therapy Collections, No. 20: Eating Disorders.* Gaithersburg, MD: Aspen Publishers, 1986.

Harkaway, Jill Elka. *Eating Disorders.* Rockville, MD: Aspen Publishers, 1987, 136p.

Haskew, Paul, & Cynthia H. Adams. *When Food Is a Four-Letter Word.* Englewood Cliffs, NJ: Prentice-Hall, 1984.

Hollis, Judi. *Relapse for Eating Disorder Sufferers.* Center City, MN: Hazelden Foundation, 1985, 28p.

Hornyak, Lynne M., & Ellen K. Baker, eds. *Experiential Therapies for Eating Disorders.* New York: Guilford Press, 1989, 339p.

Hsu, L. K. George. *Eating Disorders.* New York: Guilford Press, 1990, 248p.

Jantz, Gregory L. *Living Beyond Food.* Edmonds, WA: Center for Counseling and Health Resources Inc., 1991.

Johnson, William G., ed. *Advances in Eating Disorders.* Greenwich, CT: JAI Press Inc., 1987.

Kano, Susan. *Making Peace with Food: Freeing Yourself from the Diet/Weight Obsession.* Rev. ed. New York: Harper & Row, 1989, 256p.

Kaplan, D. W., ed. *Eating Disorders: Obesity, Anorexia Nervosa, and Bulimia in Childhood and Adolescence.* Farmington, CT: S. Karger, AG, 1986, 84p.

Katzman, M., P. Fallon, & S. Wooley. *Feminist Perspectives on the Treatment of Eating Disorders.* New York: Guilford Press, 1992.

King, Michael B. *Eating Disorders in a General Practice Population: Prevalence, Characteristics and Follow-up at 12 to 18 Months.* New York: Cambridge University Press, 1989, 34p.

Kolodny, Nancy J. *When Food's a Foe: How to Confront and Conquer Eating Disorders.* Boston: Little, Brown & Co., 1987, 143p. (Juvenile).

Krueger, David W. *Body Self and Psychological Self: A Developmental and Clinical Integration of Disorders of the Self.* New York: Brunner/Mazel, 1989, 173p.

Kushi, Michio, & David Mann. *Obesity, Weight Loss and Eating Disorders.* Japan Publications (USA), 1986.

Larocca, Felix E. F., ed. *Eating Disorders.* San Francisco, CA: Jossey-Bass, 1986, 127p.

Larocca, Felix E. F., ed. *Eating Disorders: Effective Care and Treatment, Vol. 1.* St. Louis, MO: Ishiyaku EuroAmerica, 1986.

Levine, Michael. *How Schools Can Help Combat Student Eating Disorders.* Washington, DC: National Education Association, 1987, 280p.

Lonie, John, ed. *Learning from Life: Five Plays for Young People.* Sydney, Australia: Currency Press, 1985, 208p.

Maine, Margo. *Father Hunger: Fathers, Daughters, and Food.* Carlsbad, CA: Gürze Books, 272p.

Maloney, Michael, & Rachel Kranz. *Straight Talk about Eating Disorders.* New York: Facts on File Inc., 1991, 128p.

Mathews, John R. *Eating Disorders.* New York: Facts on File Inc., 1991, 176p.

McFarland, Barbara, & Rodney Susong. *Killing Ourselves with Kindness: Consequences of Eating Disorders.* Center City, MN: Hazelden Foundation, 1985.

McGee, Robert S., & William D. Mountcastle. *Twelve-Step Program for Overcoming Eating Disorders.* Irving, TX: Word Inc., 1990.

Miller, Caroline. *Feeding the Soul: Daily Meditations for Recovering from Eating Disorders.* New York: Bantam Books, 1991, 365p.

Minirth, Frank. *Love Hunger: Recovery for Food Codependency.* Nashville, TN: Thomas Nelson Inc., 1990.

O'Neill, Cherry B. *Dear Cherry: Questions and Answers on Eating Disorders.* New York: Continuum Publishing, 1987, 138p.

Reiff, Dan W., & K. Kim Lampson Reiff. *Eating Disorders: Nutrition Therapy in the Recovery Process.* Gaithersburg, MD: Aspen Publishers, 1991, 560p.

Riebel, Linda, & Jane Kaplan. *Someone You Love Is Obsessed with Food: What You Need to Know about Eating Disorders.* Center City, MN: Hazelden Foundation, 1989, 190p.

Rossi, Linda R., ed. *Nutrition, Health, and Eating Disorders.* Frederick, MD: Aspen Publishers, 1988, 86p.

Schlundt, David G., & William G. Johnson. *Eating Disorders: Assessment and Treatment.* Boston: Allyn & Bacon, 1990, 513p.

Schneider, Linda H., Steven J. Cooper, & Katherine A. Halmi, eds. *The Psychobiology of Human Eating Disorders: Preclinical and Clinical Perspectives.* New York: New York Academy of Sciences, 1989, 626p.

Seid, Roberta Pollack. *Never Too Thin: Why Women Are at War with Their Bodies.* New York: Prentice Hall Press, 1988, 372p.

Shepherd, R., ed. *Handbook of Psychophysiology of Human Eating.* New York: Wiley, 1989, 383p.

Siegel, Michele, Judith Brisman, & Margot Weinshel. *Surviving an Eating Disorder: Strategies for Family and Friends.* New York: Harper & Row, 1988, 222p.

Strien, Tatjana van. *Eating Behavior, Personality Traits, and Body Mass.* Berwyn, PA: Swets North America, 1986, 167p.

Stunkard, Albert J., & Eliot Stellar, eds. *Eating and Its Disorders.* New York: Raven Press, 1984, 280p.

Swift, David, & Kathleen Zraly. *Anorexia, Bulimia, and Compulsive Overeating: A Practical Guide for Counselors and Families.* New York: Continuum Publishing, 1990, 176p.

Szekely, Eva. *Never Too Thin.* Toronto: The Women's Press, 1988, 210p.

Touyz, S. W., & P. J. V. Beumont, eds. *Eating Disorders: Prevalence and Treatment.* Baltimore, MD: Williams & Wilkins, 1985, 160p.

Walsh, B. Timothy, ed. *Eating Behavior in Eating Disorders.* Washington, DC: American Psychiatric Press Inc., 1988, 232p.

Weiner, Herbert, & Andrew Baum, eds. *Eating Regulation and Discontrol.* Hillsdale, NJ: L. Erlbaum, 1988, 229p.

Williamson, Donald A. with C. J. Davis. *Assessment of Eating Disorders: Obesity, Anorexia, and Bulimia Nervosa.* New York: Pergamon Press, 1990, 199p.

Wilson, C. Philip, ed. *Eating to Live or Living to Eat: Treatment of the Eating Disorders.* Northvale, NJ: Jason Aronson, 1991.

Winick, Myron, ed. *Control of Appetite.* New York: Wiley, 1988, 152p.

Woodman, Marion. *The Owl Was a Baker's Daughter: Obesity, Anorexia Nervosa and the Repressed Feminine—A Psychological Study.* Toronto, ON, Canada: Inner City Books, 1980, 139p.

Woodside, D. Blake, & Lorie Shekter-Wolfson. *Family Approaches in Treatment of Eating Disorders.* Washington, DC: American Psychiatric Press Inc., 1991, 158p.

Wooley, S.C. *A Scream in a Different Language.* New York: Guilford Press, 1992.

Wurtman, Judith. *Managing Your Mind and Mood through Food.* New York: HarperCollins Publishers, 1988, 288p.

Wurtman, Richard J., & Judith J. Wurtman, eds. *Disorders of Eating: Nutrients in Treatment of Brain Diseases.* New York: Raven Press, 1979, 309p.

Yager, Joel, ed. *Special Problems in Managing Eating Disorders.* Washington, DC: American Psychiatric Press Inc., 1991, 285p.

Yates, Alayne. *Compulsive Exercise and the Eating Disorders: Toward an Integrated Theory of Activity.* New York: Brunner/Mazel, 1991, 259p.

Zraly, Kathleen, & David Swift. *Anorexia, Bulimia, and Compulsive Overeating: A Practical Guide for Counselors and Families.* New York: Continuum Publishing, 1990, 162p.

Audiovisuals

Afraid to Eat: Eating Disorders & the Student Athlete. Video. 17 mins. NCAA. Available from: Karol Video, 350 N Pennsylvania Ave, PO Box 7600, Wilkes Barre, PA 18773-7600. (800) 524-1013.

Dieting: The Danger Point. Video. 20 mins. 1979. CRM/McGraw-Hill Films, 674 Via de la Valle, PO Box 641, Del Mar, CA 92014. (619) 453-5000.

Don't Let Weight Control You. Poster. 18 inches x 24 inches. 2-color. NCAA, 6201 College Blvd, Overland Park, KS 66211. (913) 339-1906.

Eating Disorders. Video. 28 mins. 1987. RMI Media Productions, 2807 W 47th St, Shawnee Mission, KS 66205. (800) 821-5480.

Eating Disorders. Video. 21 mins. 1986. Research Press, 2612 N Mattis Ave, Box 3177, Champaign, IL 61821. (217) 352-3273.

Eating Disorders: The Slender Trap. Video. 21 mins. 1986. AIMS Media Inc., 9710 DeSoto Ave, Chatsworth, CA 91311-4409. (800) 367-2467.

Eating Disorders: What Can You Do? (For athletes.) Video. 15 mins. NCAA. Available from: Karol Video, 350 N Pennsylvania Ave, PO Box 7600, Wilkes Barre, PA 18773-7600. (800) 524-1013.

Eating Disorders: You Are Not Alone. Video. 20 mins. 1987. RMI Media Productions, 2807 W 47th St, Shawnee Mission, KS 66205. (800) 821-5480.

Eating—Out of Control. Video. 30 mins. 1987. Cambridge Career Productions, 90 MacCorkle Ave, SW, South Charleston, WV 25303. (800) 468-4227.

Fear of Fat: Dieting and Eating Disorders. Video. 26 mins. 1987. Churchill Films, 12210 Nebraska Ave, Los Angeles, CA 90025. (310) 207-6600.

Foodfright. Video. 28 mins. 1988. Direct Cinema Ltd, Box 69799, Los Angeles, CA 90069. (800) 345-6748.

Freeing Yourself from Isolating with Food: Moving towards Relationships, Intimacy, and Sexuality. Audiocassette. 1984. The New York Center for Eating Disorders, 490 3rd St, Brooklyn, NY 11215. (718) 788-6986.

Gentle Eating: A New Approach to Disordered Eating Treatment and Recovery. 2 Audiocassettes. 1990. Brat Inc, 6 University Dr, Ste 225, Amherst, MA 01002. (413) 549-0774.

Killing Us Softly. Video. 32 mins. 1987. Cambridge Documentary Films, Inc. PO Box 385, Cambridge, MA 02139.

Learning about Eating Disorders. 5 videos. 15min. each. 1989. Churchill Films, 12210

Nebraska Ave, Los Angeles, CA 90025. (310) 207-6600.

Out of Balance: Nutrition and Weight. (Athletics.) Video. 16 mins. NCAA. Available from: Karol Video, 350 N Pennsylvania Ave, PO Box 7600, Wilkes Barre, PA 18773-7600. (800) 524-1013.

Overcoming the Fear of Success: Working through the Need to Sabotage Yourself in Resolving an Eating Problem. Audiocassette. 1984. The New York Center for Eating Disorders, 490 3rd St., Brooklyn, NY 11215. (718) 788-6986.

ISSUES RELATING TO EATING DISORDERS

Articles

Berkman, Sue. Body Image: Larger than Life? *Weight Watchers Women's Health and Fitness News.* 4(8) (Apr 1990): 1-2.

Body Image Work Leads to Heightened Spirituality. *The Addiction Letter.* 7 (July 1991): 4.

Castleman, Michael. The Sex/Food Link. *Self.* 12(11) (Nov 1990): 76.

Charken, Shelly, & Patricia Pliner. Women, But Not Men, Are What They Eat: The Effect of Meal Size and Gender on Perceived Feminity and Masculinity. *Personality and Social Psychology Bulletin.* 13(2) (1987): 166-176.

Comer, James P. Building a Positive Body Image. *Parents' Magazine.* 65 (Nov 1990): 235.

Cullari, Salvatore, & Roselyn S. Trubilla. Body-Image Distortion in Normal Weight College Women. *Perceptual and Motor Skills.* 78(3) (1989): 1195-1198.

Deveny, Kathleen. Pill Warning; Diet Drugs Teens Use, Often in Huge Doses, Bring Calls for Controls; Kids Can Buy all They Want of Nonprescription Items Despite Danger in Overuse; Case of Late Noelle Smith *The Wall Street Journal.* (Dec 26 1990): 1.

Dieting and Puberty. *Pediatrics for Parents.* 10 (May 1989): 1.

Elkind, David. Teenagers Confront Mother Nature. *Parents' Magazine.* 65 (May 1990): 216.

Great Bodies Come in Many Shapes. *University of California, Berkeley Wellness Letter.* 7 (Feb 1991): 1ff.

Harmatz, Morton G. Are You as Fat as You Think? *Shape.* 7 (Apr 1988): 128ff.

How to Help Children Learn to Eat Right. *Healthline.* (May 1990): 14.

Hunter, Beatrice Trum. Helping Children to Develop Good Eating Habits. *Consumers Research Magazine.* 71 (October 1988): 33.

Kabatznick, Ronna. True Reflections. *Weight Watchers Magazine.* 23 (June 1990): 22ff.

Koch, Jennifer J. Sizing Up Your Body Image. *Shape.* 9 (Nov 1989): 20, 123.

Kreipe, Richard E., & Gilbert B. Forbes. Osteoporosis: A"New Morbidity" for Dieting Female Adolescents? *Pediatrics.* 86 (Sept 1990): 478ff.

Lipsyte, Robert. Prisoner of Fat; A Report from the Planet of the Bods. *American Health.* 10 (July-Aug 1991): 32ff.

Male Adolescents and Body Image. *Nutrition Research Newsletter.* 9 (May 1990): 54.

Ressler, Adrienne, & Lee Randall. A Better Body Image. *Weight Watchers Magazine.* 24(7) (July 1991): 54, 56.

Sacra, Cheryl. Mirror Images: Why an Obsession with Your Reflection May Distort the Real You. *Health.* 22 (Mar 1990): 70-73ff.

Schwartzberg, Neala S. "Do I Look Fat?". *Parents' Magazine.* 65 (Jan 1990): 66-70.

Silverstein, Brett et al. The Role of the Mass Media in Promoting a Thin Standard of Bodily Attractiveness for Women. *Sex Roles.* 14 (1986): 519-532.

Weight Gain and Stress. *Pediatrics for Parents.* 11 (Sept 1990): 1.

Wilson, Glenn D. Eating Styles and Stress. *Healthline.* 8 (Nov 1989): 12ff.

Wurtman, R.J., & J.J. Wurtman. Carbohydrates and Depression. *Scientific American.* 260 (Jan 1989): 68-75.

Books

Cash, Thomas F., & Thomas Pruzinsky, eds. *Body Images: Development, Deviance and Changes.* New York: Guilford Press, 1990, 361p.

Chernin, Kim. *The Obsession: Reflections on the Tyranny of Slenderness.* New York: Harper & Row, 1981, 206p.

Freedman, Rita. *Bodylove: Learning to Like Our Looks & Ourselves.* New York: HarperCollins Publishers, 1990, 272p.

Harrison, Marvel, & Catharine Stewart-Roache. *The attrACTIVE Woman: A Physical Fitness Approach to Emotional and Spiritual Well-Being.* Park Ridge, IL: Parkside Publishing.

Hirschmann, Jane, & Lela Zaphiropoulos. *Solving Your Child's Eating Problems.* New York: Fawcett Book Group, 1990.

Hutchinson, Marcia Germaine. *Transforming Body Image: Learning to Love the Body You Have.* Freedom, CA: The Crossing Press, 1985, 149p.

Macht, J. *Poor Eaters: Helping Children Who Refuse to Eat.* New York: Plenum Publishing, 1990.

Marlatt, G. Alan, & Judith R. Gordon. *Relapse Prevention: Maintenance Strategies in the Treatment of Addictive Disorders.* New York: Guilford Press, 1985, 558p.

Minirth-Meier. *Food for the Hungry Heart.* Nashville, TN: Thomas Nelson Inc., Publishers, 1991.

Otis, Carol L., & Roger Goldingay. *Campus Health Guide: The College Student's Handbook for Healthy Living.* New York: College Entrance Examination Board, 1989, 307p.

Satter, Ellyn. *Child of Mine: Feeding with Love and Good Sense.* Menlo Park, CA: Bull Publishing, 1991, 470p.

Satter, Ellyn. *How to Get Your Kid to Eat...but Not Too Much.* Menlo Park, CA: Bull Publishing, 1987, 397p.

Sheedy, Ally. *Yesterday I Saw the Sun: Poems.* New York: Summit Books, 1991, 160p.

Stunkard, Albert J., & Andrew Baum, eds. *Eating, Sleeping, and Sex.* Hillsdale, NJ: L. Erlbaum, 1989, 262p.

Tabin, Johanna Krout. *On the Way to Self: Ego and Early Oedipal Development.* New York: Columbia University Press, 1985.

Thompson, J. Kevin. *Body Image Disturbance: Assessment and Treatment.* New York: Pergamon Press, 1990, 140p.

Wolf, Naomi. *The Beauty Myth: How Images of Beauty Are Used against Women.* New York: Morrow, 1991, 347p.

Journals, Indexes, and Other Resources

▼
▼
▼
▼

Journals

The following journals are especially concerned with eating disorders or obesity, and all of the articles in them will discuss aspects of these disorders. All of them are directed to the health professional audience. Other journals and magazines, both professional and popular, may have articles about eating disorders. To find articles in them, see "Books and Articles about Eating Disorders," above. Also see below, "Indexes," to find out how to look up more articles about this subject.

Eating Disorders Review. PM, Inc, PO Box 10702, Van Nuys, CA 91410. Bimonthly.

International Journal of Eating Disorders. John Wiley & Sons, Inc, 605 3rd Ave, New York, NY 10158. Bimonthly.

International Journal of Obesity. Macmillan Press, Ltd, Brunel Rd, Basingstoke, Hants, RG21 2XS, UK. Monthly.

Journal of Obesity and Weight Regulation. Human Sciences Press, Inc, 72 5th Ave, New York, NY 10011. Semiannual.

Obesity and Health. 402 S 14th St, Hettinger, SD 58639. Bimonthly.

Indexes and Library Searching

To find the most recent articles about eating disorders, check the indexes listed below. Checking under these headings should yield listings:
• Eating Disorders
• Anorexia Nervosa
• Body Image
• Bulimia or Bulimia Nervosa
• Compulsive Overeating or Compulsive Eating
• Obesity
• Reducing—Psychological Aspects
• Self-acceptance
• Weight control

These headings may also be used to find books in a library's card catalog or online computer catalog.

To Find Articles in Popular Magazines and Journals

Consumer Health & Nutrition Index. Oryx Press, 4041 N Central Ave, Phoenix, AZ 85012-3397. Print quarterly. Annual cumulation. (Indexes 98 consumer and popular magazines.)

New Health Reference Center. (Formerly Health Reference Center and Health Index/Plus.) Information Access Co, 362 Lakeside Dr, Foster City, CA 94404. Electronic index, available on CD-ROM. (Indexes 5 reference books, over 3,000 magazines and journals, and 800 pamphlets.)

Reader's Guide to Periodical Literature. H.W. Wilson Co, 950 University Ave, Bronx, NY 10452-9978. Print version: 17 indexes per year; annual cumulations. Also available electronically, on CD-ROM (updated monthly), and online through WILSONLINE. (Indexes 200 popular magazines.)

To Find Articles in Professional Journals

Abridged Index Medicus. Superintendent of Documents, Government Printing Office, Washington, DC 20402. Monthly. (Indexes 118 English-language journals.)

Index Medicus. Superintendent of Documents, US Government Printing Office, Washington, DC 20402. Monthly. Also available electronically as MEDLINE, both online and on CD-ROM. (Indexes 3,000 international biomedical journals.)

Psychological Abstracts. American Psychological Association, 1400 N Uhle St, Arlington, VA 22201. Monthly. Also available electronically as PyscINFO, online, and as PsycLIT, on CD-ROM. (Indexes 1200 English-language journals in psychology and the behavioral sciences. In January 1992, books will be included.)

Sociological Abstracts. PO Box 22206, San Diego, CA 92192. 6 issues per year. Also available electronically online and on CD-ROM. (Indexes over 1400 journals, dissertations, reviews, conference reports.)

Other Sources of Materials

All of the major, national eating disorders organizations publish newsletters. See "Organizations," below, for more information. Additionally, an organization called Eating Awareness Services and Education (EASE), publishes the *Eating Awareness & Self Enhancement* newsletter 6 times a year. EASE also makes available a booklet, video, and presentations to groups. Contact EASE, PO Box 27268 Philadelphia, PA 19118, (215) 242-3358.

Gürze Books publishes a catalog of more than 125 books, workbooks, videos, and audiocassettes, all of which cover eating disorders and related recovery issues. The catalog is aimed at individuals suffering from eating disorders as well as loved ones and health care professionals. The catalog is available from Gurze Books, PO Box 2238, Carlsbad, CA 92018, (800) 756-7533 or (619) 434-7533.

Organizations

▼
▼
▼

There are a number of good organizations devoted to helping those suffering from eating disorders, their families and friends, and people in the helping professions. Below are national or regional groups. The organizations listed here may also be able to provide information about groups in your area. Your physician or therapist may also recommend helpful local groups.

American Anorexia/Bulimia Association, Inc (AABA). 418 E 76th St, New York, NY 10021. (212) 734-1114

EXECUTIVE DIRECTOR: Randi E. Wirth, PhD
DATE ESTABLISHED: 1978
MEMBERSHIP: People with anorexia nervosa, bulimia nervosa, and related eating disorders; their loved ones; interested individuals; and professionals. Dues: $50/yr. To receive newsletter alone, $30.
TYPE: Nonprofir educational, professional, and self-help organization.
SERVICES: General meetings 5 times a year; free to members, open to public by donation. At meetings, professionals present current theories about anorexia and bulimia or communication workshops are held. Separate self-help groups are available for anorexics and bulimics and for parents, spouses, siblings, loved ones. Speakers' bureau. Referrals. Reading lists. Research. Local chapters.
NEWSLETTER: *American Anorexia/Bulimia Association.* Quarterly.

ANAD—National Association of Anorexia Nervosa and Associated Disorders. PO Box 7, Highland Park, IL 60035. (708) 831-3438.

EXECUTIVE DIRECTOR: Vivian Meehan
DATE ESTABLISHED: 1976
MEMBERSHIP: People with anorexia nervosa and other eating disorders, their loved ones, interested individuals, and professionals. Fees: Member, $15; Donor, $25; Guarantor, $100; any gift welcome. $15 contribution receives quarterly newsletter.

TYPE: Nonprofit educational and self-help organization.
SERVICES: All services free. Counseling. Information. Support and self-help groups for persons with eating disorders and parents. Referral list of over 2,000 therapists, hospitals, and clinics treating eating disorders. Conferences and seminars. Research. Advocacy: ANAD provides publicity about eating disorders to news and entertainment media; works to halt insurance discrimination; monitors advertising; campaigns against over-the-counter diet drugs; attends congressional hearings.
NEWSLETTER: *Working Together.* Quarterly.

Anorexia Nervosa and Related Eating Disorders, Inc (ANRED). PO Box 5102, Eugene, OR 97405. (503) 344-1144.

EXECUTIVE DIRECTOR: Jean Bradley Rubel, ThD
MEMBERSHIP: Persons with anorexia nervosa and related eating disorders, their loved ones, interested individuals, and professionals. Dues: $10/yr; includes monthly newsletter.
TYPE: Nonprofit educational, professional, and self-help organization.
SERVICES: Speakers bureau. Referral information. Support groups. Study groups. 20-week intensive group. Weekend workshops. Family-and-friends workshops. Private sessions (by appointment). Professional training and consultation (by appointment). In-service training for human services and school personnel who work with eating and exercise-disordered clients. Information line, 9 am to noon, Monday - Friday, (503) 344-1144.
NEWSLETTER: *Anred Alert.* Monthly.

National Anorexic Aid Society (NAAS). 1925 E Dublin/Granville Rd, Columbus OH 43229. (614) 436-1112.

EXECUTIVE DIRECTOR: Arline Ianicello
DATE ESTABLISHED: 1979
MEMBERSHIP: People with anorexia nervosa and other eating disorders, their loved ones, interested individuals, and professionals.

TYPE: Nonprofit educational, professional, and self-help organization.

SERVICES: Educational training seminars on national level. Annual national eating disorders conference. Research. Educational materials, including audiotapes, textbooks, for sale. International referrals. Bibliography. Speakers Bureau. Counselor training. Advocacy.

NEWSLETTER: *NAAS Newsletter*. Quarterly.

Overeaters Anonymous. Mailing Address: PO Box 92870, Los Angeles, CA 90009. (213) 618-8835. FAX: (213) 618-8836.

EXECUTIVE DIRECTOR: Jorge Sever

DATE ESTABLISHED: 1960

MEMBERSHIP: People who desire to stop compulsive overeating. Members are anonymous. Dues: None, but contributions accepted.

TYPE: A fellowship of men and women who meet to solve the problems of compulsive overeating. Patterned after the 12-Step Alcoholics Anonymous program. Extensive network of local fellowship groups (listed in telephone book under Overeaters Anonymous).

SERVICES: Fellowship groups for support and assistance. Catalog of literature, including books, pamphlets, audiotapes, group starter kits. Annual world service conference.

NEWSLETTER: *WSO Notebook*. Bimonthly.

Pennsylvania Educational Network for Eating Disorders (PENED). PO Box 16282, Pittsburgh, PA 15242. (412) 922-5922.

EXECUTIVE DIRECTOR: Anita Sinicrope

DATE ESTABLISHED: 1984

MEMBERSHIP: People with eating disorders, their loved ones, interested individuals, and professionals.

TYPE: Nonprofit organization dedicated to aiding and educating the general and professional public on the issues, causes, and treatment of anorexia nervosa, bulimia nervosa, and compulsive eating. Actively serves all of western Pennsylvania, eastern Ohio, northern West Virginia, as well as providing information and referrals to people all over the country.

SERVICES: Telephone contact line. Support groups for persons with eating disorders and their loved ones. Educational presentations and seminars. Consultations. In-service training for professionals. Referrals for professional treatment. Educational materials.

NEWSLETTER: Available quarterly.

Index

Compiled by Janet Perlman